Free Speech and Intellectual Diversity in Higher Education

POLITICAL THEORY FOR TODAY

Series Editor: Richard Avramenko, University of Wisconsin, Madison

Political Theory for Today seeks to bring the history of political thought out of the jargon-filled world of the academy into the everyday world of social and political life. The series brings the wisdom of texts and the tradition of political philosophy to bear on salient issues of our time, especially issues pertaining to human freedom and responsibility, the relationship between individuals and the state, the moral implications of public policy, health and human flourishing, public and private virtues, and more. Great thinkers of the past have thought deeply about the human condition and their situations—books in Political Theory for Today build on that insight.

Titles Published

Free Speech and Intellectual Diversity in Higher Education edited by Carol McNamara, James Stoner and Paul Carrese
Memory and the Political Art in Plato's Statesman by Catherine Craig
Character in the American Experience: An Unruly People by Bruce P. Frohnen and Ted V. McAllister
A Politics of All: Thomas Jefferson and Radical Democracy by Dean Caivano
Rethinking Utopia: Interdisciplinary Approaches edited by Ebru Deniz Ozan
Citizenship and Civic Leadership in America edited by Carol McNamara and Trevor Shelley
The Recurrence of the End Times: Voegelin, Hegel, and the Stop-History Movements by Michael J. Colebrook
Willmoore Kendall: Tribune and Teacher of the American People by Christopher Owen
The Politics of Private Property: Contested Claims to Ownership in U.S. Cultural Discourse by Simone Knewitz
The Political Philosophy of the European City: From Polis, through City-State, to Megalopolis by Ferenc Hörcher
John Locke and the Uncivilized Society: Resistance and Individualism in America Today by Scott Robinson
Welcoming the Other: Student, Stranger, and Divine edited by N. Susan Laehn and Thomas R. Laehn
Cosmopolitanism and its Discontents: Rethinking Politics in the Age of Brexit and Trump, edited by Lee Ward
Eric Voegelin's Asian Political Thought edited by Lee Trepanier
The Spartan Drama of Plato's Laws by Eli Friedland

Free Speech and Intellectual Diversity in Higher Education

Edited by
James R. Stoner Jr.
Paul O. Carrese
and Carol McNamara

LEXINGTON BOOKS
Lanham • Boulder • New York • London

Published by Lexington Books
An imprint of The Rowman & Littlefield Publishing Group, Inc.
4501 Forbes Boulevard, Suite 200, Lanham, Maryland 20706
www.rowman.com

86-90 Paul Street, London EC2A 4NE

British Library Cataloguing in Publication Information Available

Library of Congress Cataloging-in-Publication Data Available

ISBN 978-1-66690-070-5 (cloth)
ISBN 978-1-66690-071-2 (electronic)
ISBN 978-1-66690-072-9 (pbk.)

Contents

Acknowledgments

The publication of this volume would not have been possible without the direct support of the full team at the School of Civic and Economic Thought and Leadership of devoted events, communications, and business operations staff. Special thanks to Trevor Shelley and Jakub Voboril, who, then as post-doctoral fellows with the school, dedicated themselves to the careful editing of the essays in the volume. In addition, the lecture series and conference event in which these papers were first presented was generously supported by the Sarah Scaife Foundation, the Bradley Foundation, the Institute for Humane Studies, and the Jack Miller Center. Finally, we would like to thank the planning committee, whose expertise brought together the scholars and speakers in the series and at the conference, whose important work provided the substance for this volume: Stefanie Lindquist, James Weinstein, and Joseph Russomanno.

We also acknowledge permission to reprint essays that have been published elsewhere:

- Chapter 1 first appeared in Lee C. Bollinger and Geoffrey R. Stone, eds., *The Free Speech Century* (Oxford University Press, 2018), chapter 7. Reproduced with permission of the Licensor through PLSclear.
- Chapter 2 appeared in Joseph Russomanno, ed., *Speech Freedom on Campus: Past, Present, and Future* (Lexington, 2020), ch. 1.
- Chapter 3 appeared in Ulrich Baer, *What Snowflakes Get Right: Free Speech, Truth, and Equality on Campus* (Oxford University Press, 2019), ch. 2. Reproduced with permission of the Licensor through PLSclear.
- A version of chapter 4 was published in Donald Alexander Downs, *Free Speech and Liberal Education: A Plea for Intellectual Diversity and Tolerance* (Cato Institute, 2020), ch. 3, and is reprinted here by permission.
- Chapter 5 appeared in *National Affairs* (Fall 2018). Reprinted by permission.

- An expanded version of chapter 6 appears in the *Georgetown Journal of Law and Public Policy*, vol. 20, Special Issue, 2022.
- Chapter 9 appeared in *City Journal*, December 17, 2017. Reprinted with permission.

Introduction

By James R. Stoner, Jr., Paul O. Carrese, and Carol McNamara

The essays gathered here began as talks at the inaugural conference of the School of Civic and Economic Thought and Leadership at Arizona State University in 2018, or as lectures given there during the 2017–18 academic year. It had appeared to the organizers that free speech and intellectual diversity, once thought to be two animating principles of university life that existed in perfect harmony with one another, were no longer taken for granted in academic settings. If in the 1950s and '60s American universities prided themselves on the range of opinions that could be debated in the classroom and on the quad—over against the pressure toward conformity in society at large—by the 2010s, the universities themselves seemed to conform to predictable opinions, mostly liberal or progressive, which they were sometimes willing to enforce against dissent. In contrast, debate in society had become increasingly "uninhibited, robust and wide-open," as the Supreme Court had recommended, not to mention raucous, offensive, and polarized across party lines. Was it really the case that universities had turned against free speech or the intellectual diversity that might be its fuel or consequence? If so, what was the cause? Was the new consensus progressive or problematic?

Of course, in holding an academic conference and designing an academic volume, certain choices were made about the issue in the very act of discussing it. The organizers and editors sought a diversity of viewpoints and perspectives, though perhaps weighing the balance somewhat toward dissenters from the new orthodoxy, as the voices less commonly heard. This volume begins with two leading law professors who take opposing views on the question of what the constitutional law of free speech means for academic life. Robert Post, who gave the keynote address at the conference, reviews the constitutional law of free speech as it developed in the twentieth century and concludes that its rules have little applicability in the university setting, where judgment concerning the content of speech is pervasive, truth and error must be distinguished, and expression is mandatory. In contrast, Geoffrey Stone, who headed the committee that developed the Chicago Principles in 2015, argues that the fundamental values of higher education are congruent with free-speech doctrine and thus prohibit censorship, as vigorous intellectual exchange depends upon an ability to challenge ideas and to see one's ideas challenged—with curiosity, boldness, and courage. Stepping back from First Amendment law to consider the moral atmosphere on university campuses, Ulrich Baer and Donald Downs see opposite threats. Baer discusses the 2017 march and violence in Charlottesville, the political response to which he thinks not only tolerated but condoned racist speech, giving minority students cause to wonder whether they were genuinely welcome on campus. Downs, drawing on his experience at the University of Wisconsin, emphasizes the need for universities to cultivate an ethos on campus that includes a healthy skepticism about claims to authority and thus accepts or encourages vigorous debate of controversial issues.

The second group of essays examines the philosophical foundations of freedom of speech. Harvey Mansfield focuses on the value of free speech as critical to political freedom and thus to the noble claim of self-government; free speech is for the giving of reasons, which are not mere rationalizations but do tend to be predictably partisan, offering citizens choice and thereby making the polis whole. Daniel Cullen focuses on college administrators' emphasis on promoting expressions of personal identity, even at the cost of limiting rational argument, which alters the mission of the university in a direction that is incompatible with its traditional end of clarifying the truth of things. Norma Thompson points to Edmund Burke and especially C. Vann Woodward as models whose research sustained truth against dominant opinion and changed that opinion, concluding that free speech *is* liberal education. James Stoner reviews John Stuart Mill's famous arguments in favor of freedom of thought and expression, contrasts Willmoore Kendall's critique, and sorts out where Mill's argument is useful and where misleading in various academic, political, and social contexts.

Empirical assessment of the condition of intellectual life within and around the university is the task of the essays in the third part. Social psychologist Jonathan Haidt offers a trenchant analysis of contemporary society and its tendencies toward tribalism and polarization, though he is encouraged by some recent efforts by universities to support heterodox views, a project to which he has made a signal contribution. Steven Hayward analyzes the situation within universities, finding antipathy toward free speech and overwhelming uniformity of political opinion, though he also notes a few hopeful signs. Political scientist Joshua Dunn documents the paucity of conservatives on university faculties and discusses the consequences for teaching, research, and public support. Cristine Legare and David Buss, two professors of psychology at the University of Texas, describe their success in teaching the subject of evolution in a state where the religious commitments of some of their students make the subject particularly controversial. Laura Beth Nielsen, a sociologist, analyzes the spaces where campus interactions take place and makes the case for protecting students from expression that might shock or offend. Journalist Heather MacDonald documents the efforts made at a university renowned for protecting free expression to nevertheless "disinvite" a controversial speaker.

The final group of essays looks more directly at the question of practical steps that might be taken to address the problems other essayists identified. Azhar Majeed, formerly of FIRE (Foundation for Individual Rights and Expression) and now with the Center for Inquiry, proposes a series of steps to ensure sound university policy on campus speech issues. James Manley of the Goldwater Institute discusses draft legislation his organization has proposed and the steps taken toward its implementation by the regents in Wisconsin. Two law professors conclude the volume, as two began it. Eugene Volokh offers a detailed review of proposals for regulating campus speech and assesses their compatibility with current legal doctrine, while Larry Alexander addresses the problem and the cost of protecting campus speakers against others on campus who intend to disrupt.

Our aim in this volume is to promote reflection on our topic, not to present a strategy for reform. If some of the suggestions made in its pages prove useful to those who face decisions about controversial matters, the book will have served one purpose. If some of the essays provoke readers to think afresh about freedom of speech and intellectual diversity, it will have served another. It would be too facile to say that airing these issues proves that free speech remains secure and intellectual diversity remains viable. We hope, however, that the book contributes to both goals.

As noted in opening, this volume is an extension of the annual speaker series, entitled The Civic Discourse Project, organized by a new kind of department at an American public university. Our broader hope for this volume is that those who care both about universities and about a healthy American polity will consider that universities owe to this polity—which offers them so much freedom and support for their vocation—a renewed commitment by faculty and administration to assess for their own campuses whether there is space for, let alone a student requirement to undertake, the blend of liberal inquiry and civic education offered by this speaker series and this volume.

PART I

The Concept of Free Speech in Law and Higher Education

Chapter 1

The Classic First Amendment Tradition Under Stress

Freedom of Speech and the University

Robert C. Post

The First Amendment was ratified in 1791, and ever since, Americans have enjoyed a robust civic culture that celebrates freedom of expression. But courts played virtually no role in protecting free speech rights before the 1930s. As late as 1907, Justice Oliver Wendell Holmes could easily summarize the dominant doctrinal view of the First Amendment as having the "main purpose" of preventing "all such previous restraints upon publications as had been practiced by other governments," and not of preventing "the subsequent punishment of such as may be deemed contrary to the public welfare."[1]

THE EMERGENCE OF THE CLASSIC FIRST AMENDMENT TRADITION

Holmes's narrow view of the First Amendment evolved during the twentieth century due to altered understandings of self-government.[2] The nation began to equate democracy with "the organized sway of public opinion."[3] The efforts of the Wilson administration to control public opinion by prosecuting those opposed to World War I prompted American jurists to rethink the role of courts in protecting freedom of speech. As Learned Hand wrote to his friend, Zechariah Chafee, "any State which professes to be controlled by public opinion, cannot take sides against any opinion except that which must express itself in the violation of law. On the contrary, it must regard all other expression of opinion as tolerable, if not good."[4]

When the Supreme Court at last began to protect First Amendment rights in the 1930s, it explicitly theorized First Amendment rights in terms of the political value of self-government. In the early and decisive case of *Stromberg v. California*, for example, the Court proclaimed that the "maintenance of the opportunity for free political discussion to the end that government may be responsive to the will of the people and that changes may be obtained by lawful means, an opportunity essential to the security of the Republic, is a fundamental principle of our constitutional system."[5] A decade later the magnificent opinion by Justice Roberts in *Thornhill v. Alabama* affirmed that: "Those who won our independence had confidence in the power of free and fearless reasoning and communication of ideas to discover and spread political and economic truth. Noxious doctrines in those fields may be refuted, and their evil averted, by the courageous exercise of the right of free discussion. Abridgment of freedom of speech and of the press, however, impairs those opportunities for public education that are essential to effective exercise of the power of correcting error through the processes of popular government."[6]

The classic First Amendment tradition thus protected speech insofar as it was deemed necessary for the formation "of that public opinion which is the final source of government in a democratic state."[7] The corollary of this conceptual framework was that speech deemed irrelevant for the free formation of public opinion was not protected by the First Amendment. Only two years after *Thornhill*, for example, Justice Roberts could hold for a unanimous Court that "the Constitution imposes no . . . restraint on government as respects purely commercial advertising,"[8] evidently because such advertising was regarded as exogenous to the discovery and spread of political and economic truth.

Over the years, the Court developed core First Amendment rules that give content to the right to participate in the formation of public opinion in the public sphere. Here are three such rules that are essential to modern First Amendment jurisprudence:

> *Rule 1:* "It is axiomatic that the government may not regulate speech based on its substantive content or the message it conveys. . . . When the government targets not subject matter, but particular views taken by speakers on a subject, the violation of the First Amendment is all the more blatant. Viewpoint discrimination is thus an egregious form of content discrimination."[9]

> *Rule 2:* "We have therefore been particularly vigilant to ensure that individual expressions of ideas remain free from governmentally imposed sanctions. The First Amendment recognizes no such thing as a 'false' idea. As Justice Holmes wrote, 'when men have realized that time has upset many fighting faiths, they may come to believe even more than they believe the very foundations of their own conduct that the ultimate good desired is better reached by free trade in

> ideas—that the best test of truth is the power of the thought to get itself accepted in the competition of the market. . . . '"[10]
>
> *Rule 3:* "It is . . . a basic First Amendment principle that 'freedom of speech prohibits the government from telling people what they must say.' . . . 'At the heart of the First Amendment lies the principle that each person should decide for himself or herself the ideas and beliefs deserving of expression, consideration, and adherence.'"[11] "'The essential thrust of the First Amendment is to prohibit improper restraints on the *voluntary* public expression of ideas. . . . There is necessarily . . . a concomitant freedom *not* to speak publicly, one which serves the same ultimate end as freedom of speech in its affirmative aspect.'"[12]

First Amendment doctrine incorporates these three very stringent rules because they enable the First Amendment to serve "as the guardian of our democracy."[13] The First Amendment underwrites democratic legitimacy insofar as we are free to influence public opinion and insofar as we believe that the state is responsive to public opinion.[14] If these two conditions hold, we can believe that our government is also potentially responsive to us.[15] The three essential rules of First Amendment jurisprudence are designed to safeguard the first of these conditions.

The three rules thus apply to the set of communicative acts judged necessary for the formation of public opinion. I shall call this set "public discourse." In the context of public discourse, the rule against content discrimination ensures that persons set the agenda for government action rather than the reverse. The state cannot rule out topics or viewpoints that persons wish to place on the national agenda. The rule establishing the equality of ideas stands for the proposition that every democratic citizen has an equal right to influence the contents of public opinion. As John Rawls once put it, in public debate "there are no experts: a philosopher has no more authority than other citizens."[16] The equality of ideas flows from the premise of political equality, not from any postulated epistemological equality, which would be incompatible with the very concepts of truth and falsity.[17] Finally, the rule against compelled speech prevents forms of coercion that would interfere with the ability of persons to imagine that the state is potentially responsive to them. We are not the free authors of our own government if we are compelled to participate in the formation of public opinion in a manner that is contrary to our own will.

THE CLASSIC TRADITION UNDER SIEGE

When persons participate in the formation of public opinion, they are sovereign. They decide the destiny the nation. The three essential rules of First Amendment jurisprudence define and codify this sovereignty. But, as Alexander Meiklejohn famously noted, in a democracy "the governors and the governed are not two distinct groups of persons. There is only one group—the self-governing people. Rulers and ruled are the same individuals. We, the People, are our own masters, our own subjects."[18]

Meiklejohn's insight is fundamental. The people could not be sovereigns if they could not also sometimes be subjects, for there would then be nothing left to govern. That is why classic First Amendment doctrine does not and cannot apply to "speech as such."[19] Almost all human action is communicative, and if First Amendment rights were interpreted to endow persons with sovereignty every time they spoke, the People would be constitutionally prohibited from almost all forms of regulation. They would pro tanto lose their sovereignty.

The Court stumbled across this dilemma in 1976 when it reversed its own precedent and extended constitutional protection to commercial speech.[20] The commercial marketplace exists through acts of communication, and if all such speech were protected by the three essential rules of First Amendment doctrine, the people would be stripped of the power to regulate their own economic circumstances. The Court thus very self-consciously created forms of protection for commercial speech that are far less strict than those accorded to public discourse.[21] It said that commercial speech could be compelled,[22] for example, and that the state could engage in content discrimination by suppressing "misleading" advertisements.[23] In the commercial marketplace all opinions are not equal; some are downright fraudulent.[24]

The classic First Amendment tradition has in the past two decades come under severe strain because the Court seems to have lost track of *why* the First Amendment protects speech. It has begun to apply First Amendment doctrine to all kinds of communication that have nothing to do with the formation of public opinion. A clear sign of this confusion are judicial efforts to extend to the professional speech of doctors the same protections that it accords to the formation of public opinion. As the Third Circuit recently opined in a case involving a statute regulating the speech of physicians, "[S]peech is speech, and it must be analyzed as such for purposes of the First Amendment."[25]

Taken literally, the Third Circuit's approach would transform every malpractice case involving communication—every failure to warn, every misleading medical opinion—into a question of constitutional law.

The same tendency to overreach has become visible in the context of commercial speech.[26] The overextension of First Amendment doctrine has led to repeated condemnations of modern First Amendment decisions as creating "The New Lochner,"[27] as establishing a powerful rationale for striking down ordinary commercial regulations.[28] In this chapter, I shall illustrate this contemporary failure to appreciate the fundamental purpose of the First Amendment by examining recent controversies about freedom of speech and universities.

FREEDOM OF SPEECH WITHIN UNIVERSITIES: MISAPPLYING THE CLASSIC FIRST AMENDMENT TRADITION

The Contemporary Controversy

One hears now everywhere the cry that First Amendment rights are at risk because universities have failed to protect freedom of expression. Within weeks of her confirmation, the new secretary of education, Betsy DeVos, proclaimed that "the real threat" in modern universities "is silencing the First Amendment rights of people with whom you disagree."[29] And in September, Attorney General Jeff Sessions complained that "Freedom of . . . speech on the American campus [is] under attack."[30] Universities, Sessions announced, should abide by "what the late Justice Antonin Scalia rightly called 'the first axiom of the First Amendment,' which is that, 'as a general rule, the state has no power to ban speech on the basis of its content'"[31] Certainly, Sessions asserted, failure to comply with such "free speech rights" was "not an option" for public universities, "but an unshakable requirement of the First Amendment."[32]

Controversies currently roiling American campuses are characterized as pitting "a sharp increase in attention to students' psychological health" against "a somewhat diminished concern—sometimes bordering on outright skepticism—about the right to free speech."[33] They are said to reveal "an 'apparent chasm' between free speech advocates and student activists."[34] Efforts to curb micro-aggression are resisted as "nothing less than an attack on free speech"[35] and as provoking the question whether "racist expression should be allowed as long as it's cloaked in the First Amendment."[36] "The 'safety'-crusaders who equate words with violence" are charged with nullifying "the First Amendment on account of feelings."[37] Cancelling university speakers is condemned as inconsistent with "the First Amendment."[38] The upshot is the enactment of statutes like the Campus Free Speech Protection Act of Tennessee, which provides:

a. The general assembly finds and declares that public institutions of higher education in Tennessee are not immune from the sweep of the First Amendment to the United States Constitution . . . which guarantees freedom of speech and expression.
b. It is the intent of the general assembly that the public institutions of higher education embrace a commitment to the freedom of speech and expression for all students and all faculty.[39]

On one side of the spectrum, the president of the University of California system, invoking "First Amendment protections," complains that "we have moved from freedom *of* speech on campuses to freedom *from* speech."[40] On the other side of the spectrum, right leaning commentators argue that "Pro-life speakers are unwelcome, and conservatives are demonized, even banned from campuses for believing that ideas written into America's Constitution have meaning in modern America. Farewell 1st Amendment and the remainder of the Bill of Rights."[41]

The organization that is most influential in advocating the application of First Amendment jurisprudence to universities is the Foundation for Individual Rights in Education ("FIRE"). "FIRE's mission is to defend and sustain the individual rights of students and faculty members at America's colleges and universities. These rights include freedom of speech, freedom of association, due process, legal equality, religious liberty, and sanctity of conscience—the essential qualities of liberty."[42] FIRE's mission statement explicitly affirms:

Why is free speech important on campus?

Freedom of speech is a fundamental American freedom and a human right, and there's no place that this right should be more valued and protected than America's colleges and universities. A university exists to educate students and advance the frontiers of human knowledge and does so by acting as a "marketplace of ideas" where ideas compete. The intellectual vitality of a university depends on this competition—something that cannot happen properly when students or faculty members fear punishment for expressing views that might be unpopular with the public at large or disfavored by university administrators.

Nevertheless, freedom of speech is under continuous threat at many of America's campuses, pushed aside in favor of politics, comfort, or simply a desire to avoid controversy. As a result, speech codes dictating what may or may not be said, "free speech zones" confining free speech to tiny areas of campus, and administrative attempts to punish or repress speech on a case-by-case basis are common today in academia.

What is the First Amendment?

> The First Amendment to the US Constitution is the part of the Bill of Rights that expressly prohibits the United States Congress from making laws "respecting an establishment of religion," prohibiting the free exercise of religion, infringing freedom of speech, infringing freedom of the press, limiting the right to peaceably assemble, or limiting the right to petition the government for a redress of grievances. The protections of the First Amendment are extended to state governments and public university campuses by the Fourteenth Amendment.[43]

FIRE aggressively proclaims that First Amendment protections of free speech ought to apply within the domain of universities. The assumption is apparently that First Amendment protections attach to speech, and that speech occurs within universities.

The Classic First Amendment and the Campus

The question I wish to explore is what it might mean to apply the classic First Amendment to universities. The purpose of classic First Amendment principles is to protect the process of self-government. But speech within universities does not serve this purpose. It serves the purpose of education, which requires an entirely different framework of speech regulation and protection. Speech within campus is ordinarily protected according to principles of academic freedom, as distinct from freedom of speech.

Consider, for example, speech within a classroom. Classroom communication is not about influencing public opinion; it is about educating students. When students express themselves in a classroom, they are not acting as sovereign agents of self-government. They are acting as students who are tasked with learning from their instructors. The plain implication is that their speech may be regulated in ways that facilitate their education.

It is for this reason that the three cardinal rules of First Amendment jurisprudence are manifestly inapplicable to student speech in the classroom. First, content discrimination is rampant in all classrooms. Students must address the subject under class discussion rather than whatever happens to be on their minds. If I am teaching a class on the Constitution, my students cannot ramble on about the World Series. Second, all ideas are not equal within classroom discussion. Each student should be respected, but the function of classroom conversation is to instruct students in the art of distinguishing good from poor ideas.[44] No competent teacher would conduct a class on the premise that all ideas were equal. Third, compelled speech is normal within classrooms. Students are called upon to answer questions and required to take examinations.

Consider other important First Amendment doctrines. To preserve equality of participation within public discourse, the First Amendment precludes the state from regulating public discourse by suppressing speech that is offensive or outrageous or abusive.[45] But no competent teacher would permit a class to descend into name-calling and insults. Even if the object of classroom education is to expose students to ideas that they might not otherwise encounter and that they might find disturbing or threatening, it is nevertheless inconsistent with learning for students to experience this encounter in settings in which they are personally abused or degraded.[46] Competent teachers therefore insist on respect within the classroom to promote the effectiveness of the educational experience. Personal insults and incivility are inconsistent with deliberation and learning.

A similar analysis applies if we focus on the speech of professors within the classroom. The three essential rules of First Amendment jurisprudence do not apply to professorial communication in the classroom. The mission of the classroom is instruction, and professors are regularly judged on the competence of their performance in successfully educating students. Universities routinely engage in content discrimination in assessing professorial classroom communication. If I am supposed to be teaching constitutional law, I can't spend my classroom time talking about auto mechanics. Universities also assess the quality of the ideas conveyed by professors. If a mathematics professor continuously gets her equations wrong, her competence will be called into question. Universities also compel professors to show up to class, to teach, and therefore to speak. Within the classroom, university professors do not have freedom of speech, as measured by the classic First Amendment tradition.

Professors do, however, have *academic freedom* within the classroom.[47] The scope of academic freedom is not determined by First Amendment principles of freedom of speech, but by the requirements of professional competence. Professors are free to teach in ways that are required by the educational mission of a university and that are thus conceptualized as professionally competent.

The function of higher education is ordinarily said to be the inculcation of what Cardinal Newman called "real cultivation of mind."[48] As the American Association of University Professors put it in its classic 1915 *Declaration of the Principles on Academic Freedom and Tenure*, the purpose of university education is "not to provide . . . students with ready-made conclusions, but to train them to think for themselves, and to provide them access to those materials which they need if they are to think intelligently."[49] This training can occur only if students and faculty in a classroom are "free . . . to express the widest range of viewpoints in accord with the standards of scholarly inquiry and professional ethics."[50]

Independence of mind is not a form of information that can be handed from teachers to students. It is instead a characterological trait that students must be inspired to embrace. The hope is that students who witness actual independence of mind will be moved to internalize autonomous thinking as a form of living. As Richard Rorty puts it "Students need to have freedom enacted before their eyes by actual human beings" if higher education is to achieve its purpose of becoming a "provocation to self-creation."[51]

No doubt much of higher education requires the transmission of information and skills. But if our most important goal is to inspire a mature independence of mind, professorial speech within a classroom must be given great latitude. Professors must be allowed to demonstrate their own independence. As the 1915 *Declaration* reasons:

> No man can be a successful teacher unless he enjoys the respect of his students, and their confidence in his intellectual integrity. It is clear, however, that this confidence will be impaired if there is suspicion on the part of the student that the teacher is not expressing himself fully or frankly. . . . It is not only the character of the instruction but also the character of the instructor that counts; and if the student has reason to believe that the instructor is not true to himself, the virtue of the instruction as an educative force is incalculably diminished. There must be in the mind of the teacher no mental reservation. He must give the student the best of what he has and what he is.[52]

Academic freedom of teaching is thus quite encompassing. But it does not derive from, nor is it homologous with, the classic First Amendment tradition. Freedom of teaching is not about self-government; it is about education. That is why the three essential rules of First Amendment jurisprudence do not apply to professors in the classroom.

It is also why professors who bully, abuse, degrade, or demean their students risk being found professionally incompetent in achieving the university's mission of education. Professional ethics require professors to "demonstrate respect for students as individuals and adhere to their proper roles as intellectual guides and counselors."[53] They also require professors to "avoid any exploitation, harassment, or discriminatory treatment of students."[54] Professors must walk a narrow and difficult line between maintaining student trust and identification and provoking students to consider new, unfamiliar, and perhaps even threatening ideas.

If the classic First Amendment tradition does not apply to speech in the classroom, it also does not apply to the professional research of faculty. The mission of universities includes the expansion of knowledge. Universities are not especially concerned with the kind of knowledge that derives from immediate sensory apprehension; nor do they typically dedicate themselves to the production of the charismatic knowledge characteristic of art. Instead, universities seek to advance the *expert knowledge* produced by what we call *disciplines*.[55] One cannot know whether cigarettes cause cancer merely by smoking; one cannot measure climate change by taking the temperature on a winter's day; one cannot know the half-life of Plutonium-230 merely by staring at a lump of metal. To know, or even to formulate these questions, one must understand the practices of disciplines like medicine, climatography, or nuclear physics.

Universities provide an institutional home for such disciplines. Other organizations like private corporations may create knowledge, but *only* universities reproduce, refine, and conserve the practices, beliefs, and methods of knowing that define the disciplines that certify expert knowledge. Universities are the only major institution that systematically train the experts on whom we must inevitably rely in deploying disciplinary knowledge.[56] We depend upon doctors to create vaccines to immunize us against Zika; we rely upon engineers to build bridges. We do not crowdsource such questions or decide them by public opinion polls or by popular vote. We use universities to train engineers and to educate doctors in their respective disciplines.

Disciplines may be defined as "communities of the competent."[57] In contrast to public discourse, which postulates the democratic equality of all citizens, disciplines are inherently hierarchical. To speak with authority within a discipline requires training in relevant beliefs, practices, and methods of knowing. It takes long years of preparation to become an authority within a discipline. That is why disciplines subject new devotees to long and arduous apprenticeships during graduate education. Disciplines are grounded on the premise that some ideas are better than others; disciplinary communities claim the prerogative to discriminate between competent and incompetent work.

Healthy disciplines also require freedom of inquiry. As Thomas Haskell writes, "*The price of participation in the community of the competent is perpetual exposure to criticism.*"[58] The reason for this price is not complicated to discern:

> The . . . function of seeking new truths will sometimes mean . . . the undermining of widely or generally accepted beliefs. It is rendered impossible if the work of the investigator is shackled by the requirement that his conclusions shall never seriously deviate either from generally accepted beliefs or from those accepted by the persons, private or official, through whom society provides the means for the maintenance of universities.[59]

The freedom of inquiry characteristic of a disciplinary community differs starkly from the classic First Amendment tradition. The distinction is often carelessly ignored, probably because of the old saw that "it is the purpose of the First Amendment to preserve an uninhibited marketplace of ideas in which truths will ultimately prevail,"[60] and that the First Amendment advances "knowledge . . . by fostering a free marketplace of ideas and an 'uninhibited, robust, wide-open debate on public issues.'"[61] But these bromides about the marketplace of ideas are quite misleading.

Disciplines do not create expert knowledge through a marketplace of ideas in which content discrimination is prohibited and in which all ideas are deemed equal. No professionally edited journal runs on the principle of the marketplace of ideas. Instead, disciplinary journals authorize experts to make judgments of quality that acknowledge the possibility of critique and discovery. The marketplace of ideas is inimical to such judgments.

The marketplace of ideas prohibits such judgments because each person is endowed with an equal right to influence the content of public opinion. As Michael Walzer writes, "[e]very citizen is a potential participant, a potential politician. That potentiality is the necessary condition of the citizen's self-respect."[62] If the value of political equality entitles all to participate in the marketplace of ideas, disciplinary debates are not subject to this value. Disciplinary disputes occur among those who are already trained within existing disciplinary practices. Authority and competence matter within disciplinary debates.

Disciplines thus live in the tension between freedom of inquiry and judgments of competence. Disciplines that do not allow freedom of inquiry wither and atrophy; but disciplines that do not evaluate the quality and merit of disciplinary work disintegrate and become incoherent. The three essential rules of the classic First Amendment apply to the marketplace of ideas precisely because it is not afflicted by any such tension.

It would make no sense, therefore, to apply these three rules to university regulations of faculty research. In pursuing their mission to advance knowledge, universities regularly and routinely exercise content and viewpoint discrimination. Universities offer grants to research projects they consider likely to be productive; they do not operate as passive marketplaces of ideas. Universities hire faculty based upon considerations of content, focusing on areas they believe especially important to the development of disciplinary fields. Universities continuously assess the competence of faculty. They do not consider all ideas to be equal. If there were no such thing as a false idea, there would be no such thing as a true idea, and the entire aspiration of disciplines to produce expert knowledge would collapse. That is why history professors who deny the holocaust are not hired or promoted. Universities also compel speech. The rule is publish or perish. Universities hire and promote faculty based upon their certification as experts, and consequently faculty must demonstrate their expertise by speaking.

The classic First Amendment tradition is thus a very bad guide to the way that universities control the professional speech of faculty. Within universities, research faculty are not entitled to classic First Amendment protections for speech. They are entitled instead to *academic freedom* of research.[63] Academic freedom of research is, in the words of the *Declaration of the Principles on Academic Freedom and Tenure*, the freedom to pursue the "scholar's profession"[64] according to the standards of that profession. The *Declaration* asserts that the "liberty of the scholar within the university to set forth his conclusions, be they what they may, is conditioned by their being conclusions gained by a scholar's method and held in a scholar's spirit; that is to say, they must be the fruits of competent and patient and sincere inquiry."[65] Academic freedom, the *Declaration* precisely notes, upholds "not the absolute freedom of utterance of the individual scholar, but the absolute freedom of thought, of inquiry, of discussion and of teaching, of the academic profession."[66]

The classic First Amendment tradition protects the right of *individuals* to speak. This is because democratic legitimation attaches to individual persons. But the freedom of inquiry that is relevant to a university's mission of research attaches instead to disciplinary communities. It is designed to allow such communities to develop autonomously according to their own internal logic.

To get a concrete sense of what this might mean in practice, consider the case of a young assistant professor who is denied tenure because a university has judged his work to be incompetent. If the professor sues for damages, a court will rule in his favor if it believes that his work was not substandard when measured by relevant disciplinary criteria. But a court will rule in the university's favor if it concludes that the professor's work was indeed substandard when assessed by pertinent disciplinary criteria. In effect, therefore, a court will not protect the right of the professor to publish what he individually wishes to say; it will not protect the professor's right to freedom of speech. It will instead protect the integrity of relevant disciplinary standards.

The Source of the Confusion

When seen from this angle, it seems so obvious that speech within universities cannot be governed by classic First Amendment doctrine that we may ask how constitutional First Amendment rights could ever have come to be confused with the regulation of speech within universities. Why do people now complain, as they so often do, that universities are denying First Amendment rights? I suggest that confusion occurs in circumstances where the educational or research functions of a university are neither salient nor well theorized and where academic freedom is thus not a very useful concept.

Disputes over invited speakers, for example, often involve uncertainty over the educational and research missions of the university. Such speakers are responsible neither for disciplinary competence nor for competence in teaching. Their research does not add to the productivity of the university, nor are they expected to establish long-term relationships with students that can inspire the development of intellectual independence. Outside speakers thus appear almost as strangers to the essential missions of the university. It is not clear how academic freedom applies to them. It is a small step from this ambiguity to the conclusion that outside speakers should be regarded as participants in public discourse and therefore accorded full First Amendment rights.

But this conclusion obscures the essential logic of how outside speakers enter university environs. Universities are not public fora. Whatever happens under the aegis of a university must be justified by reference to the university's twin missions of research and education. This means that outside speakers are invited to universities *because* they serve these missions. Universities betray their fiduciary responsibilities to the extent they expend resources on speakers who fail to serve these missions.[67] It follows that although the conceptual framework of academic freedom has not been elaborated to include outside speakers, the scope and bounds of the proper regulation of the speech of outside speakers must nevertheless be justified in terms of their contribution to the twin missions of the modern university.

Exactly how outside invited speakers contribute to the educational or research missions of a university is a complicated question. Relevant circumstances and distinctions proliferate indefinitely. So, for example, consider the case of a faculty member who invites an outside speaker to lecture in her class because she believes that the speaker will contribute to her research or to her pedagogical responsibilities. If the university administration believes that the outside speaker is inconsistent with the research or educational functions of the university, there is a conflict between faculty and administration about how to attain university goals. Principles of academic freedom require the university administration to give great (if not decisive) deference to the judgment of faculty in such contexts.[68] First Amendment free speech principles have little to do with the matter.

Outside speakers are often invited in ways that do not implicate the academic freedom of faculty. Especially difficult cases often arise in the context of student-invited outside speakers. Students are accountable neither for the research mission of the university nor for its educational responsibilities. It is puzzling, therefore, how to analyze student-invited speakers in terms of the purposive goals of the university.

We must begin our analysis from the premise that universities are not Hyde Parks. Unless they are wasting their resources on a frolic and detour, they can authorize students to expend university resources to invite speakers[69] *only* because it serves university purposes to do so. In the case of student-invited speakers, universities delegate to students the determination whether particular speakers serve university educational or research purposes. Outside speakers are not selected at random, even by students. Students invite speakers because they believe the speakers have something worthwhile to say. The first two cardinal rules of First Amendment jurisprudence are thus inapplicable, because students exercise content (and perhaps viewpoint) discrimination, and they also determine that certain ideas are more worth hearing than others.

Yet content and viewpoint discrimination, as well as judgments of value, are acceptable in universities, so long as they serve educational and research purposes. The difficulty is that universities typically undertheorize the relationship between student-invited speakers and its own education and research mission.[70] Universities might support student-invited speakers because they wish to empower students to pursue research interests different from those offered by faculty. Or universities might support student-invited speakers because they wish to create a diverse and heterogeneous campus climate in which students can learn the democratic skills necessary to negotiate a public sphere filled with alien and cacophonous voices. Universities may wish to educate students in practices of citizenship by encouraging a wide variety of student groups to invite outside speakers to recreate within the campus a marketplace of ideas.

As universities clarify *why* they authorize student-invited outside speakers, they will concomitantly clarify the circumstances in which the communication of such speakers is and is not appropriate. The First Amendment rights of invited speakers are irrelevant to this clarification. The question is how policies that authorize students to invite speakers to campus do and do not advance institutional purposes of education and the expansion of knowledge. It is mistaken to invoke freedom of speech principles to pre-empt this inquiry.

Apart from the question of invited speakers, recent years have witnessed controversies about the regulation of student speech that occurs off campus and that does not arise in the context of university activities. Often the rationale given for such regulation is the protection of the campus "environment" from hostile racist or misogynist influences.[71] But as the connection between off-campus student speech and the campus environment grows more tenuous, this rationale becomes more difficult to credit. Freedom of speech principles become a concomitantly more attractive lens of analysis.

In such circumstances, analysis must begin from the premise that if student speech has literally no connection with a university's mission, either positive or negative, then a university cannot justify regulating that speech by a purposive account of its own goals.[72] The fact that universities are nevertheless reaching out to regulate off-campus behavior suggests that they in fact do believe that it somehow relates to their educational mission. I suspect that this is because a new definition of educational goals is now emerging. Student pleas for "safe spaces" and for expurgated environments reflect a desire for universities to adopt an educational commitment that can properly be called *in loco parentis*.

If universities were indeed to formulate their educational mission in this way, they would accept the obligation to educate the *entire* student, not just those aspects of students that directly interact with the university environment. Just as parents assert control over every dimension of their children's lives, so universities under an *in loco parentis* conception of their educational mission would not compartmentalize distinct aspects of their students' lives. They would seek comprehensively to educate persons who are students. Hence if universities adopt an *in loco parentis* conception of education, they might be justified in asserting jurisdiction over all aspects of student speech, including speech off campus and seemingly unrelated to university matters.[73]

This comprehensive educational ambition was rejected by most universities in the 1960s. Its resurrection now is neither well understood nor widely accepted. University efforts to regulate student speech based upon this account of their educational mission are hotly disputed.[74] Ultimately, however, this controversy cannot be resolved by the classic First Amendment tradition; it can be settled only by clarifying the educational mission of universities, which is a challenge well worth meeting.

Public Universities

I have so far discussed freedom of speech in the context of universities in general. But public universities are state institutions that must abide by the First Amendment. It is therefore tempting to believe that ordinary principles of freedom of speech should (at a minimum) apply in the context of public universities.

Public universities, however, no less than private ones, are designed to serve particular purposes. All government institutions established to achieve particular goals must regulate speech as necessary to achieve those goals, on pain of becoming ineffective.[75] That is why, in the context of higher education, the Court has explicitly announced that "a university's mission is education" and that the First Amendment does not deny a university's "authority to impose reasonable regulations compatible with that mission upon the use of its campus and facilities,"[76] which includes "a university's right to exclude . . . First Amendment activities that . . . substantially interfere with the opportunity of other students to obtain an education."[77]

If state universities could not regulate speech as required to achieve their mission, they would be forced to abstain from content discrimination; they would be compelled to treat all ideas equally; they would be disabled from compelling speech. Neither private nor public universities could function under such severe constraints. Public universities, no less than private ones, must evaluate the competence of both students and faculty; they must compel students and faculty to speak; they must routinely and pervasively engage in content discrimination. FIRE and overblown public rhetoric notwithstanding, it makes little sense to apply core First Amendment principles of freedom of speech to public universities.

The constitutional question for public universities is thus whether and how communicative restraints are necessary to realize the twin objectives of research and education. The fullest account we have of the relationship between freedom of expression and the achievement of these objectives is contained within the long and distinguished tradition of *academic freedom*, which starkly contrasts with ordinary principles of First Amendment doctrine. Academic freedom turns on judgments of competence, whereas ordinary First Amendment principles forbid such judgments. Academic freedom protects the autonomy of a profession, whereas First Amendment rights protect the freedom of individuals. Because public universities must achieve the purposes for which they are created, First Amendment doctrine as applied to them is best conceived within the functional framework established by principles of academic freedom.

First Amendment restraints on public universities are therefore most difficult to understand when the requirements of academic freedom are most obscure. Many contemporary controversies involving freedom of expression on university campuses simply do not implicate academic freedom, as it is traditionally understood. In such circumstances First Amendment analysis must revert to first principles. It must begin from the premise that public universities may regulate speech as necessary to achieve their institutional objectives.

This raises the constitutionally difficult question of how the mission of public higher education is to be understood. It is true that the Constitution contains no explicit account of this mission, but whenever speech is regulated within the context of a government institution, this same basic constitutional question of mission is raised.[78] In the context of public universities, we can make it visible in a relatively simple case. Suppose students march through campus chanting, "No means yes; yes means anal."[79]

Traditional principles of academic freedom do not tell us much about how to handle such a demonstration. Such a demonstration could not be excluded from a public park, because it would be protected by the cardinal rules of First Amendment jurisprudence. The march would be deemed public discourse and immunized from regulation despite its offensive and outrageous nature. But because public universities are not public parks, and because they are dedicated to the mission of educating their students, the constitutional inquiry whether student demonstrations of this nature seriously interfere with the educational mission of a public university cannot be evaded.

Ordinary First Amendment doctrine concerning offensive or outrageous speech is not helpful with regard to this inquiry, because such doctrine is rooted in the requirements of self-governance in the context of a heterogeneous nation.[80] Instead a court must determine the nature of a public university's educational mission and the extent to which student demonstrations of this kind obstruct that mission.[81] These are no doubt truly difficult issues, but classic First Amendment doctrine does not help us resolve them.[82]

CONCLUSION

Modern debates rely heavily on the constitutional rhetoric of freedom of speech because in recent years so many have contended that First Amendment protections ought to be applied to "speech as such"[83] rather than to public discourse. This tendency derives from a failure to understand the *purposive* nature of First Amendment rights. Because communication inheres in all aspects of life, this failure poses a great threat to the classic First Amendment tradition. The predictable overextension of First Amendment rights will in the long run prove unsustainable. We ought to stop traveling down that path while there is still time. Contemporary controversies about the regulation of speech within universities well illustrate the danger.

NOTES

1. *Patterson v. Colorado*, 205 U.S. 454, 462 (1907) (Holmes, J.). Even as late as 1915, Harlan Fiske Stone, the future author of footnote four of *Carolene Products*, could summarize "the more important" aspects of the Bill of Rights as including "freedom of religious worship, the right peaceably to assemble, the right to bear arms, the right to be free from unreasonable searches and seizures, the right to a speedy trial by jury, the right not to be compelled to testify against oneself in a criminal trial, the right not to be deprived of life, liberty, or property without due process of law, and the like." Harlan F. Stone, *Law and Its Administration* (New York: Columbia University Press, 1915), p. 140. It is remarkable that in this long list Stone does not even mention freedom of expression.

2. Robert C. Post, *Citizens Divided: Campaign Finance Reform and the Constitution* (Harvard University Press, 2014).

3. Charles Horton Cooley, *Social Organization: A Study of the Larger Mind* (Glencoe, IL: Free Press, 1956), p. 118.

4. Letter from Learned Hand to Zechariah Chafee, Jr., Jan. 8, 1920 (on file in the Chafee Papers, Box 4, Folder 20, Harvard Law Library, Treasure Room), as reprinted

in Gerald Gunther, "Learned Hand and the Origins of Modern First Amendment Doctrine: Some Fragments of History," *Stanford Law Review* 27 (1975): 764–766.

5. *Stromberg v. California*, 283 U.S. 359, 369 (1931).

6. *Thornhill v. Alabama*, 310 U.S. 88, 95 (1940).

7. *Masses Publishing Co. v. Patten*, 244 F. 535 (S.D.N.Y.), *rev'd*, 246 F. 24 (2d Cir. 1917). Hence *Thornhill*: "The freedom of speech and of the press guaranteed by the Constitution embraces at the least the liberty to discuss publicly and truthfully all matters of public concern, without previous restraint or fear of subsequent punishment. The exigencies of the colonial period and the efforts to secure freedom from oppressive administration developed a broadened conception of these liberties as adequate to supply the public need for information and education with respect to the significant issues of the times. . . . Freedom of discussion, if it would fulfill its historic function in this nation, must embrace all issues about which information is needed or appropriate to enable the members of society to cope with the exigencies of their period" (101–102).

8. *Valentine v. Chrestensen*, 316 U.S. 52, 54 (1942).

9. *Rosenberger v. Rectors and Visitors of the University of Virginia*, 515 U.S. 819, 828–29 (1995). See *Reed v. Town of Gilbert*, 135 S.Ct. 2218, 2226 (2015) (The state "'has no power to restrict expression because of its message, its ideas, its subject matter, or its content.' Content-based laws—those that target speech based on its communicative content—are presumptively unconstitutional and may be justified only if the government proves that they are narrowly tailored to serve compelling state interests.").

10. *Hustler Magazine, Inc. v. Falwell*, 485 U.S. 46, 51 (1988). See *Bose Corp. v. Consumers Union of U.S., Inc.*, 466 U.S. 485, 504 (1984); *Old Dominion Branch No. 496 v. Austin*, 418 U.S. 264, 284 (1974).

11. *Agency for Intern. Development v. Alliance for Open Society Intern.*, Inc., 570 U.S. 205, 213 (2013) (quoting *Rumsfeld v. Forum for Academic and Institutional Rights, Inc.*, 547 U.S. 47, 61 [2006] and *Turner Broadcasting System, Inc. v. FCC*, 512 U.S. 622 [1994]).

12. *Harper & Row Publishers, Inc. v. Nation Enters.*, 471 U.S. 539, 559 (1985) (quoting *Estate of Hemingway v. Random House, Inc.*, 244 N.E.2d 250, 255 [1968]; emphasis added). "There is certainly some difference between compelled speech and compelled silence, but in the context of protected speech, the difference is without constitutional significance, for the First Amendment guarantees 'freedom of speech,' a term necessarily comprising the decision of both what to say and what *not* to say" (*Riley v. Nat'l Fed'n of the Blind of N.C., Inc.*, 487 U.S. 781, 796-97 [1988]). "Just as the First Amendment may prevent the government from prohibiting speech, the Amendment may prevent the government from compelling individuals to express certain views" (*United States v. United Foods*, 533 U.S. 405, 410 [2001]). See *Wooley v. Maynard*, 430 U.S. 705, 714 (1977); *West Virginia Bd. of Ed. v. Barnette*, 319 U.S. 624 (1943).

13. *Brown v. Hartlage*, 456 U.S. 45, 60 (1982).

14. Post, *Citizens Divided*.

15. See Robert C. Post, *Democracy, Expertise, Academic Freedom: A First Amendment Jurisprudence for the Modern State* (Yale University Press, 2012).

16. See John Rawls, "Reply to Habermas," *Journal of Philosophy* 92 (1995): 140–141.

17. Hence the Court's ruling that within public discourse even deliberate falsehoods can receive First Amendment protection. *United States v. Alvarez*, 567 US 709 (2012).

18. Alexander Meiklejohn, *Political Freedom: The Constitutional Powers of the People* (New York: Harper, 1960), 12.

19. *Glickman v. Wileman Brothers and Elliott, Inc.*, 521 U.S. 457, 478 (1997) (Souter, J., dissenting).

20. *Va. State Bd. of Pharmacy v. Va. Citizens Consumer Council, Inc.*, 425 U.S. 748 (1976).

21. Robert C. Post, "Compelled Commercial Speech," *West Virginia Law Review* 117 (2015): 867–919.

22. *Zauderer v. Office of Disciplinary Counsel*, 471 U.S. 626 (1985).

23. *Central Hudson Gas & Electric Corp. v. Public Service Commission*, 447 U.S. 557, 566 (1980).

24. *Illinois ex Rel. Lisa Madigan v. Telemarketing Associates, Inc.*, 538 U.S. 600 (2003).

25. *King v. Governor of New Jersey,* 767 F.3d 216, 229 (3d Cir. 2014); see *Wollschlaeger v. Florida*, 848 F.3d 1293, 1307 (11th Cir. 2017) (en banc).

26. See, e.g., *Sorrell v. IMS Health Inc.*, 131 S.Ct. 2653 (2011); *United States v. United Foods*, Inc., 533 U.S. 405 (2001).

27. See, e.g., Amanda Shanor, "The New Lochner," *Wisconsin Law Review* 2016: 133–208.

28. See Robert C. Post and Amanda Shanor, "Adam Smith's First Amendment," *Harvard Law Review Forum* 128 (2015): 165–182.

29. Scott Jaschick, "DeVos vs. the Faculty," *Inside Higher Education*, February 24, 2017, https://www.insidehighered.com/news/2017/02/24/education-secretary-criticizes-professors-telling-students-what-think. See Graham W. Bishai, "With Provocative Speakers, New Group Aims to 'Test' Free Speech Values," *Harvard Crimson*, April 7, 2017, https://www.thecrimson.com/article/2017/4/7/free-speech-club.

30. Lisa Marie Segarra, "Colleges Are an 'Echo Chamber of Political Correctness.' Read Jeff Sessions' Speech on Campus Free Speech," *Time*, September 26, 2017, http://time.com/4957604/jeff-sessions-georgetown-law-speech-transcript/.

31. Ibid.

32. Ibid.

33. Jonathan Zimmerman, *Campus Politics: What Everyone Needs to Know* (Oxford University Press, 2016), 5. See Jacqueline Pfeffer Merrill, "YES: Students must consider all ideas." *The Chronicle* (Willimantic, Connecticut), November 3, 2016: (referring to "rising campus ambivalence about free expression").

34. Jennifer Schuessler, "Can Cries of 'Free Speech' Be a Weapon? Students Say Yes," *New York Times*, October 16, 2016, https://www.nytimes.com/2016/10/17/arts/pen-warns-that-college-students-often-see-free-speech-as-a-cudgel.html.

35. Cindi Andrews, "Academic fascism begins with curbing free speech," *Cincinnati Inquirer*, August 16, 2015: ("Once leftists gain control, as they have at many universities, free speech becomes a liability and must be suppressed.").

36. Editorial, "Standing for Campus Free Speech," *Tampa Bay Times*, October 8, 2016. See Amanda Hoover, "Can a Halloween costume be hate speech?: A costume depicting Donald Trump hanging Hillary Clinton and President Obama from a noose sparked outrage at a University of Wisconsin football game. Are there controversial costumes that don't fall under free speech protections?" *Christian Science Monitor*, October 31, 2016, https://www.csmonitor.com/USA/Society/2016/1031/Can-a-Halloween-costume-be-hate-speech.

37. Sally Jenkins, "Free Speech? Columbia wrestlers can pay the price," *Washington Post*, November 16, 2016.

38. Susan Svrluga, "Writer's Speech at U-Md canceled," *Washington Post*, October 26, 2016.

39. Campus Free Speech Protection Act, 2017 Bill Text TN S.B. 723, http://www.capitol.tn.gov/Bills/110/Amend/SA0333.pdf. See Peter Schmidt, "Tennessee Law Is Hailed as Offering Unprecedented Protection of Campus Speech," *The Chronicle of Higher Education*, May 10, 2017, http://www.chronicle.com/blogs/ticker/tennessee-law-is-hailed-as-offering-unprecedented-protection-of-campus-speech/ Peter Schmidt, "A State's Effort to Head Off Campus-Speech Fights Gets Mixed Reviews," *Chronicle of Higher Education*, May 16, 2017, https://www.chronicle.com/article/A-State-s-Effort-to-Head-Off/240088. The Tennessee statute is evidently the leading edge of a coming wave of state legislative protections for free speech on campus. See Chris Quintana and Andy Thomason, "The States Where Campus Free-Speech Bills Are Being Born: A Rundown," *Chronicle of Higher Education*, May 15, 2017, https://www.chronicle.com/article/The-States-Where-Campus/240073.

40. Janet Napolitano, "It's time to free speech on campus again," *Boston Globe*, October 2, 2016, https://www.bostonglobe.com/opinion/2016/10/01/time-free-speech-campus-again/v5jDCzjuv710Mc92AhaAqL/story.html (emphasis in original).

41. Jerry Shenk, "How political correctness will kill higher ed," *Lebanon Daily News*, October 8, 2016.

42. Website of FIRE, https://www.thefire.org.

43. https://www.thefire.org/about-us/mission.

44. On distinguishing respect for students from respect for their ideas, see Matthew W. Finkin and Robert C. Post, *For the Common Good: Principles of American Academic Freedom* (Yale University Press, 2009), 105.

45. See Robert C. Post, "Community and the First Amendment," *Arizona State Law Journal* 29 (1997): 479–480. Abusive, degrading, offensive, and outrageous speech is protected in public discourse for reasons that derive from the value of self-governance. See Robert C. Post, "The Constitutional Concept of Public Discourse: Outrageous Opinion, Democratic Deliberation, and *Hustler Magazine v. Falwell*," *Harvard Law Review* 103 (1990): 603–686.

46. "Students are entitled to an atmosphere conducive to learning . . . ," AAUP, *A Statement of the Association's Council: Freedom and Responsibility*, https://www.aaup.org/report/freedom-and-responsibility.

47. Finkin and Post, *For the Common Good*, pp. 79–111.

48. John Henry Newman, *The Idea of the University Defined and Illustrated* (London: Longmans, Green, and Co.: 1888), xvi.

49. American Association of University Professors, *Declaration of Principles on Academic Freedom and Tenure* (1915), reproduced in Finkin and Post, *For the Common Good*, p. 174.

50. Ibid.

51. Richard Rorty, *Philosophy and Social Hope* (New York: Penguin, 1999), pp. 123, 125.

52. AAUP, *Declaration of Principles*, pp. 167–168.

53. AAUP, *Statement on Professional Ethics*, https://www.aaup.org/report/statement-professional-ethics.

54. Ibid.

55. See Robert C. Post, "Debating Disciplinarity," *Critical Inquiry* 35 (2009): 749–770.

56. Allan Gibbard, *Thinking How to Live* (Harvard University Press, 2003), pp. 226–227.

57. Thomas L. Haskell, "Justifying the Rights of Academic Freedom in the Era of 'Power/Knowledge,'" in *The Future of Academic Freedom*, edited by Louis Menand (University of Chicago Press, 1996), 45–46.

58. Haskell, "Justifying the Rights of Academic Freedom," 47 (emphasis in original).

59. Arthur O. Lovejoy, "Academic Freedom," in *Encyclopedia of the Social Sciences*, edited by Edwin R. A. Seligman and Alvin Johnson, volume 1 (New York: MacMillan Company, 1930), 384.

60. *Red Lion Broad. v. FCC*, 395 U.S. 367, 390 (1969).

61. Gloria Franke, "The Right of Publicity vs. The First Amendment: Will One Test Ever Capture the Starring Role," *California Law Review*, 79 (2006): 958.

62. Michael Walzer, *Spheres of Justice: A Defense of Pluralism and Equality* (New York: Basic Books, 1983), 310.

63. Finkin and Post, *For the Common Good*, pp. 53–77.

64. AAUP, *Declaration*, 163.

65. Ibid., 173. On the relationship between academic freedom and a theory of knowledge, see John R. Searle, "Two Concepts of Academic Freedom," in *The Concept of Academic Freedom*, edited by Edmund L. Pincoffs (University of Texas Press, 1975), pp. 88–89.

66. AAUP, *Declaration*, 179–180. Hence the conclusion of Thomas Haskell: "Historically speaking, the heart and soul of academic freedom lie not in free speech but in professional autonomy and collegial self-governance. Academic freedom came into being as a defense of the disciplinary community (or, more exactly, the university conceived as an ensemble of such communities)" (Haskell, "Justifying the Rights of Academic Freedom," 54).

67. In this chapter I do not consider situations where speakers come to campus based exclusively on private resources and without explicit university sanction, because in such circumstances the connection between speakers and universities

becomes particularly difficult to define. I consider instead situations in which universities are asked to expend their resources to sustain speakers.

68. Under ordinary principles of academic freedom, students have little standing to challenge the professional judgments of faculty about the value of an outside speaker with respect the attainment of either educational or research goals. Universities therefore have little tolerance for student efforts to shut down faculty-invited outside speakers.

69. See note 68 above.

70. The Supreme Court has approved a Law School policy authorizing student programs in order to encourage "tolerance, cooperation, and learning among students." *Christian Legal Society v. Martinez*, 561 U.S. 661, 689 (2010). The Court held that the school could limit expressive association to serve these goals. The school policy supporting student organizations was theorized as a limited purpose public forum.

71. See, e.g., Manny Fernandez and Richard Pérez-Peña, "As Two Oklahoma Students are Expelled for Racist Chants, Sigma Alpha Epsilon Vows Wider Inquiry," *New York Times*, March 10, 2015, https://www.nytimes.com/2015/03/11/us/university-of-oklahoma-sigma-alpha-epsilon-racist-fraternity-video.html.

72. See, e.g., *Pickering v. Board of Education*, 391 U.S. 563 (1968).

73. In the 1960s, the freedom of speech movement sought precisely to oppose this concept of education. See Robert C. Post, "Constitutionally Interpreting the FSM Controversy," in *The Free Speech Movement: Reflections on Berkeley in the 1960s*, edited by Robert Cohen and Reginald E. Zelnik (Berkeley: University of California Press, 2002), p. 401–421.

74. See, e.g., Eliza Gray, "Civil Libertarians Say Expelling Oklahoma Frat Students May Be Illegal," *Time*, March 10, 2015, http://time.com/3739268/sigma-alpha-epsilon-university-of-oklahoma-expel-free-speech.

75. See Robert C. Post, "Between Governance and Management: The History and Theory of the Public Forum," *UCLA Law Review* 34 (1987): 1713–1835. Another way to put this point is that the First Amendment does not require the state to protect speech within courtrooms, bureaucracies, and prisons as though the values of self-government were at stake.

76. Widmar v. Vincent, 454 U.S. 263, 267 n.5 (1981).

77. Ibid. at 277 (citing *Healy v. James*, 408 U.S. 169, 189 [1972]).

78. See Post, "Between Governance and Management."

79. See Tyler Kingkade, "Texas Tech Frat Loses Charter Following 'No Means Yes, Yes Means Anal' Display," *Huffington Post*, October 9, 2014, http://www.huffingtonpost.com/2014/10/08/texas-tech-frat-nomeans-yes_n_5953302.html.

80. See Post, "Community and the First Amendment," and Post, "The Constitutional Concept of Public Discourse."

81. The famous Woodward Report issued by Yale University on December 23, 1974, effectively obscures these questions when it simultaneously asserts *both* that "The primary function of a university is to discover and disseminate knowledge by means of research and teaching," *and* that a university "is not primarily a fellowship, a club, a circle of friends. . . . Without sacrificing its central purpose it cannot make its primary and dominant value the fostering of friendship, solidarity, harmony, civility,

or mutual respect." *The Woodward Report*, http://yalecollege.yale.edu/deans-office/policies-reports/report-committee-freedom-expression-yale. These two propositions are in serious tension; in extreme situations, they cannot be reconciled except through a theory of education that runs contrary to the experience of virtually all university teachers and administrators. It is no wonder, therefore, that the Report is almost always read to subordinate the goal of teaching and to elevate "free speech over every other university goal or purpose" (Zimmerman, *Campus Politics*, 113). But a university that abandons the goal of teaching can no longer remain true to its *raison d'etre.*

82. Note that under the recently enacted "Campus Individual Rights Act" of Utah, available at https://le.utah.gov/~2017/bills/static/HB0054.html#53b-27-101, the direct imposition of First Amendment "public forum" principles onto public campuses would prevent a university from regulating this demonstration on the grounds of content or viewpoint. See *Reed.*

83. *Glickman* at 478.

REFERENCES

AAUP, *A Statement of the Association's Council: Freedom and Responsibility*, https://www.aaup.org/report/freedom-and-responsibility.

Agency for Intern. Development v. Alliance for Open Society Intern., Inc., 570 U.S. 205 (2013).

Andrews, Cindi. "Academic fascism begins with curbing free speech," *Cincinnati Inquirer*, August 16, 2015

Bishai, Graham W. "With Provocative Speakers, New Group Aims to 'Test' Free Speech Values," *Harvard Crimson*, April 7, 2017, https://www.thecrimson.com/article/2017/4/7/free-speech-club.

Bose Corp. v. Consumers Union of U.S., Inc., 466 U.S. 485 (1984).

Brown v. Hartlage, 456 U.S. 45, 60 (1982).

Campus Free Speech Protection Act, 2017 Bill Text TN S.B. 723, http://www.capitol.tn.gov/Bills/110/Amend/SA0333.pdf.

Campus Individual Rights Act" of Utah, https://le.utah.gov/~2017/bills/static/HB0054.html#53b-27-101

Central Hudson Gas & Electric Corp. v. Public Service Commission, 447 U.S. 557 (1980).

Christian Legal Society v. Martinez, 561 U.S. 661 (2010).

Cooley, Charles Horton. *Social Organization: A Study of the Larger Mind* (Glencoe, IL: Free Press, 1956).

Editorial, "Standing for Campus Free Speech," *Tampa Bay Times*, October 8, 2016.

Estate of Hemingway v. Random House, Inc., 244 N.E.2d 250 (1968).

Fernandez, Manny, and Richard Pérez-Peña, "As Two Oklahoma Students are Expelled for Racist Chants, Sigma Alpha Epsilon Vows Wider Inquiry," *New York Times*, March 10, 2015, https://www.nytimes.com/2015/03/11/us/university-of-oklahoma-sigma-alpha-epsilon-racist-fraternity-video.html.

Finkin, Matthew W., and Robert C. Post, *For the Common Good: Principles of American Academic Freedom* (New Haven, CT: Yale University Press, 2009).

FIRE (website), https://www.thefire.org.

Franke, Gloria. "The Right of Publicity vs. The First Amendment: Will One Test Ever Capture the Starring Role," *California Law Review*, 79 (2006): 958.

Gibbard, Allan. *Thinking How to Live* (Cambridge, MA: Harvard University Press, 2003)

Glickman v. Wileman Brothers and Elliott, Inc., 521 U.S. 457 (1997).

Gray, Eliza. "Civil Libertarians Say Expelling Oklahoma Frat Students May Be Illegal," *Time*, March 10, 2015, http://time.com/3739268/sigma-alpha-epsilon-university-of-oklahoma-expel-free-speech.

Gunther, Gerald. "Learned Hand and the Origins of Modern First Amendment Doctrine: Some Fragments of History," *Stanford Law Review* 27 (1975): 764.

Harper & Row Publishers, Inc. v. Nation Enters., 471 U.S. 539 (1985).

Haskell, Thomas L. "Justifying the Rights of Academic Freedom in the Era of 'Power/Knowledge,'" in *The Future of Academic Freedom*, edited by Louis Menand (Chicago: University of Chicago Press, 1996).

Healy v. James, 408 U.S. 169 (1972).

Hoover, Amanda. "Can a Halloween costume be hate speech?: A costume depicting Donald Trump hanging Hillary Clinton and President Obama from a noose sparked outrage at a University of Wisconsin football game. Are there controversial costumes that don't fall under free speech protections?" *Christian Science Monitor*, October 31, 2016, https://www.csmonitor.com/USA/Society/2016/1031/Can-a-Halloween-costume-be-hate-speech.

Hustler Magazine, Inc. v. Falwell, 485 U.S. 46 (1988).

Illinois ex Rel. Lisa Madigan v. Telemarketing Associates, Inc., 538 U.S. 600 (2003).

Jaschick, Scott. "DeVos vs. the Faculty," *Inside Higher Education*, February 24, 2017, https://www.insidehighered.com/news/2017/02/24/education-secretary-criticizes-professors-telling-students-what-think.

Jenkins, Sally. "Free Speech? Columbia wrestlers can pay the price," *Washington Post*, November 16, 2016.

King v. Governor of New Jersey, 767 F.3d 216 (3d Cir. 2014).

Kingkade, Tyler. "Texas Tech Frat Loses Charter Following 'No Means Yes, Yes Means Anal' Display," *Huffington Post*, October 9, 2014, http://www.huffingtonpost.com/2014/10/08/texas-tech-frat-nomeans-yes_n_5953302.html.

Lovejoy, Arthur O. "Academic Freedom," in *Encyclopedia of the Social Sciences*, edited by Edwin R. A. Seligman and Alvin Johnson, volume 1 (New York: MacMillan Company, 1930)

Masses Publishing Co. v. Patten, 244 F. 535 (S.D.N.Y.), *rev'd,* 246 F. 24 (2d Cir. 1917).

Meiklejohn, Alexander. *Political Freedom: The Constitutional Powers of the People* (New York: Harper, 1960).

Merrill, Jacqueline Pfeffer. "YES: Students must consider all ideas." *The Chronicle* (Willimantic, Connecticut), November 3, 2016.

Napolitano, Janet. "It's time to free speech on campus again," *Boston Globe*, October 2, 2016, https://www.bostonglobe.com/opinion/2016/10/01/time-free-speech-campus-again/v5jDCzjuv710Mc92AhaAqL/story.html.

Newman, John Henry. *The Idea of the University Defined and Illustrated* (London: Longmans, Green, and Co.: 1888).

Old Dominion Branch No. 496 v. Austin, 418 U.S. 264 (1974).

Patterson v. Colorado, 205 U.S. 454 (1907).

Pickering v. Board of Education, 391 U.S. 563 (1968).

Post, Robert C. "Between Governance and Management: The History and Theory of the Public Forum," *UCLA Law Review* 34 (1987): 1713–1835.

Post, Robert C. *Citizens Divided: Campaign Finance Reform and the Constitution* (Cambridge, MA: Harvard University Press, 2014).

Post, Robert C. "Community and the First Amendment," *Arizona State Law Journal* 29 (1997): 479–480.

Post, Robert C. "Compelled Commercial Speech," *West Virginia Law Review* 117 (2015): 867–919.

Post, Robert C. "Constitutionally Interpreting the FSM Controversy." In *The Free Speech Movement: Reflections on Berkeley in the 1960s*, edited by Robert Cohen and Reginald E. Zelnik (Berkeley: University of California Press, 2002)

Post, Robert C. "Debating Disciplinarity," *Critical Inquiry* 35 (2009): 749–770.

Post, Robert C. *Democracy Expertise, Academic Freedom: A First Amendment Jurisprudence for the Modern State* (New Haven, CT: Yale University Press, 2012).

Post, Robert C. "The Constitutional Concept of Public Discourse: Outrageous Opinion, Democratic Deliberation, and *Hustler Magazine v. Falwell*," *Harvard Law Review* 103 (1990): 603–686.

Post Robert C., and Amanda Shanor, "Adam Smith's First Amendment," *Harvard Law Review Forum* 128 (2015): 165–182.

Quintana, Chris, and Andy Thomason, "The States Where Campus Free-Speech Bills Are Being Born: A Rundown," *Chronicle of Higher Education*, May 15, 2017, https://www.chronicle.com/article/The-States-Where-Campus/240073.

Rawls, John. "Reply to Habermas," *Journal of Philosophy* 92 (1995): 140–141.

Red Lion Broad. v. FCC, 395 U.S. 367 (1969).

Reed v. Town of Gilbert, 135 S.Ct. 2218 (2015).

Riley v. Nat'l Fed'n of the Blind of N.C., Inc., 487 U.S. 781 (1988).

Rorty, Richard. *Philosophy and Social Hope* (New York: Penguin, 1999).

Rosenberger v. Rectors and Visitors of the University of Virginia, 515 U.S. 819 (1995).

Rumsfeld v. Forum for Academic and Institutional Rights, Inc., 547 U.S. 47 (2006).

Searle, John R. "Two Concepts of Academic Freedom." In *The Concept of Academic Freedom*, edited by Edmund L. Pincoffs (Austin: University of Texas Press, 1975)

Segarra, Lisa Marie. "Colleges Are an 'Echo Chamber of Political Correctness.' Read Jeff Sessions' Speech on Campus Free Speech." *Time*, September 26, 2017, http://time.com/4957604/jeff-sessions-georgetown-law-speech-transcript/.

Schmidt, Peter. "A State's Effort to Head Off Campus-Speech Fights Gets Mixed Reviews." *Chronicle of Higher Education*, May 16, 2017, https://www.chronicle.com/article/A-State-s-Effort-to-Head-Off/240088.

Schmidt, Peter. "Tennessee Law Is Hailed as Offering Unprecedented Protection of Campus Speech," *The Chronicle of Higher Education*, May 10, 2017, http://www.chronicle.com/blogs/ticker/tennessee-law-is-hailed-as-offering-unprecedented-protection-of-campus-speech/118311

Schuessler, Jennifer. "Can Cries of 'Free Speech' Be a Weapon? Students Say Yes," *New York Times*, October 16, 2016, https://www.nytimes.com/2016/10/17/arts/pen-warns-that-college-students-often-see-free-speech-as-a-cudgel.html.

Shanor, Amanda. "The New Lochner." *Wisconsin Law Review* 2016: 133–208.

Shenk, Jerry. "How political correctness will kill higher ed." *Lebanon Daily News*, October 8, 2016.

Sorrell v. IMS Health Inc., 131 S.Ct. 2653 (2011).

Stone, Harlan F. *Law and Its Administration* (New York: Columbia University Press, 1915).

Stromberg v. California, 283 U.S. 359 (1931).

Svrluga, Susan. "Writer's Speech at U-Md canceled." *Washington Post*, October 26, 2016.

Thornhill v. Alabama, 310 U.S. 88 (1940).

Turner Broadcasting System, Inc. v. FCC, 512 U.S. 622 (1994).

United States v. Alvarez, 567 US 709 (2012).

United States v. United Foods, 533 U.S. 405 (2001).

Valentine v. Chrestensen, 316 U.S. 52 (1942).

Va. State Bd. of Pharmacy v. Va. Citizens Consumer Council, Inc., 425 U.S. 748 (1976).

Walzer, Michael. *Spheres of Justice: A Defense of Pluralism and Equality* (New York: Basic Books, 1983).

West Virginia Bd. of Ed. v. Barnette, 319 U.S. 624 (1943).

Widmar v. Vincent, 454 U.S. 263 (1981).

Wollschlaeger v. Florida, 848 F.3d 1293 (11th Cir. 2017) (en banc).

Woodward Report, http://yalecollege.yale.edu/deans-office/policies-reports/report-committee-freedom-expression-yale.

Wooley v. Maynard, 430 U.S. 705 (1977).

Zauderer v. Office of Disciplinary Counsel, 471 U.S. 626 (1985).

Zimmerman, Jonathan. *Campus Politics: What Everyone Needs to Know* (New York: Oxford University Press, 2016),

Chapter 2

Free Speech on Campus

A Challenge of Our Times

Geoffrey R. Stone

Whenever I speak to students, I can't help but recall an incident involving Justice Oliver Wendell Holmes. At the time of this incident, Holmes was a very old man, nearing ninety years of age, in the autumn of his very long and very distinguished career as a Justice on the Supreme Court of the United States.

On this particular occasion, Holmes was on a train headed north from Washington. He was deeply engrossed in reading a legal brief when the conductor knocked on the door to his compartment. Recognizing Holmes, the conductor respectfully asked for his ticket. Holmes looked in his coat pocket—no ticket. He looked in his vest pocket—no ticket. He reached into his trouser pocket—no ticket. Growing ever more frantic, Holmes began rummaging desperately through his briefcase—still no ticket. At this point, the conductor, trying to calm Holmes, said, "Never mind, Mr. Justice. It's really not a problem. When you find the ticket, just mail it in to the company." To which Holmes exploded: "You dolt! I don't give a damn about your ticket, I just want to know where the hell I'm supposed to be going!"

As a student, you must often feel a bit like Justice Holmes—you want to know where the hell you're supposed to be going. My task today is to offer at least some sense of direction. I should like to begin by telling you a bit about my world. It is the world of the law. More specifically, it is the world of constitutional law. Law is about stories. It is about real people involved in real disputes with real consequences. So, I shall tell you a story.

This story begins during World War I. As you may or may not know, World War I was not a particularly popular war with the American people, whose sympathies were divided. Many Americans vigorously opposed the Wilson administration's decision to intervene in the brutal conflict that was then raging in Europe, arguing that our intervention was both unwise and immoral.

Not surprisingly, such opposition did not sit well with the government. In 1917, Attorney General Thomas Gregory, attacking the loyalty of war opponents, declared: "May God have mercy on them, for they can expect none from . . . an avenging government." Gregory wasn't kidding about the "avenging" government. In 1918, Congress enacted the Sedition Act, which made it a crime for any person to utter "any disloyal, . . . scurrilous, or abusive language intended to cause contempt . . . for the . . . government of the United States, the Constitution, or the flag." True to the Attorney General's threat, federal authorities launched more than 2,000 prosecutions against individuals who wrote or spoke against the war or the draft.

One such prosecution involved five young Russian-Jewish emigrants who were roughly your age at the time. In the summer of 1918, the United States sent a contingent of marines to Vladivostok in Russia. Fearing that this was the first step of an American effort to crush the Russian Revolution, these five self-proclaimed socialists threw several thousand copies of each of two leaflets—one in English, the other in Yiddish—from several rooftops on the lower east side of New York City.

The leaflets, which were boldly signed "The Rebels," were addressed to other Russian emigrants. After stating that the Rebels hated "German militarism," they warned those who worked in ammunition factories that they were "producing bullets, bayonets and cannon to murder not only the Germans, but also your dearest, your best, who are in Russia and who are arc fighting for their freedom."

The "Rebels" were immediately arrested by the military police. After a controversial trial, they were convicted of violating the Sedition Act of 1918. The trial judge, disgusted by their behavior and their beliefs, sentenced the Rebels to terms ranging up to twenty years in prison. The Rebels appealed their convictions to the Supreme Court of the United States, claiming that their convictions violated the First Amendment, which guarantees that "Congress shall make no law . . . abridging the freedom of speech." In *Abrams v. United States*, the Supreme Court, in a 7–2 decision, rejected this claim and upheld the convictions. For the majority of the Court, this was an easy case. Because the natural tendency of the defendants' speech was to generate opposition to the war, it was not within "the freedom of speech" protected by the Constitution.

Justice Oliver Wendell Holmes, the same Justice Holmes who some years later was to lose his railway ticket, dissented. Holmes's dissenting opinion in *Abrams* is worth reading, for it remains one of the most eloquent statements ever written by a Justice of the Supreme Court about the freedom of expression. Holmes wrote: "Persecution for the expression of opinions seems to me perfectly logical. If you have no doubt of your premises . . . and want a certain result with all your heart you naturally [want to] sweep away all opposition. . . . "[1]

"But," he added, "when men have realized that time has upset many fighting faiths, they may come to believe . . . that the ultimate good desired is better reached by free trade in ideas — that the best test of truth is the power of the thought to get itself accepted in the competition of the market, and that truth is the *only* ground upon which our wishes safely can be carried out."[2] Holmes therefore concluded that "we should be eternally vigilant against attempts to check the expression" even of "opinions that we loathe and believe to be fraught with death, unless they so imminently threaten" compelling government interests that an immediate check is necessary to save the nation.[3]

I first read this passage, written almost a century ago, when I was a law student at the University of Chicago, almost half a century ago. It has engaged my energy and curiosity ever since. Indeed, I think it's fair to say that it was my puzzling over this passage that, for better or worse, put me on the path to my career and, indeed, to where I stand before you today.

But now I must change direction, for this is not to be a discourse on the First Amendment. It is, rather, to be a talk about academic freedom. Happily, these are not unrelated subjects. To the contrary, the longer I have puzzled over the meaning of free expression, and the longer I have thought about education, the more the two seem to me to converge. Indeed, neither really is worth all that much without the other. And, with that in mind, I would like to turn to what I see as the intersection of free expression and education, and to the subject of academic freedom, for it is at this intersection that we will find the most fundamental values of the world of higher education.

I hope to accomplish two things in this part of my talk. First, I will trace briefly for you the history of academic freedom, for it is only by understanding where we have been that we can appreciate—in both senses of the word—where we are today. Second, I will offer some thoughts about what all this means for you and about the responsibilities that we today bear in common.

It is important to understand that, like the freedom of speech, academic freedom is not a law of nature. It does not exist of its own force. It is always vulnerable, and should never be taken for granted. Indeed, until well into the nineteenth century, real freedom of thought was neither practiced nor professed in American colleges. To the contrary, any real freedom of inquiry or expression in American colleges in this era was smothered by the dominance of religion and by the prevailing theory of "doctrinal moralism," which assumed that the worth of an idea must be judged by what the institution's leaders declared its moral value to be.

Thus, through the first half of the nineteenth century American colleges squelched any notion of free and open discussion or intellectual curiosity.

Any student or faculty member who dared argue, for example, that women were equal to men, that Blacks were equal to whites, or that homosexuality was not immoral would surely be expelled from most colleges or fired without hesitation.

Similarly, through the first half of the nineteenth century, as the nation moved toward Civil War, any professor or student in the North who openly defended slavery, or any professor or student in the South who openly challenged slavery, could readily be dismissed, disciplined, or expelled. When a professor at the University of North Carolina expressed sympathy for the 1856 Republican presidential candidate, the students burned him in effigy, and he was dismissed by the trustees. When a professor at Franklin College in Pennsylvania admitted he was not an abolitionist, he was promptly fired.

Several decades later, a furious battle arose over Charles Darwin's theory of evolution, with traditionalists charging not only that Darwin was wrong, but also that his beliefs were dangerous, immoral, and ungodly. Because of this conflict in the academy over evolution versus creationism, new academic goals came to be embraced. For the first time, to criticize, as well as to preserve, traditional moral values and understandings became an accepted function of higher education, and by 1892, William Rainey Harper, the first president of the University of Chicago, could boldly assert: "When for any reason the administration of a university attempts to dislodge a professor or punish a student because of his political or religious sentiments at that moment the institution has ceased to be a university."

But despite such noble sentiments, the battle for academic freedom has been a continuing and fiercely contentious one. In the closing years of the nineteenth century, for example, businessmen who had accumulated vast industrial wealth began to support colleges and universities on an unprecedented scale. But that support was not without strings, and during this era professors who offended wealthy donors by criticizing their business practices were dismissed from such leading institutions as Cornell and Stanford.

Then, during World War I, patriotic zealots persecuted and, as we have seen, even prosecuted those who questioned the wisdom or morality of the war. In the face of such outrage, universities collapsed almost completely in their defense of academic freedom. Students and professors were systematically expelled and fired at colleges and universities across the nation merely for encouraging a spirit of indifference toward the war.

Similar issues arose again, with a vengeance, during the Cold War in the age of Joseph McCarthy. In the late 1940s and '50s, most colleges and universities excluded those even suspected of Communist sympathies from university life. Yale president Charles Seymour, for example, went so far as to boast that "there will be no witch hunts at Yale, because there will be no witches. We will neither admit nor hire anyone with Communist sympathies."

As this history demonstrates, the freedom to question, the freedom to challenge, the freedom to inquire are not to be taken for granted. Academic freedom is, in fact, a hard-bought acquisition in an endless struggle to preserve the right of each individual, student and faculty alike, to seek wisdom, knowledge, and truth, free of the censor's sword.

But what does all of this have to do with *you*? Well, in a radio address to America in 1931, the Irish playwright George Bernard Shaw startled his audience with the following proposition: "Every person who owes his life to civilized society and who has enjoyed . . . its very costly protections and advantages," he declared, "should appear at reasonable intervals before a properly qualified jury to justify his existence, which should be summarily and painlessly terminated if he fails to justify it." I do not advocate such a program. But I do suggest that every one of us who enjoys the protections and advantages of our hard-won system of academic freedom has a responsibility to justify her existence under it.

There are several ways in which we can meet this responsibility. First, we must defend academic freedom when it comes under attack. Like every liberty that is precious to us, the preservation of academic freedom demands vigilance, determination and, sometimes, courage.

Second, we must struggle to define the meaning of academic freedom in our time. As we saw in *Abrams*, the Constitution's guarantee of freedom of speech is not self-defining. Neither is academic freedom. Each generation must give life to this concept in the face of the distinctive conflicts that arise over time.

Today, the principal challenge to academic freedom comes not from outside the academy, but from within it—from students themselves, some of whom demand censorship of ideas that they find distasteful and offensive, and from faculty members and university administrators who, afraid to disappoint their students, too often surrender academic freedom to charges of offense.

To give just a few examples, several colleges and universities, including Johns Hopkins, Brown and Williams, have recently withdrawn speaker invitations because of student objections to the views of the invited speakers; Colorado College suspended a student for making a joke that made fun of feminism; the State University of New York denied promotion to a professor who criticized the university's affirmative action program; William and Mary and the University of Colorado disciplined students for criticizing their affirmative action programs; students at Vanderbilt University demanded that a tenured professor be fired for writing an op-ed in which she raised questions about Islam and violence; the University of Kansas disciplined a professor for mocking the National Rifle Association; and Louisiana State University fired a professor because some of her women students complained that they had been made to feel uncomfortable by her use of profanity in class.

At Wesleyan University, after the school newspaper published a student op-ed criticizing the Black Lives Matter movement, students demanded that the University defund the school paper; at Amherst College, students demanded that the administration remove posters stating that "All Lives Matter"; at Emory University, students demanded that students who had chalked "Trump in 2016" on the university's sidewalks should be punished because, in their words, a university is "supposed to be a safe place for students and this made us feel unsafe"; and at a number of institutions, including DePaul University, Claremont-McKenna, the University of California at Irvine, San Francisco State, the University of Pennsylvania and Middlebury College, students physically obstructed access to venues or shouted down speakers whose views they opposed, causing the events to be cancelled.

To put all this in perspective, a recent survey revealed that 72 percent of current college students support disciplinary action against any student or faculty member who expresses views deemed by them to be "racist, sexist, homophobic or otherwise offensive."[4]

So, where did all this come from? It was not too long ago when students were demanding the right to free speech. Now, at least some students demand the right to be free from speech that they find to be offensive, upsetting, or emotionally disturbing. What explains this profound shift in attitude?

One often-expressed theory is that at least some members of this generation of students have been raised by so-called helicopter parents who protected and celebrated them in every way, shielding them at every turn from the risks of failure, frustration, and defeat. On this theory, these students, unlike their predecessors, have never learned to deal effectively with challenge, uncertainty, insult, or fear. They therefore demand the right to be protected from speech that they find to be offensive, hurtful, or demeaning. If this is so, then the proper role of an institution of higher learning is not to shield those students from distressing and offensive ideas, but to prepare them for the challenges of the real world. The goal of a university should not be to insulate students from discomfort and insecurity, but to enable them to be strong and effective citizens of the world—a world that will not shield them from such expression.

Another possible explanation of the current situation is that this generation of students is more attuned than their predecessors to the injustices of society, to the harmful impact of hateful expression, and to the inequalities that poison our nation. To the extent this is so, it might in part be a response to the creation of social media. When I was your age, we were rarely exposed to hateful expression. The media never carried it, and although we knew it existed, we rarely confronted it. The world of social media has changed that. Today, it is difficult not to encounter hateful expression. On this view of the matter, students today are not timid, but bold. They seek not shelter, but justice. They understand the ugliness of such expression and they want to protect both themselves and their classmates from the vitriol that now poisons some forms of expression.

Still another possible explanation is that some students, particularly those who come from disadvantaged, marginalized, and discriminated against backgrounds, have *always* felt unwelcome on college campuses, but in the past they simply remained silent. On this view of the matter, this generation of college students, particularly those who themselves feel unwelcome and alienated, deserves credit, because instead of remaining silent in the face of oppression, they have the courage to demand equality and respect.

My own view, for what it's worth, is that there is an element of truth in all of these perspectives. The question is what to do about all this.

Faced with the ongoing challenge to academic freedom at American universities, in 2014 University of Chicago president Robert Zimmer charged a faculty committee with the task of drafting a formal statement for the University on Freedom of Expression. The goal of that committee, which I chaired, was to stake out *our* university's position on these issues. The committee consisted of seven distinguished faculty members from across the University. After broad consultation, we produced a brief, three-page report. At the risk of being self-indulgent, I want to read you some excerpts from that report:

> Because the University [of Chicago] is committed to free and open inquiry in all matters, it guarantees all members of our community the broadest possible latitude to speak, write, listen, challenge, and learn. Except insofar as limitations on that freedom are necessary to the functioning of the University, the University of Chicago fully respects and supports the freedom of all members of the community "to discuss any problem that presents itself."
>
> Of course, the ideas of different members of the University community will often and quite naturally conflict. But it is not the proper role of the University to attempt to shield individuals from ideas and opinions they find unwelcome, disagreeable, or even deeply offensive. Although the University greatly values civility, and although all members of the University community share in the responsibility for maintaining a climate of mutual respect, concerns about civility and mutual respect can never be used as a justification for closing off discussion of ideas, however offensive or disagreeable those ideas may be to some members of our community.
>
> The freedom to debate and discuss the merits of competing ideas does not, of course, mean that individuals may say whatever they wish, wherever they wish. The University may restrict expression that violates the law, that falsely defames a specific individual, that constitutes a genuine threat or harassment, that unjustifiably invades substantial privacy or confidentiality interests, or that is otherwise directly incompatible with the core functioning of the University.

> But these are narrow exceptions to the general principle of freedom of expression, and it is vitally important that these exceptions never be used in a manner that is inconsistent with the University's commitment to a completely free and open discussion of ideas.
>
> In a word, the University's fundamental commitment is to the principle that debate or deliberation may not be suppressed because the ideas put forth are thought by some or even by most members of the University community to be offensive, unwise, immoral, or wrong-headed. It is for the individual members of the University community, not for the University as an institution, to make those judgments for themselves, and to act on those judgments not by seeking to suppress speech, but by openly and vigorously contesting the ideas that they oppose. Indeed, fostering the ability of members of the University community to engage in such debate and deliberation in an effective and responsible manner is an essential part of the University's educational mission.
>
> As a corollary to the University's commitment to protect and promote free expression, members of the University community must also act in conformity with the principle of free expression. Although members of the University community are free to criticize and contest the views expressed on campus, and to criticize and contest speakers who are invited to express their views on campus, they may not obstruct or otherwise interfere with the freedom of others to express views they reject or even loathe. To this end, the University has a solemn responsibility not only to promote a lively and fearless freedom of debate and deliberation, but also to protect that freedom when others attempt to restrict it.[5]

Interestingly, when we wrote this report, we were thinking only about the University of Chicago. To our surprise, the report has had a national and even international impact. Indeed, it has now been adopted by more than thirty-five other colleges and universities, including such diverse institutions as Princeton, Columbia, the University of Minnesota, the University of Missouri, Purdue, Johns Hopkins, American University, and the University of Wisconsin, to name just a few.

OK, now that I've finished congratulating myself, let me elaborate a bit. Why should a university take the position that faculty and students should be free to advance all ideas, however offensive, obnoxious, and wrong-headed they might be?

First, one thing we have learned from bitter experience is that even the ideas we hold to be most certain might in fact turn out to be wrong. As confident as we might be in our own wisdom, experience teaches that certainty is different from truth. If those who believed with absolute certainty that the earth was the center of the universe were wrong, if those who believed with absolute certainty in creationism were wrong, if those who believed that slavery was natural, right, and proper were wrong, if those who believed that a woman's place is in the home were wrong, if those who believed that homosexuals were degraded perverts were wrong, then why should we have the arrogance to think that *we* are unquestionably right about our own beliefs today? The only wise approach, as Justice Holmes made clear, is to acknowledge the risk that *our* certainties might be wrong as well, and that they too must always be open to challenge and question.

Second, experience teaches that the suppression of speech breeds the suppression of speech. If today I am permitted to silence those whose views I find distasteful, I have then opened the door to allow others down the road to silence me. The neutral principle of no suppression of ideas protects us all. This is especially important in the current situation, for in the long run it is likely to be minorities, whether religious minorities, racial minorities, or political minorities, who are most likely to be silenced once censorship is deemed acceptable. Indeed, without a vibrant commitment to freedom of speech, our nation would never have seen a civil rights movement, a women's rights movement, or a gay rights movement, all of which would have been suppressed by intolerant majorities. Censorship is never a one-way street, and this is a door we do not want to open, perhaps especially in the era of Trump. Indeed, it is important to remember that a robust protection of free speech is especially important to dissenters and to minority groups, because if censorship is permitted, it is ultimately they who will suffer the most.

Third, a central precept of free expression is the concern with chilling effect. That problem is especially acute today because of the effects of social media. It used to be the case that students and faculty members were willing to take controversial positions, in part because the risks were relatively modest. One could say something provocative or outrageous, and the statement soon disappeared. But in a world of social media, where every comment you make can be circulated to the world and can be called up later by prospective employers or graduate schools or neighbors with the mere click of a button, the potential cost of speaking courageously—of taking controversial positions, of taking risks—is greater than ever before in history. Indeed, according to a recent survey, 65 percent of all college students now say that it is "unsafe" for them to express unpopular views, and this clearly has influenced faculty as well. In this setting, it is especially important for institutions of higher learning to stand up for free expression.

So, how should this work in practice? Should students, faculty and other speakers be allowed to express whatever views they want—however offensive they might be to others? Yes. Absolutely.

Should those who disagree and are offended by the views and speech of others be allowed to condemn those views and those speakers in the most vehement terms? Yes. Absolutely.

Should students, faculty, and community members who oppose a speaker be permitted to disrupt an event to prevent that individual from speaking? Absolutely not.

Although nondisruptive protests are both permitted and encouraged, disruption of the rights of others to speak and to listen is wholly incompatible with the central principle of academic freedom.

Should those who are offended and who disagree with the views of others be allowed to demand that the institution punish those who have offended them? Yes. Absolutely.

Should a university punish those whose speech annoys, offends, and insults others? Absolutely not.

What, though, *should* a university do? First, a university should educate its students and faculty about the importance of civility and mutual respect. As a former student wrote to me recently, a university "has an obligation to create a community of people as well as 'a community of ideas,' a place where everyone feels certain that they are unambiguously welcomed." This must be a core institutional value, but it is a value that must be reinforced and reaffirmed by education and by example, not by censorship.

Second, a university should encourage free, open, and robust disagreement, argument, and debate. It should educate its students about the history, the importance, and the fragility of free speech, and it should instill in its students and faculty the importance of winning the day by facts, by ideas, and by persuasion, rather than by force, disruption, or censorship. Indeed, for an institution of higher education to fulfill its most fundamental mission, it must be a safe space for even the most loathsome, offensive, and disloyal arguments.

As a former colleague of mine at the University of Chicago Law School, who stepped down in 2017 as President of the United States, observed in a commencement address: "No matter how much you might disagree" with certain speakers, "don't try to shut them down. . . . Let them talk," but "have the confidence to challenge them." "If the other side has a point, learn from them. If they're wrong, rebut them. . . . Beat them on the battlefield of ideas. And you might as well start practicing now, because one thing I can guarantee you—you will have to deal with ignorance, hatred, racism" and stupidity "at every stage of your life."[6]

Third, a university must recognize that, our society being flawed as it is, the costs of free speech will often fall most heavily on those groups and individuals who feel the most marginalized, unwelcome, and disrespected. All of us feel that way sometimes, but in our often-unjust society the individuals who most often bear the brunt of free speech—or at least of certain types of free speech—tend to be racial and ethnic minorities; religious minorities; women; gays, lesbians and transsexuals; immigrants; ideological dissidents; and the like. Colleges and universities must be sensitive to this reality. Even if they cannot "solve" this problem by censorship, they can and should take other steps to address the special challenges faced by groups and individuals who are most often made to feel unwelcome and unvalued by others. Institutions of higher learning must take this challenge seriously. They should encourage civility and mutual respect. They should support students who feel vulnerable, marginalized, silenced, and demeaned. They should help those students learn how to speak up, how to respond effectively, how to challenge those whose attitudes, whose words, and whose beliefs offend, appall, and outrage them. This is a core responsibility of these institutions, for the world is not a safe space, and it is our job to enable our graduates to win the battles they will need to fight in the years and decades to come. This is not a challenge that universities can or should ignore.

Speaking of the responsibility of universities, I should address one other critical facet of these issues. Suppose those who oppose a speaker—whether they be students, faculty, or community members—disregard their responsibility to respect the freedom of speech and threaten violence or otherwise disrupt an event in order to prevent an invited speaker from speaking. What should the university do? After the events of Charlottesville in July 2017, this is an especially important question. The simple solution is for the institution to "play it safe" and just refuse to permit the speaker to come to campus. Indeed, this is the approach several institutions have now adopted. The University of Florida and Texas A&M, for example, have announced that they will not permit alt-right leader Richard Spencer to speak on campus for fear of disruption and even violence.

But if universities adopt this approach, and thus empower those who oppose a speaker to prevent the event from taking place by threatening violence or disruption, what will happen? Such a response will inevitably encourage others who want to exclude speakers to adopt this strategy, knowing that they, too, can shut down speech they oppose merely by threatening violence or disruption. This invites what the Supreme Court has termed the "heckler's veto."

Such a course invites other groups to wield the power of censorship over whatever views they wish to suppress, whether those views be anti-war, pro–Black Lives Matter, anti-immigration, pro-Israel, anti-Trump, pro-abortion, anti–affirmative action, pro–gay rights, or whatever. In effect, the heckler's veto turns the right to free speech over to those who oppose the ideas being espoused.

It is noteworthy, by the way, the Supreme Court first learned this lesson during the Civil Rights era when white Southerners threatened violence to shut down civil rights marches. What the Court concluded is that the responsibility of the city, the police, or the university in such circumstances is to take all reasonable measures to protect the speaker and to enable the event to take place, and that it can terminate the event only if it is impossible for it to prevent a clear and present danger of serious harm. Short of that, though, the heckler's veto cannot prevail.

I should make one other important point about the strategy of disruption. It is counterproductive. What it does is to give the speaker and her ideas greater visibility, turns her into a martyr, and enables her to sell books, get on cable news, and promote her views more effectively than ever. People like Richard Spencer, Ann Coulter, and Milo Yiannopoulos, for example, were complete unknowns until they were made famous by violent protests against their views. Now, they are household names and evermore sought-after speakers.

As the Southern Poverty Law Center recently explained in a policy statement on The Alt-Right on Campus, "when an alt-right personality is scheduled to speak on campus, the most effective course of action is to deny the speaker of the thing he or she wants most—a spectacle. Alt-right personalities know their cause is helped by news footage of large jeering crowds, heated confrontations and outright violence at their events. It allows them to play the victim and gives them a larger platform for their racist message. Denying an alt-right speaker of such a spectacle is the worst insult they can endure."[7] What the Southern Poverty Law Center wisely recommends instead is that the best strategy is for those who oppose a speaker's views is to "hold an alternative event—away from the alt-right event—to highlight your campus' commitment to inclusion and our nation's democratic values."[8] This response is the right one across the boards, whether the speaker is a member of the Alt-Right, an opponent of gay rights, a supporter of abortion rights, or any other speaker whose views you oppose.

Let me now, though, return to my central theme. What is it that makes for a great educational institution? It is, I submit, "the intense, strenuous and constant intellectual activity of the place. . . . Presented with many points of view, [students must be] compelled to think for [themselves]." At a great educational institution, "the air is electric" with ideas and questions, and it is from that environment that students derive an intellectual stimulation that should last them "the rest of [their] lives." This is the true meaning of education.

Your responsibility as a student is to test what you are taught at every turn, to challenge your teachers, your classmates and yourselves, to choose your own values and your own beliefs. To meet this responsibility, you will have to be independent, you will have to be daring, you will have to take risks. It is not easy to tell your professor, who has devoted years, perhaps decades, to mastering her subject, that you disagree with her latest observation or theory. But the discourse of a great institution of learning should be an incitement to risk and to boldness. If you find yourself hesitating, if your feel timid, if you wonder if it's worth it, think of the Rebels in *Abrams*. At an age not much older than you, they dared to take on the government of the United States.

You certainly can take on a mere professor. The faculty of a great institution of higher learning ask nothing of you that they do not also ask of themselves. Even the most distinguished teacher and scholar routinely suffers frustration and failure. It is only by taking risks, by daring to ask questions no one else has ever asked, that real contributions are achieved. Thus, if your professors ask you to take risks, know that they take risks as well. At an institution like Arizona State, you should never forget that "the only appropriate response to even the most withering question is not resentment, but gratitude."

Fulfilling the responsibility of academic freedom means more than challenging your classmates and your teachers; it also means challenging yourself. It means being willing to reconsider what you yourself have come to accept as true. In 1921, after two years in prison, Mollie Steimer, one of the *Abrams* Rebels, was deported to the Soviet Union. It was not what she expected. Disappointed in the political and economic system she found there, Steimer again agitated against the government. Again, she was arrested, prosecuted and convicted of sedition. In 1923, she was deported from the Soviet Union. I don't know for sure, but I rather suspect that this was an unparalleled achievement—to be convicted of sedition and deported within five years from both the United States and the Soviet Union. Whatever else one might think of her, Mollie Steimer was not afraid to reconsider her positions.

In 1919, a majority of the Supreme Court in *Abrams* rejected the bold approach of Justice Holmes and opted for a "safe" view of the First Amendment. Fifty years later, the Supreme Court unanimously overruled the majority opinion in *Abrams* and, embracing Justice's Holmes's dissenting opinion, held that the government may not punish even speech that we "loathe and believe to be fraught with death" unless that speech is both intended and likely to incite imminent lawless action.[9] To reach this result, the Court had to challenge the first principles of its predecessors and to overturn half a century of precedent.

A great university, like a successful Court, must dedicate itself to the rigorous, open-minded, unyielding search for truth. You will learn here to ask the hard questions. But it is not enough to examine the premises, beliefs and assumptions of an earlier time and find them wanting. It is too easy to dismiss those who thought that the earth was the center of the universe, that its resources were boundless, that only men should vote, that marriage is only for people of the opposite sex, or that separate could ever be equal. You must remember that you, too, hold beliefs that your children or your children's children will rightly regard as naive, foolish, perhaps even obscene. You must be prepared to challenge your beliefs, to reform your world, just as the Rebels in *Abrams* struggled to reform theirs. You, too, must challenge the nature of things.

So, to return to the question with which I began, "Where the hell are you supposed to be going?" As you've no doubt surmised, your adventure has no predetermined path, no assigned destination. Let the journey engage you, for as the humorist Will Rogers observed almost a century ago, "even if you are on the right track, you'll get run over if you just sit there." At an institution like Arizona State, the faculty warmly welcome their students "because students are where the future lies." From this place, you will take away an intellectual stimulation and curiosity that will last the rest of your days. As Justice Holmes mused in *Abrams*, "all life is an experiment."[10] May your life's experiment be filled with curiosity, boldness and courage.

NOTES

1. *Abrams v. United States*, 250 U.S. 616, 630 (1919).
2. Ibid. (emphasis added).
3. Ibid.
4. "The William F. Buckley, Jr. Program at Yale: ALMOST HALF (49%) OF U.S. COLLEGE STUDENTS 'INTIMIDATED' BY PROFESSORS WHEN SHARING DIFFERING BELIEFS: SURVEY," October 26, 2015, http://mclaughlinonline.com/2015/10/26/the-william-f-buckley-jr-program-at-yale-almost-half-49-of-u-s-college-students-intimidated-by-professors-when-sharing-differing-beliefs-survey.
5. University of Chicago, *Report of the Committee on Freedom of Expression*, January 2015, https://provost.uchicago.edu/sites/default/files/documents/reports/FOECommitteeReport.pdf.
6. "Obama's full remarks at Howard University commencement ceremony," *Politico*, May 7, 2016, https://www.politico.com/story/2016/05/obamas-howard-commencement-transcript-222931.
7. Southern Poverty Law Center, "The Alt-Right on Campus: What Students Need to Know," August 10, 2017. https://www.splcenter.org/20170810/alt-right-campus-what-students-need-know.
8. Ibid.
9. *Abrams* at 630.
10. Ibid.

Chapter 3

From Skokie to Charlottesville

Free Speech, Moral Leadership, and the Line between Tolerating and Condoning Speech

Ulrich Baer

In 1977, the ACLU defended on speech grounds a planned march by neo-Nazis through the village of Skokie, Illinois, the home of many Holocaust survivors.[1] The town had sought to stop the march based on a local ordinance regulating inflammatory speech. In a state supreme court ruling during an appeal, the neo-Nazis won the right to march, carrying swastika flags and shouting antisemitic chants, which they eventually did without much incident in another township in nearby Chicago. Despite the small number of participants, the march gained national prominence as a test case for our country's enduring commitment to free speech. When the ACLU decided to take up the neo-Nazis' case to defend their speech, while explicitly condemning their hateful message and its impact on the people in the town, some thirty-five thousand members left the ACLU in protest. Nobody was injured or killed during the march, and to this day the ACLU cites the neo-Nazis' court victory against the Village of Skokie as proof of its nonpartisan defense of the First Amendment against the impulse to prohibit offensive or injurious speech. It serves as a case study for law students and is a frequent reference for free speech absolutists. A slew of books and documentaries parse its legal implications.

What would today's America look like if the neo-Nazis had lost their case? The counterfactual question reveals some implicit assumptions about today's speech debates. According to the ACLU, if the march had been prohibited, our nation would have taken a step on a slippery slope to tyranny.[2] What could have appeared as a sensible ruling at the time could lead to undesirable restrictions of political speech in the future. If the neo-Nazis had not marched that day, some supporters of the ACLU's actions declare without a trace of irony, America would have shifted close to fascism today. The neo-Nazis' victory and other defenses of hate speech, including and perhaps especially the advocacy of anti-democratic ideas, commentators maintain, safeguarded our democracy. But if we believe those who criticized the decision, America would have continued to function as a democracy, though perhaps with fewer instances of emboldened neo-Nazis and other virulent racists marching under the First Amendment banner. Fewer minorities would have been targeted by hate speech without consequences for the speaker; there would be less hate speech in today's mainstream political debate. While the ACLU's defense of the neo-Nazis was intended to protect democracy, one result of this engagement was to alter the public's attitude toward racist speech. Today, many commentators draw implicitly or explicitly on Skokie to argue that protecting racist speech means protecting democracy itself. But does this position embolden racist expression, challenge its occurrence, or limit it?

THE DIFFERENCE BETWEEN TOLERATING AND CONDONING SPEECH

The crux of the argument made by the Illinois Supreme Court in allowing the march to proceed, and by thoughtful defenders of this decision that a swastika is protected speech rather than a category of "fighting words"—which can be regulated in specific cases—is that virulent anti-Semitism, as objectionable as it may be, poses no significant threat to our democratic life. Put differently, racism and antisemitism do not play a sufficiently significant role in American public life to cause concern.[3] Lee Bollinger's 1986 landmark study of the Skokie case puts it succinctly: "While anti-Semitism is a problem in American society (just how serious would have been a potential issue in this case), it is not of such magnitude, or so pervasive, as to transform toleration into an act of implicit condonation."[4] The claim that antisemitism is not sufficiently pervasive in the United States to make the defense of neo-Nazis appear like an implicit condonation of their tactics or ideas, however, begs the question of who determines when such speech rises from a low-level irritant to a genuine threat. But legal theorists and philosophers decide based on principles, not personal experience. Differently put, the risks posed by exclusionary and hate speech are evaluated not based on the experiences of those targeted by such speech, but on the basis of abstraction. While theorists recognize that allowing virulent hate speech creates risks for some members of society, they place a general commitment to ideas of liberty above personal injury, as long as the threat is not immediate. Although the concerns of minority groups are understandable, we are told, they are rooted in the emotion of fear and the feeling of being offended. Since they are not based on reason, and since the experience of fear is not validated by a presumed reasonable observer, they cannot dictate legal outcomes or public life.

But to put the abstract principle of speech above any individual's concerns, the defenders of the Skokie decision make a tacit assumption. When they state that the public must tolerate anti-democratic and anti-egalitarian speech, which attacks freedom, justice, and equality, at any cost, they insist in the same breath on our nation's non-negotiable commitment to freedom, justice and equality. In fact, their defense of speech rights for the enemies of our democracy, they insist, is the strongest expression of this commitment. Bollinger's point about the limited and containable role played by antisemitism in American public life during the events in Skokie relies on a qualitative assessment. America's commitment to racial equality and its legal and cultural condemnation of race-based discrimination is sufficiently robust to tolerate fringe expressions of hatred, as long as those ideas remain peripheral. This echoes James Madison's assessment of the American populace as a great and pluralistic whole in *Federalist* 55, where many radically opposed opinions flourish but the good will ultimately outweigh the bad. Defenders of hate speech as playing only a marginal role in America's self-understanding follow Madison in presupposing "the existence of [. . .] sufficient virtue among men for self-government."[5] These ideals of freedom and equality, which are our nation's bedrock principles in whose name the pundits, legal scholars, and the ACLU then speak, trump any fringe group's destructive, anti-democratic, and anti-American ideas. When extending this logic to campus speech controversies, universities can demonstrate their commitment to equality in other ways. The University of California at Berkeley's 2018 Commission on Free Speech recommends that "campus leaders could exercise their own free speech rights by speaking out forcefully against hate speech."[6] But in addition to rhetorical and often boilerplate rebuttals, universities ought to express their disagreement with hate speech by funding programs and enforcing policies that protect the equality of all students and faculty as mandated by law. Without such a long-term commitment of resources, the rejection of hate could look like a platitude.[7]

When the ACLU defended the Neo-Nazis' rights to march, the organization stressed its commitment to democratic ideals. This means that they had to say two things at once. They defended the Nazis' right to speak to the point of providing them with free legal counsel, and also assured the public that they disagreed with everything the Nazis said. To explain this way of saying two seemingly contradictory things at once, pundits often invoke a sentence attributed to the seventeenth century French philosopher Voltaire: "I disapprove of what you say, but will defend to the death your right to say it."

SUPPORTING SPEECH RIGHTS, NOT THE SPEECH

To defend even the vilest speaker's rights, many people make this crystal-clear, quasi-Voltairean distinction between defending someone's speech rights and condemning the specific things they say. In defending the rights of speakers whose message they abhor, the neo-Nazis' defenders look rigorous. They have placed reason above emotion. By relying on an abstract principle and not on fear, offense, or disagreement, and by banking on greater tolerance, they are morally pure. When the Skokie case made its way through the courts, President Jimmy Carter was asked about it. The country was riled up and unsure; the conflict between the neo-Nazis' rights and the rights of Skokie's Jewish citizens, including Holocaust survivors, to live without targeted harassment, seemed intractable. Carter's response was a textbook example of delegating the protection of the right to speak to the courts while absolutely condemning the ideas:

> I deplore it. I wish that this demonstration of an abhorrent political and social philosophy would not be present at all . . . We have the same problem, as you know, in other parts of the Nation—in the South with the Ku Klux Klan, and others . . . I think it's best to leave it in the hands of the court.[8]

The president's unequivocal condemnation of Nazi ideas was critical. By drawing the sharpest possible line between American values and Nazi ideas, he allowed the strongest defense of speech rights not to look like a tacit condoning of anti-democratic ideas. President Carter also insisted that in the struggle over ideas, America's commitment to freedom for all as different equals, found in the Declaration of Independence, would always prevail over the idea that certain groups of people are inherently inferior.

Today, something has changed. The conditions are not only that white supremacists invade college campuses in states with open-carry laws, that people have died in speech conflicts, and that white supremacists have murdered individuals in churches, synagogues, and other places in the name of racism and antisemitism. Today's universities also enroll more diverse students. Furthermore, there is a vibrant public debate about the relevance of racism in mainstream American politics and public life.[9] In 1976, American colleges and universities had enrolled 84 percent white students of a total of about eleven million students, of which 53 percent were men. By 2014, these numbers had changed to 58 percent white students out of a total of twenty-one million students, with women being 57 percent of all enrolled students. White supremacists who lament this demographic shift rather than recognize it as the realization of the American dream have regularly sued universities for the right to speak. They want to use the right of free speech that is closely linked to the ethos of America to advance ideas of violently enforced racial superiority, which they also link to America. When the organizers invoked speech rights to receive the necessary permits for their rally in Charlottesville, which partly took place on a university campus, they insisted on their speech rights with Skokie as precedent.

Although that case concerned a march in a public space and not a university, the analogy is flawed. What has changed on a deeper level, and what we have yet to fully grasp, is that the abstract option of defending speech rights for those whose viewpoints we abhor—at once tolerating and condemning—has become compromised. The defense of speech rights is a crucial, serious, and morally taxing matter. But it requires more than a simplistic invocation of the court's current interpretation of the First Amendment, which is indeed a bedrock principle in our nation, but neither a self-enforcing nor self-explanatory law. The insistence on speech rights requires an equally powerful insistence on our nation's equally non-negotiable principle, namely equality. When speech rights are invoked as an abstraction available to all, but a speaker's message of another group's inherent inferiority and fundamental inequality is not challenged, we operate in a moral vacuum. This vacuum has direct implications for how universities handle speech matters.

President Trump was the first president in modern memory not to condemn the Neo-Nazis and the Ku Klux Klan unequivocally. In his hesitation to distance himself strongly from virulent racists while leaving the matter of their rights to speech and assembly entirely to the courts, President Trump differed from every president, regardless of party affiliation, from Carter onward.

We might view the statements offered by Carter, Reagan, George H. W. Bush, Clinton, George W. Bush, and Obama about the abhorrence of virulent racism to be little more than symbolic platitudes, or empty political statements belied by policy decisions. All issues concerning speech rights are a legal matter to be decided in the courts, and not something determined by the President. While we may wish for moral leadership, we can rely on our laws and our court's wise interpretation of them, and proceed without presidential guidance when it may be lacking.

What has changed, however, is that the bright line between tolerating a speaker's rights and condoning his views, which is the principle behind the law, is no longer as clear as it needs to be. The critical distinction between tolerating and condoning hateful speech was put to the test in 2007 when Lee Bollinger, as president of Columbia University, hosted then Iranian president Mahmoud Ahmadinejad. In his introduction, Bollinger criticized the invited speaker. This criticism was the indispensable flipside of the coin which constitutes speech absolutism in Bollinger's own exposition. Defend an objectionable speaker's right to speak but be sure not to let this defense be understood as an implicit endorsement.

In this example, the balancing act of tolerating but not condoning the speech tested the conventions of hospitality. President Ahmadinejad censured Bollinger for disparaging him, for not allowing the student audience to make up their own minds, and for not upholding the rules of open debate. The visiting head of state invoked all the principles cherished by free speech absolutists in America. The fact that he routinely spread deliberate falsehoods and denied proven facts made his remarks perhaps sound hypocritical. But he exploited the tension in Bollinger's balanced approach to speech rights, which requires upholding an abstract principle while forcefully condemning the content of protected speech and tried to portray it as an untenable contradiction.

The question is not to decide who was right; the question is neither to reveal that a philosophical principle, such as free speech, can be pushed to the point where it flips into its opposite. The point is to highlight the role of power when it comes to the distinction between tolerating versus condoning speech: the power to host a debate, the power to set and enforce the ground rules, the power to address the audience, and the power of running an institution such as a university or a country. The point is also to stress that the university is the site where political power is checked by more than power, namely by the language of argument rather than the language of emotion or force, and by respect for the truth. This, of course, is the crux of all debates about the danger of speech: the proponents of absolute speech rights insist that arguments, no matter how vile or absurd, must be met with counterarguments rather than force. But some arguments, namely those that deny a speaker's right to speak not based on the merit of their ideas but on their identity, cannot be resolved through debate.

President Ahmadinejad considered it a breach of protocol for his host to criticize his views before his talk. For him, in an overly rigid interpretation of a point that Bollinger had made in his study of the virtues of tolerating offensive speech, the host's function is to tolerate the speaker's right to speak but to refrain from condoning or condemning him so that the audience can make up their minds freely. But the political leader sought out the university to introduce politics into that space by force, and to gain legitimacy in that space where it is not power but reasoning and expertise that allows listeners to differentiate between truth, lies, and mere opinion. The event at Columbia is a useful case for understanding the difficulty of properly balancing an abstract defense of speech rights without inadvertently providing prestige and tacitly endorsing an objectionable point of view.

When members of the alt-right have arrived on campuses in more recent years, university leaders were put in a similarly difficult position. They had to reassure students, faculty, and staff that allowing and paying for a white supremacist's visit with scarce resources meant upholding American laws *and* principles, all of which are staked on equality, and that honoring such an invitation did not mean upholding his views of some racial group's inherent inferiority. The university leaders had to insist that speech rights must not be compromised, but that granting a platform to a racist, when unqualified laymen who espouse unscientific views are routinely denied their wish to lecture at a university, does not mean endorsing the view.

Once President Trump equivocated on condemning the white supremacists and identified "very fine people" on all sides, all other assurances, by university presidents, lawyers, and commentators, sounded different. There are two issues with the President's statement, which prompted widespread criticism. He failed to condemn the message of hate in his defense of the speakers' right to speak. In this regard, he echoed the bi-partisan support to absolute speech rights, and the forceful defense of hate speech as contributing to rather than harming our nation. He also pursued his consistent strategy of erasing any difference between racial groups in terms of social position, power, and history, which allows him to depict whites as disadvantaged by government actions.

As long as the nation's highest office routinely condemned virulent racism as incompatible with our nation's principles, as represented by our elected government's commitment to equality, then racist speech could be defended on the premise that such ideas will never be permitted to take root. The vigorous defense of hate speech had always been linked to an equally vigorous defense, and indeed a commitment shared and led by the country's highest office, to liberty and equality. Once the highest office hesitated to affirm this consensus, the absolute defense of speech rights looked like the condonation of hateful views. Over the past sixty years, the courts have defended the expression of racist speech, including group libel, but the same courts, and the government, prohibits institutionalized segregation and inequality before the law from becoming policy. There is surely a range of widely divergent assessments of our courts' and governments' record of protecting, ensuring and advancing equality.[10] Free speech absolutism, however, which nearly always centers on the defense of hate speech, depends on an equally absolute and articulated commitment to fundamental equality. Otherwise, it looks like an empty intellectual exercise, or, and this is the cause of many campus controversies, it looks like supporting, endorsing, and emboldening anti-American and anti-democratic values.

Once the forceful official condemnation of the neo-Nazis' views (but not a restriction of their right to speak) had gone missing from our country's highest office, the line between reluctantly tolerating and tacitly condoning such ideas became blurred. Protecting extreme speech is a stress test for all democracies; in the United States, there had been a governing assumption that democracy faces no internal threats.

Even though the public sphere is largely unregulated, the president's remarks after Charlottesville, thanks to the power of his office, broadened the scope of what may be reasonably discussed in public. The president's rhetoric, I would submit, has generally expanded the range of acceptable things to say in public discourse. It is not the place here to decide whether this is a symptom of larger social tendencies, energized by the advent of social media, or whether his divisive rhetoric constitutes a complete strategy and newly emboldened stance. However you wish to interpret the president's statements, as either defining a strategy or simply coarse and folksy, in the wake of his statements the abstract defense of speech rights has begun to look like the defense of particular speech. Virulent racism, and formal segregation, had remained beyond the pale of being considered as viable policy before. Or, to draw on the work of Ian Haney López, previously racism had been communicated only through dog whistle statements, audible to everyone but deniable when called out, rather than direct endorsement.[11]

By leaving things momentarily unclear, the president introduced the possibility that the executive branch might condone the message of some of these speakers, and not just tolerate their right to speak. In the context of universities, this has prompted students, faculty, and others to regard the abstract defense of absolute speech rights not as an expression of viewpoint neutrality, but as the politicization of such rights to advance an ultra-conservative agenda.

THE QUESTION OF SPEECH IS LINKED TO POWER

The point is that the question of free speech is inseparable from the question of power. When the nation's most powerful office does not make a crystal-clear distinction between tolerating and condoning speech that defines minorities as undeserving of legal and social equality in our country, and when elected politicians leave doubts about the legitimacy of a violent attack on the Capitol, such an absence of clear condemnation is problematic because the president and elected officials have actual power. If a regular citizen, a lower-ranking official, or a political candidate made similar claims, which people often do, such statements can be countered, refuted, or debated by others in comparable positions. When a person with great institutional or political power, and especially a person who can shape the terms of public debate and implement policies by accessing a popular or prestigious platform, creates the impression that he is defending not an abstract speech right but tacitly endorsing a speaker's point of view, this shifts the dynamic. It is at this point that university leaders tend to make an error identified by the political scientist Judith Shklar.[12] It is possible to politicize the rules of the game, which are supposed to be the neutral and shared guardrails to political debate. This means that speakers can score a symbolic victory merely by appearing on a college stage, even if their ideas are presumably defeated. It means that simply being invited to campus, even if the event must be canceled, is a form of symbolic speech. The idea that hateful speech can be defeated by more speech is powerful. But this idea, to which most universities resort with the idea of counterprogramming, disregards the fact that a speaker can win over listeners even when other speakers offer better arguments.

The assurance that hateful fringe groups are entitled to speak but that their speech constitutes no threat to civic life, the safety of which is guaranteed by our government for all people, is no longer a simple and bright line. The claim that protecting hate speech indeed results in a more tolerant society, as Bollinger argues, and that the presence of hate speech produces a stronger democracy, as Nadine Strossen and others have proposed, cannot be proven.[13] It is an assumption based on the idea that it's always possible to uphold speech rights while condemning those who advocate the abolition of such rights. When Erwin Chemerinsky and Howard claim that regulating hate speech is bad for democracy and "has always led to disaster," instead of assessing relevant historical precedents they cite an opinion piece.[14]

There are at least three things worth questioning about the assertion that regulating hate speech is always worse than protecting such speech. First, our country through the past century has moved from less to more robust speech protection. Such progress would not have been possible if earlier restrictions of speech, for instance the successful suppression of communist speech for several decades, had inevitably led to disaster. Second, U.S. jurisprudence has always recognized the need to regulate speech in specific areas, which include libel, commercial speech, treason, defamation, and certain types of incitement, in addition to falsely yelling fire in a crowded theater to incite panic. This means that the regulation of speech deemed harmful does not inevitably result in more regulation of harmless speech. Third, other democracies—among them Canada, South Africa, France, Germany, Britain, Italy, Spain, and others—have regulated speech in different ways without sliding into totalitarianism.[15] It is not correct, as Nadine Strossen asserts, that "'hate speech' laws undermine universal principles of liberty, equality, and democracy." No such universal principles exist, and we have evidence of different approaches to hate speech that do not conflict with specific conceptions of liberty, equality, and democracy.[16] Lastly, it remains an open question whether the court's robust protection especially of group defamation, which is the legal term for racist expression, over the past forty years has inevitably improved the situation for everyone in the United States, and whether it has improved or harmed race relations and equality.

Indeed, the entire question of free speech hinges on this last question, and today's students are asking a far more profound question about democracy than their critics like to admit. Has the robust protection of group defamation, ushered in by court decisions in the early 1960s, after the Supreme Court had initially restricted hate speech in the 1950s, when the threat of fascism and anti-Semitism was considered more immediate and real, helped, or hindered the cause of equality? According to Strossen, Floyd Abrams, Timothy Garton Ash, and others, allowing and indeed especially protecting hate and ignorance exposes such ideas to light and reason, where they will wither and die. Penalizing certain specific forms of such expression, according to Strossen, undermines democracy itself.[17] The idea is that protecting people's rights to insult, demean, and degrade strengthens democracy. But has protecting hate speech improved conditions? Or has the persistence of racism harmed the country as a whole? In the setting of the university, this question is put into sharp relief. Does the presence, and the administration's explicit protection of hate speech help or hinder the equal conditions of learning for students? Are deliberate falsehoods and the intentional denial of proven facts conducive to study and research when they are not properly presented as part of a pedagogical exercise but up for open debate? How can universities defend hate speech on a principle of content-neutrality that is not applicable to countless other ideas in academia, without letting this defense of hate speech above other types of speech become an attack on the guarantee of equality?

The case of Skokie concerned a town, where a group of neo-Nazis claimed their constitutional right to march in a public street. Today, neo-Nazis take aim at the university, where additional and distinct rules apply, even in public institutions that operate as extensions of the government. These rules include everyone's right to participate on equal terms, even while their contributions will be vetted and graded as having different value, the obligation to protect everyone from harm, and the principle that unfettered debate occurs for the purpose of advancing and instilling in students the value of respecting the truth. When virulent racists arrive on campus, waving the First Amendment banner and sporting ACLU pins alongside swastikas, do they follow these rules? When an external speaker with no credentials nor valuable life experience openly disregards facts and does not honor the truth, what do the students learn? They wonder, even if they have not studied the writings of Hannah Arendt, whether "freedom of opinion," as Arendt wrote in a 1967 essay, "is a farce unless factual information is guaranteed and the facts themselves are not in dispute."[18] University leaders, faculty and students are deeply invested in not allowing free speech to become a farce. This is why many absolutist defenses of free speech identify the problem as one of offensive, controversial, uncomfortable, and upsetting ideas, rather than one of deliberate falsehood, the revival of settled ideas, and invective. To prevent free speech from becoming a farce, members of a university community must not make the error of defending speakers who deny the existence of proven facts on an empty principle, instead of pairing this defense of free speech with an equally vigorous defense of upholding respect for the truth and equality. Without this latter part, the defense of free speech as an abstraction is easily weaponized by those who wish to undermine its very purpose, which is the advancement of knowledge and the truth.

When the university provides extremist speakers with a platform, can students be sure that the administration, which also sets policies about admissions and equal participation, draws a clear line between supporting a speaker's right to speak and condemning the views which undermine the university's enterprise? In his book, *When the State Speaks*, Corey Brettschneider has proposed that toleration of hate speech must be paired with strong institutional declarations of opposing values.[19] I do not mean that every conservative speaker's visit must be matched by liberal visitors. But I am suspicious of descriptions of speech controversies as a matter of protecting offended feelings and creating a climate of inclusion. A university's toleration of virulent speech must be matched by the institution's commitment to prevent and counter discrimination actively, and to work affirmatively, through policies and resources, to create equal conditions of access. But when our nation's leader does not unequivocally distinguish between the government's position and such ideas, how can we be sure that the First Amendment will not undo other constitutional guarantees, and does not become, in the 1949 words of Supreme Court Justice Robert H. Jackson, who cautioned against rigidly enforcing principles that undermine our democracy, "a suicide pact"?

IS VIOLENCE THE ONLY LIMIT ON SPEECH?

The highest price for our liberties, free speech absolutists maintain, is the discomfort we experience when encountering vile ideas. The risk that those ideas could engulf our rights at some point, they argue, is less than the risk of curtailing someone's liberty to spread falsehoods or dangerous ideas. In the case of Skokie, the ACLU had defended a hate group's rights not in order to advance the cause of fascism but in order to uphold our nation's democratic values. The risk had been worth it, many commentators maintain, since nobody was injured or killed, since antisemitism is regarded, by some as explained above, to be a minor issue in America, and because the neo-Nazis did not carry the day. Charlottesville, where the ACLU once again provided the neo-Nazis with free counsel, presents an opportune moment to clarify whether deadly violence is the only place to draw a line. It is not only naïve but historically uninformed to believe that the marchers' goal was to persuade the students with arguments. Their point was to threaten them with force. In my recorded conversations with faculty members and students at the University of Virginia, during the summer of 2018, I was reminded repeatedly that the events in Charlottesville were not a matter of speech, but of violent attack. Framing these events exclusively as a matter of speech is already a debatable premise, rather than a neutral lens through which we can then discern the truth.

In the university, where speech serves a specific rather than general purpose, the line must be drawn to distinguish speech that advances learning and research from speech that materially undermines the equal participation of students in the quest for knowledge. In the university, the right to equal participation cannot be taken for granted. It became a legal requirement, as Title IX, only in 1972. But aside from legal protection, speech serves a specific purpose in the university's mission. It carries more weight, rather than less, than on a street corner.

Today's students, and many scholars, are not willing to dismiss virulent racism and white supremacy as mere ideas that do not materially impact them or are inconsequential to American public life. They are unwilling to defend a torch-wielding, weapons-bearing group of men and women in the name of freedom, rather than identify them as incitement to unfreedom, division and hatred. They are less trusting that university leaders who defend speech principles above all also uphold the university's commitment to equality, and question whether the defense of abstract speech rights does not contain a sliver of agreement with these points of view. Nojan Rostami, a senior at the University of Virginia during the time of the alt-right rally, identified the struggle to maintain trust in moral leadership: "[T]he president of University of Virginia sent out a statement that reminded us that the college 'is a public institution and follows state and federal law regarding the public's right to access open spaces.' She wrote that the University of Virginia supports First Amendment rights but rejects 'the ideology of intolerance and hate.' [. . .] I'm trying to be sympathetic [. . .] but it's hard to do that when I'm staying up on Saturday night fending off nightmares of armed militiamen dragging me out of my dorm room [. . .] Those men beat and pepper-sprayed my friends and killed a young woman in the town I have come to call home."[20] The University of Virginia committed enormous resources to restore the students' faith in their institution. This effort meant assuring everyone that permitting hate speech on campus does not materially undermine the equality guarantees of all students, faculty, and staff. This is as much a legal as a moral and political question.

COUNTER SPEECH WITH MORE SPEECH

After Charlottesville, faculty, university leaders, and national commentators exhorted the students to counter unreason with reason, hate speech with more speech, and to defeat hatred with tolerance, kindness, and love. Rise above provocation and bigotry, commentators said. Stage a counterrally. Trust that the university is committed to your equal participation, even if your administration sponsors a speaker who disputes your right to exist. Trust that we are really defending everyone's interests, even when we are most vocal in the defense of racist hatemongers.

But universities depend not on vague ideas of love and good intentions but on ground rules of mutual respect, on the premise of equal participation, and on the idea that debate serves a purpose. Speech enjoys a privileged status in universities not for its own sake, so that there can be as much debate about any conceivable topic, but as a means to reaching the end of informed consensus that approaches the truth.[21] When commentators counseled students to practice forbearance and civility, as did newspaper columnist David Brooks in reference to Steven Carter, a Yale professor of law, and that "the only way to confront fanaticism is with love," they essentially asked them to follow these rules.[22] But in asking students, faculty and staff to adhere to the ground rules and accommodate people who materially undermine the same rules of equal participation, the university applies a double standard. When the issue is one of someone being offended, the university might be able to maintain this tension. In instances when the speaker refuses to adhere to the rules, however, this double standard undoes the university's purpose. It is then no longer a community of people who share the goal of advancing knowledge and respecting the truth but becomes an unregulated public space indistinguishable from any street corner or online forum.

The issue is not that the students were offended when the neo-Nazis came to their university. The current generation of students takes seriously the self-evident truth that once admitted to the university, as far as group belonging, they have a right to equal participation. The issue is that the next generation is standing up for equality and brings hard questions to bear on the sixty-plus years of a very specific interpretation of speech law which has allegedly led everyone to a better place.

They do not accept that they must defend a neo-Nazis' right to speak who disputes Jewish, Black, and other minority students' right to exist, and asserts that such students are inherently inferior. They also do not accept at face value the hypocrisy of people who defend a neo-Nazi's right to speech, ostensibly to uphold his constitutional rights against state suppression, and at the same time submit legislative bills mandating the expulsion of students who exercise their right to political protest.[23] One would think that such measures, meant to suppress political expression, fly in the face of upholding vigorous debate. They certainly make a mockery of the values and principles of Mario Savio and other forebears of today's campus free speech absolutists, who insisted on the rights of political expression to advance and not abolish racial justice and equality.

The result of such selective and dishonest application of free speech rights is to cloak the intention of subjugating others, most often racial minorities and women, under the mantle of free speech.

Charlottesville brought to light deeper problems than how to balance individual speech rights and equality. Our nation's universities have regularly admitted women and minority students for more than half a century but still struggle with providing all students with legally required equal participation. When a speaker disputes the rights of minority students to participate in a university on equal terms, this imposition harks back to a time, which perhaps persists even today, when women and minority students, in every class, every day, at every classroom door and college gate, had to prove their right to belong. Let them prove it, some may say. But such an unequal requirement, which is not expected of all students, is prohibited by Title IX, which is the law. To refer to the arguments made in the wake of Skokie, I offer no opinion whether today's neo-Nazis and white supremacists should not be barred from a public space, such as a park or street corner. Like their forebears in Skokie, they may march in the streets to promote obsolete and long-settled ideas of racial supremacy. But in a university, they undermine the very premise of education, which depends on the equal participation of all members of the community, regardless of background and race. Inviting them in means for the university to abdicate its role in deciding what speech advances the truth, and what speech undermines this collective project.

The nation's political landscape has shifted after Charlottesville. I think Charlottesville requires us to be more honest about the difference between absolute speech rights and academic freedom of inquiry, which admits ideas, after appropriate vetting, for unfettered debate to advance knowledge. Charlottesville encourages us to insist on our constitutional obligation to uphold educational equality, even when the courts wrongheadedly subordinate educational equality in a narrow application of libertarian First Amendment orthodoxy. I also think that these events force us to think about how the impact of any given speaker depends not only on the content of their speech but also on the platform. The violence wrought by the white supremacists is not a reason to enact draconian speech codes. But a speaker's refusal to accept the protocol and rules of university life should motivate us to articulate these ground rules more clearly, and to show that upholding speech rights on campus must not mean relinquishing the educational enterprise itself.

NOTES

1. A different version of this essay appears in *What Snowflakes Get Right: Free Speech, Truth and Equality on Campus* (Oxford: Oxford University Press, 2019).

2. Eugene Volokh has shown that the fear of a slippery slope as an automatic development is based on neither philosophical nor legal reasoning. There is no automatic deleterious effect of a given ruling, unless one presumes that all future legal decisions will not be based on sound reasoning and proceed as if without restraint. What is needed is the ability to identify "the various slippery-slope mechanisms." See Volokh, "The Mechanism of the Slippery Slope," *Harvard Law Review* 116 (2003): 1127.

3. The conviction that incendiary political speech will never constitute a threat to the United States as an idea and a reality is occasionally rooted in a denial of our nation's history. Floyd Abrams maintains that American history includes no episodes of disturbing violence linked to political beliefs: "In some nations, limitations on speech arise directly from disturbing, even sickening, events of their past [. . .]

It is understandable that some nations have sometimes responded by limiting particularly hateful speech that may have contributed to past tragedies. The United States has been fortunate not to have suffered such horrific events, and I am unwilling to criticize nations that have responded to such calamities by urging them to change their policies. For this nation, though, strict constitutionally imposed limitations on such legislation have served us well." *The Soul of the First Amendment* (New Haven: Yale University Press, 2017), 88.

4. Lee Bollinger, *The Tolerant Society: Freedom of Speech and Extremist Speech in America* (New York: Oxford University Press, 1986), 199.

5. Alexander Hamilton, James Madison, and John Jay, *The Federalist Papers* (New York: Signet, 2003).

6. *Report of the Chancellor's Commission on Free Speech*, April 9, 2018, p. 12, https://chancellor.berkeley.edu/sites/default/files/report_of_the_commission_on_free_speech.pdf

7. Pamela Newkirk offers concrete ideas for promoting diversity beyond paying lipservice to equity and inclusion, in *Diversity, Inc.: The Failed Promise of a Billion-Dollar Industry* (New York: Bold Type Books, 2019).

8. President Jimmy Carter, press conference, January 30, 1978, cited at https://www.presidency.ucsb.edu/documents/the-presidents-news-conference-1016.

9. The debates about Nikole Hannah-Jones book, *1619*, are a symptom of this larger shift. See *The 1619 Project; A New Origin Story* (New York: One World, 2021).

10. On the Supreme Court's history of protecting minority rights, see Erwin Chemerinsky, *The Case Against the Supreme Court* (New York: Penguin, 2015).

11. Ian Haney López, *Dog Whistle Politics*: *How Coded Racial Appeals Have Reinvented Racism and Wrecked the Middle Class* (New York and Oxford: Oxford University Press, 2014).

12. Judith Shklar, "Political Theory and the Rule of Law," in Allan Hutchinson and Patrick J. Monahan (eds.), *The Rule of Law: Ideal or Ideology* (Toronto: Carswell, 1987), ps. 1–16.

13. Nadine Strossen, *Hate: Why We Should Resist it With Free Speech, Not Censorship* (Oxford: Oxford University Press, 2017).

14. Erwin Chemerinsky and Howard Gillman, *Free Speech on Campus* (New Haven: Yale University Press, 2017).

15. The literature on comparative approaches to speech law is vast. An indispensable discussion is found in Norman Dorsen, Michel Rosenfeld, Andras Sajo, and Susanne Baer, *Comparative Constitutionalism: Cases and Materials* (New York: West, 2010).

16. Strossen, *Hate: Why We Should Resist it with Free Speech, Not Censorship* (op. cit.), p. 23. Timothy Garton Ash, *Free Speech: Ten Principles for a Connected World* (New Haven: Yale University Press, 2016).

17. Ibid., 25. Strossen introduces a list of cases where hate speech has resulted in what she considers questionable legal rulings. She does not list counterexamples, where communities have benefited from restraining the expression of targeted hate. It is clearly more difficult to prove the beneficial effects of restrictive laws, but this does not prove conclusively that such regulation does not have positive outcomes.

18. Hannah Arendt, "Truth and Politics" (1967), in *Between Past and Future: Eight Exercises in Political Thought* (New York: Penguin, 2006), p. 234.

19. Corey Brettschneider, *When the State Speaks, What Should it Say? How Democracies Can Protect Expression and Promote Equality* (Princeton, NJ: Princeton University Press, 2012).

20. "What UVA Students Saw in Charlottesville," *New York Times*, August 13, 2017.

21. On the purpose of speech in a university, see Baer, "What Universities Get Wrong About Free Speech," November 16, 2019, https://blog.oup.com/2019/11/universities-get-wrong-free-speech/.

22. David Brooks, "How to Engage a Fanatic," *The New York Times*, October 23, 2017, https://www.nytimes.com/2017/10/23/opinion/engaging-fanatics.html.

23. Jonathan Friedman, "Wrong Answer: How Good-Faith Efforts to Address Free Speech and Anti-Semitism on Campus Could Backfire," PEN publications, https://pen.org/research-resources/wrong-answer/.

REFERENCES

Abrams, Floyd. *The Soul of the First Amendment* (New Haven: Yale University Press, 2017).

Arendt, Hannah. "Truth and Politics" (1967). In *Between Past and Future: Eight Exercises in Political Thought* (New York: Penguin, 2006).

Ash, Timothy Garton. *Free Speech: Ten Principles for a Connected World* (New Haven: Yale University Press, 2016).

Baer, Ulrich. *What Snowflakes Get Right: Free Speech, Truth and Equality on Campus* (Oxford: Oxford University Press, 2019).

Baer, Ulrich. "What Universities Get Wrong About Free Speech," November 16, 2019, https://blog.oup.com/2019/11/universities-get-wrong-free-speech/

Bollinger, Lee. *The Tolerant Society: Freedom of Speech and Extremist Speech in America* (New York: Oxford University Press, 1986).

Brettschneider, Corey. *When The State Speaks, What Should it Say? How Democracies Can Protect Expression and Promote Equality* (Princeton, NJ: Princeton University Press, 2012).

Brooks, David. "How to Engage a Fanatic," *The New York Times*, October 23, 2017, https://www.nytimes.com/2017/10/23/opinion/engaging-fanatics.html.

Chemerinsky, Erwin. *The Case Against the Supreme Court* (New York: Penguin, 2015).

Chemerinsky, Erwin, and Howard Gillman, *Free Speech on Campus* (New Haven: Yale University Press, 2017).

Dorsen, Norman, Michel Rosenfeld, Andras Sajo, and Susanne Baer, *Comparative Constitutionalism: Cases and Materials* (New York: West, 2010).

Friedman, Jonathan. "Wrong Answer: How Good-Faith Efforts to Address Free Speech and Anti-Semitism on Campus Could Backfire," PEN publications, https://pen.org/research-resources/wrong-answer/

Hamilton, Alexander, James Madison, and John Jay, *The Federalist Papers* (New York: Signet, 2003).

Hannah-Jones, Nikole. *The 1619 Project; A New Origin Story* (New York: One World, 2021).

López, Ian Haney. *Dog Whistle Politics: How Coded Racial Appeals Have Reinvented Racism and Wrecked the Middle Class* (New York and Oxford: Oxford University Press, 2014).

Newkirk, Pamela. *Diversity, Inc.: The Failed Promise of a Billion-Dollar Industry* (New York: Bold Type Books, 2019).

Report of the Chancellor's Commission on Free Speech, April 9, 2018. https://chancellor.berkeley.edu/sites/default/files/report_of_the_commission_on_free_speech.pdf

Shklar, Judith. "Political Theory and the Rule of Law." In Allan Hutchinson and Patrick J. Monahan (eds.), The rule of law: Ideal or ideology (Toronto: Carswell, 1987), pp. 1–16.

Strossen, Nadine. *Hate: Why We Should Resist it With Free Speech, Not Censorship* (Oxford: Oxford University Press, 2017).

Volokh, Eugene. "The Mechanism of the Slippery Slope." *Harvard Law Review* 116 (2003): 1127.

"What UVA Students Saw in Charlottesville." *New York Times*, August 13, 2017.

Chapter 4

The First Amendment and Academic Freedom

Principles, Law, and Politics

Donald Alexander Downs

I would like to address the distinction that Robert Post advocated in his keynote address between "academic freedom" and "freedom of speech," and the implications of this distinction for free speech and academic theory and practice. Post's address raised a central concern that is of vital importance to the ongoing national debate over intellectual freedom on campus today. Though it has manifestations in law, the question of the relationship between free speech and academic freedom is primarily normative, so this short paper will not delve into many legalistic details, rather addressing this issue largely in policy and theoretical terms.

I am grateful to Post for presenting this thesis. His take has taught me much, and I agree that the distinction between these realms is essential if we want to preserve the fiduciary mission and integrity of the university. At the same time, I draw different conclusions regarding the balance or relationship between the two freedoms. Though the university's distinctive mission is premised on the principles and contours of academic freedom more than freedom of speech, freedom of speech also plays a crucial role when we consider the university as an intellectual *polis* consisting of different realms. In this essay, I will try to make a case for why this is so.

ACADEMIC FREEDOM AND FREE SPEECH

Post's keynote address was a condensed version of his noteworthy book on the relationship among free speech, democratic theory and practice, and expertise, *Democracy, Expertise, and Academic Freedom*.[1] Post discussed how the fundamental doctrinal principles of First Amendment and free speech jurisprudence are inappropriate when applied to the specialized context of academic life and higher education institutions. There *is* a fundamental distinction between free speech and academic freedom that speaks to the special fiduciary obligations of colleges and universities in our constitutional polity—their *raison d'être*. Indeed, the tension over the proper relationship between academic freedom and more general freedom of speech has become a major topic in current debate over free speech in higher education today.[2]

Higher education's fundamental mission is to pursue the truth and teach through competent and trained personnel. This mission is premised upon what my university, the University of Wisconsin, has declared to be "that continual and fearless sifting and winnowing [of ideas] by which alone truth may be found."[3] This process requires not only strong protections of intellectual freedom, but also the ability and willingness to separate truth from half-truth and falsehood. (Ptolemy's vision of the universe is wrong, period; astrology is not scientifically verified, etc.) It entails respect for freedom, but also commitment to intellectual standards. Post referred to Cardinal Newman's concept of the university's mission: "A University training . . . aims at raising the intellectual tone of society, at cultivating the public mind, at purifying the national taste."[4] That said, I will argue that classic First Amendment doctrine should play more of a role than a clear distinction between free speech and academic freedom implies. Classic free speech doctrine might be secondary compared to the strictures of academic freedom, but its presence is nonetheless necessary to a meaningful education. And to the extent that the law does not support this proposition, practical action by campus citizens should be undertaken to fill the gap, as I will discuss in a brief postscript to this essay.

At the risk of oversimplification, I boil Post's position down to its most basic points. I will add a couple of fundamental points to the list below for reasons I will mention, though the principles Post stresses are sufficient to support his main argument about the distinction between free speech and academic freedom. They are also familiar to anyone conversant in First Amendment law and jurisprudence. Though scholars have posited many different justifications or purposes for freedom of speech, Post premised his depiction of classic doctrine on the self-government philosophy of democratic theory, which is a widely respected principal justification:[5]

1. Under our system of government, the ultimate truth and strength of ideas are to be determined by We the People in the marketplace of ideas, the public forum, or in our own minds, not by the state in its different guises.[6] Accordingly, in regulating speech, the state may not engage in content discrimination or, especially, viewpoint discrimination. I would add that this rule also entails an *anti-paternalism principle* when it comes to the speaking and reception of ideas. Except in limited and distinct circumstances, the state may not treat adults like children who need the state to protect them from exposure to controversial or potentially harmful ideas.
2. All ideas are equal under the First Amendment. As the Supreme Court declared in an important libel case to which Post alluded, "We begin with the common ground. Under the First Amendment, there is no such thing as a false idea. However pernicious an opinion may seem, we depend for its correction not on the conscience of judges and juries, but on the competition of other ideas."[7] Post mentions a related condition in John Rawls' theory of equality and liberty that is pertinent to this cardinal operating assumption: in democracy and the marketplace of ideas, there are no experts.[8]
3. The state may not compel a person to speak, especially when the speech entails ideas or beliefs. This is the rule against "compelled speech" or "compelled association."
4. Let me add a fourth principle that Post did not mention but is consistent with his portrayal of predominant free speech theory and jurisprudence: *lack of trust* in government to make the decision regarding what people should be allowed to hear or say. Indeed, after an exhaustive analysis of the various justifications of free speech, First Amendment scholar Frederick Schauer concludes that lack of trust in government ("Who decides?") is the best plausible justification for protecting free speech from government control.[9]

As Post makes clear, anyone who insouciantly equates academic freedom with freedom of speech must reckon with the ways in which academic practice deviates from each of these essential rules. The following points seal the case:

1. Pedagogy is replete with content and viewpoint discrimination. For example, the academic freedom of faculty and students in the classroom is limited to speech that is "germane" or "relevant" to the academic matter at hand. (To be sure, what is relevant or germane should be generously construed because of heuristic aspirations stemming from the interconnectedness of knowledge and the need to give "breathing space"

to the valid discretion of instructors, as Post and Matthew Finkin have maintained.)[10] In addition, the kind of willful and obvious hate speech that is protected in the general public forum or realm may be restricted in classroom situations, where a basic distinction between gratuitous offense—substantial offense uttered simply for its own sake—and incidental offense based on the presentation of ideas is operative, subject to appropriate safeguards for intellectual freedom. In his book, *The Harm in Hate Speech*, our conference participant Jeremy Waldron defines "hate speech" as views "that express profound disrespect, hatred, and vilification for the members of minority groups."[11] Debate rages about the legal, normative, and practical aspects of enforcing this restriction, and Waldron would apply the standard to the general public forum as well the domains of academic speech. I do not wish to engage this debate here, except to say that at the least I would want more safeguards for class discussion, and that I am not prepared to accept Waldron's thesis in broader contexts. And there are valid concerns about how campus administrators today could abuse Waldron's thesis in application because of their disrespect for intellectual freedom and the pains unavoidably attendant to the "courageous sifting and winnowing of ideas."[12] The point is simply that such restriction is at least potentially more acceptable in classroom contexts than in the general free speech world because of the special obligations of the classroom. And Waldron himself stresses that his exception to speech must not pertain to the presentation of *ideas* that have racially unsettling or offensive implications, and the harm he is talking about is not the same thing as offensiveness. As Jonathan Rauch has convincingly demonstrated, the honest pursuit of truth often causes offense, so offense alone can never in itself trump academic freedom or freedom of speech, even in the classroom.[13]

2. The pursuit of truth, especially in academia, means distinguishing truth from falsehood. Some ideas are better than others, even if we concede the imperative Millian principle about human fallibility. (The universality of fallibility is one reason intellectual freedom must be protected.) And except at institutions that remain suspect in the eyes of many, students receive grades that reflect differences in the quality of their work. Furthermore, colleges and universities correctly strive to place experts in the roles of instructors, not charlatans. We don't hire specialists in the study of the Middle Ages to teach calculus, for example.
3. Finally, students may be compelled to speak or write all the time. They may be called on in class, and required to write exams lest they fail the course. For example, in *Axson-Flynn v. Johnson*, a federal court ruled that a religiously conservative theater student could be compelled to use language she considered sacrilegious so long as the requirement was

"reasonably related to pedagogical concerns."[14] The compelled speech doctrine does not apply in such cases. And, of course, faculty members are compelled to do quality research in institutions that live by the "publish or perish" rule.

4. Regarding my additional point above on "trust": In higher education, a great deal of trust is delegated to scholarly authorities—instructors, departments, scholarly review committees, and so on—to decide core academic matters, including what Justice Frankfurter considered the "four essential" pillars of academic freedom in *Sweazy v. New Hampshire*: the university must be allowed "to determine for itself on academic grounds who may teach, what may be taught, how it shall be taught, and who may be admitted to study."[15] (Note that Frankfurter's emphasis here is on the freedom of *the institution* to decide such matters based on the deference society owes to the expertise of academics to determine academic matters. This emphasis will prove to be problematic a few decades after Frankfurter wrote, as I explain below.) It is important to note that this trust has been bequeathed by not only students and their parents, but also by society as a whole. The institutional autonomy that is a hallmark of academic freedom was bestowed as part of an (at least) implicit social contract: *We the People give you institutional academic freedom to be autonomous, but only if you do your job, which is to teach and pursue the truth in an unbiased fashion with intellectual ability, freedom, integrity, and honesty*. Included in this compact is a responsibility that the American Association of University Professors (AAUP) has declared is an academic responsibility attached to the right of academic freedom: *the affirmative duty to do what is necessary to defend academic freedom itself*—the duty to protect the right at stake.[16] Below I will have something to say about this particular responsibility and its relationship to the distinction between academic freedom and free speech.

Hence, maintaining a fundamental distinction between academic freedom and free speech is necessary to the mission of the university. The distinction applies most readily to the professional academic realms of teaching and research, and such professional and scholarly activities as decisions regarding curricula, hiring, tenure, and in professional meetings on campus. What about speech outside of these contexts that seems to entail more classic contexts of free speech, such as the public forum on campus, student advocacy and free speech groups, and outside speakers? Like some other writers who have stressed the special nature of the university, Post also contends that classic First Amendment doctrine is not appropriately applicable to these realms, either. In a 2017 essay in *Vox*, Post wrote, "No university, public or private, could perform its mission were it not permitted to evaluate the merit of ideas" even in these realms.[17] Post was thinking about the right of such inflammatory and racist speakers as white nationalist Richard Spencer to speak on campus. In October 2017, for example, Spencer's appearance at the University of Florida, Gainesville, occasioned much controversy.

Beyond the question of a right to be invited, Post goes further and argues that even public universities should be able to limit the speech of outside speakers in two contexts: (1) speakers invited by students and even faculty if the university appropriately deems the speech inconsistent with the intellectual missions of the institution; (2) uninvited speakers who show up in open public forums on campus if their speech is similarly inconsistent with the institutional pedagogical mission. Post would authorize limits on speech in both contexts because he holds that the academic and pedagogical mission of the university may properly be extended to the public forum and invitees as well as to such places as the classroom.

Even if we accept Post's position that general public forum constitutional doctrine applicable outside of educational institutions should not apply to speakers at universities, a potential case could be made to allow such speakers as Spencer on policy and pedagogical grounds that also track classic free speech theory as well as Post's stricture that pedagogical value be the primary concern: there can be intellectual and political value in being exposed to ideas we find highly objectionable for two fundamental reasons. First, such exposure can more genuinely make us aware of the nature of the realities of political life and what is happening in the world, including the human capacity for injustice and evil. Second, as a civil rights leader once replied to me when I asked him if the First Amendment should protect hate groups like the Klan, "Letting them speak makes me more aware of their existence and where they stand so I can more responsibly deal with the reality of their presence."[18]

Post's point that no person has *a right* to be invited to give a talk on campus is certainly correct, though he is clear that as a normative matter non-invitations should not be motivated by concerns unrelated to intellectual quality, such as undue concerns for sensitivity or ideological postures—problems too prevalent in higher education today, unfortunately. But should his concern about intellectual standards extend to university decisions regarding campus areas that are classic or limited public forums, such as the place where Spencer spoke at the University of Florida in October 2017? According to the university's chief legal counsel, such areas at the university have long been places where uninvited speakers may speak so long as they do not violate legitimate laws. As "limited" public forums under the First Amendment, the University of Florida may shut such forums down, even though it is a public school—but only if it does so for all speakers to avoid the norms against viewpoint discrimination. The University of Florida chose not to do so, and to let Spencer speak, but only after legitimately delaying the speech to properly prepare for it. The university made this decision for two reasons. First, it desired to keep the forum open to provide a venue for other speakers to come to enhance the student experience. Second, given First Amendment requirements, it then had to allow Spencer to speak eventually at great effort and cost.[19]

Post would resolve this dilemma by making classic First Amendment doctrine inapplicable not only to the classroom, but also to public forums on campus. Let me now make a case for why higher education institutions should take classic First Amendment principles seriously even as they maintain the fundamental distinction between academic freedom and free speech. Whether this commitment should be required by First Amendment law is a matter of importance, but I will leave that question aside, resting my case on Post's own grounds, which are normative in the name of pedagogical mission. Let me also note that it is good that private schools may limit speech in the name of their proprietary missions unless they promise otherwise. Such commitments contribute to intellectual and moral diversity in the polity taken as a whole and are consistent with freedom of association.

THE RELATIONSHIP BETWEEN FREE SPEECH AND ACADEMIC FREEDOM RECONSIDERED: THE UNIVERSITY AS AN INTELLECTUAL *POLIS*

I veer from Post's position in several respects, though I agree with his understanding that academic freedom is the *sine qua non* of higher education, that which makes it distinctive. If instructors were given green lights without qualification to teach such things as Holocaust denial and Ptolemy as factual truth without qualification, the university as we know it would not exist.[20] But there are good reasons that most higher education institutions should adhere to classic First Amendment standards in other domains, for at least normative, if not legal, reasons. An appropriate balance between the standards of academic freedom and free speech jurisprudence is truer to the mission of higher education than upholding only the pillar of academic freedom.

First, consider the argument of Erwin Chemerinsky and Howard Gillman in their 2017 book, *Free Speech on Campus*. They posit two realms of campus life in the wake of the Berkeley Free Speech Movement of 1964: "Rather than view the university as a heavily regulated space of professional instruction and scholarly activity [the realm of 'academic freedom,' which is more circumscribed: D.A.D.], the students [at Berkeley] demanded that it also be recognized as a public forum for free speech . . . We should think of campuses as having two different zones of free expression: a *professional zone*, which protects the expression of ideas but imposes an obligation of responsible discourse and responsible conduct in formal educational and scholarly settings; and a larger *free speech zone*, which exists outside scholarly and administrative settings and where the only restrictions are those of society at large."[21] The university is a complex institution with different realms and activities. When it functions best, it is a kind of intellectual *polis*. The concept of the "Open University" speaks to this type of *polis*. And what affects intellectual freedom in one realm can influence intellectual freedom in other realms. In its section "Of Values and Priorities," the famous 1974 *Report of the Committee on Free Expression at Yale* (also known as the *Woodward Report* in honor of the committee's chair, C. Vann Woodward), wrote:

> The primary function of a university is to discover and disseminate knowledge by means of research and teaching. *To fulfill this function a free interchange of ideas is necessary not only within its walls but with the world beyond as well.* It follows that the university must do everything possible to ensure within it the fullest degree of intellectual freedom. The history of intellectual growth and discovery clearly demonstrates the need for unfettered freedom, the right to think the unthinkable, discuss the unmentionable, and challenge the unchallengeable. To curtail free expression strikes twice at intellectual freedom, for whoever deprives another of the right to state unpopular views necessarily also deprives others of the right to listen to those views.[22]

I would go further than Chemerinsky and Gillman. There is also a third dimension beyond the public forum: the countless interactions where campus citizens engage in the numerous nooks, crannies, and venues outside of libraries, classrooms, and speaker forums. Colleges and universities should be alive with Socratic exchanges in many domains. The seminal 1968 Supreme Court case dealing with the First Amendment right of a high school student to wear a black arm band to school to protest the Vietnam War championed the broad institutional aspect of student free speech I have in mind; and the point is even more pertinent to higher education, where intellectual freedom properly reigns more supreme than in high school, as both pedagogical theory and numerous court decisions have acknowledged:

> That [schools] are educating the young for citizenship is reason for scrupulous protection of Constitutional freedoms of the individual, if we are not to strangle the free mind at its source and teach youth to discount important principles of our government as mere platitudes . . .
>
> The principle of these cases is not confined to the supervised and ordained discussion which takes place in the classroom. The principal use to which the schools are dedicated is to accommodate students during prescribed hours for the purpose of certain types of activities. Among those activities is personal

> intercommunication among the students. This is not only an inevitable part of the process of attending school; it is also an important part of the educational process. A student's rights, therefore, do not embrace merely the classroom hours. When he is in the cafeteria, or on the playing field, or on the campus during the authorized hours, he may express his opinions, even on controversial subjects like the conflict in Vietnam, if he does so without "materially and substantially interfer[ing] with the requirements of appropriate discipline in the operation of the school" and without colliding with the rights of others.[23]

Protecting free speech in all three domains is important for both practical and normative reasons. It is practical simply because it acknowledges that a vital college or university is an institutional community or *polis*. If we deny this reality, we blind ourselves to the ways in which free thought can flourish in different realms, and how the suppression of speech in the informal realms can readily spill over to the formal realms—and vice versa. Controversial views should not be relegated to the bathroom or subway walls, or the "sounds of silence." ("The words of the prophets are / Written on the subway walls / And tenement halls / And whispered in the sounds of silence.")[24] And it is normative because so much learning and intellectual growth occur outside formal settings. When I taught, I considered my classes to be springboards for student discussions in different campus domains, and always relished the countless intellectual interchanges I had with students in the various domains of the campus. I considered it a moral victory when students would tell me about debates that they had undertaken about my class in their dorm rooms and apartments, Memorial Union, or in the watering holes that line State Street. But the formal learning that takes place also elevates and gives more substance to the exchanges and engagements that arise in the informal spheres. Each realm nourishes the other in a dialectical process.

We could even add a fourth realm of speech. Burkay Ozturk and Bob Fisher, drawing on the work of political theorist Jacob Levy and the constitutional doctrine of private association rights, refer to what we may discern to be another realm of campus speech activity:

> the right of individuals and communities to pursue their lives quite independently of one another, at least in certain crucial respects. So perhaps, the Framers established a system of rights in which speech isn't just a tool for the dissemination of ideas: It's also [a] way of telling the world who you are and for aligning yourself with like-minded people.[25]

In 1982, the late constitutional scholar Robert Cover analyzed this important aspect of freedom of thought and conscience in a prominent law review essay: the right to establish your own community of meaning and truth in opposition to state and community truths, so long as you accept legitimate general laws that do not unnecessarily infringe upon this right. Similar to political scientist Samuel Huntington, Cover explored how constitutional meaning is forged by the "constant struggle" of groups to define their own meanings and to "maintain the independence and authority of their own *nomos*."[26]

It is useful to think of the connections among the four realms in terms of the relationship between formal activities and play. Whereas formal situations and presentations constitute specialized contexts for the achievement of excellence, play is the realm where we can be more experimental and open our wings more readily. This is especially important for young adults, who are experimenting and feeling their way in a trial-and-error respect. As Hans-Georg Gadamer has discerned, truth about human qualities and nature is often disclosed in acts of play, commitment, and creation.[27] The highest form of excellence is when we combine the two forms, making official performance itself a form of play, or elevating play itself to a higher level. This understanding is much like the German *Bildung* tradition, which envisions individual learning and maturation as a process of self-definition and discovery in relation to a community of meaning. Seek and ye shall find. As one essay on *Bildung* relates:

> [A]ccording to the German *Bildung* tradition, philosophy and education are virtually synonymous terms that designate an ongoing process of both personal and cultural maturation. This maturation is evidenced in a harmonization of the individual's mind and heart and in a unification of society. Harmonization of the self is achieved through a wide variety of experiences and challenges to the individual's accepted beliefs; in Hegel's writings, these challenges entail agonizing alienation from one's "natural consciousness" that leads to a reunification and development of the self.[28]

FIVE OTHER CONSIDERATIONS

Let me advance five additional and related reasons for giving free speech jurisprudence more, yet appropriately balanced, influence in higher education. *First*, though the realms of academic freedom and free speech are distinct for the reasons we have articulated, they also share an essential common ground: the commitment to the pursuit of truth and the intellectual freedom that is essential to that end. (See the observation of the Woodward Committee above.) This is one reason that efforts to define free speech and academic freedom often overlap or are conceptually complex. An example might be the University of Chicago's famous "Statement on Principles of Free Expression," which focuses on free "expression," but is also meant to have at least some meaningful application to academic freedom.[29] The University of Wisconsin-Madison's definition of "academic freedom" in its official rules governing faculty rights and responsibilities, enacted by the faculty senate in 2010, also reflects this balance or tension. This definition has the effect of state law because the Board of Regents let it stand after passage in the senate. The definition of "academic freedom" is followed by a definition of "academic responsibility." The two sections embody the appropriate balance under discussion as such:

> B. Academic freedom is the freedom to discuss and present scholarly opinions and conclusions regarding all relevant matters in the classroom, to explore all avenues of scholarship, research, and creative expression, and to reach conclusions according to one's scholarly discernment. It also includes the right to speak or write—as a private citizen or within the context of one's activities as an employee of the university—without institutional discipline or restraint on matters of public concern as well as on matters related to professional duties, the functioning of the university, and university positions and policies.
>
> C. Academic responsibility implies the faithful performance of professional duties and obligations, the recognition of the demands of the scholarly enterprise, and the candor to make it clear that when one is speaking on matters of public interest or concern, one is speaking on behalf of oneself, not the institution.[30]

Note also that this definition also extends protection to faculty members' public criticism of the university, which the Supreme Court potentially precluded from First Amendment protection in the infamous *Ceballos* case. This enactment by the faculty senate was led by the Committee for Academic Freedom and Rights, an independent, nonpartisan faculty group that was the campus leader in promoting and protecting free speech and academic freedom between 1996 and 2016. During its tenure, CAFAR also successfully defended over twenty individuals at Madison and in the state whose academic freedom or free speech had been harmed or jeopardized.[31]

Second, courts have applied First Amendment standards to contexts in public institutions that mirror contexts in the real world where free speech principles reign. For example, courts have struck down rules that limit campus speech to restrictive "free speech zones." (In my eyes, restrictive free speech zones imply that the institution needs to "quarantine" free speech on campus, as if free speech is some kind of disease!) And in the *Southworth* case, the Supreme Court ruled that schools must abide by the viewpoint neutrality rule when they require students to pay fees to support a system of student groups for purposes of association or advocacy. (If such a student forum for ideas is not viewpoint neutral, requiring the payment of fees can constitute "compelled association.") In addition, courts have been highly suspicious of speech codes directed at students, typically applying general First Amendment principles.[32] And consider a hypothetical case of a school requiring students to take an oath supporting some institutional policy, such as diversity or sustainability of energy. Would not such a requirement run afoul of basic First Amendment rights against compelled association?

Third, and one of the more informative points, the best universities have historically been places where academic principles and vibrant free speech have coexisted. In this respect I am reminded of the vision of the university that Jose Ortega presents in *Mission of the University*. On the one hand, Ortega makes it clear that the foundation of the university is the cultivation of the mind through an emphasis upon "science," by which he means the pursuit of truth through rigorous scholarly standards. Intellectual freedom is crucial to the pursuit of science, but such freedom must ultimately bow to academic rigor and standards. Ortega's concept of science is similar to the German concept of *Wissenschaft*, which in philosopher Brian Leiter's words means "any systematic form of inquiry into nature, history, literature, or society marked by rigorous methods that secure the reliability or truth of its findings."[33]

On the other hand, Ortega praises the concept of an open university that faces the pressing issues and controversies of the day. His emphasis is similar to that of the Woodward Report, but also somewhat different, deriving from Ortega's general philosophy of historical vitality, struggle, and phenomenology:

> Not only does [the university] need perpetual contact with science, on pain of atrophy, it needs contact, likewise, with public life, with historical reality, with the present, which is essentially a whole to be dealt with only in its totality . . . The university must be in the midst of life, and saturated with it.[34]

But even if the university includes a zone for public discourse and student activism, its primary mission is to instill the intellectual virtues—*to make students more thoughtful and knowledgeable in whatever they do on campus and in life*—to cultivate the mind. The university must engage the world "in its totality," *but it must do so on its own terms*, which combine intellectual freedom with a commitment to intellectual standards. Ortega continued:

> The original sin stems from the pretension to be other than one's true self. It is our *privilege* to be whatever we wish; but it is vicious to pretend to be what we are not, to delude ourselves by growing habituated to a radically false idea of what we are. When the habitual behavior of a man or an institution is false, the next step is complete demoralization.[35]

From Ortega's perspective, a university can become "demoralized" in three ways. First, by losing its commitment to "science" broadly understood, which typically happens when politicization and other forms of bias infect it, or if it loses its duty to foster the rigorous inquiry into truth. Second, by not properly distinguishing the realms of academic freedom/responsibility and free speech, by becoming only or primarily a marketplace of ideas rather than a cultivator of the mind. And third, by closing itself off from the vitality of what Ortega called "life" in the world that surrounds it. Think of "life" as the energy that helps to motivate and engage the mind. Most of the political theorists we study in political science and philosophy were deeply committed to engaging the pressing public issues of their time in one form or another, so the involvement with the "life" around the university gives students who simultaneously study the great thinkers a taste of the actual intellectual circumstances of these thinkers. The great international relations theorist Hans Morgenthau called this combination of rigorous intellectual study and engagement with contemporary issues a form of "higher practicality." When properly conducted, the "higher practicality" makes the big questions of social and political existence come alive for students, showing them how historically notable political thought is often forged in conflict and pressure, entailing not only the intellect, but also entailing emotion, character, and commitment—all themes one finds in the history and theory of free speech, by the way. Such inquiry broadens, deepens, and enlivens the pursuit of truth, while taking the best works of political thought seriously adds depth and intellectual responsibility to the quest. Contra Marx's critique of Hegel, the purpose of philosophy is to understand the world before trying to change it.[36]

"Science" cultivates and elevates the mind, submitting passion to reason. "Life" motivates and energizes the mind, giving it force and presence. One is reminded of Plato's depiction of how the passion of love can serve the pursuit of philosophy in the *Symposium*. In terms of liberal democracy, what the proper balance between free speech and academic freedom/responsibility does is to make the passion play of democracy more amenable to the constraints of knowledge, reason, and a sense of justice. In Tocqueville's terms, higher education should be a "remedy" or "check" for the passions and darker inclinations of democratic societies.

The *fourth* reason for striving to maintain a proper balance of free speech and academic freedom is the way in which such a balance represents a due commitment to both intellectual standards and a healthy regard for human fallibility, which is a hallmark of free speech theory. After Mill, respect for the fallibility principle is mandatory, which means maintaining due doubt about truth claims, however compelling they may be. Indeed, such healthy skepticism lies at the heart of our constitutional system, which promotes checks and balances to guard against the imperfections—intellectual and moral—of those who govern us at the same time that it establishes requisite power for the government to constitutionally govern citizens in order to protect us from our own fallibilities. As Madison put it, "In framing a government which is to be administered by men over men, the great difficulty lies in this: you must first enable the government to control the governed; and in the next place to oblige it to control itself." Political theorist Paul Eidelberg explains the intellectual/political rationale behind American checks and balances: "It means that the first object of government is to prevent any attempt to bring about a massive uniformity of opinions, passions, and interests . . . Madison wished to institute a system of checks and balances to preserve the republic from the leveling spirit. To guard against that spirit is to guard against the degradation of the republican form of government."[37]

For the *fifth* and final point, let us return to the question of *trust* that I added to Post's list of core free speech principles above. Lack of trust in government and authority is a classic free speech value that is different from the institutional autonomy higher education leaders have traditionally enjoyed in practice and in law. But given the threats to intellectual freedom on campus today, is such trust merited? As I mentioned earlier, academic freedom was originally conceived as an institutional right more than an individual right. And this is how courts have tended to treat it even to this day, though the relationship between individual and institutional autonomy is not crystal clear.[38]

There are different reasons for this emphasis, one of which is the fact that most of the historical threats to academic freedom hailed from outside the university's gates, largely from the right. Accordingly, individual and institutional interests in academic freedom coexisted largely in harmony, at least compared to more recent times. But this arrangement has changed over the course of the last few decades. Though threats from the right continue—often in response to universities not protecting worthy intellectual diversity—most threats today have come from the academic left, and from *inside* higher education itself. This is a long yet familiar story, but the fundamental fact is indisputable. The policies and actions that threaten academic freedom and free speech today are progressive in nature (hence the term "progressive censorship"): aggressive forms of identity politics that do not tolerate the criticism that is a hallmark of free discourse; speech codes; overly expansive harassment codes; trigger warnings; microaggression policies; expansive bias-reporting programs that have expanded into the classroom; safe-space policies; speaker shout downs and speaker dis-invitation—many pushed by a growing administrative class with agendas that are not consistent with the intellectual mission that Post correctly posits as the university's *sine qua non*. As former Stanford provost John Etchemendy wrote in a recent article in the *Chronicle of Higher Education*, "Intellectual intolerance poses an existential danger to the university."[39] The "existential danger" is due to higher education not living up to its end of the social contract.

To the degree that this situation reigns—the main debate today is over the *extent* of the problem, not its *existence*—it is no longer as feasible as it once was to blithely trust the judgments of academic leaders to determine academic policy for themselves. At best, the situation should be one of "trust, but verify." Sadly, the due distrust that is a linchpin of free speech jurisprudence should be applied to the realm of academic politics and discretion. The question is how distrust should be manifested.

POSTSCRIPT: POLITICAL—NOT LEGAL—MOBILIZATION ON BEHALF OF ACADEMIC FREEDOM AND RIGHTS

Given the history and actuality of problems associated with outside intervention, by far the best remedy is for faculty who care about intellectual freedom on campus to do what the AAUP touts as a duty attached to the right of academic freedom: to mobilize to defend academic freedom against its detractors and enemies. Others and I have written about this remedy and have been involved in such movements. Such mobilization is also needed because, as I have only intimated in this essay, First Amendment law is clearer about the protection of student speech than of faculty speech. Faculty are employees, so courts have traditionally been less willing to defend faculty speech than the speech of students, though there are exceptions to this difference. This is especially the situation after *Garcetti*.

Back in the mid-1990s, I asked the national director of the American Civil Liberties Union, Nadine Strossen, if the ACLU would be willing to challenge UW-Madison's deeply troubling faculty speech code for the classroom in court. (The student speech code, which exempted the classroom, had nonetheless been invalidated by a federal court in 1991 for being overly broad.) She said yes and contacted the director of the Wisconsin Civil Liberties Union to consider the matter. But the WCLU declined to take the case, maintaining that faculty speech in that context was less protected than student speech. My allies in the newly formed independent Committee for Academic Freedom and Rights at Madison and I had learned enough about the application of the faculty code to know that it had to be abolished or severely reformed; so, we mobilized a movement that crossed political and ideological lines. This movement eventuated in a vote in the faculty senate on March 1, 1999, to abolish the code. Henceforth, all faculty speech "relevant" to the subject matter at hand would be protected in the classroom—a standard beholden to both academic freedom and freedom of speech principles. We were the first known case of a university abolishing a speech code through campus politics rather than a court order. This victory for intellectual freedom set the stage for other successes over the years.[40]

In the end, we were glad that the WCLU turned us down because it is always better to achieve such results through a political process the success of which requires achieving a voluntary consensus than to rely upon the external authority of a court that might be resisted or disrespected. As H.L.A. Hart has written, there is a difference between being "obliged" and being "obligated." As Hart puts it, you are "obliged" to give a gunman the money he demands, but not "obligated." To be "obligated," one must feel a normative commitment or reason for so acting.[41] Proper mobilization on campus can achieve a sense of obligation among faculty, whereas court orders are often taken as coercive orders that merely oblige. That was the case at Madison regarding the court decision on the student code in 1991, as I personally witnessed. Equally important, the necessity of mobilizing a campus movement through CAFAR necessitated establishing a political infrastructure on campus that lasted two decades, establishing a power base to defend both free speech and academic freedom on campus.

I have much more to say about different approaches to mobilization, internal and external, but space constraints oblige—I mean obligate—me to leave that for another occasion.[42]

NOTES

1. Robert Post, *Democracy, Expertise, and Academic Freedom: A First Amendment Jurisprudence for the Modern State* (Yale University Press, 2013).

2. See, e.g., James R. Stoner, "Are Academic Freedom and Freedom of Speech Congruent or Opposed?" in *The Value and Limits of Academic Free Speech*, edited by Donald Alexander Downs and Chris W. Surprenant (New York: Routledge, 2018), ch. 4.

3. Official Statement of Board of Regents, University of Wisconsin, 1894. See, e.g., Theodore Herfurth, *Sifting and Winnowing* (1949), ch. 6, http://digicoll.library.wisc.edu/WIReader/WER1035-Chpt6.html

4. John Henry Newman, *The Idea of a University*, edited by Frank M. Turner (Yale University Press, 1996), 126.

5. Other justifications of free speech include such things as the elusive pursuit of truth, self-realization and happiness, social change, speech as a safety valve for dissent, inherent individual right, consent theory, and distrust of government, among others.

6. The education philosopher and democratic theorist Alexander Meiklejohn is perhaps the most prominent advocate of this theory of free speech. See Meiklejohn, "Free Speech and Its Relation to Self-Government," in Meiklejohn, *Political Freedom: The Constitutional Powers of the People* (Oxford University Press, 1960).

7. *Gertz v. Robert Welch*, 418 U.S. 323, 339–340 (1974).

8. In *Kindly Inquisitors*, Jonathan Rauch defends what he calls the "empirical rule," which means that truth claims must be demonstrated by relevant facts rather than simply deferring to the conclusions of people with authority or prestige. But note that Rauch also correctly stresses that it is profoundly wrong to hold that all ideas are entitled to equal respect. (He critiques the "Egalitarian Principle" in this regard.) *Kindly Inquisitors: The New Attacks on Free Thought* (University of Chicago Press, 1993), Chs. 1 and 2.

9. Frederick Schauer, *Free Speech: A Philosophical Enquiry* (Harvard University Press, 1982).

10. See, e.g., Matthew Finkin and Robert Post, *For the Common Good: Principles of American Academic Freedom* (Yale University Press, 2009), esp. p. 94.

11. Waldron, *The Harm in Hate Speech* (Harvard University Press, 2012), p. 27.

12. On the practical and administrative slippery slope regarding Waldron's definition of hate speech in the higher education context, see C. K. Miles, "Skepticism About Title IX Culture," in Downs and Surprenant, *The Value and Limits of Academic Free Speech*, ch. 15.

13. Rauch, *Kindly Inquisitors*.

14. *Axson-Flynn v. Johnson*, 356 F.3d 1277, 1285 (10th Cir. 2004).

15. *Sweazy v. New Hampshire*, 354 U.S. 234, 263 (1957).

16. AAUP, *A Statement of the Association's Council: Freedom and Responsibility*, October 1970, https://www.aaup.org/file/freedom-and-responsibility.pdf.

17. Robert Post, "There Is No First Amendment Right to Speak on a College Campus," *Vox*, October 25, 2017, https://www.vox.com/the-big-idea/2017/10/25/16526442/first-amendment-college-campuses-milo-spencer-protests.

18. See also Aryeh Neier, *Defending My Enemy: American Nazis, the Skokie Case, and the Risks of Freedom* (New York: Dutton, 1979); Donald Alexander Downs, *Nazis in Skokie: Freedom, Community, and the First Amendment* (University of Notre Dame Press, 1985), Ch. 6.

19. University of Florida general counsel Amy M. Hass made these points at a conference at the University of Tampa on April 6, 2019, on "Free Speech and Academic Freedom." She and I served as two of the panelists.

20. See, e.g., Mary Lefkowitz, *History Lesson: A Race Odyssey* (Yale University Press, 2008).

21. Chemerinsky and Gillman, *Free Speech on Campus* (Yale University Press, 2017), pp. 75, 77 (emphasis in original).

22. *Report of the Committee on Free Expression at Yale* (1974), Section 1, "Of Values and Priorities." https://yalecollege.yale.edu/deans-office/reports/report-committee-freedom-expression-yale (emphasis in original).

23. *Tinker v. Des Moines School District*, 393 U.S. 503, 507 and 512–513 (1969).

24. In the wake of California Proposition 209 in the late 1990s that limited the use of race as a criterion for admission to public higher education, a climate of severe intolerance of different viewpoints on race arose at Berkeley's Boalt Law School. Many students chose to express their disagreements with this silencing on the bathroom stalls rather than in more public domains. Even students opposed to 209 were

upset at the effect of the broad silencing on their educations. See David Wienir and Marc Berley, eds., *The Diversity Hoax: Law Students Report from Berkeley* (New York: Foundation for Academic Standards and Tradition, 1999), pp. 52–53, 155. See also Downs, *Restoring Free Speech and Liberty on Campus* (Cambridge University Press, 2006), Ch. 4. Simon and Garfunkel, "The Sounds of Silence."

25. Burkay Ozturk and Bob Fischer, "Speech and War: Rethinking the Ethics of Speech Restrictions," in Downs and Surprenant, *The Value and Limits of Academic Free Speech*, p. 190.

26. Robert Cover, "Foreword: *Nomos* and Narrative," *Harvard Law Review*, 97 (1983): 25. Samuel Huntington, *American Politics: The Promise of Disharmony* (Harvard University Press, 1981).

27. Gadamer, *Truth and Method*, trans. Garrett Barden and John Cumming (New York: Seabury Press, 1975), pp. 92–110.

28. Antonie Dubbelman, "The German *Bildung* Tradition," https://www.academia.edu/8055120/The_German_Bildung_Tradition. See also, Alexander Nehamas, *Nietzsche: Life as Literature* (Harvard University Press, 1985).

29. *Report of the Committee on Freedom of Expression*, University of Chicago, 2015, https://provost.uchicago.edu/sites/default/files/documents/reports/FOECommitteeReport.pdf.

30. Chapter 8, UW-Madison, Faculty Procedures and Policies: Faculty Rights and Responsibilities, Sections 8.01: https://secfac.wisc.edu/wp-content/uploads/sites/50/2017/06/FPP-chapter-8-2016-May-17.pdf.

31. Donald A. Downs, "The University of Wisconsin Counters *Garcetti v. Ceballos*," AAUP,https://www.aaup.org/get-involved/issue-campaigns/speak-speak-out-protect-faculty-voice/how-and-success-stories/wisconsin. On CAFAR in general, see Downs, *Restoring Free Speech and Liberty on Campus,* Ch.s 1, 7, and 8.

32. *Board of Regents of the University of Wisconsin System v. Southworth*, 529 U.S. 217 (2000); *UWM Post v. Board of Regents*, 773 F. Supp. 1163 (E.D. Wis., 1991). The latter case on the University of Wisconsin's student speech code applied fighting words doctrine, concluding that First Amendment rights trumped Title VII.

33. Brian Leiter, "Why Academic Freedom?" in Downs and Surprenant, *The Value and Limits of Academic Free Speech*, 33.

34. Ortega, *Mission of the University* (New York: Norton, 1966).

35. Ibid.

36. Hans J. Morgenthau, "The Purpose of Political Science," in James C. Charlesworth, editor, *A Design for Political Science: Scope, Objectives, and Methods* (American Academy of Political and Social Science, 1966). Marx, "Theses on Feuerbach," in *Selected Writings*, edited by Lawrence H. Simon (Indianapolis: Hackett, 1994), p. 101.

37. James Madison, *Federalist* 51 in Alexander Hamilton, John Jay, and James Madison, *The Federalist*, edited by George W. Carey and James McClellan, Gideon Edition (Indianapolis: Liberty Fund, 2001), 269. Paul Eidelberg, *The Philosophy of the American Constitution: A Reinterpretation of the Intentions of the Founding Fathers* (New York: Free Press, 1968), p. 153.

38. See, e.g., David M. Rabban, "Academic Freedom, Individual or Institutional? Most Federal Courts Agree that Academic Freedom Is a First Amendment Right, But Whose Right Is It?" *Academe Online*, November-December, 2001, http://www/aaup.org/AAuP/pubres/academe/2001/Feat/Rabb/htm.

39. John Etchemendy, "The Threat from Within: Intellectual Intolerance Poses an Existential Danger to the University," *Chronicle Review*, March 3, 2017, https://www.chronicle.com/article/The-Threat-From-Within/239391. Many works have chronicled the ideological and intellectual imbalance in higher education today, as well as the unequal effects of the policies mentioned. See, e.g., Jon A. Shields and Joshua M. Dunn, Sr., *Passing on the Right: Conservatives in the Progressive University* (Oxford University Press, 2016). Alan Charles Kors and Harvey A. Silverglate, *The Shadow University: The Betrayal of Liberty on America's Campuses* (New York: Free Press, 1998).

40. For histories of this movement, see Donald A. Downs and Stanley G. Payne, "The Wisconsin Fight for Academic Freedom," *Academic Questions*, Summer 2016; Downs, *Restoring Free Speech and Liberty on Campus*, Chs. 6 and 7.

41. H.L.A. Hart, *The Concept of Law* (Oxford: Clarendon Press, 1961).

42. See, e.g., *Free Speech and Liberal Education* (Washington, D.C.: Cato Institute, 2020).

REFERENCES

AAUP, *A Statement of the Association's Council: Freedom and Responsibility*, October 1970, https://www.aaup.org/file/freedom-and-responsibility.pdf.

Axson-Flynn v. Johnson, 356 F.3d 1277, 1285 (10th Cir. 2004).

Board of Regents of the University of Wisconsin System v. Southworth, 529 U.S. 217 (2000).

Chemerinsky, Erwin, and Howard Gillman, *Free Speech on Campus* (Yale University Press, 2017).

Robert Cover, "Foreword: *Nomos* and Narrative," *Harvard Law Review*, 97 (1983): 25.

Downs, Donald Alexander. *Free Speech and Liberal Education* (Washington, D.C.: Cato Institute, 2020).

Downs, Donald Alexander. *Nazis in Skokie: Freedom, Community, and the First Amendment* (University of Notre Dame Press, 1985).

Downs, Donald Alexander. *Restoring Free Speech and Liberty on Campus* (Cambridge University Press, 2006).

Downs, Donald Alexander. "The University of Wisconsin Counters *Garcetti v. Ceballos*," AAUP, https://www.aaup.org/get-involved/issue-campaigns/speak-speak-out-protect-faculty-voice/how-and-success-stories/wisconsin.

Downs, Donald A., and Stanley G. Payne, "The Wisconsin Fight for Academic Freedom," *Academic Questions*, Summer 2016.

Dubbelman, Antonie. "The German *Bildung* Tradition," https://www.academia.edu/8055120/The_German_Bildung_Tradition.

Eidelberg, Paul. *The Philosophy of the American Constitution: A Reinterpretation of the Intentions of the Founding Fathers* (New York: Free Press, 1968).

John Etchemendy, "The Threat from Within: Intellectual Intolerance Poses an Existential Danger to the University," *Chronicle Review*, March 3, 2017, https://www.chronicle.com/article/The-Threat-From-Within/239391.

Finkin, Matthew, and Robert Post, *For the Common Good: Principles of American Academic Freedom* (Yale University Press, 2009).

Gadamer, Hans-Georg. *Truth and Method*, trans. Garrett Barden and John Cumming (New York: Seabury Press, 1975).

Gertz v. Robert Welch, 418 U.S. 323 (1974).

Hamilton, Alexander, John Jay, and James Madison. *The Federalist*, edited by George W. Carey and James McClellan, Gideon Edition (Indianapolis: Liberty Fund, 2001).

Hart, H. L. A. *The Concept of Law* (Oxford: Clarendon Press, 1961).

Herfurth, Theodore. *Sifting and Winnowing* (1949), ch.6, http://digicoll.library.wisc.edu/WIReader/WER1035-Chpt6.html

Huntington, Samuel. *American Politics: The Promise of Disharmony* (Harvard University Press, 1981).

Kors, Alan Charles, and Harvey A. Silverglate. *The Shadow University: The Betrayal of Liberty on America's Campuses* (New York: Free Press, 1998).

Lefkowitz, Mary. *History Lesson: A Race Odyssey* (Yale University Press, 2008).

Leiter, Brian. "Why Academic Freedom?" In *The Value and Limits of Academic Free Speech*, edited by Donald Alexander Downs and Chris W. Surprenant (New York: Routledge, 2018), ch. 2.

Marx, Karl. "Theses on Feuerbach." In *Selected Writings*, edited by Lawrence H. Simon (Indianapolis: Hackett, 1994).

Meiklejohn, Alexander. *Political Freedom: The Constitutional Powers of the People* (Oxford University Press, 1960).

Miles, C. K. "Skepticism About Title IX Culture." In *The Value and Limits of Academic Free Speech*, edited by Donald Alexander Downs and Chris W. Surprenant (New York: Routledge, 2018), ch. 15.

Morgenthau, Hans J. "The Purpose of Political Science," in James C. Charlesworth, editor, *A Design for Political Science: Scope, Objectives, and Methods* (American Academy of Political and Social Science, 1966).

Nehamas, Alexander. *Nietzsche: Life as Literature* (Harvard University Press, 1985).

Neier, Aryeh. *Defending My Enemy: American Nazis, the Skokie Case, and the Risks of Freedom* (New York: Dutton, 1979).

Newman, John Henry. *The Idea of a University*, edited by Frank M. Turner (Yale University Press, 1996).

Ortega y Gasset, Jose. *Mission of the University* (New York: Norton, 1966).

Ozturk, Burkay, and Bob Fischer. "Speech and War: Rethinking the Ethics of Speech Restrictions." In *The Value and Limits of Academic Free Speech*, edited by Donald Alexander Downs and Chris W. Surprenant (New York: Routledge, 2018), ch. 11.

Post, Robert. *Democracy, Expertise, and Academic Freedom: A First Amendment Jurisprudence for the Modern State* (Yale University Press, 2013).

Post, Robert. "There Is No First Amendment Right to Speak on a College Campus," *Vox*, October 25, 2017, https://www.vox.com/the-big-idea/2017/10/25/16526442/first-amendment-college-campuses-milo-spencer-protests.

Rabban, David M. "Academic Freedom, Individual or Institutional? Most Federal Courts Agree that Academic Freedom Is a First Amendment Right, But Whose Right Is It?" *Academe Online*, November–December 2001, http://www/aaup.org/AAuP/pubres/academe/2001/Feat/Rabb/htm.

Rauch, Jonathan. *Kindly Inquisitors: The New Attacks on Free Thought* (University of Chicago Press, 1993).

Report of the Committee on Free Expression at Yale (1974). https://yalecollege.yale.edu/deans-office/reports/report-committee-freedom-expression-yale

Report of the Committee on Freedom of Expression, University of Chicago, 2015: https://provost.uchicago.edu/sites/default/files/documents/reports/FOECommitteeReport.pdf.

Schauer, Frederick. *Free Speech: A Philosophical Enquiry* (Harvard University Press, 1982).

Shields, Jon A., and Joshua M. Dunn, Sr., *Passing on the Right: Conservatives in the Progressive University* (Oxford University Press, 2016).

Stoner, James R. "Are Academic Freedom and Freedom of Speech Congruent or Opposed?" In *The Value and Limits of Academic Free Speech*, edited by Donald Alexander Downs and Chris W. Surprenant (New York: Routledge, 2018), ch. 4.

Sweazy v. New Hampshire, 354 U.S. 234 (1957).

Tinker v. Des Moines School District, 393 U.S. 503 (1969).

UW-Madison, Faculty Procedures and Policies: Faculty Rights and Responsibilities, Sections 8.01: https://secfac.wisc.edu/wp-content/uploads/sites/50/2017/06/FPP-chapter-8-2016-May-17.pdf.

UWM Post v. Board of Regents, 773 F. Supp. 1163 (E.D. Wis., 1991).

Waldron, Jeremy. *The Harm in Hate Speech* (Harvard University Press, 2012).

Wienir, David, and Marc Berley, eds., *The Diversity Hoax: Law Students Report from Berkeley* (New York: Foundation for Academic Standards and Tradition, 1999).

PART II

Free Inquiry on Campus

Philosophy

Chapter 5

The Value of Free Speech

Harvey C. Mansfield

Our usual debate over the extent of free speech takes the value of free speech for granted. As we argue over the boundaries or limits of free speech, we pass over the value of what is normally said in order to consider the extremes in which speech incites dangerous deeds or has to be inferred from ritual deeds like flag-saluting or provocative deeds like flag-burning. In keeping with liberal philosophical tradition and with the free-speech issues decided by the Supreme Court, we concentrate on the extremes of speech. By so doing we overlook how we benefit from normal free speech that does not test the permissible limits but rather expresses in argument the normal human differences that occur in any society and can be heard only in a free society. In what follows I shall try to identify the one normal human difference that is the most salient issue in normal free speech. The argument will be an outline designed not to explain in depth but to cover ground.

NORMAL SPEECH

There is a reason why our normal view of speech overlooks the normal practice of free speech. Our disinterest in the value of free speech, sometimes amounting to a refusal to define it, can be found in the principles of our liberalism, which enshrines free speech as one right, perhaps the principal right, among the rights that deserve protection in a liberal society. To protect this particular right, it seems, one must not specify the value of what will normally be said lest by such definition society take away what it wants to protect. For to discuss the value of free speech one would expose less valued or valueless speech to disdain, or worse, prohibition. A society of rights must above all protect its boundaries in the definition of rights rather than concern itself too much, or at all, with what is said within the protected territory. Thus, the protection of unlimited, or nearly unlimited, speech eclipses our view of worthy speech.

Everybody admits the exception to unlimited speech in the dangerous but exemplary circumstance of the crowded theater, but no one wants to pursue the distinction implied in that exception. Yet to condemn or punish the act of falsely shouting "fire!" in that situation is indeed to distinguish between helpful and harmful speech. At times we will find value in apparently harmful speech, as in the "redeeming social value" awarded by the Supreme Court to speech that might appear obscene and thus dangerous to our morals. From this example one could infer that there is no such thing as a "content-free" attitude toward free speech. Our need to define permissible speech tempts or compels us to find value in any speech that is permitted. We pass from permitting speech because it is valuable to valuing speech because we permit it. However much our liberalism demands that we withhold judgment upon what is said, by the same token it impels us to find value in what we permit. Hence, one may ask, not from without but from within liberalism, what is this value—the value of normal non-obscene speech?

The right of free speech makes presuppositions. To prize it is to hold that free speech has some value, which in turn requires that speech have value. Speech consists in giving reasons. It is not just communication that other animals can give, often very effectively, without supplying reasons; only humans give reasons. Speaking is an appeal to fellow human beings who share the power of reason; so, speech presupposes that man is a rational animal. As it would be feckless to use reason if reason had no power, speech presupposes the power of reason. The power of reason is to appeal to others persuasively at some level of generality with which to gain the assent of someone besides yourself. It is more than a cry of pain or a grunt of pleasure, and it must issue in a complaint or a statement of gratitude that lifts the communication above your private feeling. It is the "rational" that rises above the "animal." Speech is a claim upon the attention of another, a prayer or a demand to be heard; it is an argument if nothing else against indifference.

So far, one might nod in agreement, having seen the point being made—but it seems too simple. Is it so clear that speech lifts one above personal motives? Perhaps speech is not reason but rationalization, the reasons giving effect to one's motives by concealing them rather than transcending them. And what of the joke: "Shut up," he explained. Do not many arguments end in the attempt to silence the other side's reasons? Isn't this maneuver characteristic of political speech above all? Surely reason comes wrapped in illustrations, examples, metaphors, and fables; speech comes often (or always?) in poetry, seeking alluring or frightening images and disdaining manly frankness. Speech certainly includes rhetoric and comes expressed in a language, not in purely deductive propositions.

One might allege, therefore, that the point of arguing is to win, not merely to appeal to reason, and that the power of reason is to serve as a cloak for the desire to win. But to say this admits that reason has a certain power and the desire to win a certain limit. Reason makes domination respectable while it requires the winner to make himself acceptable. Language too is not merely arbitrary; it has a structure, a grammar enabling it to make sense. Even a lie must make sense. The "shut up" joke makes sense by pointing to the fact that it is sometimes courageous and not always wise to speak. Reason makes its way often with apparent rationality, but the appearance of reason indicates the presence of reason. Even silencing requires an argument, as in George Orwell's rationalization from Napoleon the pig that "all animals are equal but some animals are more equal than others." The power of reason, one may conclude, is shown in its very abuse. But this is an objection to which one must return. Somehow the power of reason must be shown to be compatible with, rather than merely subordinated to, the power of rulers. Somehow one must understand reason as not merely poetry and rhetoric, or in today's ugly word, "ideological"—in sum, not merely partisan.

Preoccupation with the limits rather than the content of free speech can be seen in John Stuart Mill's iconic pamphlet *On Liberty*. Mill wishes to expand the limits of free speech as against the "tyranny of the majority" that menaces his country in his time, and to do this he magnifies the benefits of free speech and minimizes the harms.[1] The benefits culminate in more "originality and genius," the harms are no worse than the need for intellectuals like himself sometimes to "keep . . . their convictions within their own breast."[2] But discussion of the consequences of free speech detracts from Mill's principle that all concern for them constitutes "interference" with individual freedom. Within the permissible limits of free speech all speech is substantially equal, for "permissible" means deserving an audience. Mill divides speech into true and false, not good and bad, for true speech brings progress "as mankind improve" and false speech merely tests and corrects true speech.[3] All speech is good, though it is not said to address other rational animals and does not have to be argumentative. The benefits of speech do exist, though Mill seems naively to exaggerate the power of reason in discussion. Yet in his view the right to free speech holds sway over its benefits, and the benefits do not arise from the nature of speech as giving reasons. Mill's society heads toward progress but has no sense of direction other than a vague goal of replacing "despotism" and "barbarism" with "civilization." Instead, Mill's undescribed civilization has itself been replaced in our time by value relativism that makes it a point of pride to renounce its ability to distinguish "civilization" from the "culture" of any society whatever.

The U.S. Supreme Court has charged ahead of Mill to extend speech to "expression." This is a step beyond the First Amendment, which speaks of free *speech*, to the assertion that it meant to say free *expression* or perhaps to express that word without saying it. The change has developed in a number of cases over years, but it seems to have been introduced in the famous flag-salute case in 1943, *West Virginia v. Barnette*, when the Court decided that it was permissible for Jehovah's Witnesses not to salute the flag in schoolrooms. Their refusal to salute was taken as a symbolic exercise of free speech because the command to salute was declared to be an impermissible compulsion to speak. So refusing to speak was concluded to be speech and protected as such. In oft-quoted words Justice Robert Jackson said that "if there is any fixed star in our constitutional constellation, it is that no official, high or petty, can prescribe what is orthodox in politics . . . " and force citizens to do so "by word or act."[4] Here "act" is added to "word," apparently as not the same, but the act is then taken as a kind of word. "Symbolic speech" and "expressive conduct" emerge in later cases dealing with flag-burning, draft-card burning, wearing of armbands, and nude dancing. In 1941, Franklin D. Roosevelt had listed "freedom of speech and expression" among the Four Freedoms America would defend, and after the Court developed its meaning, "expression" has come to be accepted as an equivalent of speech or indeed as the generic term of which "speech" is one variety. Law school courses in constitutional law now routinely use the title of "freedom of expression" for the subject of free speech.

Two questionable consequences can be seen to emerge in the words of Justice Jackson's *Barnette* opinion. First, he denies that there is any constitutional fixed star of political orthodoxy in the very act of declaring the political orthodoxy of free speech. The "very purpose of a Bill of Rights," he says, "was to withdraw certain subjects from the vicissitudes of political controversy . . . "[5] Are not those subjects declared to be beyond controversy thereby made orthodox? The implication is that free speech must be regarded as sacred and hence has no value that can or needs to be disputed. This is a proposition I am disputing.

Second, Justice Jackson says that free speech cannot be compelled because the Bill of Rights "guards the individual's right to speak his own mind."[6] But to speak one's own *mind* is to address other minds, not merely to squeak or bark or chirp like an animal. The flag salute and the other, later examples of "expressive conduct" that the Court found to be akin to free speech are symbols or gestures to which one can impute a meaning, but they are not rational argument. When speech is taken as expression and "expression" becomes the general category of which speech is one type, then the rational in speech is subordinated to the irrationality of symbolic expression. Yet a symbol is only a symbol by virtue of its imputed rational meaning in words. The irrational is rightly subordinate to the rational from which alone it gains its sense. Both of these consequences imply that free speech is fundamentally irrational: the first, that free speech cannot be rationally disputed as good or bad by partisans in politics; the second, that a symbol is not inferior to an argument but rather an argument is a kind of symbol.

A refusal to consider the content of speech so as to recognize its value leads to a minimal definition of free speech so as to include as much as one would not wish to prohibit. One would not wish to do away with theater and poetry just because they add symbol, style and gesture to reasonable speech. But though the beauties of speech add to its power, they distract from its thought, or at least conceal it. And since a thought is almost always disputable, as is beauty, so a less strict definition of speech is more exact; one can be surer of the boundary between speech and act. So the Supreme Court has found that although flag burning is acceptable as legal speech, draft-card burning can be prohibited as an illegal act. That is how it happens that our speech over free speech tends to concentrate on the extremes of riot, rebellion, eccentricity, and obscenity where reason seems to be at its weakest. We liberals are occupied with challenges to normal speech rather than the normal speech it rejects. We so far forget that "expression" is a dilution of speech that it comes to be held the essence of it. Shouting and screaming take precedence over persuasion or threaten to become the normal means of persuasion. The more intense the expression, the freer it ought to be; the test of free speech is to show how far it can tolerate departures from free speech. In the latest instance a baker's message on the icing of a cake is taken as protected speech.[7] If I mush someone's face in it, do I send a message or commit an assault? That is the kind of discussion we have over free speech.

ENEMIES OF SPEECH

To see the value of free speech, therefore, one must leave the precincts of constitutional legality and not focus on what should be allowed, what prohibited. Such matters are necessary, to be sure, but they are significant only because we assume that free speech is a good thing. With this assumption "expressive conduct" gains respectability and constitutional legality to the extent that through our thoughtful interpretation it is seen to contain rational speech. Even expressive conduct deprecating or attacking rational speech conveys its lesson in rational speech.

Speech is free, we have seen, insofar as it is rational, but our argument needs to develop the point. Reason prompts human beings to set their minds on their situation and find reasons for what they do. Having to give a reason compels one to lift oneself above one's own trouble or problem in order to convince someone else that he would act or think the same as oneself. Thinking requires detachment from one's own, and from the body with its pleasures and pains that is the source of one's own. This detachment is freedom from the immediate constraints of the body in a manner that distinguishes humans from other animals. Human life has its necessities because humans have animal bodies, but human reason can act and reflect on these necessities. Free speech makes the metaphysical assumption that human reason can be capable within bounds if not self-sufficient. Not all free speech is reasonable of course, but it is reasonable speech that is the cause of its freedom, even of the freedom to reject reason that is always expressed in some kind of reason. Speech is essentially reason, but that is the best speech, the speech that defines speech. Normal speech is not wise but always more or less reasonable, and normal when people within the bounds of political convention listen to one another. "Expression" of one's speech deliberately prefers slogans, avoids arguments and occurs when people want to impress others by a show of determination (a protest) or indicate that they want to put loyalty to country or God beyond dispute. All human speech has some reason in it, but normally it is bound by unspoken conventions and often perverted by attempts to bend logic to one's will.

In presuming the capability of human reason, free speech has two present-day enemies seeking to pervert it or make it irrelevant. One we have seen, the notion that speech is dictated by the urge to express oneself; the other is that speech is directed by self-interest. All speech comes from the self, but as speech, it rises above the self when one has to give a reason. The reason may be urged with an implicit demand for attention to one's self—listen to me!—but the reason is a call to justice, not merely for one's own advantage. Socrates in Plato's *Apology of Socrates* defends himself to be sure, but also "someone like himself," a person in his position, not himself alone. The notion of self-expression, however, denies the power of reason and the existence of justice to say that all reason is rationalization, all generalization a fraud, a mask for the irrational id or urge, which is directing you. That your speech is not really free because you are not free, and your reason is the theme (the argument!) of Nietzsche, very powerful today though often not advanced under his name. In this view, the purpose of argument is to win and the result is not to learn, as when one's argument is refuted, but to triumph in a contest when no telling refutation can be readily produced. The ancient Sophists without the help of Nietzsche practiced their belief that rhetoric is clever maneuver to get the best of your opponent. They were opposed by Socrates as enemies who did not understand the value of free speech and therefore felt free to abuse it.

Self-interest, the other enemy of free speech, also has an argument. Its proponents say that one's speech follows from one's interest, reflects it, and cannot change it. You can change your mind but not your interest: your mind is the prisoner and slave of your interest. While self-expression is heated and demanding, self-interest is cool and calculating. It has two forms, one very old and unsophisticated, the other modern (dating from the eighteenth century) and philosophically sophisticated.

Personal denunciation, or "character assassination," is the first form. One's opponent is said to have a bad character, a perverse sense of his self-interest that determines what he says. Hence his words are spoken in bad faith and his argument, whatever it is, can safely be ignored while focusing attention on his personal failings. The reason that this bad character deploys is the captive of his character and does not have the power to rise above it. Such a person can be defeated by reasoning that is *ad hoc* and *ad hominem*. Do not listen to him! It's better to insinuate and insult than to argue with him, which would give his argument more dignity than it deserves. This tactic, found in both mild and strong samples, is endemic to politics; it is sometimes true and always tempting, particularly in a democracy where the multitude enjoys the spectacle of bringing down the elite—the high, the mighty and the presumptuous. The office of the demagogue has been denounced from Plato to *The Federalist*, by friends and by opponents of popular government. Today the term is used frequently and demagogically by politicians, and never by political scientists, who refuse it the certificate of scientific credibility.

The political scientists (and their confreres in social science) have a second method of refusing to listen to speech. Their science says that speech cannot cause action; it can only be caused by action. It assumes that humans speak and act according to their interests, open or concealed. Humans speak in opinions, but they act according to their interests, which they give as opinions as if freely chosen but actually hold in consequence of their interests. These subjective opinions can be studied by social science in such magical fashion that they become objective "data"—i.e., facts obtained and certified by science. Social science surveys are baptized as "survey data" and then explained by the interest of the group that holds them. The explanation is a study of cause and effect with a view to making predictions, which are either in the past (as "analysis") or in the future (truly as predictions). This procedure assumes that human beings cannot choose for themselves or guide themselves, meaning not as they describe themselves. They may say "I did it," but in scientific fact they were *caused* to do what they boastfully claim to do. Thus, humans are essentially slaves to the causes that science imputes to them. "You vote by your interest" would often be taken by a voter as an insult (and rightly so), but science is not troubled by such subjective reactions. It says that speech cannot be a cause of human behavior—which means that free speech has no value. Free speech in whole and every part is nothing but a boast.

FREE SPEECH WELL SAID

At this point we have finished the beginning of the argument; there is now more to come. Every stage reached so far could reasonably be disputed, but the purpose here is to lay out the whole of it. One point needs to be reiterated, however: present-day discussion of free speech is understandably but deplorably dominated by the question of what speech should be permitted, what forbidden. By this standard, everything not forbidden is permitted and is—here is the rub—considered equal because equally permitted. But all free speech does not have equal value; speech that attacks free speech has less value than speech that explains it, endorses it, and practices it. Free speech needs to define itself in order to address its enemies, as described so far. Speech that explains and uses free speech has greater value and should have precedence over speech that denies the value of speech. This does not mean that free speech should be denied to its enemies (which are self-expression and self-interest). This would be censorship, and censorship has the preliminary but fatal flaw of being impractical in a free society. Tocqueville supplies a beautiful demonstration of the point.[8] But more than impracticability, the citizens of a free society have an interest (caused by their faith in the reason of free speech) in listening to the enemies of free speech. Those enemies may not be entirely wrong, and they certainly provide food for thought. They point to the assumptions on which free speech rests and the weaknesses that exist in supposing so confidently that free speech is really speech and really free. These weaknesses must be addressed by free citizens. The direction of my argument can be discerned by this switch of addressee from humans to citizens.

Now to take a further step: What is free speech supposed to say? The question will seem strange, even inappropriate, from the standpoint of free speech as a right. A right to free speech presupposes that what one says, or how one exercises the right, is left undefined. The government protects the right; the citizens in society ("civil society") say what they please. Yet clearly some free speech is more appropriate than the rest. Some free speech contributes to free speech by helping to define freedom and free speech in general and for that society. In so doing such speech defends and promotes the right of free speech. This would be the main task of free speech: to use reason to show why free speech is valuable and to make it active and lively. The task would include the investigation of the presuppositions of free speech in political philosophy, to see whether reason can guide our lives and how. In saying this, I do not mean to abridge or deny the right of free speech but only to specify what is valuable as opposed to what is tolerated. Tolerated but not valuable is the free speech understood as self-expression or self-interest, as stated above. You should have the right to speak (almost) as you please, and the right should be protected by law. But it is important to understand and to sustain the value of the free speech that contributes to free speech rather than that which abuses the right by denying or belittling the value of free speech. Not everything said is said well, and the right of free speech needs to be exercised well.

What is it in free speech that is said well? Let the definition be positive so that we do not proceed by excluding or proscribing any speech but rather by asking what good free speech supports. We have seen that free speech presupposes the freedom of human beings. Freedom means being in charge of yourself as opposed to being a slave. More specifically, freedom is the power of the self to cause its own action and reflection as opposed to the slavery of being under the power of necessity, when one is only *being caused*. Self-caused is both individual and social, and it amounts to the power to choose. The individual can choose by himself or with others. In choosing, one governs oneself as a whole individual or as one among a political whole that includes other free individuals. This choosing together is self-government or political liberty. Is it the essential liberty?

Political liberty might not seem to be the greatest good, greater than other uses of free speech such as freedom of thought and freedom of artistic expression that protect individual excellence. Yet human beings are not fully self-sufficient as individuals, however much they sometimes wish to be. Men are social because they must live together, depending on one another to supply their needs, above all those bodily needs that ambitious thinkers like philosophers and poets cannot be troubled to satisfy on their own. And more than merely social, men are political because they do not have the necessary instincts to cooperate but are compelled to invent the conventions by which they live and to use the rationality they have in their nature instead of instincts.These conventions are based on principles by which they rule in societies. Conventions are disputable and humans argue in politics over what they should be and who should make them. Such argument is the content of free speech, and it makes use of the rationality that is the most distinctive feature of a human. At the same time that it is distinctive, this sort of argument addresses the needs of the body, needs that humans share with other animals. Politics thus features the rule of reason over unreason, the rule of what is distinctive about humans over the necessities of animals, including the mortality common to all living things. Man in the whole is the topic of politics as much as it is the arena of philosophy and poetry. Philosophers and poets might wish to learn from politics in order better to instruct politics, as they do and frequently like to do.

Liberalism, as shown above, wants to distinguish politics from what it calls "civil society" in order to prevent the full operation of political liberty.

It distinguishes public from private to the advantage of the latter, reducing politics to providing the means of securing the private sphere, to the "pursuit of [sc. private] happiness." It has, therefore, a strong resistance to the idea of "rule," an animus displayed in attempts made to subvert or overthrow the sovereignty of political liberty. One of these is the discipline of "economics," a science distinct from politics that seeks to establish economic laws that are independent of political rule. Another is the "right of consent" to government, made central to all other rights, which depend on government, in such manner as to provide a lesser substitute for the comprehensiveness of "rule." The people do not rule but consent to the rule of those whom they elect, who also do not rule because they are creatures of the sovereign people. Consent is passive, as consent to *be ruled*; government is active but restrained from ruling. Political liberty in these constructions of liberalism is reduced to one liberty among others such as economic liberty or to the central but subordinate liberty as the liberty to consent. Fortunately there are wiser liberals, above all the two greatest authorities of American politics, the author of *The Federalist* and Alexis de Tocqueville in his *Democracy in America*, who by observation and interpretation show that liberal consent in America amounts to political liberty in its fuller meaning. They show that the "Blessings of Liberty" promised in the preamble of the Constitution center on the free self-government over free men that is the same as "the rule of the free." Political liberty becomes responsible for economic liberty, ruling it with encouragement and restriction as partisan elections decide, and democratic consent becomes active in private life as well as sovereign in public decisions.

Free thought can exist without political liberty, as we know from the great philosophical works written in times of tyranny and of threatening religious censorship. The same is true for great works of poetry, art, and music, which seem to have become scarcer as a grave but almost unnoticed consequence of more democracy. Liberty for the few can be available if exercised with care so that it does not reach the attention of the public authority. One might conclude that this liberty is the most that can be achieved, indeed that all human achievement is reserved for the few who accomplish their thoughts and deeds by themselves beyond the notice of the many and the powerful. Yet a free society in which the many are the powerful has achieved greatness and nobility in its deeds, and in a crucial situation under the watchful attention of the world. This is America in the twentieth century, which with its allies saved civilization from the barbarism of Nazism and Communism. This great deed (or series of deeds) was done not out of self-expression or self-interest nor by mere commitment or calculation but out of nobility, a democratic nobility shared by all though led by a few.

NOBILITY AND FREE SPEECH

Nobility means rising above necessity, or above the seeming necessity of living as you wish and calculating for present advantage, by finding it necessary to face a daunting task, thus using necessity against itself. One must refuse to accept the slavery of seeming necessity and instead insist on the human capacity for choice. Free men preserve their freedom only through acts of nobility that elevate them above ordinary necessities that seem to provide excuses for indifference and inaction. These acts are not constantly necessary as if human life were one long war, but they are occasionally necessary and they reveal the extent of human freedom over circumstances. On this point one can again criticize the official liberalism of our time, which, guided by the great thinkers at its inception, sought to make freedom easy by connecting it to motives of necessity. John Locke, for example, began from the "perfect freedom" of men in the state of nature, and then tried to maintain this freedom by resorting to the right of self-preservation rather than to moral virtue to protect one's freedom. America, however, fought to preserve itself as America, a free country, not to keep its population alive as separate individuals (which might have justified indifference or even surrender). This it did as a choice, neither blindly nor automatically.

Freedom is life by choice, in some serious degree conscious and voluntary and for both the individual and society. Choice requires rising above an urge or a whim or a passion. To do this requires moral virtue to rise above slavery to one's human body. The human body rules us by pain and pleasure, and one can become a slave to fear if one is without courage, and to pleasure if without moderation. A human cannot deny the fact of pain and pleasure but one can learn through good upbringing to control the extremes of bodily passions in a reasonable mean. Courage is a mean between rashness and timidity, moderation a mean between greed and insensitivity, as we know from Aristotle's report of what we naturally know. Free speech—to return to the topic—has a stake in moral virtue as the cause of free persons. Morality demands a free person because an action is not moral unless it is chosen, and morality makes free action possible by lifting an individual or a society above slavish necessities. It's a virtuous circle of cause and effect. It implies a natural capacity for virtue that has to be actuated by virtue—a capacity for freedom that requires the exercise of freedom.

To repeat, I am not proposing to forbid immoral speech, assuming it has been identified as speech succumbing to human necessities. Humans need an occasional holiday from the seriousness of moral virtue, pleasant as it is to moral people. Aristotle puts the fun of wit on his list of virtues. Free speech can serve as a safety valve for letting off steam, a purging function often claimed for it that is featured by Machiavelli. We also need other, subordinate liberties to political liberty, economic liberty to make us prosperous, artistic liberty to make our lives beautiful, but these are not as serious as political liberty. With political liberty we speak to one another about our liberty; we argue over a course of action, a policy, and our ruling principles. Political liberty is the use of free speech to determine who and what principle should rule us.

FREE SPEECH AND FREE RULE

Societies stay together through rulers who rule by ruling principles, which are about the whole and the common good. The debate over abortion today is about the kind of society we want. One could suppose that those who want abortion to be legal should have abortions, and those opposed should refrain from them, with the result that both sides are happy. But in fact both sides would be unhappy. Those who favor legal abortion want a society in which a woman freely controls her own body, and those opposed want a society in which a woman does not have a right to kill a potential human for the sake of her convenience. Politics is not about "preferences," as is often said by those using the analogy of consumer preferences. One can prefer vanilla to chocolate without wanting to abolish chocolate, but this is not the case in politics. Political liberty is distinctive because it consists in free speech over the choice of which principle, under which rulers, should rule the whole.

This much—or little—is said to show what is distinctive about free speech as political liberty. Now what is the typical choice of free speech as to rule? One can approach this question through a consideration of the freest human being, the philosopher. The philosopher is the freest because he questions and studies things that most people take for granted—on the ground that taking fundamental principles for granted is a form of slavery. Freedom in the strongest, or the strictest, sense is to break free of the principles that normal people do not question. To break free does not necessarily mean to abandon them and live as a hermit or madman or rogue. One can question the presuppositions behind free speech and find them reasonable, as in this attempt.[9] But then one's embrace of or accommodation to the principle of freedom has been responsibly addressed and found more or less reasonable. This is the highest or best freedom, one might reluctantly agree, but is it the only freedom? There seems also to be freedom in a loose sense, attainable by many if not all of those who do not want or are not able to be a philosopher. This would be political liberty.

Then within political liberty is there a typical argument, one found in most every free society? Indeed there is, and it is an argument analogous to the distinction between strict philosophical liberty and loose political liberty.

According to Aristotle, there are two parties in every regime, visible in a free regime. The party of the many, democracy, and the party of the few, oligarchy, can be found everywhere, and they engage in argument with each other, sometimes muted and implied, sometimes open. The many are more than the few in quantity. They are the larger part of all, that is, of all individuals in the whole. How is this possible? One needs a little metaphysics to see; one must carry the logic of politics into the whole universe to clarify the democratic argument. "All" can be a whole if all are equal parts, and they can be equal if seen as bodies that are parts of a whole body. Human beings are equal with reference to their bodies and their bodily necessities. When however one looks to their souls or minds, they are unequal, sometimes greatly unequal. Bodies are most equal, most bodies, when considered for their matter, in which they are the same as all matter, as if human beings were nothing but matter, like the rest of the universe. By the logic of the democratic argument, humans would have nothing special, nothing outstanding or distinctive, from the rest of nature.

Can the many make a whole, given this stringent extension of the argument on their behalf? Aristotle's answer is "No," and to make it he distinguishes *demotic* from *democratic*. Demotic individuals are simply equal, but as such they cannot form a government, having no distinctive capacities. Without a government there is no rule, no common good. A government needs officials and its society needs artisans, workers, experts; all of these are unequal. It seems that certain inequalities are needed to make a whole even of equal parts. Aristotle's distinction is like James Madison's in *Federalist 10* between democracy (meaning pure democracy) and republic (representative democracy). A republic needs institutions that will (likely) select "fit characters," as Madison calls them, which are no longer simply among the many whom they are selected to serve. The "-cracy" in democracy enables it to function at the cost of departure from strict equality.

Aristotle does not make this objection to demotic equality in his own name but puts in the mouth of a spokesman for oligarchy. Oligarchy, government of the few, stands for "the better sort," or the best, altogether for excellence, and in sum for quality. The need for quality is a need for the few who have the most of it, whatever it may be. Even democratic qualities found quite generally, like courage, are distinctive of some democrats, not all of them as such. The whole of quantity fails because it is quite homogeneous; to succeed it needs those who are outstanding and needs to give them the rank they deserve as outstanding. Democracy speaks for mankind as one individual human to another; oligarchy speaks for humanity as a whole vis-à-vis the rest of the world or the universe. Mankind is the part of the whole of nature that has an awareness of the whole; it can reflect on the whole—theory—and react on it—practice. Thus the oligarchical argument *asserts* the claim of humanity to be outstanding, for its awareness perhaps the best part of the whole. To assert something is more than merely to say it when nothing is at stake; it is to speak with passion and to demand to be honored and listened to in a situation where one's statements are contested. Assertiveness is the most outstanding, the freest quality of free speech. The Declaration of Independence begins from the "self-evident" truth Americans hold that all men are created equal. But this is not enough. At the end its signers go beyond what is self-evident; they mutually pledge "our lives, our fortunes and our sacred honor" to affirm it. In so doing they stand out from the equality they assert on behalf of those they excel by the very act of pledging their distinctive honor.

The two parties are those of quantity and of quality. But all nature has both quantity and quality. Humans are quantity insofar as each counts for one, but quality insofar as human beings have the special honor of claiming superiority over the rest of nature. Humans are a democracy among themselves as a species, and an aristocracy with respect to the rest of nature. Then both parties are correct or true: quality counts for more because it is more important, and quantity counts for more because many are more than one or few. There are two meanings of "count" in regard to humans. "I count" means I am special; "we count" means "we count up." Every quantity is a quantity of a certain quality, and when counting one adds up the quality or qualities that have been identified as "counting." Yet conversely quality also depends on quantity; the quality when identified becomes something countable, as every "one" is potentially more than one, namely, few or many. As seen above, in a rational claim every personal "I" becomes "someone" like me with my qualities and deserts.

THE PARTIES OF FREE SPEECH

Tocqueville applies Aristotle's analysis to our democratic era, saying that every free society has two great parties, one that wishes to extend and another that wishes to restrict the power of the people. We may now apply the distinction to American parties today, the Democrats and the Republicans, who seem as liberals versus conservatives to fit this general description. Other free countries with more parties also maintain despite their complication the wider political difference between left and right. This is to continue the search for the value of free speech in the typical speech of the two American parties that inhabit the whole of our political liberty. What do they argue to each other? Let us see what they say, condensed as is appropriate for an outline and equipped with the occasional insertions of an arbitrator.

The Democrats desire to extend the power of the people. In their understanding, democracy is not so much the rule of the people that presently exists as it is a future condition toward which our imperfectly democratic society is moving if with the fits and starts corresponding to electoral triumphs and disappointments. Its actual movement accords with both the way things *should go* and the grander movement of history. Democracy must democratize itself; it is essentially not a settled state as in "we live in a democracy," but rather a revolution bringing ever more democracy. In becoming ever more democratic, democracy moves in the direction of what Aristotle calls the demotic, toward ever-greater simplicity and universality, or as said today, toward *inclusiveness*. Inclusiveness in what? In a whole—but which whole? America, of course, but Democrats want an America that is not distinct from the rest of the world but rather as part of it. Are the Democrats therefore not patriotic? Their patriotism exists, but not for an America superior to other countries. It is a patriotism mindful of other patriotisms. An American citizen should aspire to be a world citizen rather than strut around dressed in the garb of Uncle Sam disparaging other countries.

Inclusiveness becomes visible in practice in the foreign policy of Democrats, for example in the tour of apologetic speeches for American conduct made by President Obama in 2009 at the beginning of his presidency. "Leading from behind" (the phrase of a supporter) was for him not Machiavellian cunning but genuine deference to the sensibilities of other countries representing other "cultures" equal to the American. It was the farthest thing from an insistence on being first in any regard except that of deference. The immigration issue that is lively now shows Democrats eager for welcoming more new citizens, especially the needy and least advantaged who come to America to be safe rather than because it is free. If in coming they should happen to break immigration law, this is no more serious than coming without documents. The environment is a favorite issue for Democrats, as it affects everybody across barriers and boundaries. It is a world problem all countries must address so as to cooperate in the interest of all humanity—even all life. It gets more attention today than assuring world peace by preventing war, perhaps because it lacks the ambiguity in the means to the goal of world peace between frightening aggressors, as Republicans support, and pacifying them, as Democrats prefer. Awareness of danger to the environment seems to unite, hence include, all humans unequivocally in a common and mutual awareness of our vulnerability. Democrats look to vulnerability, to the most vulnerable humans as the most representative of the vulnerability of all humans. A liberal, one could say, is a person who spends his life looking for people (and animals) to feel sorry for. Vulnerability is the most universal feature of human life and so, paradoxically, the most secure basis for life as a whole.

Now let us turn to the Republicans, whom I call the party of *virtue* as opposed to inclusiveness, even though I know that many will gag in astonished disgust. Even Republicans fear to assert such a claim; they prefer to be known as the party of liberty. But they demand liberty without license, liberty properly exercised, which means liberty with virtue. Because they insist on the good behavior that follows from virtue they look down on those who lack it. Democrats would say that Republicans are the party of money, not virtue, but Republicans believe that they earned their money; it is the regular result of their virtue. Democrats doubt this claim; they think that money is luck and that perhaps even virtue is luck to the extent that it is inherited rather than achieved or "earned," as Republicans want to say of virtue. "It takes a village," that is, a community, a whole, to achieve what achievers fondly and wrongly believe is their own doing. Republicans reply that a whole composed of equal participants would be indifferent to the virtue that went into its creation and continues in its maintenance and supervision, virtue that deserves honor and reward.

The virtue that Republicans prize, though without speaking much of it, is what people who think little of it call "bourgeois virtue," with the qualities of honesty, respectability, and responsibility. It is wrapped in conventions of conduct and speech that make possible trust and comity in everyday dealings and are found in both law and custom. To practice these conventions one must take notice of them, which leads to a state of soul that Democrats would criticize as "uptight." Frowning Republicans would consider this view too relaxed. Though partisans of both parties commit crimes, Democrats generally have fewer scruples than Republicans. They are the people's party, and for this important assignment the moral goal excuses occasional departures from moral means. The party difference can be seen in the greatest recent scandal of each party. The Republican Richard Nixon, not a relaxed man, was almost impeached and was forced to resign because his party in Congress, shocked by the disrespect for law shown in his desire to cover up a petty misdeed, turned against him. Bill Clinton, a Democrat, was impeached but not convicted, though guilty of perjury, because his party in Congress supported him. His offense was sexual and not serious enough for Democrats, including feminist Democrats, to desert him. Democrats, being more relaxed, are easier to be with; they make better dinner companions than a Republican, who smiles only for relief from the effort of a frown.

Donald Trump, elected by Republicans but not much of one himself, has an adversarial relationship with virtue and particularly with its accompanying conventions. He does appeal to virtue by loudly emphasizing the application of vulgar versions of it that are attractive to his supporters, almost all of whom are more honest than he is. These rough copies of virtue are united in his insistence that winners are superior to losers, as if there were no lucky winner or noble loser and no ground for tragedy in life. It is true enough that a winner has some superiority over a loser, if only in luck, but it is unmanly to boast. At their best Republicans admire; they look up to their heroes.

Their party was founded by Abraham Lincoln, and it was never sullied by engagement with slavery and segregation, like the Democrats, who from Andrew Jackson to George Wallace were the party of White supremacy in America. But Democrats are now the party of African Americans voting as a bloc. They have lived down their dubious past by enshrining the civil rights movement of the 1960s as a sacred event with an undying power today to inspire Democrats to attack Republicans. Democrats believe in the "living Constitution," and they have moved on in order to get and stay on the right side of history.

Republicans would ignore the poor much more than they actually do if the poor did not have votes and Democrats to speak for them and to vote for. Republicans prefer the greater virtue of generosity, which is voluntary, to the compulsory virtue of justice, which requires obedience to the law when it does not demand protest and disobedience. Arthur Brooks discovered that the average family in the rich, liberal city of San Francisco, gives 75 percent less of its annual income to charity than in the much less rich conservative state of South Dakota with the same population.[10] Republicans are church-goers to a greater degree than Democrats, among whom secularism thrives. Going to church makes you a better citizen, as we know from the bipartisan social science research of Charles Murray and Robert Putnam.

For Democrats, generosity is too accidental, hence not dependable for the policy of a country. It is they who are primarily responsible for the entitlements of America's Welfare State. Moreover, the pride givers feel in their generosity puffs them up and makes them feel superior to those they benefit with their haphazard gifts. Democrats praise compassion for the vulnerable as they enact taxes to aid and support them. Rather than look up to or admire, they look down at the plight of so many unlucky persons. They deprecate or deny the power of virtue as episodic and unsteady. If asked they would claim to possess virtue themselves for not relying on virtue as Republicans do. For Republicans, America is overall a just society in which those with status deserve what they have. Their favorite private institution is the church and their favorite public one is the military; for Democrats, their favorites are the university and the social welfare workers. Democrats have come to depend greatly on professors, who carry on the Social Science studies that expose the underside of American society. Republicans look down on professors but they need think-tanks outside them to do counter-studies that end inevitably in the exposure of government programs that do not work. Republicans are the respectable party, the party of the status quo, but they are also the judgmental party that does not hesitate to blame. Democrats are non-judgmental so as to be equal, and equal so as to be inclusive. They want progress, but don't ask them to define it. "Progress" is progress in equality, but just how far and why not further are questions not discussed. Other issues between the parties could be discussed to elaborate and qualify the general difference between them, but let this much suffice. This much also abstracts from the current situation of polarized parties and the strategies they puzzle over for the future.

Both parties are forgivably rather self-righteous because unlike the ordinary citizens who compose them, they are always arguing with each other and in doing so always compelled to make a point of themselves. They argue over the character of the whole, the whole of our country and also the whole of all things. Is it a homogeneous whole of equal or similar individuals, as the Democrats intend, or a heterogeneous whole of diverse parts of different rank and importance, as Republicans imply? The argument between these two wholes, we may now conclude, is free speech about the character of free human beings. Each is a partial truth, but each is tempted to make the partial truth a partisan whole. In doing so each makes an attempt to explain the other side and claim it for themselves: Democrats want virtue but in pursuit of equality; Republicans want popularity but from a virtuous people. Each reveals itself when trying to answer the other.

Democrats imply a whole that is inclusive of all, when each is understood as equal to everyone else; Republicans imply a whole with hierarchy and ranking of those who are better or best at the top. One can understand this political difference as a disagreement over our non-political thinking. When defining a thing it is necessary to speak of what it is when it is perfect or complete, in its best instance, and yet also to speak of the quality or qualities that cover all instances of that thing so as not to omit what must be included. Thus, a tree is defined by the complete tree and by all instances of objects that one would call a tree. The best instance is the standard that a tree should fit, and the class of tree holds together all its instances. Every definition needs to combine standard and class; it needs to have a standard to state a class. The difficulty is in defining a human being, where the best instance is far distant from the average or worst instances—so that a definition combining class and standard is very difficult to specify. The standard of the best human is too strict to include all humans, and the class of all humans is too loose to do justice to the best. Our two parties represent these two tendencies, and each tries to see the whole in terms of its partial or partisan view.

There is no freedom without choice, and no choice without choice-worthy choices, those that make sense and can be defended as reasonable. Our free country is more a dualism of our two parties than a pluralism of any number. There are many ways in which a people can be made more alike and more unlike, but Nietzsche is wrong to say that man has one thousand and one goals. Our politics is not indeterminate, chaotic, or arbitrary; it is connected to human nature, to the grand question raised by human nature, and to the choice we make in the exercise of our natural capacity for choice. That capacity depends on the speech with which we form and state a choice. Our liberalism—and here I include conservatives with those now called "liberals"—should cease its feckless quest to overturn any rational basis for freedom and thereby deny any value to free speech. What a surprise that in our very partisan differences, fickle and arbitrary as they often seem, we should turn out to be rational beings.

NOTES

1. John Stuart Mill, *On Liberty* (Indianapolis: Hackett Publishing Co., 1978 [1859]), 4.
2. Mill, 62, 31.
3. Mill, 42.
4. *West Virginia Board of Education v. Barnette*, 319 U.S. 624, 642 (1943).
5. Ibid. at 638.
6. Ibid. at 634.
7. *Masterpiece Cakeshop v. Colorado Civil Rights Commission*, 584 U.S. __ (2018).
8. Alexis de Tocqueville, *Democracy in America*, 1.2.3.
9. For a fuller philosophical statement, see Delba Winthrop, *Aristotle: Democracy and Political Science*, edited by Harvey C. Mansfield (Chicago: University of Chicago Press, 2019).
10. Arthur Brooks, *Who Really Cares? The Surprising Truth About Compassionate Conservatism* (New York: Basic Books, 2006), 31–33.

REFERENCES

Brooks, Arthur. *Who Really Cares? The Surprising Truth About Compassionate Conservatism* (New York: Basic Books, 2006).
Masterpiece Cakeshop v. Colorado Civil Rights Commission, 584 U.S. __ (2018).
Mill, John Stuart. *On Liberty* (Indianapolis: Hackett Publishing Co., 1978 [1859]).
Tocqueville, Alexis de. *Democracy in America*. Trans. By Harvey C. Mansfield and Delba Winthrop (Chicago: University of Chicago Press, 2000 [1835, 1840]).
West Virginia Board of Education v. Barnette, 319 U.S. 624 (1943).
Winthrop, Delba. *Aristotle: Democracy and Political Science*. Edited by Harvey C. Mansfield (Chicago: University of Chicago Press, 2019).

Chapter 6

What Is Free Speech For?

Daniel Cullen

The year 2017 will be remembered for a watershed moment regarding free speech on college campuses. Tax- and tuition-paying citizens were taken aback by the spectacle of students demanding freedom *from* speech and using disruption and force to achieve it. At Middlebury College the "free speech under assault" storyline moved beyond metaphor and seemed to bring the entire country to an inflection point. The details are well known: Having successfully prevented a public talk by a controversial speaker, student protestors descended on the bunker that had been arranged as a secure fallback position for a livestreamed interview conducted by a Middlebury professor. Banging on windows and setting off fire alarms, the mob did its best to disrupt plan B, and completed the trifecta by physically harassing the speaker, a senior administrator, and the professor (who was injured in the process) as they tried to leave campus. The evening ended well enough for the trio, but only after literally being chased out of town.[1]

The intolerable provocation was an appearance by Charles Murray, the most soft-spoken controversialist imaginable, but branded nonetheless by the Southern Poverty Law Center (SPLC) as a "white nationalist." The evening began with the friendliest reminder of college policies regarding the disruption of invited speakers. Stage one would be a "request" to cease and desist; "college discipline" might follow. Next, Middlebury president Laurie Patton expressed sympathy with Murray's critics and belabored the obvious: that Murray's appearance did not entail an institutional endorsement of his views. To her credit, she urged the crowd to suffer the Murray talk—"rhetorical resilience" being a signature Middlebury value—reminding that "the very premise of free speech on this campus is that a speaker has a right to be heard." The protestors responded with disdain, ritually turned their backs as Murray took the podium, and chanted a prepared statement, which ran: "This is not a respectful discourse or a debate about free speech. These are not ideas that can be fairly debated. There is no potential for an equal exchange of ideas. . . . We see this talk as hate speech." Leave aside that Murray had yet to say a word, that his topic had nothing to do with his notorious 1994 co-authored book, *The Bell Curve*, and that what the students knew of Murray's ideas derived from a cheat sheet provided by the SPLC; the sententious indictment illuminates the problem of free speech and the universities by revealing the shifting rationale for the shout down. On one hand, the problem is inequality: Murray's ideas (whatever they might turn out to be) had an unfair advantage. Murray was the beneficiary of a "platform" that literally and figuratively elevated his ideas above dissenting views, notwithstanding the fact that his argument would be subjected to scrutiny by a professor unsympathetic to his perspective and who had come, as she said, "loaded for bear." On the other hand, Murray's words would be "hate speech," not words expressive of ideas but weapons designed to injure, an intention (or an effect) that provided sufficient warrant to suppress rather than rebut them. Both points were confirmed the day after in an anonymous, self-exculpatory message from the protest leaders to the Middlebury campus: "The administration's support of a platform for white nationalist speech was an intense act of aggression towards the most marginalized members of the Middlebury community." This extraordinary charge echoed one made in a joint letter from several hundred Middlebury alumni protesting Murray's appearance before the fact: Murray's ideas, it was said, had been discredited and were thus "not worth engaging"; but, more importantly, his views were a "threat," "a message to every woman, every person of color, every first-generation student, every poor and working class person, every disabled person and every queer person that not only their acceptance to and presence at Middlebury, but also their safety, their agency, their humanity and even their very right to exist are all up for 'debate.'" In sum, "hate speech" is an act of "violence" and Murray's ideas are not merely erroneous but pose an existential threat to the most vulnerable members of the college community. No wonder the joint letter dismissed in advance "hollow appeals to tolerance and dialogue," or that the student protestors were prepared to meet "violence" with violence. To give Charles Murray a hearing would, in their view, violate Middlebury's commitment to both "intellectual rigor" and "compassionate inclusivity."

Such hyperbolic accusations invite ridicule, and the critical response outside academia has indeed been fierce; but to simply mock the protestors as "snowflakes" and re-assert free speech principles is inadequate for two reasons. The students pounding on the administrator's getaway car at Middlebury were many things—snowflakes they were not. Characterizing their militancy as "hypersensitivity" obscures the fact that their offendedness is more than the effect of a generational experience of overprotection; it is a choice to take offense. If the student protestors were triggered, they were already locked and loaded. What transpired at Middlebury was a performance of offendedness, and it was informed by a theory. Secondly, although our free speech principles are indeed poorly understood, their reaffirmation alone will not defuse campus tensions. For one thing, while freedom of speech and academic freedom overlap, they are not congruent. Both have a place in the university, and both are at risk, but they serve different ends and entail different norms. Academic freedom is more than the practice of "free speech" in the academic realm, and different rules apply in the classroom and the forum. Clarifying the distinction would also, however, get us beyond the rote invocation by college administrators of a "balance" between "free speech" and "inclusivity," a compromise that characteristically ignores the question: Inclusion in what? Attending to that matter brings to the foreground the identitarian assumptions that drive both the campus protests and the administrative reaction to them.

The shoutdown of Charles Murray was defended as an appropriate response to the symbolic violence his speech would have enacted. In the protestors' minds, Murray's views attacked the identity of groups already victimized along multiple axes of race, gender, sexual orientation, and class (the list is not exhaustive), groups whose complex oppression can only be grasped "intersectionally." The public sensed the irony of students at an elite institution resisting the voice of "privilege," but the latter were burdened with the paradoxical task of exposing a hierarchy of dominance so pervasive as to be invisible. Their point was that Charles Murray was *effectively* a white supremacist. To expect evidence or argument for such lurid claims would be to underscore one's obtuseness, to display the very "misrecognition" or "induced misunderstanding" that, according to the sociologist Pierre Bourdieu, renders social domination legitimate even in the eyes of those subject to it.[2] The protestors hadn't bothered to read Murray, but enough Bourdieu, Spivak and Foucault had trickled down to instill in them the ideological confidence of the "woke."

It is not so much that free speech principles are forgotten or misunderstood on the left-leaning campus (as President Patton candidly described Middlebury) as there is an insurrection against them inspired by a complex worldview that emphasizes the social construction of identities while condemning their non-recognition by means of "epistemic violence."[3] Because non-recognition imposes their lower status, the "safety" of vulnerable identities trumps protection for speech or expression that marginalizes or "silences" them. To regard speech as a method of peaceful social regulation is to "misrecognize" the way in which a hierarchical social system is rigged and how "free speech" can subordinate by "otherizing." This is heady stuff to be sure, but its cogency is accepted as a matter of faith on the progressive campus. The authoritative source is Marcuse, for whom the task of theory in the unequal society was "to break the concreteness of oppression in order to open the mental space in which this society can be recognized as what it is and does." The *practice* of liberation, he added, may well require "apparently undemocratic means" such as the withdrawal of toleration of speech by those who reinforce or benefit from social discrimination. In other words, free speech principles beg the question of their own validity. In an oppressive society, "suppression of the regressive" *is* the path of progress. On some issues, Marcuse concludes, "there is no 'other side.'"[4] It follows, that "tolerance cannot be indiscriminate and equal with respect to the contents of expression, neither in word nor in deed; it cannot protect false words and wrong deeds which demonstrate that they contradict and counteract the possibilities of liberation."[5]

This baleful reasoning may explain the otherwise surprising finding that many college students now believe that the Constitution already prohibits hate speech or that it should.[6] Shortly after the Middlebury protest, the Supreme Court of the United States, as if on cue, doubled down on traditional free speech principles in rejecting the claim of a governmental interest in blocking the expression of offensive ideas. The ruling in *Matal v. Tam* did not deny that "Speech that demeans on the basis of race, ethnicity, gender, religion, age, disability, or any other similar ground is hateful," nor did it ignore the fact that the costs of toleration are imposed disproportionately on minorities. Nevertheless, Justice Alito averred, "the proudest boast of our free speech jurisprudence is that we protect the freedom to express 'the thought that we hate.'"[7]

Let us stipulate that the trademark registration victory by "The Slants," an Asian-American rock band bent on reappropriating a racial slur, might, in its way, be an occasion of constitutional pride; the aforementioned student majority is loath to embrace the irony. When it comes to "hate speech" they do not find tolerance ennobling. To suggest that students find a thicker skin misses the point that compassionate inclusivity requires a thinner one. Students remain solicitous of free speech rights and inclined generally toward a "liberal" campus atmosphere, but they are unpersuaded of the virtue of tolerating the thought we hate if it threatens the progress of diversity and inclusion. In preferring to err on *that* side, students and college administrators find themselves, for once, on the same page regarding college discipline.

Though the elaboration is typically elided in administrative parlance, diversity means diversity of *identities* associated especially with race, gender, non-Christian religion, and sexual orientation. And because such identities remain stigmatized by the broader culture, "diversity" is nothing without "inclusion," without the feeling of being genuinely welcomed rather than grudgingly tolerated.[8] The anodyne intentions of college administrators seem far removed from the severities contemplated by Marcuse, but the belated and mild official response to the Middlebury protest is consistent with the logic of "resistance." The protestors may have been a minority, and yes, their violence was inexcusable, but they were expressing the new moral sense of the progressive campus that takes "dignitary safety" as seriously as the freedom of inquiry.

Sigal R. Ben-Porath has coined the term "inclusive freedom" to describe a framework that seeks the broadest protection for campus speech compatible with the assurance that "all members of the campus community are recognized—and know they are recognized—as members in good standing." But there lies the rub, for the composite goal "becomes harder to realize when instructors, speakers, and students express views that some members of the community see as undermining their basic dignity, casting them as less than full members."[9]

The concept of inclusive freedom denies any basic incompatibility between free speech and respect for identity, but assumption of their mutual dependence allows the *practice* of inclusive freedom to take a Marcusean turn. Free speech serves democracy, but democracy is never served by anything less than more democracy. And insofar as the progress of democracy is measured by increasing respect for identity, the latter functions as a barometer of freedom itself. It follows that "[a] call for creating an inclusive environment in which all members are respected and where all voices can be heard should be framed and recognized as furthering rather than impeding the realization of a free and open campus."[10] And thus spoke the Middlebury protestors whose point was precisely that unequal freedom is not genuine freedom. As they "framed" it, the campus problem was not about striking a balance between equality and liberty interests; their practice of inclusive freedom was predicated on the idea that freedom itself is limited when the vulnerable are "effectively barred" from speaking their minds out of fear of ridicule, "or when they do not feel that they belong or that they are appreciated."[11] For her part, Ben-Porath credits the "rejection of Murray's views" by the (non-violent) student protestors as an "effort to expand the democratic reach of speech to groups they see as harmed and silenced," where they might have sought merely "to protect themselves within a liberal cocoon."[12] By the latter phrase she seems to mean, as one conflicted student protestor put it, the choice to "protect Murray's academic freedom and [Middlebury's] commitment to intellectual debate" at the expense of a failure to express solidarity with those students who felt stigmatized by Murray's arguments.[13] In this reframing, silencing Murray expands the benefit of speech by redistributing it more inclusively and without, presumably, generating an even larger cocoon.

The conviction that genuine inclusion will do the work of freedom seems to be both a cause and effect of the metamorphosis in academic culture at

Middlebury and beyond. The now-fraying "liberal" academic culture was, however, nurtured by the converse proposition that genuine freedom would do the work of inclusion. For the humane concern for the feelings of others is warranted on intellectual as well as compassionate grounds. Speech is directed at other selves, and even the most vehement speaker implicitly accepts that his speech expresses not mere grunts but an argument, thereby conceding that even his opponent is a rational agent capable of receiving it.[14] This inadvertent tribute that intellectual vice pays to virtue bears interestingly on the fraught matter of criminalizing hate speech. It is the denial of equal social standing that is said to constitute the harm sufficient to exclude hate speech from legal protection.[15] The philosopher Bernard Williams once remarked on the curious fact that even those bent on social domination strangely felt the need to invent what they assumed to be a morally relevant reason for the denial of equality. Hence the Nazis cultivated bizarre theories about the inferiority of the Jews as a way of making themselves believe in it.[16] All stripes of "supremacists" follow the same pattern, submitting themselves unwittingly and, for their "cause," disastrously, to the bar of reason—better for them to stick to grunting. It is faith in the intrinsic discipline of reason that underwrites the liberal confidence that exposure to argument is the best response to pernicious ideas, yet that discipline has implications for the proponents of compassionate inclusivity as well.

The principal weakness of the inclusive freedom framework is that there is no arguing with people's subjective feelings, and *a fortiori* with their identities. Granted we should be mindful of the feelings of others and take pains to convey the message that minority students are not only admitted but welcome. Still, we are welcoming them to an academic community where their membership or "standing" is independent of their identities. To put it bluntly, as Alan Ryan does, in the academic realm professors should be focused not on who the student is "as a person" but on what the student thinks: "The point of insulating the classroom from the forum is to allow, indeed to force, participants to leave their identities as whatever it might be that is most salient to them outside the door.""[17]

Civic life requires the equal protection of the laws and in that way assures respect for different identities, but a crucial assumption of academic life is that our beliefs are separable from our identities, and the trend toward equating critical appraisals of ideas with attacks on personhood negates it. Blurring the distinction between what one is and what one thinks risks putting beliefs beyond the bounds of criticism. For this reason, while making the case for an actionable harm in hate speech, Jeremy Waldron cautions against conflating attacks on one's social standing with criticism of one's beliefs: "If I identify my *self* with my beliefs, then criticisms of them will seem like an assault on me."[18]

Insofar as academic culture depends on boundaries between the classroom and the forum, and distinctions between ideas and identities, the well-intentioned excesses of diversity and inclusion rhetoric must be opposed. To valorize students' "lived experiences," or to suggest that their academic work involves the expression of their extra-academic identities, is to send precisely the wrong message about inclusion in the university and their eligibility for it. Of course, men and women, whites and blacks, gays and straights have different experiences and perspectives on the world, but the intersectional insight that identity is always a complex amalgam might remind us that in the final analysis, we can speak only for ourselves.

These are strong claims about the character of academic community, and they are hotly contested by those suspicious of "essentializing" arguments. It is worth remembering that whatever free inquiry obtained in the medieval university was subordinated to the clarification of orthodoxy and the exposure of heresy. It was a radical change to redefine the mission of the university as the advancement of enlightenment generally, and the emergence of the research university and the secular liberal arts college we know represent still further shifts. Nevertheless, there is reason to think that what I have described advisedly as a "liberal" academic culture offers better guidance on free speech and academic freedom than the professedly democratic culture of inclusive freedom. In the former view, academic freedom is the freedom of inquiry, and such investigation is rigorous, disciplined, and, in an important sense, self-effacing. What the teacher is after is not the student's "opinion" but his or her critical appraisal of a book or an argument.[19] Academic freedom is the fence against illegitimate interference with research and teaching, or with the ability to express one's ideas and hypotheses; it includes the correlative right to challenge the conclusions of others. But academic speech is highly structured, constrained as much as free. At every juncture, the expression of students and professors is graded, vetted, scrutinized for error; and individuals themselves are promoted, demoted, or excluded along with their more or less successful exposition of ideas.

The university is hardly a "marketplace of ideas," if one means a mall where every intellectual product can be offered for consumption. As Stanley Fish emphasizes, the academy "is in the business of excluding what it has judged to be unworthy."[20] Far from being democratic, the academic community is pervasively authoritarian. Whereas government can neither authorize nor de-authorize anyone's voice, the academic community does it all the time because the advancement of knowledge depends on carefully-wrought structures of exclusion. This ethos of exclusion applies even more strenuously to political demands: "A passion for justice is of course a good thing; it's just not an academic good thing," says Fish, and the infiltration of causes necessarily subverts academic culture.[21] In an acerbic flourish, Fish admonishes progressive students to "save the world on your own time."[22] He is equally caustic in dismissing affirmative action for "conservative" viewpoints on grounds of intellectual pluralism, despite their well-documented underrepresentation in academia. Equal representation, Fish retorts, is a political not an academic principle: "The business of the academy is to sort the wheat from the chaff and discard, not represent, points of view it judges unworthy; it does not give points of view a place at the table simply because someone out there is asserting them."[23]

The narrow justification of academic freedom is the preservation of the authority of communities of inquiry, and that authority in turn presupposes the possibility of disinterested scholarship. Contrary to the rhetoric of admissions brochures, good professors can be dispassionate about their subject, skeptical of the urgencies of the here and now invoked on behalf of the "socially relevant" curriculum. Self-preservation requires that they find a way to be "relatable," but in their professional capacity they are interested in the head rather than in "the whole person." The enterprise of education is always vulnerable because other minds must be permanently recruited to the task of preserving and expanding knowledge.

Enough has been said perhaps to indicate why "free speech on campus" is a more complex problem than meets the eye and why the assimilation of First Amendment freedom to academic freedom is not its solution. Freedom of thought *is* endangered on campus, but our political free-speech principles necessarily protect the kind of thoughtless expression academic rigor seeks to exclude. The conundrum is illustrated in a recent and worthy effort by Erwin Chemerinsky and Howard Gillman to reconcile free speech protections with the creation of "inclusive learning environments for all students."[24] All arguments for hate-speech bans fail, and Chemerinsky and Gillman insist that colleges cannot legitimately *prohibit* any ideas or views "no matter how offensive or how uncomfortable they make people feel."[25] On the other hand, they too distinguish free speech precepts from the principles of academic freedom, concluding that a campus ought to contain a free-speech zone regulated by nothing more than First Amendment principles without constituting itself as a free-speech zone per se. In the final analysis they defend the right of administrators to "sensitize students and faculty to the impact that certain words may have, as part of an effort to create a respectful work and learning environment."[26]

Chemerinsky and Gillman (who happen to be both professors and administrators) grant such latitude to sensitivity training efforts that one wonders about the efficacy of their red line: "There is an enormous difference between advocating norms of civility in expression—which always exist and which we are all taught from a young age—and enforcing these norms by censorship or punishment."[27] Thus, a campus can't *prohibit* microaggressions;

it can "sensitize" students and faculty to the impact of offensive words or ideas. Campuses can create safe spaces to "ensure that individuals feel free to express the widest array of viewpoints" (or, one assumes, the *narrowest*); but campuses "can't use the concept of safe spaces to censor the expression of ideas considered too offensive for students to hear."[28]

The distinction between a safe space and the *concept* thereof is intriguing. It turns out that while safe spaces themselves are natural features of the educational environment—the classroom wherein one feels safe enough to express an opinion being the obvious example—the *concept* of safe spaces has transmogrified into the ideological demand for protection *from* the expression of ideas. Chemerinsky and Gillman contrast legitimate and illegitimate demands for intellectual safety: the first seeks protection *for* the expression of one's ideas, the second seeks protection *from* exposure to the offensive ideas of others. But the brightness of the distinction is dulled by mounting qualifications. It is wrong, the authors say, for universities to *require* faculty to issue trigger warnings about potentially offensive material; but if a *recommendation* such as Oberlin's that faculty "Be aware of racism, classism, sexism, heterosexism, cissexism, ableism, and other issues of privilege or oppression" can pass muster, is the distinction between prohibition and sensitizing any longer meaningful? The checklist of microaggressive errors is a not-so-friendly reminder of the burgeoning number of topics on which there is no "other side."

And here a deeper problem manifests itself in Chemerinsky and Gillman's otherwise compelling defense of the freedom of speech. Their primary argument is that free speech is essential to free thought, without which "a person cannot develop an independent point of view about the world," and without which no true diversity of identities is possible. More importantly, such diversity is nothing without the freedom to express those identities: "To hide who you are and what you believe" out of fear is "an exceedingly cruel and oppressive circumstance."[29] All of this is doubtless true as a conclusion about equal citizenship in the social and civic spheres, but the emphasis on freedom as the expression of one's unique identity is the very notion that threatens to displace freedom for the pursuit of truth when carried into the academic realm.

The Oberlin faculty guide mirrors the Middlebury alumni protest letter, minus the latter's existential dread. Oppression is everywhere yet distributed unequally across different identities such that the naïve observer who might acknowledge discrimination in one regard misses its "multidimensionality" and thereby "theoretically erases" the victim. This was the thought that stood behind the earnest belief that Charles Murray's wonky arguments put various identities at risk. The implication is that to suggest, as Murray does, that culture counts, that responsibility is a neglected virtue, and that a class divide has arisen on behavioral rather than economic lines threatens the safety, agency, and humanity of each and every marginalized group. Could any of Murray's propositions be true? That there is a choice to be made among better or worse proposals to advance the public good, that markets and the rule of law might benefit the entire social order, or that power might be exercised through institutions that constrain personal domination? These propositions are so at odds with the narrative of powerlessness as to make dialogue impossible. Such at least was the view of the Middlebury protestors; it is ascendant on our campuses, and the justification of free speech for the sake of free expression makes little headway against it.

In oppressive conditions, Marcuse explained, tolerance does not and cannot fulfill "the civilizing function" attributed to it by liberals. When there is no "other side," he added, "tolerance cannot be indiscriminate and equal with respect to the contents of expression, neither in word nor in deed; it cannot protect false words and wrong deeds which demonstrate that they contradict and counteract the possibilities of liberation."[30] Inclusive freedom might seem to solve the problem of balance by transcending its zero sum formulation, but for the fact that inclusion has been defined in terms of social liberation, the freedom to express one's identity, rather than admission to the company of truth-seekers.

Another view is available, an understanding of intellectual autonomy in which thinking for ourselves is neither thinking what we please nor "saying whatever comes into our heads next." As Alan Ryan puts it, "A condition of thinking for oneself is that we subordinate our wills to the demands of logical argument and sound evidence."[31] Such academic discipline has virtually nothing to do with self-expression as the latter is usually understood. Free inquiry is thinking for ourselves by subjecting our thoughts to scrutiny and abandoning them when they fail the test. Insofar as our thoughts are indeed *considered* judgments and not mere reflexes, they are ultimately not our own but are available to others with minds open to receive them. In this way, the deeply private activity of thinking includes an element of generosity. Its self-effacing tendency is also manifest in the vulnerability that accompanies "allowing another's thoughts to re-enact themselves in one's own mind."[32] The strange reality of intellectual freedom is that it is ultimately not for our own sake but that of others, which is another way of saying: for the sake of truth. In an academic setting there is nothing significant about my opinions flowing from the fact that they are contingently mine; and strictly speaking, I have no right to my opinion other than the freedom to offer arguments on its behalf. Should those arguments fail I ought reasonably to revise or abandon my opinion. Similarly, no damage is done to *me* if I lose an argument; I continue to stand but stand corrected. But if my thoughts and my opinions are indissolubly linked to my "identity," they risk becoming mechanisms of self-protection or "validation" and argument necessarily becomes fraught with personal risk.

The tenacity of our opinions is indicative of our need for intellectual comfort, and there is no gainsaying that the truth often hurts. Precisely because of such personal stakes in truth, the justice that obtains in an academic community is justice to the argument, and the only force tolerable is the force of reason. If we made justice in this sense our virtue, we might accomplish all that we hope for by the pursuit of compassionate inclusivity. Students would owe and show each other mutual respect, not because of their chosen or unchosen identities, but insofar as their arguments were sincere attempts to clarify the truth of things. Discussions would remain heated—it bears remembering that to "discuss" means to break apart, the destruction making possible the examination of minute parts of things. But our challenges to one another would be motivated by a desire to "get it right," they would be attributions of error, made tolerable by the common interest in avoiding the burden of bad ideas.

"'School,'" Michael Oakeshott remarked, "is an emancipation achieved in a continuous redirection of attention," where the learner is animated "not by the inclinations he brings with him, but by intimations of excellence and aspirations he has never dreamed of."[33] We cannot but bring our identities with us to school, but our purpose is the cultivation of reason. Fortunately, "inclusion in the pursuit of knowledge is the truest form of inclusion that college makes possible."[34] Let academic freedom do its transformative work.

NOTES

1. "Charles Murray at Middlebury: Unacceptable and Unethical, Say Over 500 Alumni," *Beyond the Green: Collective of Middlebury Voices* (March 2, 2017), https://beyondthegreenmidd.wordpress.com/2017/03/02/charles-murray-at-middlebury-unacceptable-and-unethical-say-over-500-alumni/ [https://perma.cc/58T4-LXFM].

2. Pierre Bourdieu, *Outline of A Theory of Practice* (Cambridge: Cambridge University Press, 1977).

3. The seminal argument is Gayatri Spivak, "Can the Subaltern Speak?" In Cary Nelson and Lawrence Grossberg, eds., *Marxism and the Interpretation of Culture* (Urbana: University of Illinois Press, 1988).

4. Herbert Marcuse, "Repressive Tolerance" in Robert Paul Wolff et. al., *A Critique of Pure Tolerance* (Boston: Beacon Press, 1969), 81–82, 100, 106, 120.

5. Marcuse adds: "Such indiscriminate tolerance is justified in harmless, in conversation, in academic discussion; it is indispensable in the scientific enterprise, in private religion." Ibid., 88. Brian Leiter argues that this surprising but significant exception to the justification of repressive tolerance brings Marcuse into alignment with a positively Millian defense of academic speech and inquiry. Brian Leiter, "Why Academic Freedom?" in Donald A. Downs and Chris W. Surprenant, eds., *The Value*

and Limits of Academic Speech (New York and London: Routledge, 2018), 34–37, 40–41. How Marcuse might exempt what progressives today dub "the corporate university" from his indictment of a comprehensive system of social oppression that vitiates freedom at every turn in what he called "the established reality" is, as Leiter demonstrates, worthy of further reflection, especially by Marcuse's critics. But the point remains that Marcuse's general critique of rational inquiry leaves "[the] defense of the of the university to teach and to research as it will in more danger immediately from Marcuse's student allies than from any other quarter—even although Marcuse himself has on occasion exempted the university from his critique." Alasdair McIntyre, *Herbert Marcuse: An Exposition and a Polemic* (New York: Viking Press, 1970), 104–5.

6. "Free Expression on Campus: What College Students Think about First Amendment Issues." March 12, 2018. https://knightfoundation.org/reports/free-expression-on-campus-what-college-students-think-about-first-amendment-issues

7. *Matal v. Tam*, 582 U.S. ___ (2017). Justice Kennedy's separate opinion added the prudent reminder that "A law that can be directed against speech found offensive to some portion of the public can be turned against minority and dissenting views to the detriment of all."

8. Diversity and inclusion consultants like to stress the distinction between being invited to a party and being asked to dance, to distinguish between diversity and inclusion, respectively. "Equity" has recently been added as the third component of a unified egalitarian imperative, in acknowledgment of the invisible barriers to equal opportunity said to operate behind the veil of equal treatment.

9. Sigal R. Ben-Porath, *Free Speech on Campus* (Philadelphia: University of Pennsylvania Press, 2017), 56–57.

10. Ibid., 37.

11. Ibid., 62.

12. Ibid., 53.

13. Ibid.

14. See Harvey Mansfield's essay in this volume.

15. See Jeremy Waldron, *The Harm in Hate Speech* (Cambridge: Harvard University Press, 2014).

16. Bernard Williams, "The Idea of Equality," in *Problems of The Self: Philosophical Papers 1956–1972* (Cambridge: Cambridge University Press, 1973).

17. Alan Ryan, "Academic Freedom and the 'Truth Function,'" in Cheryl Hudson and Joanna Williams eds., and *Why Academic Freedom Matters* (Civitas, 2016), 63.

18. Waldron, *The Harm in Hate Speech*, 135. Italics in the original.

19. This is a point stressed in Alan Ryan, "Free Inquiry: Easy Times Can Be Difficult Too," *Social Research* 76 (Fall 2009).

20. Stanley Fish, *Versions of Academic Freedom* (Chicago: University of Chicago Press, 2014), 148.

21. Ibid., 17.

22. Stanley Fish, *Save the World on Your Own Time* (Oxford and New York: Oxford University Press, 2008).

23. Ibid., 72.

24. Erwin Chemerinsky and Howard Gillman, *Free Speech on Campus* (New Haven: Yale University Press, 2017), x.

25. Ibid., 19.

26. Ibid., 140.

27. Ibid., 141.

28. Ibid., 138–39.

29. Ibid., 24–25.

30. Marcuse, "Repressive Tolerance," 117, 123, 88.

31. Ryan, "Free Inquiry," 951.

32. Michael Oakeshott, *The Voice of Liberal Learning* ed., Timothy Fuller (New Haven: Yale University Press, 1989), 68.

33. Ibid., 69

34. James R. Stoner, "Free Speech, Diversity and Inclusion: Is There a Balance?," *Jack Miller Center*, https://jackmillercenter.org/constitution-day/constitution-day-conversation-2017/#essay [https://perma.cc/7MNE-WMER].

REFERENCES

Ben-Porath, Sigal R. *Free Speech on Campus* (Philadelphia: University of Pennsylvania Press, 2017).

Bourdieu, Pierre. *Outline of A Theory of Practice* (Cambridge: Cambridge University Press, 1977).

"Charles Murray at Middlebury: Unacceptable and Unethical, Say Over 500 Alumni," *Beyond the Green: Collective of Middlebury Voices* (March 2, 2017), https://beyondthegreenmidd.wordpress.com/2017/03/02/charles-murray-at-middlebury-unacceptable-and-unethical-say-over-500-alumni/ [https://perma.cc/58T4-LXFM].

Chemerinsky, Erwin, and Howard Gillman, *Free Speech on Campus* (New Haven: Yale University Press, 2017).

Fish, Stanley. *Save the World on Your Own Time* (Oxford and New York: Oxford University Press, 2008).

Fish, Stanley. *Versions of Academic Freedom* (Chicago: University of Chicago Press, 2014).

"Free Expression on Campus: What College Students Think about First Amendment Issues." March 12, 2018. https://knightfoundation.org/reports/free-expression-on-campus-what-college-students-think-about-first-amendment-issues

Leiter, Brian. "Why Academic Freedom?" In Donald A. Downs and Chris W. Surprenant, eds. *The Value and Limits of Academic Speech* (New York and London: Routledge, 2018), ch. 2.

Marcuse, Herbert. "Repressive Tolerance." In Robert Paul Wolff et. al., *A Critique of Pure Tolerance* (Boston: Beacon Press, 1969).

McIntyre, Alasdair. *Herbert Marcuse: An Exposition and a Polemic* (New York: Viking Press, 1970).

Oakeshott, Michael. *The Voice of Liberal Learning.* Ed., Timothy Fuller (New Haven: Yale University Press, 1989).

Ryan, Alan. "Academic Freedom and the 'Truth Function.'" In Cheryl Hudson and Joanna Williams, eds. *Why Academic Freedom Matters* (Civitas, 2016).

Ryan, Alan. "Free Inquiry: Easy Times Can Be Difficult Too." *Social Research* 76 (Fall 2009).

Spivak, Gayatri. "Can the Subaltern Speak?" In Cary Nelson and Lawrence Grossberg, eds., *Marxism and the Interpretation of Culture* (Urbana: University of Illinois Press, 1988).

Stoner, James R. "Free Speech, Diversity and Inclusion: Is There a Balance?," *Jack Miller Center,* https://jackmillercenter.org/constitution-day/constitution-day-conversation-2017/#essay [https://perma.cc/7MNE-WMER].

Waldron, Jeremy. *The Harm in Hate Speech* (Cambridge: Harvard University Press, 2014).

Williams, Bernard. "The Idea of Equality," in *Problems of The Self: Philosophical Papers 1956–1972* (Cambridge: Cambridge University Press, 1973).

Chapter 7

Free Speech and Liberal Education

Norma Thompson

The Woodward Report of 1974 may or may not be a high point in the classical free speech tradition, but it was a crowning moment for Yale College. It was produced after the controversial speaker William Shockley was shouted down by Yale undergraduates for his statements on genetics and for his advocacy of sterilization among certain populations. The report urged the university to commit to the idea that "the results of free expression are to the general benefit in the long run, however unpleasant they may appear at the time,"[1] that no matter how outrageous the speech of the latest agitator, the tumult will die out and the speaker's words will fall away or take hold because of their own error or merit. Accordingly, speech that is inherently hateful will reveal itself in time with ever increasing clarity. As Edmund Burke noted, people tend to be fifty years behind in their politics, such that "men are wise with but little reflection, and good with little self-denial, in the business of all times except their own."[2] Thankfully, time and cool reflection may do substantial work on their own. Why dignify extreme speech by suggesting that undergraduates need to be protected from it? The judgment in 1974 at Yale was that it is far better to assume that students are equipped with the intellectual resources to deal with illiberal expressions of opinion than it is for faculty and administrators to get into the business of policing the parameters of acceptable speech. This is, and has always been, the cornerstone of liberal argumentation; truth is to be sought through the incessant process of argumentation, not dictated once and for all from below or above.

There was one dissenting voice in the 1974 Woodward Report, a Yale graduate student in economics and law, who was given ample space in the finished product to air his disagreements. His stipulated authorities featured Herbert Marcuse. He derided the majority for being facile and simplistic, and for inserting value judgments in the historical review; he stressed instead that "power relationships enter into our language" and must be accounted for. Insisting that liberation of the oppressed must be prior to the cause of free speech, he put the "free marketplace of ideas" in scare quotes and dismissed the majority's belief that "good ideas will beat out bad ideas."[3]

Such denunciations were common in the late 1970s when I was in college and in *my* Marxist phase. I, too, was obsessing about how all knowledge is relative and the result of social conditioning; the code word was "alienation." For a while, Marcuse answered everything. "Free election of masters does not abolish the masters or the slaves," he wrote, intriguingly. "Free choice among a wide variety of goods and services does not signify freedom if these goods and services sustain social controls over a life of toil and fear—that is, if they sustain alienation."[4] Marx's early writings about alienation were alluring, and I devoured the *Economic and Philosophic Manuscripts*. But an abrupt shock to my Marxism came in a standard course in the history of political thought. Edmund Burke, who I had been led to believe was the enemy, seemed to make a lot of sense, once I actually attended to his writings. Everyone granted that his speeches on Ireland, America, and India were not only persuasive; they were also politically spotless. But his *Reflections on the Revolution in France* also turned out to be masterful and persuasive, though in the late 1970s, not politically acceptable at all to the intellectual establishment. Here was a puzzle. Concerning radical political change, Burke pummeled one easy assumption after another, compelling me to think anew about the most constructive means to achieving political freedom.

If Burke was correct about being fifty years or so behind in our abilities to comprehend our politics, how did he get so much *right* about the French Revolution, before the event? He anticipated the Terror, the radicalization of the leaders, the King's execution, and the outcome (the charismatic general who would take power) *years* before they occurred. Even if I couldn't explain this, one thing was sure: my fellow-traveling days with Marx and Marxists were over. I was drawn to the practical politician who was also a political philosopher. I had shopped in my own personal marketplace of ideas, and yes, I had to conclude that the good ones beat out the bad.

Those who have sought to explain Burke's prescience have credited his ability to comprehend the *whole* of reality by, as his contemporary Oliver Goldsmith said, "[winding] into his subject like a serpent." As Peter Stanlis elaborated, "this simile reflects perfectly Burke's most characteristic method of treating a subject—his mind grasped it, penetrated to its core, and enveloped it in a three-dimensional hold that included his senses, his intuitional reason, and his emotions and imagination."[5] Significantly, Burke *earns* that "three-dimensional hold" through his immersion in and mastery of detail, as the historian Thomas Macaulay attests, in speaking of Burke's massive research on Warren Hastings' career as governor-general of British-ruled

Bengal: "The manner in which Burke brought his higher powers of intellect to work on statements of facts, and on tables of figures, was peculiar to himself. In every part of those huge bales of Indian information which repelled almost all other readers, his mind, at once philosophical and poetical, found something to instruct or to delight."[6] It seems that Burke is so good at seeing what will happen in the future because he is so fastidious at putting together a narrative of what has transpired in the past, who it effects, and how. His observations of character are uncommonly penetrating.[7]

This consideration of Burke's methodology brought me back to an off-putting comment that Aristotle makes in his *Rhetoric* that I had always wanted to understand better. The context is his opening move against Plato, in which Aristotle seems to be taking the philosopher to task for giving rhetoric a bad name. "Rhetoric *is* useful," Aristotle counters, "because the true and the just are by nature stronger than their opposite."[8] Aristotle was no fool: he knew that truth and politics do not mix well, and that bad things happen to good people. So what is the enigma, if we really are "natured" to be receptive to truth and justice? Now I came to see that first of all, nature is easily *transgressed*—as Burke would affirm repeatedly in reference to the French revolutionaries who were caught up in their metaphysical schemes. "This sort of people are so taken up with their theories about the rights of man that they have totally forgotten his nature."[9] Then Aristotle qualified his assertion: if you have truth and justice on your side, you *should* have the advantage. But you *still* need to package that truth, to promote it rhetorically, to *defend* it. This insight has resonance in our contemporary debates: new and old entries into the canon need *packaging*, they need to be promoted, and they require a strong defense—in perpetuity.

It would be prudent here to anticipate objections. No doubt power relationships enter into our language, and politicians intentionally mischaracterize actions and events. But among the serf, the slave, the oppressed—who does *not* recognize this? Those without power often have recourse to a secret, shared language amid the everyday dissimulation—that is called learning to read between the lines and communicating accordingly. This isn't news; see, for example, the eloquent work of James C. Scott, and most recently *Weapons of the Weak*, about which Ramachandra Guha writes: "A moving account of the poor's refusal to accept the terms of their subordination. It effectively disposes of the belief (common to both radical and conservative sociology) that theoretical sophistication and intelligible prose are somehow at odds."[10] Perhaps the claim that the true and the just are by nature stronger than their opposite is just to recognize the wisdom of *folk* wisdom.

To honor the perceptive powers of the common man and woman, however, goes against the grain of our times. At least on college campuses, the default historicist assumption is that all cultural phenomena are determined by their time and place in history, so preferred topics of study frequently are the ways that we *don't* have control over our thoughts. Social science has become "an invasive species" informing us almost daily that new "studies show" that our assumption of free will is a delusion. Arthur Melzer has written brilliantly about the consequences of this historicist view. He chronicles a "numbing" of intellects such that ideas have lost the power to shock, making us susceptible to great lies: "We no longer reason with our whole souls," Melzer charges. "We don't connect."[11] This is all to justify why Burke, the man who *connects*, is such an important author for our times, and how he became one of my fondest intellectual heroes, right up there with Aristotle and Jane Austen. But as usual, I went one way, and the world went another.

Back at Yale, the views of that dissenting graduate student in 1974 have now won the day, and the minority voice has become the majority. There is nothing in his original list of charges that departs significantly from the way in 2015 several infamous Yale controversies were portrayed on campus, and from the way events transpired around the time of Halloween that year. Two events in particular keep rising to the surface narrative, one of doubtful authenticity and the other decidedly real.

The first controversy had to do with the charge that three African American female undergraduates at Yale were turned away from a fraternity, after being told the party was "white girls only." There is little evidence that this event actually happened.[12] This has made no difference to those who continue to repeat it, apparently because they *want* it to be true—to bolster their assertion that power matters above all.

The second controversy was thoroughly documented. Erika Christakis, Associate Master of Silliman College, had objected to what seemed to her to be a paternalistic letter sent from one branch of the administration encouraging students to choose their Halloween costumes thoughtfully, lest they offend the sensitivities of their peers. She disagreed with the intervention, and countered with an email to Silliman students claiming that they were mature enough to make their own decisions. Christakis intended her letter to respect the dignity of students, but by some it was received as hostile. Referring to her husband, the Master of the college, she wrote: "Nicholas says, if you don't like a costume someone is wearing, look away, or tell them you are offended. Talk to each other. Free speech and the ability to tolerate offence are the hallmarks of a free and open society."[13] Many students were enraged, and more than seven hundred members of the Yale community went on to sign an open letter taking issue with the way her words invalidated the voices of minority students.

To discuss the controversy, Nicholas Christakis agreed to meet with concerned students. This encounter was captured on video and replayed endlessly by the media as the latest campus outrage. An undergraduate tells Christakis that it is his role as Master to "create a place of comfort and home" for the students. When he disagreed with that definition, she shrieked "who the fuck hired you?" demanding that he step down because being Master is "not about creating an intellectual space," but about "creating a home."[14]

Directly following that explosive time at Yale, it was difficult to get a handle on events, but more recently the grievances have come into focus. In one 2016 *Atlantic* magazine interview, a Yale undergraduate declared that "the right of *some* people to express themselves does not trump the right of people of color to live free of harassment,"[15] and went on to charge that white students don't understand the depth of the issue because they avoid taking courses in AFAM where the history of racism is studied. I could sympathize with this complaint, because these Yale students were not taking *my* courses in Humanities, either. I thought about her advice and jotted down a list of authors whom she recommended for anyone who wanted a deeper understanding of the racial divide. Ta-Nehisi Coates was familiar to me, but not Michelle Alexander, among others.[16]

It seemed providential shortly thereafter when I walked into a bookstore to find the highly recommended Michelle Alexander's *The New Jim Crow* featured prominently. Why providential? Well, in the foreword to Alexander's book, Cornel West puts *The New Jim Crow* in the direct lineage of *The Strange Career of Jim Crow* by C. Vann Woodward—the very same author of Yale's 1974 Woodward Report.[17] Here was a ready-made thought experiment, and I decided to read the two books in tandem.

Woodward's book is grim reading, as its subject is an ugly swath of American history. Yet few would deny that it is nevertheless a superb analysis. Woodward names the villains, traces a complex story, indicates how things could have gone otherwise, and throughout, is modest in his aims and claims. His preface sets the tone: "I shall expect and hope to be corrected."[18] The tone of *The Strange Career of Jim Crow* is calm, measured, and open to amendment. We used to say "objective." If the work is dated, it is only in the genteel mannerisms of its author. Having read the history through, I saw how fitting it was that Woodward had been turned to for leadership in the explosive early 1970's on the Yale campus.

The Michelle Alexander book presents the strongest possible contrast, as it presents a horrific picture of Black incarceration—and blames the whole of it on white racists who have conspired to create the "new" Jim Crow. To paint the villains with such broad strokes means, of course, that individual malefactors go unnamed as the "class" takes the hit. Real actors are not in clear view. I thought back to Herbert Marcuse's *One-Dimensional Man*, where abstract nouns similarly are made to assume the role of "acting" subject.[19] I recognized the familiar Marxist stipulations: the world-historical scope of the issue; the need for total revolution; the irrelevance of facts contrary to the narrative; and the anticipations of false consciousness wherever characters in the account do not act as predicted.[20]

The New Jim Crow is not just Marxist, however—and thereby silently beholden to a dead white male. It is full of questionable rhetorical practices such as leaning on passive constructions to insinuate vast racial conspiracies. Alexander writes, for example: "A new race-neutral language was developed for appealing to old racist sentiments, a language accompanied by a political movement that succeeded in putting the vast majority of Blacks back in their place."[21] Marcuse does this, too, in a way that passed unnoticed my first time around but that provokes me now.[22] But Michelle Alexander's version is more incendiary, which is presumably why two state prisons initially banned the book from their libraries.[23]

Without question, the subject of Alexander's work is alarming, and there is cause to be wholly sympathetic to her concerns about the way that mass incarceration in the United States has affected Blacks out of all proportion to convictions for minor drug offenses. But what is unacceptable is that she explains this phenomenon because of a nefarious scheme. Alexander attributes a conspiracy to whites opposed to racial reform, claiming that they have orchestrated the mass incarceration, while concealing their bias through race-neutral language.[24] Why compromise the seriousness of the topic by insisting on its analogy to Jim Crow laws? When Alexander presents the "new" Jim Crow as factual, she minimizes the evil of the "old," which had nothing metaphorical about it. And, of course, her students are not hearing any rejoinders to this rendition of history. My concern is that it is not just the white students who are not taking AFAM classes; it is also the Black students who are *only* taking AFAM classes and may encounter polemical work without further context.

Consider Michelle Alexander's opening statement, which she uses to prove how *little* things have changed since Jim Crow laws were in force.

> Jarvious Cotton cannot vote. Like his father, grandfather, great-grandfather, and great-great-grandfather, he has been denied the right to participate in our electoral democracy. Cotton's family tree tells the story of several generations of Black men who were born in the United States but who were denied the most basic freedom that democracy promises—the freedom to vote for those who will make the rules and laws that govern one's life.[25]

But there is at least one Yale professor who is bold enough to take issue with how she frames this picture and who is willing to label its rhetoric as underhanded. James Forman Jr., Professor of Law at Yale Law School, notes that "there is one salient difference between Cotton and his ancestors. They couldn't vote because they were black; Cotton lost his right to vote when he was convicted of murder."[26] Later, when Alexander writes: "Today mass incarceration defines the meaning of blackness in America: black people, especially black men, are criminals. That is what it means to be black."[27] Forman responds simply: "Today nothing 'defines the meaning of blackness in America.'"[28]

How admirably blunt! James Forman Jr. is himself Black, the son of a Civil Rights hero, and the author of his own outstanding book on mass incarceration. Yet Forman transcends these characterizations when he declares that the Jim Crow analogy is objectionable because it "neglects some important truths and must be criticized in the service of truth."[29] He includes no scare quotes, as if it were an unproblematic aspiration for a legal scholar to write in the service of truth. Forman thus appears suspiciously like a single "Woodward" holdover from earlier times at Yale; his formulation is completely in line with the majority conclusions of 1974.

Two generations later, when the majority Woodward view of 1974 has become the minority view, the circle appears to be complete. But what does all of this have to do with free speech? I contend that the narrative traced here points beyond campus speech codes and the shouting down of unpopular speakers: the target looks more like the entire tradition of liberal education. This is a culture war of a different order, not about adding diverse voices, but about stipulating in advance which voice can be heard. Cornel West declares that Michelle Alexander's work is an "instant classic," as if her work can *skip* the stage of critical review. That is a dangerous game, to abdicate standards of evidence for some pre-approved writers, who get a free pass on political grounds. This treatment may intimidate other scholars, who might be laboring to produce more careful and defensible inquiries. Worse, it makes a mockery of standards of evidence—and you never know when you yourself will need to appeal to the sanctity of truth. Today we have reason to fear that the integrity of language will erode if it is not respected in everyday speech and action.

It is perfectly understandable that people who feel they have been excluded from the liberal arts tradition should want their voices to be heard—almost at any cost. But I would like to pause at that "almost," because there is a case that needs to be made that some costs are too high. We can and should put contemporary works in the conversation with established works. But that is not the same as declaring favorites from our time to be classics; that is just not our call to make. Works get into the canon by fighting their way in, by providing insights into enduring human concerns, by speaking insightfully to human nature and more powerfully of the human condition than do their tendentious critics. Classics aren't born overnight. There really is something to the test of time.

This would suggest that we pay attention to which stories have lasted, which ones have endured these battles along the way. We *can* do something to sharpen our judgment: we can study together in good faith across fields, and talk about injustices, using rigorous argument. We can attempt to banish polemics and all forms of conspiracy thinking. We can honor Woodward not for having written an untouchable document, but for his humility in standing perpetually open to contradiction. We can honor Alexander by dignifying her political analysis with a deeper historical background. Call me hopelessly optimistic, but I'm asking the dissenters not to outlaw dissent.

What we call liberal education may be traceable to the work of Cicero, who pulled together the greatest expressions of thought and action from ancient Athens and from his own Roman heritage, providing generations to come with a sense of a canon for the widest range of learning—and challenging—humanity's record of intellectual and moral achievement.

In doing so, Cicero invented, or at least institutionalized, the concept which liberal education, or educators, have come to take for granted yet has never ceased to be under assault from those who claim to be the sole possessors of the truth. But the word "liberal" in liberal education requires plurality, multifarity, unbounded forays of expression in contests before, and for, consideration by the people. Cicero's career in the law was realized through *in utramque partem*, the court structure in which arguments can be made from either side of a disputed question because only in this way is language *productive of knowledge*. And the linchpin of this is language which must be freely protected.

Thus, the title of this forum "Free Speech and Liberal Education" can be best understood as "Free Speech *is* Liberal Education."

NOTES

1. *Report of the Committee on Freedom of Expression at Yale* (1974), p. 6, https://yalecollege.yale.edu/get-know-yale-college/office-dean/reports/report-committee-freedom-expression-yale. Hereafter, "Woodward Report."

2. Edmund Burke, "Thoughts on the Cause of the Present Discontents. . . . 1770," in *Edmund Burke: Selected Writings and Speeches*, ed. with intro. by Peter J. Stanlis (Washington, D.C.: Regnery Publishing, Inc., 1963), p. 128.

3. Woodward Report, pp. 37–41, 51.

4. Herbert Marcuse, *One-Dimensional Man: Studies in the Ideology of Advanced Industrial Society* (Boston: Beacon Press, 1964), p. 7.

5. Peter J. Stanlis, Introduction, *Edmund Burke: Selected Writings and Speeches*, p. 15.

6. Macaulay continues: "India and its inhabitants were not to him, as to most Englishmen, mere names and abstractions, but a real country and a real people. . . . All India was present to the eye of his mind . . . Oppression in Bengal was to him the same thing as oppression in the streets of London." Lord Macaulay, *Critical and Historical*

Essays, selected and introduced by Hugh Trevor-Roper (London: Fontana Library, 1965), pp. 485–486.

7. There cannot be many goals more challenging than to capture the character of a whole people, without being reductive. Burke excels here, as when he identified the way the people of New England "carry on" their whale-fishery: "Neither the perseverance of Holland, nor the activity of France, nor the dexterous and firm sagacity of English enterprise, ever carried this most perilous mode of hardy industry to the extent to which it has been pushed by this recent people . . . " Burke, "Speech on Conciliation," in Stanlis ed. *Selected Writings*, p. 187.

8. Aristotle, *On Rhetoric: A Theory of Civic Discourse*, 2nd ed., trans. with intro., notes and appendices by George A. Kennedy (New York: Oxford University Press, 2007), 1355a21–23, p. 35.

9. Edmund Burke, *Reflections on the Revolution in France,* ed. with intro. and notes by J. G. A. Pocock (Indianapolis: Hackett Publishing Company, 1987), p. 56.

10. Ramachandra Guha, "Presentation of Class in Everyday Life," *Economic and Political Weekly*, Vol 22, No. 47 (21 November 1987): 2001–2002. https://www.epw.in/journal/1987/47/reviews-uncategorised/presentation-class-everyday-life.html. http://www.jstor.org/stable/4377757.

11. Arthur M. Melzer, *Philosophy Between the Lines: The Lost History of Esoteric Writing* (Chicago: University of Chicago Press, 2014), p. 202. Melzer's book has been little noticed by the academic mainstream. But see the non-mainstream *Symposium on Arthur Melzer's Philosophy Between the Lines*, ed. Peter Lawler, *Perspectives on Political Science*, Summer 2015.

12. Michael E. Miller, "Yale investigation finds 'no evidence' of racism at frat party alleged to have been for 'white girls only,'" *The Washington Post*, December 11, 2015.

13. FIRE, "Email from Erika Christakis: 'Dressing Yourselves,' email to Silliman College (Yale) Students on Halloween Costumes," October 30, 2015, https://www.thefire.org/email-from-erika-christakis-dressing-yourselves-email-to-silliman-college-yale-students-on-halloween-costumes. Note that the title of "Master" in the residential colleges was changed to "head of college" in 2016, after this event.

14. FIRE, "Yale Halloween Costume Controversy," November 6, 2015, https://www.youtube.com/playlist?list=PLvIqJIL2kOMefn77xg6-6yrvek5kbNf3Z.

15. Conor Friedersdorf, "A Dialogue on Race and Speech at Yale," *The Atlantic*, March 24, 2016, https://www.theatlantic.com/politics/archive/2016/03/yale-silliman-race/475152 (emphasis added).

16. At the time of this writing (for the free speech conference at Arizona State University in February 2018), Michelle Alexander had not yet joined the *New York Times* as opinion columnist; that occurred in September, 2018.

17. Cornel West, Foreword to Michelle Alexander, *The New Jim Crow: Mass Incarceration in the Age of Colorblindness,* rev. edition (New York: The New Press, 2010, 2012), p. ix.

18. C. Vann Woodward, *The Strange Career of Jim Crow*, 3rd rev. edition (New York: Oxford University Press, 1974), p. xvii. An example of Woodward's typically cautious appraisal appears on page 33: "Under these circumstances a great deal of

variety and inconsistency prevailed in race relations from state to state and within a state. It was a time of experiment, testing, and uncertainty—quite different from the time of repression and rigid uniformity that was to come toward the end of the century. Alternatives were still open and real choices had to be made."

19. "Technology serves to institute new, more effective, and more pleasant forms of social control and social cohesion. The totalitarian tendency of these controls seems to assert itself in still another sense—by spreading to the less developed and even to the pre-industrial areas of the world, and by creating similarities in the development of capitalism and communism." Marcuse, *One-Dimensional Man*, pp. xv-xvi.

20. From Marx, *The Communist Manifesto* pp. 172, 174: "the middle-class owner of property . . . must, indeed, be swept out of the way, and made impossible. . . . The ruling ideas of each age have ever been the ideas of its ruling class." From *The German Ideology*, pp. 124–125: "the alteration of men on a mass scale is required. . . . In each historical epoch they have had to *share the illusion of that epoch*" (emphasis in the original). Karl Marx, *Selected Writings*, ed. with intro. by Lawrence H. Simon (Indianapolis: Hackett Publishing Co., Inc., 1994).

21. Alexander, *The New Jim Crow*, p. 40.

22. Marcuse, *One-Dimensional Man*, p. 7: "Under the rule of a repressive whole, liberty can be made into a powerful instrument of domination." By whom? How? Why? And why didn't I ask these questions the first time through?

23. Jonah Engel Bromwich, "Why Are American Prisons So Afraid of This Book?" *New York Times,* January 18, 2018, https://www.nytimes.com/2018/01/18/us/new-jim-crow-book-ban-prison.html. Bromwich insinuates that the prisons are afraid of the truth, whereas I contend it is the reverse: it is the *exaggerations* that they feared—probably rightly.

24. Alexander, *The New Jim Crow*, e.g., pp. x, 40, 42, 49.

25. Ibid., 1.

26. James Forman, Jr., "Racial Critiques of Mass Incarceration: Beyond the New Jim Crow," *New York University Law Review* 87 (2012): 50.

27. Alexander, *The New Jim Crow*, 197.

28. Forman, "Racial Critiques of Mass Incarceration," 58.

29. Ibid., 24.

REFERENCES

Alexander, Michelle. *The New Jim Crow: Mass Incarceration in the Age of Colorblindness.* Rev. edition (New York: The New Press, 2010, 2012).

Aristotle. *On Rhetoric: A Theory of Civic Discourse*, 2nd ed. Trans. with intro., notes, and appendices by George A. Kennedy (New York: Oxford University Press, 2007).

Bromwich, Jonah Engel. "Why Are American Prisons So Afraid of This Book?" *New York Times,* January 18, 2018. https://www.nytimes.com/2018/01/18/us/new-jim-crow-book-ban-prison.html.

Burke, Edmund. *Reflections on the Revolution in France*. Ed. with intro. and notes by J.G.A. Pocock (Indianapolis: Hackett Publishing Company, 1987).

Burke, Edmund. "Thoughts on the Cause of the Present Discontents. . . . 1770." In *Edmund Burke: Selected Writings and Speeches*. Ed. with intro. by Peter J. Stanlis (Washington, D.C.: Regnery Publishing, Inc., 1963).

FIRE, "Email from Erika Christakis: 'Dressing Yourselves,' email to Silliman College (Yale) Students on Halloween Costumes." October 30, 2015. https://www.the-fire.org/email-from-erika-christakis-dressing-yourselves-email-to-silliman-college-yale-students-on-halloween-costumes.

FIRE, "Yale Halloween Costume Controversy." November 6, 2015, https://www.youtube.com/playlist?list=PLvIqJIL2kOMefn77xg6-6yrvek5kbNf3Z.

Forman, James, Jr. "Racial Critiques of Mass Incarceration: Beyond the New Jim Crow." *New York University Law Review* 87 (2012): 50.

Friedersdorf, Conor. "A Dialogue on Race and Speech at Yale." *The Atlantic*, March 24, 2016, https://www.theatlantic.com/politics/archive/2016/03/yale-silliman-race/475152

Guha, Ramachandra. "Presentation of Class in Everyday Life." *Economic and Political Weekly*, Vol 22, No. 47 (21 November 1987): 2001–2002. https://www.epw.in/journal/1987/47/reviews-uncategorised/presentation-class-everyday-life.html. [http://www.jstor.org/stable/4377757].

Lawler, Peter, ed. "Symposium on Arthur Melzer's Philosophy Between the Lines." *Perspectives on Political Science*. Summer 2015.

Macaulay, Thomas Babington (Lord). *Critical and Historical Essays*. Selected and introduced by Hugh Trevor-Roper (London: Fontana Library, 1965).

Marcuse, Herbert. *One-Dimensional Man: Studies in the Ideology of Advanced Industrial Society* (Boston: Beacon Press, 1964).

Marx, Karl. *Selected Writings*, ed. with intro. by Lawrence H. Simon (Indianapolis: Hackett Publishing Co., Inc., 1994).

Melzer, Arthur M. *Philosophy Between the Lines: The Lost History of Esoteric Writing* (Chicago: University of Chicago Press, 2014).

Miller, Michael E. "Yale investigation finds 'no evidence' of racism at frat party alleged to have been for 'white girls only.'" *The Washington Post*, December 11, 2015.

Report of the Committee on Freedom of Expression at Yale (1974). https://yalecollege.yale.edu/get-know-yale-college/office-dean/reports/report-committee-freedom-expression-yale.

Stanlis, Peter J. Introduction, *Edmund Burke: Selected Writings and Speeches* (Washington, D.C.: Regnery Publishing, Inc., 1963).

Woodward, C. Vann. *The Strange Career of Jim Crow*. 3rd rev. edition (New York: Oxford University Press, 1974).

Chapter 8

Was John Stuart Mill Right about Freedom of Speech?

James R. Stoner, Jr.

As Earth's magnetic poles have flipped over the course of geological time, so in our politically polarized society we have seen a sort of reversal of the parties in recent years on the question of free speech. In the middle of the twentieth century, it was almost the definition of being a liberal that you were a champion of expanding free speech, removing censorship (for example, of movies or library books or sex education) and encouraging what Justice William Brennan called "uninhibited, robust, and wide-open" public debate.[1] Conservatives then were wary, concerned that lifting censorship on obscene materials would encourage moral degeneracy and that removing the protection of reputation by the law of libel would harm innocent people and drive good people out of political life. At least one conservative professor raised the question of whether free speech even contributed to the advance of knowledge, suggesting upon newly uncovered evidence that the wise can communicate with one another esoterically even under censorious regimes, and that no regime, even a liberal one, could avoid being censorious, if only through the influence of dominant opinion.[2]

But today, as I said, the poles have flipped. It is usually from the Left that free speech is attacked or at least called into question. Sometimes, it is even said that the term "free speech" is a codeword or "dog whistle" for "hate speech," and hate speech is treated as a form of assault.[3] Indeed, even or especially at universities, once the avant garde of free speech, certain ideas, even those not long ago taken for granted or at least regnant, are seen to violate the universities' commitment to an inclusive learning environment, pitting one key principle—that learning should be open to all who are able—against another—that all ideas should be open to critical examination. Meanwhile, conservatives have found themselves defending free speech by using arguments that not long ago belonged to liberals. Now part of this might simply be the phenomenon of conservatives being comfortable with the familiar, and since until recently robust free expression was familiar, conservatives are reluctant to see that change. And then, at some schools, traditional rules protecting free speech remain in place, and conservatives tend to feel comfortable with old rules. But what I notice is that conservative thinkers and groups are using liberal arguments, especially the arguments of that quintessential nineteenth-century liberal John Stuart Mill, whose little book, *On Liberty*, and especially its second chapter, has become the *locus classicus* in defense of free speech. One sees this, for example, in Princeton professor Keith Whittington's fine book, *Speak Freely: Why Universities Must Defend Free Speech*, which works through Mill's argument and explicitly endorses it, as well as in the advocacy of the Foundation for Individual Rights and Expression, or FIRE, an organization implacably opposed to anything resembling a campus speech code.[4] On the Supreme Court, it has often been the purportedly conservative justices, or most of them, who have endorsed a constitutional law of free speech that grew out of the 1960s, allowing suppression of speech only when there is imminent danger of serious harm, and in fact promoting affirmative steps by government to give police protection to the most provocative speakers, begun when protection was given to neo-Nazis marching in a Jewish suburb inhabited by Holocaust survivors; not to mention squelching even the most hesitant steps by Congress when it still had the will to limit the proliferation of pornography on the internet.[5] How did conservatives become champions of liberal arguments about free speech, and are they right to use such arguments?

WHAT CHANGED?

I think there are three possible explanations for the switching of the polarities on free speech, particularly with reference to Mill. First, Mill's liberalism on freedom of speech might be indicative of his classical liberalism and his essential continuity with seventeenth- and eighteenth-century liberals like John Locke and Adam Smith. It has been widely noted that today's conservatives, particularly in the United States, are actually classical liberals in their respect for market freedom and distrust of government regulation, so perhaps it is merely that conservative economic opinions and free-speech opinions have now come into alignment, extending conservatives' economic libertarianism into the social field. Something like this is proposed by Nicholas Capaldi, one of Mill's premier intellectual biographers, who notes Mill's general sympathy with free-market principles and his recognition of their transformative effect on society.[6] The problem with this argument is that, while Mill might have begun as an advocate of free markets, he concluded his writing career as a friend of socialism, or at least by the twentieth century his greatest admirers were those who were friendly to socialist reform of the free market system.[7] Mill might have been right in his early career about the market and in his later career about free speech, but the change in his thought about markets undercuts a conservative attempt to appeal to his early utilitarianism regarding markets to vindicate his later libertarianism regarding speech.

A second attempt to align Mill with conservatives might be traced to scholars such as Nancy Rosenblum, who see in Mill "another liberalism" in contrast to the rationalist liberalism of his teacher Jeremy Bentham, himself the intellectual descendant of Locke and Smith.[8] To Rosenblum, Mill is essentially a romantic, determined to vindicate individual passion against the uniformity of economic man, searching for an account of the human good that transcends wealth and narrow utilitarianism—and since much of nineteenth-century conservatism was romantic in its sensibility, perhaps conservative use of Mill should not be surprising. The difficulty here is that the very social institutions and practices that European conservatives admired—throne and altar, aristocracy and tradition, government and religion—are directly challenged by the freedom of speech Mill proposes, which is willing if not eager to call into question all existing institutions and to refuse to act unless an adequate reason can be given, a reason that goes beyond the assertion, "we've always done things that way," a statement that can never literally be true.

Finally, there is the possibility that liberalism itself has changed, perhaps even according to its inner logic, so that Mill's arguments in favor of freedom of speech transform, paradoxically, into the very arguments used against it. This, I think, is the better explanation. As is plain in *On Liberty*, Mill is an advocate of progress, and he makes clear that, not any set of principles or "abstract right," but the "interests of man as a progressive being" are the ultimate point of reference in his thinking.[9] If classical liberalism should yield to socialism in the name of economic progress, why won't free-speech liberalism yield to progressive objections in the name of social equality? Even more to the point, if Mill's case in favor of free speech rests principally on his case in favor of individuality, as I intend to show, and if this promotes "experiments of living" unanchored in any kind of knowledge of what constitutes the individual human being, then there is nothing enduring in his case for freedom of speech and one should expect, given the variability of human affairs, that it will eventually be abandoned by its advocates if the "experimenters" grow impatient with the possibility of further change under the system of liberty.[10] In short, except perhaps as a matter of prudence in winning allies among older liberals, I think conservatives should be reluctant to rely on Millian arguments—unless such arguments can be grounded on sturdier principles and thus perhaps understood in a different way.

MILL'S ARGUMENTS

That said, Mill's case for freedom of speech—or to use his precise terminology, "freedom of thought and discussion"—is clear and powerful, and before I critique it any further, I want to lay it out in such a way as to make it as persuasive as possible. In the first place, Mill writes, suppression of speech supposes infallibility in the suppresser; it assumes the dominant power—government or social opinion, for Mill means to argue against them both—is in possession of the truth and cannot profit from objections or corrections. But, says Mill, if history has shown us anything, it is that mankind is slow to learn the truth about things, and many things thought true by the wisest of men have eventually been proven mistaken or merely partially true. Error has no ordinary corrective except objection and argument, and this is possible only under a regime of freedom of speech. He gives several examples, both of persecution by the authorities of their day of those nowadays thought to have introduced new truth—most dramatically, the examples of Socrates and Jesus—and of wise men who themselves were persecutors, for example, the Stoic emperor Marcus Aurelius. Passing over the fact that neither Socrates nor Jesus—though both put to death for their teaching—argued for freedom of speech as a general proposition, Mill insists that the progress of truth depends on free expression, for "intellectual pacification is the sacrifice of the entire moral courage of the human mind."[11] While acknowledging that great minds have sometimes thrived in the face of repression, he expresses concern for "the multitude of promising intellects combined with timid characters" who fall silent when threatened, and he adds that freedom to think "is as much and even more indispensable to enable average human beings to attain the mental stature they are capable of."[12] Human progress—remember, Mill's ultimate reference—depends not only and perhaps not even especially on great genius, though he praises this in another place, but on a society alive with thought and argument, eager to develop and willing to change. He makes it clear that he does not think the victory of truth is inevitable, against the rhetoric of his great English forebear advocating free expression, the poet John Milton, nor define truth as whatever wins, like his great American disciple, Justice Oliver Wendell Holmes.

Mill's second argument asserts that even if the prevailing opinion is certainly right, freedom to challenge it ought to be permitted, because there is a difference between knowing a truth and holding even a correct opinion. The best way to be sure that the person with the true opinion really knows and doesn't merely repeat a formula of words is to force him to defend the truth against a challenge, and that, he says, requires freedom of speech. Mill is aware of scientific progress, which even in his day had exploded many a view about physical nature held by the leading philosophers of the ancient world, and he seems to suppose some moral opinions have similarly been decisively refuted; indeed, he even writes that over time, fewer and fewer issues will be contested, as human knowledge grows and grows.[13] Nevertheless, noting that Plato wrote in dialogues and that even the Catholic Church employs a "devil's advocate" before raising a saint to the honor of the altar, he insists that freedom of speech is necessary to preserve the dialectic, since the human capacity to know derives from the capacity to learn, and so continuous knowing demands continuous relearning. What better way to ensure the actuality of knowledge than to place it under constant assault?

Finally, Mill concedes or rather asserts that truth is usually found in the middle between two sides of an argument, for example moral truth between "pagan self-assertion" and "Christian self-denial."[14] Although opposition is the best test of truth, opponents tend toward extremes, even at the cost of distorting their own and others' arguments, adding vituperation to polemic. Mill can't resist taking a dig at holders of the dominant religious opinion who excoriate heretics and infidels while being unaware of their own bigotry, but in the end he is content to let them denounce one another, since "the collision of opinions works its salutary effect" not on the "impassioned partisan" but on "the calmer and more disinterested bystander."[15] Truth is not sure to win out when extreme partisans grapple with one another, but Mill seems confident that sensible people can find a point of balance between them. In a progressive society, he seems to think, the way of wisdom is between extremes.

Now in *On Liberty*, the discussion of free speech is actually preliminary to the discussion of freedom of action. He says in his introductory that

> The object of this essay is to assert one very simple principle, as entitled to govern absolutely the dealings of society with the individual by way of compulsion and control, . . . [namely] that the sole end for which mankind are warranted, individually or collectively, in interfering with the liberty of action of any of their number is self-protection.[16]

Liberty of action permits "the free development of individuality . . . one of the leading essentials of well-being," Mill writes in chapter three, something good in itself.[17] Although he concedes that "The initiation of all wise and noble things comes and must come from individuals; generally at first from some one individual," he continues:

> If a person possesses any tolerable amount of common sense and experience, his own mode of laying out his existence is the best, not because it is the best in itself, but because it is his own mode.[18]

The remainder of *On Liberty* is concerned with working out details, discussing first what individual actions should be beyond social reprobation, namely those that concern only the individual and violate no "distinct and assignable obligation" to another,[19] and second what action society is permitted or refused regarding individuals who stay within bounds, namely permitted not to associate with those whose choices and habits others don't like, but not to scold or censure through public opinion and certainly not to impose upon the individual the force of law or other forms of coercion. Mill had never seen a Twitter mob, of course, but he anticipates that sort of righteous anger and insists it should be stopped or prevented. Let every individual conduct his own "experiments of living": It's good for him, and in the long run good for us all. Avoiding the dead hand of custom is crucial to the progress of mankind.

What is the relation, then, of freedom of speech and freedom of action? At first Mill seems to suggest that the latter follows on analogy to the former: "As it is useful that while mankind are imperfect there should be different opinions, so it is that there should be different experiments of living."[20] But in fact, I think, freedom of speech is instrumental to freedom of action, and the latter assumes a certain priority over the former, as is the case with all means and ends. The opinions presented in Chapter 2 as the occasion of controversy principally concern the question how to live. Mill is certainly aware that deadly theological controversy has erupted in the past, but in his own century he seems most to fear the advocates of customary thinking about manners and morals, particularly Calvinist Christians. The concluding remarks in that chapter about finding truth in the middle surely suppose the truths in question are practical rather than theoretical: The controversy between geological and biblical accounts of the age of the Earth is hardly solved by splitting the difference (though perhaps questions concerning the judicious use of alcohol are). "The truth of an opinion is part of its utility," writes Mill,[21] in answer to the objection that sometimes social peace depends on unchallenged shared opinion, but it is hard to see how this would apply to speculative matters. Indeed, by making utility—the interests of man as a progressive being—the ultimate touchstone of the whole argument, the priority of action over thought is built into the logical structure of *On Liberty* as a whole.

While the essay is often read as a guide for when to limit government, Mill's aim is explicitly more ambitious. He makes clear that "Neither one person, nor any number of persons, is warranted in saying to another human creature of ripe years that he shall not do with his life for his own benefit what he chooses to do with it." This limit on "saying" is not accidental; while we "owe to each other help to distinguish better from worse, and encouragement to choose the former and avoid the latter," disapprobation can be expressed only for those actions that injure others or for the dispositions, such as envy and pride, that lead to such actions.[22] These are clear limits on speech, on what can be voiced in public, and while Mill hardly seems to expect government to enforce such limits, he is certainly encouraging individuals to censor themselves. This is not quite our modern non-judgmentalism, for he acknowledges that people will inevitably engage in "unfavorable judgment of others," and he does allow that those other individuals might suffer "the inconveniences which are strictly inseparable" consequences of idiosyncratic behavior—not being invited to parties, that sort of thing.[23] Still, it is remarkable that, one chapter after making the case for unlimited freedom of speech, Mill makes the case that, when it comes to expressing disapproval for how others choose to live, society should just shut up. As others have noted, Mill decries "dead dogma" in chapter two but writes the whole book to promote the dogma of societal non-interference in self-regarding actions, which has come to govern liberal societies as "absolutely" as he hoped. I for one think Mill was perfectly aware what he was doing when seeming to contradict himself in these matters: His point was to shake off Christian morals and the conformity to mediocrity he thought they encouraged, thereby to promote a dynamic, progressive society. I will say a little more about this later, but since our topic is freedom of speech, I want now to ask whether Mill's argument for freedom of thought and discussion can stand on its own, outside the context in which it was originally embedded.

KENDALL'S CRITIQUE OF MILL

The best assessment I know of Mill's free speech arguments taken on their own was written sixty years ago by Yale professor Willmoore Kendall and published in the *American Political Science Review* under the title, "The Open Society and Its Fallacies."[24] Kendall reads Mill's second chapter literally to allow, even promote, the expression of every opinion on every subject everywhere—except saying "property is theft" to a hungry mob in front of a poorly guarded mansion. No society can possibly live the way Mill advises, asserts Kendall, and he lists six objections.[25] First, Mill doesn't really mean *no* restriction, since he knew there were laws against slander and circulation of obscene materials to the young and does not object to them. Second, in promoting unlimited expression, Mill is really promoting a way of life, a society that can teach no orthodoxy whatsoever and therefore sacrifices its own freedom to order itself as anything besides a debating club. Third, despite claiming freedom in the name of discovering truth, Mill made it authoritative doctrine in society that there can be no public truth, since every truth claim is partial. Fourth, Mill's free speech is demanded by considerations of utility and progress, not taught as right, since rights imply a stable framework of justice and constitutional limits as well as immunities. Fifth, writes Kendall, what Mill has in mind is a revolutionary attack on traditional society and thus on existing religion and philosophy. Finally, Mill's whole argument is based on a false dilemma—either never silence anyone or declare oneself infallible—when in practice societies exercise a range of choice over what liberties they allow and what laws they insist on.

Moreover, Kendall says Mill holds a false notion of society—as if it could be a debating club concerned with no other goods—and a false anthropology, as if people can act indifferent when in fact they care about the good. He argues that a society admitting Mill's principles will become intolerant in the end, since forced indifference breeds the view that all opinions are equal, but then why not all equally suppressible as much as all equally admissible? And Kendall predicts that differences of opinion will deepen in a liberal society, since Mill invites the expression of irresponsible opinions and in a way acts to prefer them. I don't know how well most predictions in the *APSR* in the early 1960s have held up, but perhaps we can agree that this one was "spot on."

Kendall concludes by arguing that even if society could be constituted as a debating club, Mill's is not the way actual discussion leads toward truth, and he gives as evidence how exchange of ideas proceeds in the scholarship of an academic discipline. Here he lists eight steps or maxims.[26] First, exchange of ideas is crucial to progress toward truth, but ideas don't come randomly or from just anyone. Second, "the man or woman who wishes to exercise the right to be heard has a logically and temporally prior obligation to *prepare* for the exchange." Third, there is a duty to speak with courtesy, as if one might learn from others. Fourth, one should presume there has been worthwhile work before, so one begins from the received orthodoxy. Fifth, an argument proceeds within a frame of reference that, if it changes, changes by the decision of the scholarly community (Kendall here is anticipating the contemporaneous work of Thomas Kuhn on paradigm shifts[27]). Sixth, you should expect barriers if you challenge the orthodoxy, but these are an ordinary part of the process, which, Kendall implies, force challengers to play their best game. Seventh, one earns the right to play by "performing the obligation to produce a craftsmanlike piece of work." Finally, if you disagree with the orthodoxy but can't persuade the community, recognize you will be isolated or banished. (It is poignant to note that soon after publishing this piece, Kendall accepted Yale's offer to buy out his tenure and moved to the young University of Dallas to found its Department of Politics.)

As perhaps you can tell from this summary, I find much in Kendall's critique of Mill persuasive, but no critique can be wholly persuasive unless an alternative is proffered, so I want to spend the rest of the essay doing just that. My argument for freedom of speech is not supportive of "free speech absolutism," to use a phrase coined to describe Justice Hugo Black's approach to free-speech law, an approach based on Mill and increasingly favored by the contemporary Court, but instead will address the different contexts of free speech and will try to sort out the arguments that ought to guide our thinking in each realm. Indeed, I think the sort of speech that most deserves protection will be best secured if we don't insist on absolutism.

THREE CONTEXTS, THREE NORMS

I follow others in suggesting there are three principal rationales for protecting free speech in modern society: for the sake of discovering truth, for the sake of republican government, and for the sake of self-expression.[28] Rather than treating these as three legs on a single stool, let me take them in turn and apply them to the different institutions in modern society where they seem most applicable.

Truth

What are the institutions of society most concerned with the discovery of truth, or perhaps I should say, its discovery and transmission? Let me suggest four: the university, the Church, the press (or media), and the world of book publication. Actually, it might be more accurate to speak of each of these in the plural—since we have several kinds of universities, numerous churches, different kinds and outlets in the media, and so forth—but allow me sometimes to lapse into the old convention of speaking of each as a whole. The university seems to be the institution devoted most systematically to the discovery of truth and, insofar as it serves to guard the treasure of what has been discovered and to pass it along to the next generation, also to its transmission. As Kendall noted in his critique of Mill, the scholarly disciplines that inhabit the university do not proceed in their research in the mode Mill describes, by vituperative debate, but instead have developed complex practices designed to ensure scientific progress. The development of knowledge often proceeds by accretion, with an occasional breakthrough by penetrating genius, itself usually preceded by painstaking work. To be sure, there are exceptions: perhaps especially in the social sciences, robust political opinion sometimes suggests new avenues for research; the need for integration of the various disciplines—if only for the sake of ordering the curriculum—might prompt recourse to thought that transcends them; and not every cluster of professors who follow Kendall's rules are doing science (*Wissenschaft*), particularly if there is no reality they are seeking to uncover. Still, most scientific thinking and university research proceeds methodically or methodologically. This is not to say that radical questioning is out of order and freedom of speech unnecessary; on the contrary, there are questions the university can and probably must address that are unlikely to be raised anywhere else if they aren't asked here, for example, in our own time, questions about how slavery emerged and spread, or questions about the natural differences of the sexes, and it is probably true that genuine inquisitiveness about such matters depends upon intellectual diversity and diversity of experience. But even when the questioning is radical, the answering is cautious, gathering evidence before jumping to conclusions, following arguments even when they lead in uncomfortable directions. As for the transmission of truth, I know of no professor who would not agree with Mill that teaching mere dogma or conclusions without reproducing the reasoning is not education in a true sense.

The Church is somewhat different, in some respects radically different. No one thinks everyone ought to go to college, even if colleges ought not to exclude anyone willing and able to learn. But many think everyone should go to church! Speaking now only of the traditions that have grown around a book that transmits what they believe to be the revealed word of God—Judaism, Christianity, and Islam—the Church might be said to be less concerned with the discovery of truth than with its preservation and transmission, though all consider the present implications of their ancient truths. All three of these traditions guard what they regard as treasures of witness and wisdom, and sometimes they carefully control what can be taught authoritatively within their precincts. American constitutional law protects their ability to do so as a matter of religious liberty, allowing them simultaneously to speak freely to those outside their walls and to limit the speech of those within. Sometimes these internal limits vary among their members. In the Catholic tradition, to which I belong, for example, dogma is taught generally in catechesis, classically in the old *Baltimore Catechism* where pupils were expected to memorize a series of questions and answers: Q. "What must we do to gain the happiness of heaven?" A. "To gain the happiness of heaven we must know, love, and serve God in this world"[29]—but for Catholics who are willing and able, there is Thomas Aquinas's *Summa Theologica*, where between the questions and the answers there are a number of objections proposing opposite conclusions that demand to be weighed and replied to on their own.[30] If Mill would despise the former as mere indoctrination, he ought to acknowledge the latter as requiring more rigorous thought and reflection than reading a carefully crafted rhetorical essay like his own.

I mentioned the press or the media as the third category of truth-seeking institutions, and by the beginning of the twenty-first century they had for the most part adopted Mill's arguments altogether, in all their ambiguity: on the one hand providing a platform for the vituperative, on the other enforcing Mill's "very simple principle" against moral judgment of how others live, unless they live judgmentally. Insofar as the media intend not merely to entertain or turn a profit but to enlighten, (and recognizing the constraints of time under which they operate,) one wishes they were a little better studied in the variety of partisan opinion to be aware of their own limitations and open to seeing the world through the eyes of others. The better journalists will do this, of course, but their editors need reminding: some, it seems, have been replaced by "producers," even in the print media, whose focus is on the product, not getting at the truth, while others have abandoned the quest for objectivity and openly or surreptitiously promote partisan narratives. I discovered at a conference in Arizona that I am not the only one willing to call into question the Supreme Court's 1964 decision in *New York Times v. Sullivan* that effectively eviscerated for public officials the law of libel—that previously forbad defamation of character unless the statement in question could be proven true, putting a burden on the press to insure the accuracy of its accusations—nor am I the only one who thinks the protections of libel law ought to be considered for postings on social media. I'll say a little more about this later; here my point is that the weakening of libel law might have made the press freer but also less credible. As for book publication, my fourth institution, the battle against state (and Church) censorship, first waged by Milton in his great pamphlet, *Areopagitica*,[31] has long been won, but pressure against publication even by university presses and academic journals has reappeared in recent years, out of fear of either Islamic terrorism or Leftist outcry, and editors have shown themselves variously courageous and supine.

Self-Government

The second argument in favor of free speech and so the second locus of consideration concerns republican self-government. James Madison's 1800 *Report on the [Virginia] Resolutions of 1798–99* provides a classic formulation of the republican speech argument in the context of denying the constitutionality of the Alien and Sedition Acts passed by Congress in 1798. While best known for developing the compact theory of the Constitution and the case for interposition by the states to prevent enforcement of federal laws deemed unconstitutional, Madison's *Report* addresses not only the question of Congress' constitutional power but also the legitimacy of the common law of seditious libel in a republic. While freedom of the press in English law was interpreted to mean simply "no prior restraint"—that is, no censorship before publication, but liability afterwards for wrongful publication—in the Republican governments of America, unlike monarchical government in England, freedom of the press must be read more expansively:

> The nature of governments elective, limited, and responsible, in all their branches, may well be supposed to require a greater freedom of animadversion, than might be tolerated by the genius of such a government as that of Great Britain. In the latter, it is a maxim, that the king—an hereditary, not a responsible magistrate—can do no wrong; and that the legislature, which, in two thirds of its composition, is also hereditary, not responsible, can do what it pleases. In the United States, the executive magistrates are not held to be infallible, nor the legislatures to be omnipotent; and both, being elective, are both responsible. Is it not natural and necessary, under such different circumstances, that a different degree of freedom in the use of the press should be contemplated?[32]

Moreover, Madison continues, in both England and the American states freedom of speech and press has been greater in practice than the doctrine of the common law requires: "In every state, probably, in the Union, the press has exerted a freedom in canvassing the merits and measures of public men, of every description, which has not been confined to the strict limits of the common law."[33] Since the *Zenger* case in colonial New York, Americans (in contrast to their British brethren) had accepted truth as a defense in libel cases; now Madison goes further, protecting "opinion, and inferences, and conjectural observations" in political debate, even when they could not meet courtroom standards of proof. "The right of freely examining public characters and measures, and of communication thereon, is the only effectual guardian of every other right," he writes.[34] Electoral politics depend upon such freedom; the sovereignty of the people can be exercised in no other way.

The need for open debate and free comment in public debate is so great in a democracy that it might seem to swallow up all the other concerns and justify First Amendment "absolutism." And to be sure the Supreme Court has considered it so in recent years, for example in *Snyder v. Phelps*, the 2011 Westboro Baptist case in which the Court protected the right to yell slogans denouncing the military, homosexuality, and Catholicism down the street from the funeral of a fallen soldier on the grounds that the protestors were engaging in public debate—over the dissent of Justice Samuel Alito who argued, quite sensibly in my opinion, that this "church" was engaged in verbal assault, not in civic discussion, the latter being perfectly available to them in many forms.[35] Parliamentary discussion requires rules of order, it has long been understood, and while there is always a danger that these will be imposed to suppress one side in a debate, the rules exist to insure both that minorities can get their say and that majorities can work their will. That said, I think it was a genuine advance to the cause of free speech for self-government when the so-called Fairness Doctrine was abolished, the requirement put in place by the Federal Communications Commission in 1949 and repealed in 1987 mandating that expressions of political opinion on controversial topics be balanced—a requirement that was right in principle (Who would admit to being against fairness?) but perverse in its effects, by delegating to the government the judgment of the range and balance of opinion, by consequently discouraging broadcasters from the expression of opinion, and by creating the presumption that the news itself was "fair and balanced" and immune to bias or partisan intent.[36]

Self-Expression

The argument that speech ought to be free for the sake of self-expression arose in the nineteenth century, and although the term was not used by Mill, "self-expression" might be taken as a synonym for his own word "individuality" seen from the point of view of free speech. Every action can be said to be expressive in some way or another, and Mill's socially rebellious or eccentric individuals might certainly use speech to give an account of how they live and what they do, without necessarily making a claim to have discovered some truth or offering a proposal for public debate. Of course, expressions of personal identity nowadays often have a political purpose, and I acknowledge that the three rationales are not mutually exclusive nor their places of exercise hermetically sealed. Still, self-expression seems by its nature to be the least institutionalized of the forms of speech I have discussed, or the least subject to institutionalization, unless one counts social media on the internet as an institution, for it is hard to imagine anyone gainsaying that speech on social media principally involves self-expression, however much politicking may ensue. While I may have seemed a bit sour when discussing individuality and self-expression, I will now add—though cannot here elaborate—that this is the engine driving our modern (or post-modern) economy, not to mention some of the energy that manifests in poetry, music, and art. The recognition that individuals can best judge their own good is the truth that underlies the explosive growth of modern society. The question is whether individuals are the only judge of what is truly good even for themselves and whether there is a truly common good as well, questions that command philosophical reflection and political choice—and thus require free speech for thought and deliberation, but do not presuppose it as an absolute right.

Although I have suggested certain limitations on speech as appropriate in the different settings I have discussed, limitations implicit in the principle of self-expression are probably the most extensive, at least potentially. If we follow Mill, the limit directly consequent would be against speech that harms other individuals, and the law clearly protects against certain forms of harmful speech: true threats, fraudulent speech in commercial transactions, libel, and slander (at least for private individuals and at least in the traditional press), and even certain insults (what were called "fighting words"). Obscenity used to be strictly limited by law, on account of the harm that it might cause to the weak-willed and to minors, but most of those limits have now been relaxed in the name of self-expression. Respect for privacy can be required by law, and violations of privacy punished, even if the violation involves only saying or publishing things that are true. Symbols and other visual and musical modes of communication are expressive, of course, even though they do not entail speech; so are actions, as I argued above, although to protect every action because it is also expressive would incapacitate law. Self-expression seems, of all the justifications for free speech, the most demanding—neither truth nor justice constitutes its natural limit, as for the other forms—but it is also the most readily limited, particularly if one adopts an expansive view of what is harmful or offensive. Most European countries have taken such an expansive view, enforcing laws against "hate speech"; American law thus far has taken a narrower view of harm and so a broader view of what can be said with impunity, at least with legal impunity, it being possible to criticize the expression of hatred thanks to the protection of free speech itself.[37] In fact, I think, most calls for the suppression of hate speech, though made in the name of preventing harm and justifiable when the target is a particular individual, in practice threaten to cripple the discovery of inconvenient truth or seek to remove an issue from public debate.

So was John Stuart Mill right about freedom of speech? No, I've argued, but then I must immediately concede that he would welcome my saying so, at least for the sake of fostering debate, lest free speech itself become dead dogma. The task is to determine, considering the various ends that freedom of speech can serve—and the goods it threatens—what rules ought to govern speech in the various circumstances of intellectual, political, and social life. This at least seems clear: No "very simple principle" can do that work.

NOTES

1. *New York Times v. Sullivan*, 376 U.S. 254 (1964), at 270.

2. Leo Strauss, *Persecution and the Art of Writing* (Chicago: University of Chicago Press, 1988 [1952]). Among Strauss's students who published on free speech are Harry Clor, *Obscenity and Public Morality: Censorship in a Liberal Society* (Chicago: University of Chicago Press, 1969); Francis Canavan, *Freedom of Expression: Purpose as Limit* (Durham, NC: Carolina Academic Press, 1984); David Lowenthal, *No Liberty for License: The Forgotten Logic of the First Amendment* (Dallas: Spence Publishing, 1997); and Walter Berns, "Beyond the (Garbage) Pale, or Democracy,

Censorship, and the Arts," in *In Defense of Liberal Democracy* (Chicago: Gateway Editions, 1984).

3. For a serious argument, see Jeremy Waldron, *The Harm in Hate Speech* (Cambridge, MA: Harvard University Press, 2012).

4. Keith Whittington, *Speak Freely: Why Universities Must Defend Free Speech* (Princeton, NJ: Princeton University Press, 2018). FIRE changed its name from Foundation for Individual Rights in Education in 2022. See https://www.thefire.org/about-us/mission/.

5. See Donald Alexander Downs, *Nazis in Skokie: Freedom, Community, and the First Amendment* (Notre Dame, IN: Notre Dame University Press, 1985). For a characteristic case, see *Snyder v. Phelps*, 562 U.S. 443 (2011). The internet cases are *Reno v. ACLU*, 521 U.S. 844 (1997) and *Ashcroft v. Free Speech Coalition*, 535 U.S. 234 (2002).

6. Nicholas Capaldi, *John Stuart Mill: A Biography* (Cambridge: Cambridge University Press, 2004).

7. See John Stuart Mill, *Socialism* (Chicago: Belford, Clarke, & Co., 1879); Helen McCabe, *John Stuart Mill: Socialist* (Montreal: McGill-Queen's University Press, 2021).

8. Nancy L. Rosenblum, *Another Liberalism: Romanticism and the Reconstruction of Liberal Thought* (Cambridge, MA: Harvard University Press, 1987).

9. John Stuart Mill, *On Liberty* (Indianapolis: Hackett Publishing Co., 1978 [1859]), 10.

10. Ibid., 54.

11. Ibid., 31.

12. Ibid., 32.

13. Ibid., 42.

14. Ibid., 43 ff.; 59.

15. Ibid., 49.

16. Ibid., 9.

17. Ibid., 54.

18. Ibid., 63–64.

19. Ibid., 79.

20. Ibid., 54.

21. Ibid., 21.

22. Ibid., 74.

23. Ibid., 76.

24. Willmoore Kendall, "The 'Open Society' and its Fallacies," *American Political Science Review* 54 (4) (Dec. 1960): 972–979.

25. Ibid., 973–976.

26. Ibid., 979. The quotations are from the same page.

27. Thomas Kuhn, *The Structure of Scientific Revolutions* (Chicago: University of Chicago Press, 1970 [1962]).

28. See my "Are Academic Freedom and Freedom of Speech Congruent or Opposed?" in Donald Alexander Downs and Chris W. Surprenant, eds., *The Value and*

Limits of Academic Speech: Philosophical, Political, and Legal Perspectives (New York: Routledge, 2018).

29. *Baltimore Catechism* [orig. 1885], lesson 1, q. 4, available at https://www.catholicity.com/baltimore-catechism/lesson01.html.

30. St. Thomas Aquinas, *Summa Theologica*, tr. Fathers of the English Dominican Province, 5 vols. (New York: Benziger Bros., 1948).

31. John Milton, *Areopagitica and Other Political Writings* (Indianapolis: Liberty Fund, 1999 [orig. 1644]).

32. James Madison, "Report on the Resolutions of 1798–99," in *Debates in the Several State Conventions*, vol. 4, ed. Jonathan Elliott, http://oll.libertyfund.org/titles/elliot-the-debates-in-the-several-state-conventions-vol-4, 570.

33. Ibid.

34. Ibid., 576.

35. *Snyder v. Phelps*, 562 U.S. 443 (2011).

36. See Ronald Reagan Presidential Library and Museum, "Fairness Doctrine," https://www.reaganlibrary.gov/archives/topic-guide/fairness-doctrine

37. See Timothy Garton Ash, *Free Speech: Ten Principles for a Connected World* (New Haven, CT: Yale University Press, 2016).

REFERENCES

Ash, Timothy Garton. *Free Speech: Ten Principles for a Connected World* (New Haven, CT: Yale University Press, 2016).

Ashcroft v. Free Speech Coalition, 535 U.S. 234 (2002).

Aquinas, St. Thomas. *Summa Theologica*, tr. Fathers of the English Dominican Province, 5 vols. (New York: Benziger Bros., 1948).

Baltimore Catechism [orig. 1885]. https://www.catholicity.com/baltimore-catechism/.

Berns, Walter. "Beyond the (Garbage) Pale, or Democracy, Censorship, and the Arts." In *In Defense of Liberal Democracy* (Chicago: Gateway Editions, 1984).

Canavan, Francis. *Freedom of Expression: Purpose as Limit* (Durham, NC: Carolina Academic Press, 1984).

Capaldi, Nicholas. *John Stuart Mill: A Biography* (Cambridge: Cambridge University Press, 2004).

Clor, Harry. *Obscenity and Public Morality: Censorship in a Liberal Society* (Chicago: University of Chicago Press, 1969).

Downs, Donald Alexander. *Nazis in Skokie: Freedom, Community, and the First Amendment* (Notre Dame, IN: Notre Dame University Press, 1985).

Kendall, Willmoore. "The 'Open Society' and its Fallacies," *American Political Science Review* 54 (4) (Dec. 1960): 972–979.

Kuhn, Thomas. *The Structure of Scientific Revolutions* (Chicago: University of Chicago Press, 1970 [1962]).

Lowenthal, David. *No Liberty for License: The Forgotten Logic of the First Amendment* (Dallas: Spence Publishing, 1997).

Madison, James. "Report on the Resolutions of 1798–99." In *Debates in the Several State Conventions*, vol. 4, ed. Jonathan Elliott, http://oll.libertyfund.org/titles/elliot-the-debates-in-the-several-state-conventions-vol-4

McCabe, Helen. *John Stuart Mill: Socialist* (Montreal: McGill-Queen's University Press, 2021).

Mill, John Stuart. *On Liberty* (Indianapolis: Hackett Publishing Co., 1978 [1859]).

Mill, John Stuart. *Socialism* (Chicago: Belford, Clarke, & Co., 1879).

Milton, John. *Areopagitica and Other Political Writings* (Indianapolis: Liberty Fund, 1999 [orig. 1644]).

Reno v. ACLU, 521 U.S. 844 (1997).

Ronald Reagan Presidential Library and Museum. "Fairness Doctrine." https://www.reaganlibrary.gov/archives/topic-guide/fairness-doctrine

Snyder v. Phelps, 562 U.S. 443 (2011).

Stoner, James. "Are Academic Freedom and Freedom of Speech Congruent or Opposed?" In Donald Alexander Downs and Chris W. Surprenant, eds., *The Value and Limits of Academic Speech: Philosophical, Political, and Legal Perspectives* (New York: Routledge, 2018).

Strauss, Leo. *Persecution and the Art of Writing* (Chicago: University of Chicago Press, 1988 [1952]).

Waldron, Jeremy. *The Harm in Hate Speech* (Cambridge, MA: Harvard University Press, 2012).

Whittington, Keith. *Speak Freely: Why Universities Must Defend Free Speech* (Princeton, NJ: Princeton University Press, 2018).

PART III

Free Inquiry on Campus

The Current Landscape

Chapter 9

The Age of Outrage

What the Current Political Climate Is Doing to Our Country and Our Universities

Jonathan Haidt

What is happening to our country, particularly in our universities? It sometimes seems that everything is coming apart. To understand why, I have found it helpful to think about an idea from cosmology called "the fine-tuned universe." There are around twenty fundamental constants in physics—things like the speed of light, Newton's gravitational constant, and the charge of an electron. In the weird world of cosmology, these are constants throughout our universe, but it is thought that some of them could be set to different values in other universes. As physicists have begun to understand our universe, they have noticed that many of these physical constants seem to be set just right to allow matter to condense and life to get started.

For a few of these constants, if they were just one or two percent higher or lower, matter would have never condensed after the big bang. There would have been no stars, no planets, no life. As Stephen Hawking put it, "the remarkable fact is that the values of these numbers seem to have been very finely adjusted to make possible the development of life."

Some have suggested that this fine-tuning might be evidence for the existence of God. This would be a deist conception of God, of the sort that Thomas Jefferson, James Madison, and most of the Founding Fathers believed in—a God who set up the universe like a giant clock, with exactly the right springs and gears, and then set it in motion. I myself am not taking fine-tuning as evidence of God. I'm simply using it to open this lecture. I want to lift your attention up into the cosmos and put you into a mindset that is awestruck at our improbability. And if I have succeeded in doing that, then I'd like you to take that same mindset and apply it to the existence of our improbable country.

I'd like you to consider an idea that I'll call "the fine-tuned liberal democracy." It begins by looking backward a few million generations and tracing our ancestry, from tree-dwelling apes to land-dwelling apes, to upright-walking apes, whose hands were freed up for tool use, to larger-brained hominids who made weapons as well as tools, and then finally to homo sapiens, who painted cave walls and painted their faces and danced around campfires and worshipped gods and murdered each other in large numbers.

When we look back at the ways our ancestors lived, there's no getting around it: we are tribal primates. We are exquisitely designed and adapted by evolution for life in small societies with intense, animistic religion and violent intergroup conflict over territory. We love tribal living so much that we invented sports, fraternities, street gangs, fan clubs, and tattoos. Tribalism is in our hearts and minds. We'll never stamp it out entirely, but we can minimize its effects because we are a behaviorally flexible species. We can live in many different ways, from egalitarian hunter-gatherer groups of fifty individuals to feudal hierarchies binding together millions. And in the last two centuries, a lot of us have lived in large, multi-ethnic secular liberal democracies. So clearly that is possible. But how much margin of error do we have in such societies?

Here is the fine-tuned liberal democracy hypothesis: as tribal primates, human beings are unsuited for life in large, diverse secular democracies, unless you get certain settings finely adjusted to make possible the development of stable political life. This seems to be what the Founding Fathers believed. Jefferson, Madison, and the rest of those eighteenth-century deists clearly did think that designing a constitution was like designing a giant clock, a clock that might run forever if they chose the right springs and gears.

Thankfully, our Founders were good psychologists. They knew that we are not angels; they knew that we are tribal creatures. As Madison wrote in Federalist *No. 10*: "the latent causes of faction are thus sown in the nature of man." Our Founders were also good historians; they were well aware of Plato's belief that democracy is the second worst form of government because it inevitably decays into tyranny. Madison wrote in Federalist *No. 10* about pure or direct democracies, which he said are quickly consumed by the passions of the majority: "Such democracies have ever been spectacles of turbulence and contention . . . and have, in general, been as short in their lives as they have been violent in their deaths."[1]

So what did the Founders do? They built in safeguards against runaway factionalism, such as the division of powers among the three branches, and an elaborate series of checks and balances. But they also knew that they had to train future generations of clock mechanics. They were creating a new kind of republic, which would demand far more maturity from its citizens than was needed in nations ruled by a king or other Leviathan.

Here is the education expert E. D. Hirsch, on the founding of our nation:

> The history of tribal and racial hatred is the history and prehistory of humankind. . . . The American experiment, which now seems so natural to us, is a thoroughly artificial device designed to counterbalance the natural impulses of group suspicions and hatreds. . . . This vast, artificial, trans-tribal construct is what our Founders aimed to achieve. And they understood that it can be achieved effectively only by intelligent schooling.[2]

Thomas Jefferson wrote, in 1789, that "wherever the people are well informed they can be trusted with their own government"; he backed up that claim by founding the University of Virginia, about which he wrote, in 1820: "This institution will be based on the illimitable freedom of the human mind. For here we are not afraid to follow the truth wherever it may lead, nor to tolerate any error as long as reason is left free to combat it."[3]

So, how are we doing, as the inheritors of the clock? Are we maintaining it well? If Madison visited Washington, D.C., today, he'd find that our government is divided into two all-consuming factions, which cut right down the middle of each of the three branches, uniting the three red half-branches against the three blue half-branches, with no branch serving the original function as he had envisioned.

And how are we doing at training clock mechanics? What would Jefferson say if he were to take a tour of America's most prestigious universities in 2017? What would he think about safe spaces, microaggressions, trigger warnings, bias response teams, and the climate of fearfulness, intimidation, and conflict that is now so prevalent on campus? But first, let's ask: How did we mess things up so badly?

I've been studying political polarization since 2007. Data from Gallup and Pew show steadily rising polarization since the 1990s, whether you ask people how much they dislike the other side, how much they think the other side is a threat to the country, or how upset they'd be if their child married someone from the other side.

Why do we hate and fear each other so much more than we used to as recently as the early 1990s? The political scientist Sam Abrams and I wrote an essay in 2015, listing ten causes.[4] I won't describe them all, but I'll give you a unifying idea, another metaphor from physics: keep your eye on the balance between centrifugal and centripetal forces. Imagine three kids making a human chain with their arms, and one kid has his free hand wrapped around a pole. The kids start running around in a circle, around the pole, faster and faster. The centrifugal force increases. That's the force pulling outward as the human centrifuge speeds up. But at the same time, the kids strengthen their grip. That's the centripetal force, pulling them inward along the chain of their arms. Eventually the centrifugal force exceeds the centripetal force, and then their hands slip. The chain breaks. This, I believe, is what is happening to our country. I'll briefly mention five of the trends that Abrams and I identified, all of which can be seen as increasing centrifugal forces or weakening centripetal forces.

> External enemies: Fighting and winning two world wars, followed by the Cold War, had an enormous unifying effect. The Vietnam War was different, but in general, war is the strongest known centripetal force. Since 1989, we have had no unifying common enemy.
>
> The media: Newspapers in the early days of the republic were partisan and often quite nasty. But with the advent of television in the mid-twentieth century, America experienced something unusual: the media was a gigantic centripetal force. Americans got much of their news from three television networks, which were regulated and required to show political balance. That couldn't last, and it began to change in the 1980s with the advent of cable TV and narrowcasting, followed by the Internet in the 1990s, and social media in the 2000s. Now we are drowning in outrage stories, very high-quality outrage stories, often supported by horrifying video clips. Social media is turning out to be a gigantic centrifugal force.
>
> Immigration and diversity: This one is complicated and politically fraught. Let me be clear that I think immigration and diversity are good things, overall. The economists seem to agree that immigration brings large economic benefits. The complete dominance of America in Nobel prizes, music, and the arts, and now the technology sector, would not have happened if we had not been open to immigrants. But as a social psychologist, I must point out that immigration and diversity have many sociological effects, some of which are negative. The main one is that they reduce social capital—the bonds of trust that exist between individuals. The political scientist Robert Putnam found this in a paper titled "E Pluribus Unum," in which he followed his data to a conclusion he clearly did not relish: "In the short run, immigration and ethnic diversity tend to reduce social solidarity and social capital. New evidence from the US suggests that in ethnically diverse neighborhoods residents of all races tend to 'hunker down.' Trust (even of one's own race) is lower, altruism and community cooperation rarer, friends fewer."[5]

In short, despite its other benefits, diversity is a centrifugal force, something the Founders were well aware of. In Federalist 2, John Jay wrote that we should count it as a blessing that America possessed "one united people;

a people descended from the same ancestors, speaking the same language, professing the same religion."[6] I repeat that diversity has many good effects too, and I am grateful that America took in my grandparents from Russia and Poland, and my wife's parents from Korea. But Putnam's findings make it clear that those who want more diversity should be even more attentive to strengthening centripetal forces.

The final two causes I will mention are likely to arouse the most disagreement, because these are the two where I blame specific parties, specific sides. They are: the Republicans in Washington, and the Left on campus. Both have strengthened the centrifugal forces that are now tearing us apart.

The more radical Republican Party: When the Democrats ran the House of Representatives for almost all of six decades, before 1995, they did not treat the Republican minority particularly well. So I can understand Newt Gingrich's desire for revenge when he took over as Speaker of the House in 1995. But many of the changes he made polarized the Congress, made bipartisan cooperation more difficult, and took us into a new era of outrage and conflict in Washington. One change stands out to me, speaking as a social psychologist: he changed the legislative calendar so that all business was done Tuesday through Thursday, and he encouraged his incoming freshmen not to move to the District. He did not want them to develop personal friendships with Democrats. He did not want their spouses to serve on the same charitable boards. But personal relationships among legislators and their families in Washington had long been a massive centripetal force. Gingrich deliberately weakened it.

And this all happened along with the rise of Fox News. Many political scientists have noted that Fox News and the right-wing media ecosystem influenced the Republican Party in a manner that is unlike anything that happened on the Left.[7] It rewards more extreme statements, more grandstanding, more outrage. Many people will point out that the media leans left overall, and that the Democrats did some polarizing things, too. Fair enough. But Gingrich set out to create a more partisan, zero-sum Congress, and he succeeded. This more combative culture then filtered up to the Senate, and out to the rest of the Republican Party.

The new identity politics of the Left: Jonathan Rauch offers a simple definition of identity politics: a "political mobilization organized around group characteristics such as race, gender, and sexuality, as opposed to party, ideology, or pecuniary interest." Rauch then adds: "In America, this sort of mobilization is not new, unusual, unAmerican, illegitimate, nefarious, or particularly leftwing."[8] This definition makes it easy for us to identify two kinds of identity politics: the good kind is that which, in the long run, is a centripetal force. The bad kind is that which, in the long run, is a centrifugal force.

Injustice is centrifugal. It destroys trust and causes righteous anger. Institutionalized racism bakes injustice into the system and plants the seeds of an eventual explosion. When slavery was written into the Constitution, it set us up for the greatest explosion of our history. It was a necessary explosion, but we didn't manage the healing process well in the Reconstruction era. When Jim Crow was written into Southern laws, it led to another period of necessary explosions, in the 1960s.

The civil rights struggle was indeed identity politics, but it was an effort to fix a mistake, to make us better and stronger as a nation. Martin Luther King's rhetoric made it clear that this was a campaign to create conditions that would allow national reconciliation. He drew on the moral resources of the American civil religion to activate our shared identity and values: "When the architects of our republic wrote the magnificent words of the Constitution and the Declaration of Independence, they were signing a promissory note." And: "I still have a dream. It is a dream deeply rooted in the American dream. I have a dream that one day this nation will rise up and live out the true meaning of its creed: 'We hold these truths to be self-evident, that all men are created equal.'"[9]

Of course, some people saw the civil rights movement as divisive, or centrifugal. But King's speech is among the most famous in American history precisely because it framed our greatest moral failing as an opportunity for centripetal redemption. This is what I'm calling the good kind of identity politics.

Let us contrast King's identity politics with the version taught in universities today. There is a new variant that has swept through the academy in the last five years. It is called intersectionality. The term and concept were presented in a 1989 essay by Kimberlé Crenshaw, a law professor at UCLA, who made the very reasonable point that a Black woman's experience in America is not captured by the summation of the Black experience and the female experience. She analyzed a legal case in which black women were victims of discrimination at General Motors, even when the company could show that it hired plenty of Blacks (in factory jobs dominated by men), and it hired plenty of women (in clerical jobs dominated by whites). So even though GM was found not guilty of discriminating against Blacks or women, it ended up hiring hardly any Black women. This is an excellent argument. What academic could oppose the claim that when analyzing a complex system, we must look at interaction effects, not just main effects?

But what happens when young people study intersectionality? In some majors, it's woven into many courses. Students memorize diagrams showing matrices of privilege and oppression. It's not just white privilege causing Black oppression, and male privilege causing female oppression; its heterosexual vs. LGBTQ, able-bodied vs. disabled; young vs. old, attractive vs. unattractive, even fertile vs. infertile. Anything that a group has that is good or valued is seen as a kind of privilege, which causes a kind of oppression in those who don't have it. A funny thing happens when you take young human beings, whose minds evolved for tribal warfare and us/them thinking, and you fill those minds full of binary dimensions. You tell them that one side of each binary is good and the other is bad. You turn on their ancient tribal circuits, preparing them for battle. Many students find it thrilling; it floods them with a sense of meaning and purpose.

And here's the strategically brilliant move made by intersectionality: all of the binary dimensions of oppression are said to be interlocking and overlapping. America is said to be one giant matrix of oppression, and its victims cannot fight their battles separately. They must all come together to fight their common enemy, the group that sits at the top of the pyramid of oppression: the straight, white, cisgendered, able-bodied Christian or Jewish or possibly atheist male. This is why a perceived slight against one victim group calls forth protest from all victim groups. This is why so many campus groups now align against Israel. Intersectionality is like NATO for social-justice activists.

This means that on any campus where intersectionality thrives, conflict will be eternal, because no campus can eliminate all offense, all microaggressions, and all misunderstandings. This is why the use of shout-downs, intimidation, and even violence in response to words and ideas is most common at our most progressive universities, in the most progressive regions of the country. It's schools such as Yale, Brown, and Middlebury in New England, and UC Berkeley, Evergreen, and Reed on the West Coast. Are those the places where oppression is worst, or are they the places where this new way of thinking is most widespread?

Let me remind you of the educational vision of the Founders, by way of E. D. Hirsch: "The American experiment . . . is a thoroughly artificial device designed to counterbalance the natural impulses of group suspicions and hatreds . . . This vast, artificial, trans-tribal construct is what our Founders aimed to achieve." Intersectionality aims for the exact opposite: an inflaming of tribal suspicions and hatreds, in order to stimulate anger and activism in students, in order to recruit them as fighters for the political mission of the professor. The identity politics taught on campus today is entirely different from that of Martin Luther King. It rejects America and American values. It does not speak of forgiveness or reconciliation. It is a massive centrifugal force, which is now seeping down into high schools, especially progressive private schools.

Today's identity politics has another interesting feature: it teaches students to think in a way antithetical to what a liberal arts education should do. When I was at Yale in the 1980s, I was given so many tools for understanding the world. By the time I graduated, I could think about things as a Utilitarian or a Kantian, as a Freudian or a behaviorist, as a computer scientist or a humanist. I was given many lenses to apply to any one situation. But nowadays, students who major in departments that prioritize social justice over the disinterested pursuit of truth are given just one lens—power—and told to apply it to all situations. Everything is about power. Every situation is to be analyzed in terms of the bad people acting to preserve their power and privilege over the good people. This is not an education. This is induction into a cult, a fundamentalist religion, a paranoid worldview that separates people from each other and sends them down the road to alienation, anxiety, and intellectual impotence.

Here is how one young queer activist described the cult. The essay is titled "'Everything is Problematic': My journey into the center of a dark political world, and how I escaped." The author identifies four features of the culture: dogmatism, groupthink, a crusader mentality, and anti-intellectualism. Of greatest relevance to our exploration of tribalism, he writes: "Thinking this way quickly divides the world into an ingroup and an outgroup—believers and heathens, the righteous and the wrong-teous. . . . Every minor heresy inches you further away from the group. When I was part of groups like this, everyone was on exactly the same page about a suspiciously large range of issues. Internal disagreement was rare."[10]

Can you imagine a culture that is more antithetical to the mission of a university? Can you believe that many universities offer dozens of courses that promote this way of thinking? Some are even requiring that all students take such a course.

Let us return to Jefferson's vision: "For here we are not afraid to follow the truth wherever it may lead, nor to tolerate any error as long as reason is left free to combat it." If Jefferson were to return today and tour our nation's top universities, he would be shocked at the culture of fear, the prevalence of unchallenged error, and the shackles placed on reason.

Now that I have thoroughly depressed you, let me end with a few rays of hope and some thoughts about what can be done. I began this lecture with a discussion of the fine-tuned liberal democracy, which is the hypothesis that human beings are unsuited for life in large diverse secular democracies, unless we can get certain settings finely adjusted. I think this hypothesis is true, and I have tried to show that we have stumbled into some very bad settings. I am pessimistic about our future but let me state clearly that I have low confidence in my pessimism. It has always been wrong to bet against America, and it is probably wrong to do so now. My libertarian friends constantly remind me that people are resourceful; when problems get more severe, people get more inventive, and that might be happening to us right now. If you want hope, you need only put this quotation up on your bathroom mirror: "We cannot absolutely prove that those are in error who tell us that society has reached a turning point, that we have seen our best days. But so said all before us, and with just as much apparent reason . . . On what principle is it that, when we see nothing but improvement behind us, we are to expect nothing but deterioration before us?"

That was written by the British historian Thomas Babington Macauley in 1830. It is probably still true today. And if you want more hope, let me tell you why I think things are going to start to improve on university campuses, beginning in the fall of 2018: because as things get worse on campus, more people are beginning to stand up, and more people are searching for solutions. Some college presidents are starting to stand up. They all know they are sitting on a powder keg, and they want to defuse it. Also, they are generally liberal scholars, deeply opposed to illiberalism. Carol Christ, the new chancellor of UC Berkeley, is clearly mortified by what happened to her school's reputation last spring, and she has taken a very strong and public stand, saying that UC Berkeley supports freedom of speech and will pay to protect speakers. Robert Zimmer, the president of the University of Chicago, has been consistently excellent. I have spoken with several other college presidents who would like to stand up publicly but still feel that the illiberal factions on their campuses are too strong. But if a few more presidents stand up, and if applications to schools like the University of Chicago surge this year, then I think we'll see the floodgates open, possibly next fall.

Professors are starting to stand up, too. At Heterodox Academy, we started with twenty-five members two years ago; now we have over 1,400, evenly balanced between left and right.[11] We got a big surge of members after the violence at Middlebury because that was a tipping point. Professors are overwhelmingly on the left, but they are mostly liberal Left, not illiberal. My field—social psychology—for example, is quite sane. I have been raising the alarm about political imbalance and orthodoxy since 2011, and so far, nothing bad has happened to me. I have not been ostracized. The problem on campus—the intense illiberalism—is concentrated in a few departments that are committed to political activism. When you look at who signs the petitions denouncing professors for what they've written, or demanding that journal articles be retracted, it is mostly professors from about seven departments in the humanities and identity studies. Few professors dared risk the ire of this illiberal Left back in 2015, but with each new witch hunt, each aggressive shout-down, more members of the liberal Left are willing to stand up and say: enough is enough. This is contrary to my values.

And most importantly, some students are beginning to stand up. At Reed College, one of the most politically orthodox schools in the country, social-justice activists had been protesting and disrupting the first-year humanities course for more than a year. They called the course an act of white supremacy because it focused on dead white authors. They said the course was traumatizing to nonwhite students. They brought their signs and chants into the classroom every day, making it hard for professors to teach or for students to learn. Many Reed students and professors objected, but none dared to do so publicly, lest they be called racist themselves. Finally, in the fall of 2017, several Asian students stood up, criticized the protesters, and asked them to stop interfering with their education.[12] Once these students stood up, support for the protesters collapsed. Many people had been going along out of fear, rather than conviction.

At Heterodox Academy, we're tracking these trends very closely, and we are putting out ideas and tools that help people stand up for viewpoint diversity and open inquiry. We created a guide to colleges to steer applicants toward the schools that offer more viewpoint diversity. We created an online survey that schools can use to assess the level of orthodoxy and fear on campus, or in any classroom. And most importantly, we've created the OpenMind app.[13] It's a self-guided app that teaches students about the value of viewpoint diversity and then trains them to engage with people who don't share their values. We have many more initiatives planned.

I also want to call your attention to someone else who is searching for a solution: Lenore Skenazy has been sounding the alarm about what happens to kids when we raise them like veal, protecting them from everything including emotional harm. Answer: they ask to be protected in college, too. They expect that college will be a giant safe space, and that there will always be a designated adult to resolve their conflicts. Lenore has so many ideas for how to restore childhood to children—to give them the unsupervised time they need to become autonomous, self-supervising adults. With seed money from Daniel Shuchman, she has started a nonprofit called LetGrow.org. I serve on the board, along with Peter Gray, from Boston College. One of the reasons LetGrow is so important, and the reason I mention it now, is that unsupervised free play turns out to be crucial for the development of democratic citizenship. I just want to read you a few sentences from one of Gray's articles on the importance of unsupervised free play:

> To play with another person, you must pay attention to the other person's needs, not just your own, or the other person will quit. You must overcome narcissism. You must learn to negotiate in ways that respect the other person's ideas, not just yours. [Gray goes on to describe the way that kids learn about rules, when adults are not present.] They learn in this way that rules are not fixed by heaven,

> but are human contrivances to make life more fun and fair. This is an important lesson; it is a cornerstone of democracy.[14]

So please do not despair. Be alarmed—the situation is truly alarming. But most Americans are decent, thoughtful people who don't want to give up on their country or its universities. There are many things we can do to reduce tribalism, strengthen our kids, and repair our universities. We—the baby boomers and gen-X-ers who fill this room—we have made a mess of the clock. Left and Right, Republicans and Democrats. But we can make up for it if we can come together, admit that we messed up, and change what we are doing to kids, and to college students. We just might be able to raise a generation of kids who can care for the clock after all.

NOTES

1. Alexander Hamilton, John Jay, and James Madison, *The Federalist*, ed. George W. Carey and James McClellan (Indianapolis: Liberty Fund, 2001 [1788]), 43, 46.

2. E. D. Hirsch, Jr., *The Making of Americans: Democracy and Our Schools* (New Haven, CT: Yale University Press, 2009), 85–86.

3. Thomas Jefferson to Richard Price, January 8, 1789, https://www.loc.gov/exhibits/jefferson/60.html; Thomas Jefferson to William Roscoe, December 27, 1820, https://www.loc.gov/exhibits/jefferson/75.html.

4. Jonathan Haidt and Sam Abrams, "The Top 10 Reasons American Politics Are So Broken," *The Washington Post*, January 7, 2015, https://www.washingtonpost.com/news/wonk/wp/2015/01/07/the-top-10-reasons-american-politics-are-worse-than-ever/

5. Robert D. Putnam, "*E Pluribus Unum*: Diversity and Community in the Twenty-First Century. The 2006 Johan Skytte Prize Lecture," *Scandinavian Political Studies* 30 (2) (June 2007): 137.

6. *The Federalist*, 6.

7. Jeffrey M. Berry and Sarah Sobieraj, *The Outrage Industry: Political Opinion Media and the New Incivility* (New York: Oxford University Press, 2014).

8. Jonathan Rauch, "Speaking as a . . . ," *The New York Review*, November 9, 2017, https://www.nybooks.com/articles/2017/11/09/mark-lilla-liberal-speaking/

9. Martin Luther King, Jr., The "I Have a Dream" Speech, https://www.usconstitution.net/dream.html; on civil religion, see Robert N. Bellah, "Civil Religion in America," *Daedalus: Journal of the American Academy of Arts and Sciences* 96 (1) (Winter 1966): 1–21.

10. Yarrow Eady, "'Everything is problematic': My journey into the centre of a dark political world, and how I escaped," *The McGill Daily*, November 24, 2014, https://www.mcgilldaily.com/2014/11/everything-problematic/

11. See https://heterodoxacademy.org.

12. Chris Bodenner, "The Surprising Revolt at the Most Liberal College in the Country," *The Atlantic*, November 2, 2017, https://www.theatlantic.com/education/archive/2017/11/the-surprising-revolt-at-reed/544682/

13. https://openmindplatform.org.

14. Peter Gray, "The Culture of Childhood: We've Almost Destroyed It," *Psychology Today*, October 31, 2016, https://www.psychologytoday.com/us/blog/freedom-learn/201610/the-culture-childhood-we-ve-almost-destroyed-it

REFERENCES

Bellah, Robert N. "Civil Religion in America." *Daedalus: Journal of the American Academy of Arts and Sciences* 96 (1) (Winter 1966): 1–21.

Berry, Jeffrey M., and Sarah Sobieraj. *The Outrage Industry: Political Opinion Media and the New Incivility* (New York: Oxford University Press, 2014).

Bodenner, Chris. "The Surprising Revolt at the Most Liberal College in the Country." *The Atlantic*, November 2, 2017. https://www.theatlantic.com/education/archive/2017/11/the-surprising-revolt-at-reed/544682/.

Eady, Yarrow. "'Everything is problematic': My journey into the centre of a dark political world, and how I escaped." *The McGill Daily*, November 24, 2014. https://www.mcgilldaily.com/2014/11/everything-problematic/

Gray, Peter. "The Culture of Childhood: We've Almost Destroyed It." *Psychology Today*, October 31, 2016. https://www.psychologytoday.com/us/blog/freedom-learn/201610/the-culture-childhood-we-ve-almost-destroyed-it.

Haidt, Jonathan, and Sam Abrams. "The Top 10 Reasons American Politics Are So Broken." *The Washington Post*, January 7, 2015. https://www.washingtonpost.com/news/wonk/wp/2015/01/07/the-top-10-reasons-american-politics-are-worse-than-ever/.

Hamilton, Alexander, John Jay, and James Madison, *The Federalist*, ed. George W. Carey and James McClellan (Indianapolis: Liberty Fund, 2001 [1788]).

Hirsch, E. D., Jr., *The Making of Americans: Democracy and Our Schools* (New Haven, CT: Yale University Press, 2009).

Jefferson, Thomas, to Richard Price. January 8, 1789. https://www.loc.gov/exhibits/jefferson/60.html.

Jefferson, Thomas, to William Roscoe, December 27, 1820, https://www.loc.gov/exhibits/jefferson/75.html.

King, Martin Luther, Jr. The "I Have a Dream" Speech, https://www.usconstitution.net/dream.html.

Putnam, Robert D. "*E Pluribus Unum*: Diversity and Community in the Twenty-First Century. The 2006 Johan Skytte Prize Lecture." *Scandinavian Political Studies* 30 (2) (June 2007): 137.

Rauch, Jonathan. "Speaking as a. . . . " *The New York Review*, November 9, 2017. https://www.nybooks.com/articles/2017/11/09/mark-lilla-liberal-speaking/.

Chapter 10

The Intellectual Suicide of American Universities

Causes and Remedies

Steven F. Hayward

I want to take an unorthodox approach to the problems of universities at the present time, and begin with my conclusion, which is that the School of Civic and Economic Thought and Leadership here at ASU is the most significant and promising innovation in higher education today. I say this not to flatter my hosts or their supporters, but to set a high bar for the line of reasoning that leads to this conclusion.

I have taken as the bold title for my remarks "The Intellectual Suicide of the University: Causes and Remedies," which on the surface may seem overwrought, since student enrollment in colleges and universities today is at or near an all-time high, and universities recently reported record fundraising numbers for the previous year. Beneath the surface, however, are signs that universities are, to use a favorite term from campuses today, far along the process of "marginalizing" themselves, or at least on a road to becoming something very different than they have been in our history.

In recent years campuses have been at a boil not seen since the 1960s, over issues of identity, safety and security, the acceptable limits of provocative speech, and ideological diversity. The discussion over these campus controversies has fallen into a familiar rut.

Most discussion centers around narrow issues of free speech versus "hate speech," and the meaning and practical implementation of "diversity and inclusion," but these dimensions only scratch the surface. The real causes of campus polarization and ideological isolation lie deeper and require fresh thinking and bold experimentation as a remedy—the kind of experimentation and innovation represented by the School of Civic and Economic Thought and Leadership at ASU.

The basic problem can be stated succinctly: universities ought to be the *best* institutions for thoughtful deliberation and vigorous debate about the most controversial matters facing our society today, yet they have become the very *worst* institutions for doing so, if not in fact the source for making our divisions more severe. Critics—and not just critics on the right—have attributed most of the blame for this on a newly emboldened ideological extremism of the campus left—what we used to call merely "political correctness."

There is much to this explanation, but it is not complete or sufficient or understood as clearly as it ought. Universities have always been liberal, and often deeply left in some of their leading precincts. Conservative complaints about the leftward character of universities go back at least to the 1930s. What is new and different about the present moment?

I think there are several deeper factors that are not widely perceived. There are three parts of this story that I want to knit together in a new way. First, it should be acknowledged that the fundamental claims emanating from the radical left departments of gender studies, ethnic studies, African American studies, and cultural studies are *correct*. More on this point presently. The fanatical and obscurantist ways these grievances are often expressed and enforced are the result of the second underappreciated factor, the role of group polarization in intellectual life, whose effects are arguably more severe on campus than the polarization in our general political life that is such a big topic these days. It is surprising to me how little this phenomenon is recognized. Third and perhaps least appreciated, the ever-increasing specialization of academic inquiry, especially in large research universities, has degraded the intellectual capabilities of especially the humanities and social sciences to conduct sensible debate and discussion of our most divisive political and social issues. This, too, requires some explanation.

You can see all three of these factors come together in the—to me—astonishing new doubts about the nature and status of free speech, whether on campus or at Google—which, it may not be a coincidence, refers to its headquarters as a "campus."

Let me explain each of these three factors in order, and then knit them together in a manner that will I hope help demonstrate why the SCETL here is such an important initiative.

First, with the exception of truly vile racists like Richard Spencer, is there anyone who disagrees with the basic claim that women and minorities have experienced massive injustice and discrimination in American history, and still do today in many ways? It is eminently reasonable to suggest that progress to date is insufficient, but from the dominant campus discourse today, however, you'd think things have never been worse for women and minorities, especially when you read the various Inspector Javert-like hunts for micro- and nano-aggressions with respect to racism and sexism, inspired by highly specious and impenetrable postmodern doctrines and some rather dodgy social science.

Perhaps a helpful clue about to how to sort this out is found in the understanding of heresy by the medieval scholastics. Heresy for those thinkers of the Middle Ages was not a complete falsehood or untruth—rather, it was a part of the truth blown up to exaggerated or misleading proportions. Or perhaps another way of conceiving the problem is to apply Gresham's Law—"bad money drives out good"—to academia: extremist scholarship has driven out a sensible treatment of social controversies that would feature a robust debate. Instead, we have ended up with highly ideological approaches that explain everything in terms of pervasive, systemic, structural oppression, and condemn any dissent from orthodoxy in the most highly charged and morally censorious ways.

Coleman Hughes, as a second-year student at Columbia University, wrote a powerful article observing this problem in action:

> As a second-year undergrad student at Columbia University, I've noticed that two of my courses this semester differ greatly. One is a generic introductory philosophy course, in which we read classic papers in the philosophy of mind, identity, and morality. The second philosophy course mainly covered feminist epistemology and queer theory, in which we learn the core principles of intersectional feminism, queer theory, and feminist epistemology.
>
> Leaving aside what is taught, the courses differ greatly in how they're taught. In the generic intro course, we'll read some philosopher—say, Thomas Nagel—and learn his arguments well enough to repeat them, and then spend much of the class exposing any weaknesses that Nagel's argument might have. We don't hold anyone's views as sacred, or even special. We debate with one another; I even argue with the professor at times. The prevailing mood encourages friendly but lively debate. It's challenging, good-natured, and fun.
>
> Every Monday and Wednesday I leave my generic introductory course and go straight to the second where the mood is strikingly different. We read some philosopher—say, Foucault—and learn his arguments, but rarely does a single person even ask a question, to say nothing of making a critique. On the exceedingly rare occasion that a student asks a question that could potentially contradict what's being taught, the professor has a mysterious way of answering without ever suggesting that the argument could simply have a weakness.
>
> Of the seven philosophy courses I've taken at Columbia so far, not a single one has operated even close to this way—philosophy professors are always the first to point out logical weaknesses, strong counterarguments, and alternative points of view, even when they fundamentally agree with the course material. In this class, I got the sense that the professor was wedded to the material, such that a critique of the material would have been synonymous with a critique of

> her. As hyperbolic as this might sound, voicing a strong pushback against any idea that the Professor favored was nearly unthinkable.[1]

By the way, young Mr. Hughes is African American, so I hope there will be no nonsense about his "white privilege," though I suppose he still must bear the handicap of being male. One more excerpt:

> The professor once said that all students of color are victims of oppression (I'm Black and I view myself in no such way, but I didn't dare say so in the moment because I felt a silent pressure not to be a nuisance).[2]

There's much more extraordinary and frankly scandalous detail in his complete article, but this is enough to illustrate my point that this is the recipe for the intellectual suicide of universities. Although one out of seven philosophy courses in Hughes's experience may not sound imbalanced overall, there are reasons to think the radical conformist perspectives are steadily gaining ground over nonpoliticized courses. It is difficult to quantify this tend statistically, but a recent account of anthropologist Joseph Manson reaching the decision to resign his tenured position at UCLA draws widespread nods of recognition in many departments today:

> Gradually, one hire at a time, practitioners of "critical" (i.e. far-left postmodernist) anthropology, some of them lying about their beliefs during job interviews, came to comprise the department's most influential clique. These militant faculty recruited even more extremely militant graduate students to work with them.[3]

How did we come to this pass, which, as I suggest, goes beyond the historic left-leaning disposition of universities observable for several decades now? I think the explanation is surprisingly simple and is best explained by one of the most formidable thinkers of the center-left today, Cass Sunstein of Harvard Law School. Some years back, Prof. Sunstein wrote a long paper entitled "The Law of Group Polarization," where he went beyond the usual literature of "groupthink" to explore how homogenous groups of people will become more extreme the more they deliberate together, and paradoxically degrade deliberation.[4] Sunstein was prompted to write this paper because he was surprised at how little studied this phenomenon is. I quote him here: "Members of a deliberating group move toward a more extreme point in whatever direction is indicated by the members' pre-deliberation strategy."[5] In other words, it is not at all surprising that a homogeneous group of academics concerned with the problems of racism should, deliberating in isolation, become more extreme in their outlook, finally offering sweeping categorical generalizations that explain everything.

One of the implications, Sunstein went on to argue, is that "social homogeneity can be quite damaging to good deliberation. When people are hearing echoes of their own voices, the consequence may be far more than support and reinforcement. . . . [P]articular forms of homogeneity can be breeding grounds . . . for unjustified extremism, even fanaticism."[6] This leads, he goes on, to "social cascades. . . . The serious risk with social cascades . . . is that they can lead to widespread errors, factual or otherwise."[7] Sunstein quotes other social scientists who warn that "'the social process is polluted' by the '*dominance of conformity*.'"[8] Swap out "academic process" and "academic homogeneity" for "social process" and "social homogeneity," and I think you have an accurate description of the causes of the campus climate today.

But I think we need to add one more dimension to this line of analysis. If you go back to the 1960s when the first demands were made to set up Black studies programs or departments (and later women's studies, ethnic studies, etc.), there was vigorous debate in faculty meetings and curriculum committees about whether such new initiatives should be included inside existing departments—that is, Black studies in history, sociology, political science, anthropology, education, and so forth—or whether they should be autonomous, standalone departments operating just like all other traditional topical disciplines.

There were strongly put arguments for either scheme of organization. What we got in practice was—both. Today we find a lot of faculties with joint appointments in traditional departments along with primary appointments in gender studies, African American studies, and so forth. Hence in most departments of political science, history, English, anthropology, psychology, philosophy, sociology, and (most curious of all) geography, you will find several professors who describe their main focus as the holy trinity of "race, class and gender" and its close correlates—"post-colonialist" perspectives, or post-modern or "post-structural" analysis." (Or if the "holy trinity" simile seems infelicitous, you could go with the four horsemen of the leftist apocalypse instead: patriarchy, colonialism, "privilege," and Israel.)

Now—here's the little secret of the social sciences and humanities unknown off campus. Most of the faculty—including the most liberal members of the faculty—do not take seriously their radical colleagues in the various "studies" departments, and regard them with benign neglect. One reason for this is easy to grasp: the typical academic liberal sympathizes with the basic historical grievances of the academic left about racism and sexism as suggested before, and thus doesn't have a fundamental objection to the enthusiasm, and in many cases acts from sincere goodwill toward what we label "marginalized groups." But there's a second factor at work: there's no upside to resisting these trends, and there are a lot of downsides. Risk-averse administrators whose default position is to appease the latest mob outrage or demand offer little encouragement to any faculty members who might wish to resist. Thus, administrators and faculty embody Churchill's famous description of an appeaser as someone who "feeds a crocodile, hoping it will eat him last."

The example of Mark Lilla at Columbia University is an excellent case in point. Immediately after the 2016 election, Lilla published an op-ed article in the *New York Times* criticizing "identity politics" and the role he thinks it played in the election of Donald Trump, whom Lilla, as a liberal of long-standing and partisan Democrat, by his own profession, abhors.[9] This prompted Katherine Franke, a law professor at Columbia, to attack Lilla as a "white supremacist":

> In the new political climate we now inhabit, Duke and Lilla were contributing to the same ideological project, the former cloaked in a KKK hood, the latter in an academic gown. Both men are underwriting the whitening of American nationalism, and the re-centering of white lives as lives that matter most in the U.S. Duke is happy to own the white supremacy of his statements, while Lilla's op-ed does the more nefarious background work of making white supremacy respectable. Again.[10]

I suspect that most professors of the race-class-gender post-modernist catechism can sense that many of their colleagues don't take them seriously or regard them with benign neglect, which further fuels their rightcous indignation, self-imposed sense of "oppression," and mob mentality.

I'll mention two further examples of this in action. Several years ago, a student group occupied the President's office at Dartmouth College, demanding that a "queer studies" course be required of all students in *every* department. Physics? Chemistry? Biology? Seriously? As usual the administration earnestly proclaimed that they would take up the proposal, appoint a committee to review the matter, put it under advisement, and all of the other predictable platitudes. And then nothing was ever heard about it again—because the idea is so clearly absurd that even a college president can grasp it. Meanwhile, at a recent annual meeting of the American Economic Association, several panels were disrupted by protestors condemning the discipline for not including the perspectives of race, class, and gender, followed by the usual demands that such perspectives be made mandatory in economics curricula.

For an ideology that marks out "colonialism" as a pre-eminent sin of Western racism and oppression, it is ironic that the forces of leftist conformity do not perceive their own academic imperialism. It is not content to reside contentedly in the various "studies" fields but demands to be incorporated in every other department.

It is often suggested today that the dearth of conservative or non-liberal faculty in our universities is a leading cause of the recent descent into extreme campus conformism. This is a view that increasingly finds favor, incidentally, with some liberal college presidents, most notably Michael Roth of Wesleyan University, who has openly said this, despite his own very Left-liberal political views. I've had several people pass along to me accounts of other presidents of prominent universities who privately think the same thing but are unwilling to say so publicly. To be sure, we have good data on how the number of conservative faculty in the humanities and social sciences has declined precipitously over the last twenty-five years or so, and the reasons for this are contested. But I don't think this is the most salient factor in recent campus trends. I think a much larger and unappreciated factor is the dynamic of the modern research university, which I think has also affected the old, smaller liberal arts colleges.

Along with the decline in the number of conservative professors, it is worth taking note of another secular decline in higher education—namely, the sharp decline in the number of students majoring in the humanities or social sciences. The number of students majoring in the humanities and social sciences (excluding economics) has fallen by about two-thirds over the last generation. The old departments have been able to maintain themselves or grow somewhat because of the larger student body enrolled today, but make no mistake, they are in relative decline at many universities. The leading explanation for this trend is thought to be the high cost of college today along with a practical orientation to get a job after graduation—hence the durability of economics among the social sciences. But I don't think that's the deepest reason.

Having harshly criticized the politicized "studies" departments in universities, let me say one more thing in their favor, as a means of explaining succinctly what the meaning of this is. Why are so many students drawn to the radicalized "studies" departments? I think the answer is simple: such programs raise the problem of justice and injustice in a direct and straightforward way, while other social sciences no longer do so, or do so very poorly. However tendentious may be the accounts of injustice, however inadequate may be the proposed remedies, at least the various "studies" departments speak to a longing in the soul of the young to engage the moral problems of justice and injustice in our world. By contrast, the political science or sociology departments offer mostly—regression models. The relative sterility of the old-line social sciences and the dead-end historicism of the humanities is not lost on most students.

I could say much more about this aspect of the social sciences and humanities today, and the tussles about methodology are not new, even within the disciplines themselves. I'm trying to raise a broader point: the modern research university tends toward ever-increasing specialization, and emphasizes the discovery of new knowledge above teaching. The emphasis on new knowledge is entirely appropriate for a large research university, but it comes at a high cost.

Cast your mind back for a moment to 1943, when Harvard produced the report on "General Education in a Free Society," better known as its "Redbook." The Redbook was aiming ironically at the needs of the expected increase in diversity of the postwar student body, but also at the assimilation of immigrants—something you probably can't say on college campuses without provoking a riot. In other words, the Redbook was written with an eye toward a problem that is being talked about again today—the need for serious general civic education.

Harvard's then president, James Bryant Conant, was not entirely happy with the recommendations of the Redbook, because he presciently thought that the specialists of an elite research university would not be very good at general education. Indeed, he mused that universities like Harvard perhaps ought to maintain an entirely separate teaching faculty for general education.[11] I think he was on to something, and Harvard's general education program withered by degrees before being abandoned in the 1970s, partly because its elite, specialized research faculty didn't want to teach general education courses—say, the old freshman survey course on Western civilization—and probably weren't any good at it when they did. If you look closely, you will see that most universities today that claim to have a core curriculum have a smorgasbord of specialty courses indistinguishable from upper division courses in their departments.

There are still a few leading universities that emphasize the old general education philosophy very well, such as Columbia (though its core curriculum has become controversial with guess who among its faculty), and Yale, which still offers its Directed Studies program as an option for students. It used to be until fairly recently that a student who desired an old-fashioned liberal arts bachelor's degree would choose a small liberal arts college, but the competitive pressures and conventions of academia today have caused most professors in smaller liberal arts colleges to follow the path of narrower specialization as practiced in large research universities.

Add to the research emphasis on always breaking new ground in a field, and teaching the latest perspectives to students, the dismissal of older modes of understanding, simply because they are old—to us. The point is: what we call the "old perspectives," and old methods aren't old to the next generation of students.

This is the deeper intellectual and structural background of the free speech controversies today. Let me then summarize the precarious state of free speech.

First, the older liberal understanding of the centrality of free speech, and the consequent reverence for the First Amendment, is no longer universally accepted. It is common to hear many students say that the First Amendment is "obsolete."

The attack on free speech comes in two forms, which I label as postmodern metaphysics, and empirical social science liberalism. They are contradictory on one level, but together they form a classic pincer movement.

The metaphysical attack is that free speech is just a cover or tool for oppression by the powerful. This critique is not new. It is at least as old as Herbert Marcuse but has found new dimensions with the various philosophical and linguistic critiques of language itself, often traced back to Foucault, Derrida, or some other challenging French or German thinker. It finds unique manifestation in different disciplines, such as "critical legal studies" in law.[12] This line of argument rejects the modern liberal tradition *in toto* and has no room or respect for John Stuart Mill or Oliver Wendell Holmes.

More recently an empirical case has emerged that does not challenge any of the foundations of liberalism regarding speech; rather, it accepts it wholly, and argues that "hate speech" satisfies liberalism's limiting principle of physical harm to others. As Lisa Feldman Barrett, a psychologist at Northwestern University, argued in the *New York Times*:

> Words can have a powerful effect on your nervous system. Certain types of adversity, even those involving no physical contact, can make you sick, alter your brain—even kill neurons—and shorten your life . . . The scientific findings I described above provide empirical guidance for which kinds of controversial speech should and shouldn't be acceptable on campus and in civil society.[13]

In other words, the old playground lyric from our childhood—"sticks and stones may break my bones but your words will never harm me"—is wrong, and certain kinds of speech acts can be as physically harmful to someone as a blow to the body.

Even if we accept at face value the methodology and findings of this kind of social science, it ought to raise a lot of questions about whether attempts to pre-empt psychological harm from speech are any more sensible than trying to prevent crime by assigning every individual her own personal security force. Lots of things cause stress and anxiety. Is the presence of Milo Yiannapoulos on campus more stressful for a student than a mid-term exam or a term-paper deadline?

An analogy to the problem of childhood asthma might be relevant here. One of the medical mysteries of our time is why childhood asthma rates have been rising over the last few decades while conventional air pollution has been falling rapidly. One hypothesis is that to the extent asthma is partly an autoimmune disease, the latest generation of children, raised indoors with too much time on video games and computers (or so the cliché goes), does not spend enough time playing outdoors exposed to pathogens that make the immune system more robust.[14] This view is highly controversial among health researchers and environmental scientists, as should be the hypothesis that speech acts constitute physical harm equivalent to a hammer blow. But attempts to shield students from the harms from disagreeable speech surely risks an equivalent harm—the cultivation of an "intellectual auto-immune" response.

And what are the implications of saying that "marginalized groups" need to receive heightened protection against speech acts? Does this not tacitly if unwittingly ratify the very premise of racial supremacists?

I've only just scratched the surface here, and some of the defects outlined might at first glance suggests wholesale remedies that are simply not going to happen because the impulses behind them are so deeply embedded in our colleges now, and not just in academic departments, but increasingly in the administrative offices of universities. Just have a close look at the recent shameful episode involving Lindsay Shepherd at Laurier University in Canada for an entirely typical example.[15] Ms. Shepherd, a graduate student and teaching assistant, became the subject of international attention when the public release of her surreptitious recording of her upbraiding by the administration for the act of showing five minutes of Jordan Peterson in class proved so shocking that the university profusely apologized for her treatment. That such an encounter could not survive public scrutiny shows how out of balance the campus climate has become. One wonders how many apologies universities might have to issue if all such meetings were on the public record.

But it is idle to think that universities will do much to change their intellectual climate without some compelling forces brought to bear. It should be understood that universities are in one sense deeply reactionary institutions. University of California's legendary president Clark Kerr once observed that "few institutions are so conservative as the universities about their own affairs while their members are so liberal about the affairs of others."[16]

In thinking about remedies, it is worth thinking back to another historical analogy. Universities today can be compared to the cartels and trusts of old, especially regarding the cost of college today, which has increased at a higher rate than health care for the last thirty-five years. But I think the better comparison is to the monopolies of old, which gouged consumers and stifled competition. And one of the defects of monopolies and cartels is that they suppress innovation and lead to industry stagnation. I assert that the humanities are largely stagnating these days; the social sciences are a more mixed bag.

I think we're already seeing the beginnings of a *de facto* divorce of universities, in which the STEM fields and other "practical" disciplines essentially split off from the humanities and social sciences, not to mention the more politicized departments. One early sign—perhaps a canary in the university coal mine—can be seen in the recent announcement of the University of Wisconsin Stevens Point campus that it is shuttering thirteen departments in the humanities and social sciences, and laying off tenured faculty, on account of declining enrollment and budget pressures, and reallocating funds to STEM subjects.[17] Another sign are the economics departments that have begun subdividing themselves into "general economics" and an even more math-centric "quantitative econometrics." Several economics departments are formally reclassifying themselves as STEM departments (there are federal guidelines for this) for a variety of reasons, but among them must be wishing to disassociate themselves further from other social sciences.

Instead of insisting on unrealistic reform or transformation of individual academic departments or the mode of academic inquiry, let's try old-fashioned competition. Not just competition of ideas, but methodological competition, and interdisciplinary courses of study done right. And that is exactly what SCETL represents—competition. I hope more and more universities will follow this model. Right now, about the only comparable full-scale program like it is the Thomas Jefferson Center for the Study of Core Texts at the University of Texas at Austin. That program is extremely popular with students—its course offerings are always heavily oversubscribed—as I expect SCETL will become here.

NOTES

1. Coleman Hughes, "A Tale of Two Columbia Classes," *Heterodox Academy*, January 29, 2018, https://heterodoxacademy.org/a-tale-of-two-columbia-classes.
2. Ibid.
3. Joseph H. Manson, "Why I Am Leaving the University," Josephamanson.com, July 4, 2022, https://josephhmanson.com/2022/07/04/why-im-leaving-the-university /.
4. Cass Sunstein, "The Law of Group Polarization," University of Chicago Law School, John M. Olin Law & Economics Working Paper No. 91 (1999): 1–37, https: //ssrn.com/abstract=199668. A revised version of this paper was published under the same title in *Journal of Political Philosophy* 10 (2002): pp. 175–195.
5. Ibid., 3–4 (emphasis removed).
6. Ibid., 4.
7. Ibid., 9.
8. Ibid., 8 (emphasis added).

9. Mark Lilla, "The End of Identity Liberalism," *New York Times*, November 18, 2016, https://www.nytimes.com/2016/11/20/opinion/sunday/the-end-of-identity-liberalism.html.

10. Katherine Franke, "Making White Supremacy Respectable Again," *Los Angeles Review of Books*, November 21, 2016, http://blog.lareviewofbooks.org/essays/making-white-supremacy-respectable.

11. See Louis Menand, *The Marketplace of Ideas: Reform and Resistance in the American University* (New York: Norton, 2010), pp. 37–43.

12. See, in particular, Richard Epstein, "Linguistic Relativism and the Decline of the Rule of Law," *Harvard Journal of Law and Public Policy* 39, no. 3 (2016): 583–630, http://www.harvard-jlpp.com/wp-content/uploads/2010/01/39_3_Epstein_F.pdf. See also Daniel A. Farber and Suzanna Sherry, *Beyond All Reason: The Radical Assault on Truth in American Law* (New York: Oxford University Press, 1997).

13. See Lisa Feldman Barrett, "When Is Speech Violence?," *New York Times*, July 14, 2017, https://www.nytimes.com/2017/07/14/opinion/sunday/when-is-speech-violence.html.

14. See, e.g., John A. Bukowski and R. Jeffrey Lewis, "Is the Hygiene Hypothesis an Example of Hormesis?" *Nonlinearity in Biology, Toxicology, Medicine* 1 (2003): 155–166; David Gems and Linda Partridge, "Stress-Response Hormesis and Aging: 'That Which Does Not Kill Us Makes Us Stronger,'" *Cell Metabolism* 7 (2008): 200–203.

15. Raffi Grinberg, "Lindsay Shepherd and the Potential for Heterodoxy at Wilfrid Laurier University," *Heterodox Academy*, November 23, 2017, https://heterodoxacademy.org/lindsay-shepherd-and-the-potential-for-heterodoxy-at-wilfrid-laurier-university.

16. Clark Kerr, *The Uses of the University* (Cambridge, MA: Harvard University Press, 1963), 99.

17. Colleen Flaherty, "U Wisconsin-Stevens Point to Eliminate 13 Majors," *Inside Higher Ed*, March 6, 2018, https://www.insidehighered.com/quicktakes/2018/03/06/u-wisconsin-stevens-point-eliminate-13-majors.

REFERENCES

Barrett, Lisa Feldman. "When Is Speech Violence?" *New York Times*, July 14, 2017. https://www.nytimes.com/2017/07/14/opinion/sunday/when-is-speech-violence.html.

John A. Bukowski and R. Jeffrey Lewis, "Is the Hygiene Hypothesis an Example of Hormesis?" *Nonlinearity in Biology, Toxicology, Medicine* 1 (2003): 155–166.

Epstein, Richard. "Linguistic Relativism and the Decline of the Rule of Law." *Harvard Journal of Law and Public Policy* 39, no. 3 (2016): 583–630.

Farber, Daniel A., and Suzanna Sherry. *Beyond All Reason: The Radical Assault on Truth in American Law* (New York: Oxford University Press, 1997).

Flaherty, Colleen. "U Wisconsin-Stevens Point to Eliminate 13 Majors." *Inside Higher Ed*, March 6, 2018. https://www.insidehighered.com/quicktakes/2018/03/06/u-wisconsin-stevens-point-eliminate-13-majors.

Franke, Katherine. "Making White Supremacy Respectable Again." *Los Angeles Review of Books*, November 21, 2016. http://blog.lareviewofbooks.org/essays/making-white-supremacy-respectable.

Gems, David, and Linda Partridge. "Stress-Response Hormesis and Aging: 'That Which Does Not Kill Us Makes Us Stronger.'" *Cell Metabolism* 7 (2008): 200–203.

Grinberg, Raffi. "Lindsay Shepherd and the Potential for Heterodoxy at Wilfrid Laurier University." *Heterodox Academy*, November 23, 2017. https://heterodoxacademy.org/lindsay-shepherd-and-the-potential-for-heterodoxy-at-wilfrid-laurier-university.

Hughes, Coleman. "A Tale of Two Columbia Classes." *Heterodox Academy*, January 29, 2018. https://heterodoxacademy.org/a-tale-of-two-columbia-classes.

Kerr, Clark. *The Uses of the University* (Cambridge, MA: Harvard University Press, 1963).

Lilla, Mark. "The End of Identity Liberalism." *New York Times*, November 18, 2016. https://www.nytimes.com/2016/11/20/opinion/sunday/the-end-of-identity-liberalism.html.

Manson, Joseph H. "Why I Am Leaving the University." Josephamanson.com, July 4, 2022. https://josephhmanson.com/2022/07/04/why-im-leaving-the-university/.

Menand, Louis. *The Marketplace of Ideas: Reform and Resistance in the American University* (New York: Norton, 2010).

Sunstein, Cass. "The Law of Group Polarization." University of Chicago Law School, John M. Olin Law & Economics Working Paper No. 91 (1999): 1–37. https://ssrn.com/abstract=199668.

Chapter 11

The High Price of Political Homogeneity

Joshua M. Dunn

THE POLITICS OF THE PROFESSORIATE

Only the innumerate would deny that the academy is an overwhelmingly left-leaning institution and that its viewpoint homogeneity is increasing. According to the Higher Education Research Institute at UCLA, liberal professors outnumber conservatives five to one.[1] This ideological imbalance has grown over the past three decades. In 1989, 42 percent of professors identified as liberal or far left.[2] In 2014, 59 percent identified as liberal or far left. Over the same period, the percentage identifying as moderate declined from 40 to 27 percent and the percentage identifying as conservative and far right declined from eighteen to thirteen percent.

The lack of intellectual diversity is most acute in the social sciences and humanities, fields where politics is often central to the discipline. A 2006 survey by Neil Gross and Solon Simmons found that nearly eighteen percent of social scientists identified as Marxists while only 5 percent identified as conservative. In sociology, over 25 percent identify as Marxist.[3] Similarly, a 2016 study of five disciplines at forty universities by Mitchell Langbert, Anthony Quain, and Daniel Klein found significant imbalances in voter registration among faculty. Of the professors they identified, 3,623 were registered Democratic and 314 Republican for an overall Democrat to Republican ratio of 11.5 to 1. In the five disciplines they studied, the Democrat to Republican Ratios were: Economics 4.5 to 1, History 33.5 to 1, Journalism/Communications 20.0 to 1, Law 8.6 to 1, and Psychology 17.4 to 1.[4] They also found that younger faculty tended to be more Democratic indicating that the ratios are likely to increase in the future. An analysis of the political attitudes of social psychologists by Jonathan Haidt found that out of the sample of 327 only one had views that were right of center on social issues.[5]

The two primary explanations for this imbalance are self-selection and discrimination. Neil Gross and Ethan Fosse have argued that liberals have long found the academy to be a more attractive career option than conservatives, which has led being a professor to be seen as a liberal or left-wing occupation. Just as some fields become "typed" based on gender, some fields can be typed based on political identity.[6] Others have found significant evidence of discrimination against conservatives. In *Compromising Scholarship*, George Yancey surveyed professors in multiple disciplines and asked them if they would be inclined to hire job candidates based on their membership in different groups. He found that half would be less likely to hire someone if they knew they were a conservative Protestant.[7] Thirty percent of sociologists reported that they would be less likely to hire someone if they knew they were a Republican. A 2012 study by Yoel Inbar and Joris Lammers found a similar willingness to discriminate among social psychologists.[8] Thirty-eight percent said they would discriminate against conservatives and the most liberal respondents were the most willing to discriminate. Ironically, the most liberal respondents were also the most likely to report that conservatives did not face a hostile environment in the discipline. Yoel Inbar later expressed surprise at these findings since "usually you have to be pretty tricky to get people to say they'd discriminate against minorities."[9] Willingness to discriminate then might actually be much higher.

Considering their minority status and the willingness of many faculty to discriminate against them, it is not surprising that many conservatives often feel the need to hide their politics from their colleagues. In *Passing on the Right: Conservative Professors in the Progressive University*, Jon Shields and I found that of the 153 conservative faculty we interviewed, one-third hid their politics from their colleagues and nearly half engaged in some form of political self-censorship. If economics, the most ideologically diverse discipline in the social sciences, is excluded, half of the faculty hid their politics.[10] This means that the effective representation of conservatives is even lower since so many refuse to broadcast their politics and challenge the left-wing consensus.

While this imbalance is obvious, it is not obvious that it matters. Is there any reason to be concerned about the political monoculture of the academy? Many on the left would say that this is just the natural order of affairs. Conservatives might be fit for other kinds of occupations like business or the military, but nothing is really lost if they are underrepresented in the university. UCLA historian Russell Jacoby, for instance, declared that the mission of the university is not compromised if it is "overrun by liberals."[11] This sanguine interpretation, however, is difficult to reconcile with the two-core purposes of the university, teaching, and research. And even if one is not persuaded on that count, ideological homogeneity nevertheless creates political threats that the academy, out of its own self-interest, should find worrisome.

TEACHING

Teaching is at the heart of the university. Transmitting knowledge to new generations of students is its core mission. One of the primary conservative critiques of the academy is that this mission is corrupted by left-wing faculty determined to indoctrinate students and turn them into progressive foot soldiers. Thus, knowledge is not transmitted so much as politically curated and force-fed to a captive student population. This concern is either false or incomplete. One does not need to look far to find stories of attempted political indoctrination in the classroom. Websites like the College Fix and Campus Reform have successful business models largely built on exposing campus indoctrination. Instead, this critique is false or incomplete in that there is very little evidence that these attempts at indoctrination work. The evidence that we do have indicates that classes designed to promote an ideological end either have no effect or increase the attitudes that professors are trying to purge from their charges.[12] Thus, these classes might be a massive waste of educational resources that could be devoted to real subjects, but they do not seem to actually change political attitudes. Peer groups have a far more robust effect on student attitudes than professors so when looking for villains, conservatives would be better advised to train their sights on offices of student life and residence life where students are often selected for leadership based on their ideological fitness.

Instead, viewpoint homogeneity should primarily be seen as a lost opportunity. Universities should be the one place in American society where deliberative virtues such as civility, toleration, critical engagement, and mutual respect are modeled. However, it is difficult to do that when there are so few people of different political persuasions around. In the past few years, the university has experienced many embarrassing displays of outrage and even violence by petulant students who, apparently having not escaped the pre-operational stage of development, cannot fathom the fact that people they disagree with should be allowed to speak on campus. Perhaps, if there were more political diversity among the faculty, students might have learned that it is possible to coexist with those with whom you disagree. Or if that is asking too much, they might have learned that if there is a guest speaker who holds views so loathsome that you do not even want to hear them that there is an easy solution. Don't go.

These outbursts point to the second danger of campus echo-chambers. Students are not exposed to the necessary range of ideas to be prepared to live in a politically pluralistic society. There can, of course, be interesting debates between factions on the left, but the broader American society is not a microcosm of those on the left and the farther left. Somewhere between a third and half of all Americans would fall on the right. Thus, while debates between the left and the far left can be valuable on campus, they are not particularly useful for teaching students and the broader community how to engage with others beyond the university's walls. Whether progressive faculty like it or not, students will one day have to leave the university and actually grapple with conservative ideas. But today it is quite possible to receive an education, and an elite one at that, and never be exposed to major intellectual figures from the right like Edmund Burke, Friedrich von Hayek, Alexis de Tocqueville, and Milton Friedman.

Consider Jonathan Haidt, one of today's most preeminent social psychologists. In *The Righteous Mind*, he describes how he came across a copy of Jerry Muller's *Conservatism: An Anthology of Conservative Thought* in a used bookstore. At the time he was already a tenured professor at the University of Virginia. Haidt was puzzled by the title because "As a life-long liberal, I had always assumed that conservatism = orthodoxy = religion = faith = rejection of science." Intrigued by a title that implied that there was such a thing as conservative thought, he says, "I started reading Muller's introduction while standing in the aisle but by the third page I had to sit down on the floor." He was, he says, "quite literally floored" by discovering that "there was a kind of conservatism that could compete against liberalism in the court of social science." While Haidt did not become a conservative, he did begin to appreciate the power of conservative ideas saying, "I began to see that they had attained a crucial insight into the sociology of morality that I had *never* encountered before."[13] If Jonathan Haidt, who attended and has taught at some of our nation's most elite institutions, could make it into his forties without ever confronting conservative ideas then it must not be uncommon for undergraduates to spend four or more years blissfully oblivious that there are more than liberal ideas that they should be exposed to.

There is another important lesson to be learned from Haidt's example. Ask, for instance, if this could ever happen in reverse. Could one imagine a conservative, tenured professor in the social sciences at a major research university stumbling across an anthology of progressive thought or socialist thought in a used bookstore and being floored by what she reads? Of course not. Outside of a few religious schools, to make your way through the university means swimming in a leftist current. You might try to swim against that current, but if you are a conservative there is no doubt that you know that it exists and where it is trying to take you. Thought of this way, liberal students are done the greatest disservice by political homogeneity since they are seldom exposed to ideas that they disagree with while conservative students are constantly forced to defend their ideas and sharpen their ideas.

RESEARCH

Political homogeneity also compromises the research mission of the university. It does so both by limiting the questions that we ask and undermining our ability to eliminate error. Political biases inevitably shape what we find important and when vast swaths of researchers share the same biases, important questions go unasked. And even when researchers in the political minority find them important, they often refrain from asking them, fearing political reprisals from their colleagues. As one conservative sociologist put it, "To say a strong conservative political opinion with conviction in an academic gathering is analogous to uttering an obscenity." Heterodox researchers also don't want to appear out of step with disciplinary norms. Rather than risk political discrimination, they simply want to check the right boxes necessary for professional advancement in their field.

Think of the effects of same-sex parenting on children. After the Supreme Court's 2015 decision in *Obergefell v. Hodges* creating a constitutional right to same-sex marriage this has become an even more important subject for social scientists to study. But after the attacks on the University of Texas sociologist Mark Regnerus for his 2012 study on same-sex parenting, the probability of someone even gathering data on the subject is remote, perhaps even approaching zero. Previous studies on same-sex parenting had all relied on convenience samples making them unrepresentative and unreliable. Regnerus, however, gathered data from a random cross-section of young adults. He found that children who had a parent involved in a same-sex romantic relationship were more likely to have used drugs, have been sexually abused, and have trouble with the law among other negative outcomes.[14] Regnerus acknowledged that the reason for these outcomes was uncertain but was probably related to family instability and that his study could thus support the case for gay marriage. Distinguished scholars such as Paul Amato, the chair of the family section of the American Sociological Association, praised Regnerus's study saying it was "better situated than virtually all previous studies to detect differences between these [different family] groups in the population."[15] But that was not enough to placate the academic mob. Sociologists stampeded to denounce his study as bigoted and flawed. He was even subjected to a research misconduct investigation by the University of Texas, which confiscated all of his computers and sequestered forty-two thousand of his emails. Regnerus was fully exonerated by the investigators, but the process, as the saying goes, was the punishment. Who would be willing to expose themselves to the vitriol and professional attacks after witnessing what Regnerus endured? Today, it would be unwise for anyone to even gather data on the subject. Thus, the effects of this massive social change are likely to remain uninvestigated lest they produce politically inconvenient facts and confirm Regnerus's findings. The political echo chamber of the academy is consigning us to ignorance.

Or consider whether conservatives themselves are unfit for academic life. It takes little effort to find scholars who have argued that conservativism is incompatible with reasoned discourse and inquiry. Conservatives suffer from regrettable cognitive defects and subsist in the dark swamps of rigidity and parochialism. Liberals, in contrast, scamper gaily in the sunny uplands of cosmopolitanism and creativity. As the law school professor Michael Vitiello declared, "The fact that conservatives are more dogmatic, intolerant of ambiguity, rigid and close-minded, than are liberals, may explain why fewer of them are hired than their more open-minded, flexible colleagues."[16] It turns out that this self-flattering armchair psychological analysis is wrong. Recent research by a small but persistent group of psychologists has found that liberals are just as intolerant as conservatives on subjects that liberals care deeply about.[17]

Or consider the longstanding position of many liberal scholars that religious belief and, even worse, religious movements are incompatible with deliberative democracy. Deeply held faith makes believers unable to participate in the give-and-take required by liberal democracy. Surely there was no better example of this than the pro-life movement bristling with moralizing zealotry. But when Jon Shields actually studied evangelical activists he found that, "The vast majority of Christian-right leaders have long labored to inculcate deliberative norms in their rank-and-file activists—especially the practice of civility and respect; the cultivation of dialogue by listening and asking questions; the rejection of appeals to theology; and the practice of careful moral reasoning."[18] Peter Steinfels joked that his book's title, *The Democratic Virtues of the Christian Right*, was for liberals "akin to 'The Winning Ways of Serial Killers.'"[19]

These examples also point to the problem of confirmation bias, our tendency to accept findings and theories that are consistent with our preexisting beliefs. Francis Bacon gave one of the best descriptions of this phenomenon: "The human understanding when it has once adopted an opinion (either as being the received opinion or as being agreeable to itself) draws all things else to support and agree with it. And though there be a greater number and weight of instances to be found on the other side, yet these it either neglects and despises, or else by some distinction sets aside and rejects, in order that by this great and pernicious predetermination the authority of its former conclusions may remain inviolate."[20] Or as the psychologists Phillip Tetlock and Gregory Mitchel succinctly explained, "biased information processing is deeply wired into human nature."[21] For scholarship bearing on political and social topics this means that weaknesses in arguments supporting favored orthodoxies are less likely to be challenged when political minorities are scarce. When that happens, beliefs ossify into dead, academic dogma. Intellectual diversity, therefore, is necessary for rooting out error.

Once again, we have no shortage of examples of insular academic communities perpetuating not only false ideas but also deeply destructive ones. In 1965, Daniel Patrick Moynihan published his report, *The Negro Family: The Case for National Action*, which raised the alarm about rising illegitimacy and female-headed families. What was happening to the Black family would soon be happening to the white family as well, and, he predicted, it would be disastrous for both. The result was condemnation from the left for "blaming the victim." Afterward elite academic opinion consolidated around the idea that the nuclear family was overrated, and that family disruption was not that harmful and even came with compensating benefits such as enlarged kinship networks. James Patterson, in his history of the Moynihan report, said that, "by the late 1970s widespread rejection by liberal scholars of *The Negro Family* had not only perpetuated the great silence that Moynihan had lamented in the late 1960s, it had also hardened into an orthodoxy that virtually excused lower-class Black people from much if any responsibility for their difficulties."[22] This ethos was still evident in 1992 when Dan Quayle gave his infamous "Murphy Brown" speech lamenting the celebration of single-parenting on one the nation's most popular sitcoms. Quayle was excoriated by the left for his archaic, backward moralizing. But at the same time Quayle was being ridiculed, a small group of social scientists was compiling evidence that Moynihan was right all along. Scholars such as Sara McLanahan at Princeton were accumulating mountains of data showing that the feel-good consensus of the 1970s and '80s was false. Eventually, sociology accepted the evidence and, in fact, accepted it so much that sociologists started enlisting it in the cause of gay marriage. But it took decades and countless damaged lives for the discipline to accept it. As one sociologist put it, "Basically, sociology had to be dragged kicking and screaming until it recognized that broken families aren't . . . good things. It's like, if you have to spend decades and millions of dollars in [National Science Foundation] grants to convince astronomers that the sun rises in the east."[23]

Scholars have also connected the problem of confirmation bias to the reproducibility crisis in social science. One of the basic characteristics of scientific studies is that they are replicable by other scientists. Several leading social psychologists have argued that the embarrassing high-profile replication failures are related to its ideological isolation.[24] Perhaps one of the most glaring contemporary examples is the research on "implicit bias." According to implicit bias researchers, tests such as the Implicit Association Test (IAT), the most used of several similar measures, can identify deep unconscious prejudice. It purports to explain why racial disparities still exist even though overt racism has declined, and affirmative action programs have been established to eliminate unequal outcomes. The test allegedly works by showing test subjects a series of Black and white faces on a screen and asks them to sort them by race (other tests do the same thing with other characteristics like weight or sex) with the "i" and "e" keys on the keyboard. Then the subjects must sort words positive words and negative words using the same keys. Then the sorting process is mixed and reversed. The assumption is that the longer someone takes to associate a Black face with a good key, the more implicitly racist they are and the more they unconsciously perpetuate racism and sexism. Like the original sin, it turns out that no matter how righteous we think we are, we are all plagued by the stain of implicit bias.

There are two basic problems with the IAT and similar tests: they are unreliable and invalid. A measure is reliable if upon retesting a subject gets a similar score. But for the IAT individual scores vary wildly, far more than what is statistically acceptable. In other words, the IAT cannot replicate itself even with individual subjects. It turns out that the test is invalid as well. A test is valid if it measures the thing it purports to measure. In the case of the IAT it should measure racism. However, studies of the IAT show that it has almost no predictive power of discriminatory behavior.[25] According to the philosopher of science, Edouard Machery, the IAT is "just the most recent episode" in a "sad history of irrational exuberance followed by disappointment" of attitude measurement by psychologists. He offered this summary of its value:

> we've learned that people aren't really unaware of whatever it is that the IAT measures. So, whatever it is that the IAT measures isn't really unconscious. And we've learned that the IAT predicts very little proportion of variance. In particular, only a tiny proportion of biased behavior correlates with IAT scores. We have also learned that your IAT score today will be quite different from your IAT score tomorrow. And it is now clear that there is precious little, perhaps *no*, evidence that whatever it is that the IAT measures causes biased behavior. So, we have a measure of attitude that is not reliable, does not predict behavior well, may not measure anything causally relevant, and does not give us access to the unconscious causes of human behavior. It would be irresponsible to put much stock in it and to build theoretical castles on such quicksand.[26]

Despite these fatal problems, the test has been dogmatically accepted as scripture in vast swathes of the academy and has comfortably burrowed its way into general discussion on all the -isms that continue to plague us. One can hardly attend a faculty meeting without hearing about how we are all corrupted with implicit bias and that the university needs to do more expunge it from ourselves and our students. Universities routinely hold implicit bias retreats for faculty staff and bring speakers to raise awareness about our unconscious biases.[27] The University of Virginia has even mandated that all students receive instruction on implicit bias during their first year.[28] Given that the IAT is now an article of faith on campus, skeptics are afraid to point out that it is nothing more than pseudo-science. When a philosophy graduate student alerted Brian Leiter, an avowedly left-wing philosopher and IAT skeptic at the University of Chicago, to yet another debunking of the test, he asked not to be identified telling Leiter "Folks in my department take this stuff as gospel, so I'd rather not be targeted as a skeptic." Leiter took it as evidence of the "totalitarian environment in some departments."[29]

POLITICS AND POLICY

Even if faculty and administrators are not concerned about the danger that a political monoculture creates for the teaching and research missions of the university they should nevertheless be concerned out of a baser motivation: self-interest. Universities, it turns out, are soft budgetary targets made even softer by their political homogeneity. Publicly accountable policymakers are less likely to financially support the university when it is perceived as implacably hostile to roughly half the electorate. State institutions are particularly vulnerable to political backlash—just ask the faculty at the University of Wisconsin. Or think of the 2017 Republican tax plan which levied a 1.4 percent tax on university endowments worth at least $500,000 per student. This affects only a small number of schools but now the precedent has been set it would not be surprising to see Republicans come back for more. In fact, the original plan proposed taxing graduate student tuition waivers as income and eliminating the tax deduction for interest on student loans.

Politicians don't even have to level divisive charges of liberal bias against the hardest and farthest of the left-leaning scholars—those in the social sciences and humanities. They just have to charge these fields with being "impractical" or a "poor investment." For instance, Rick Scott, the Republican Governor of Florida called for cutting funding for the humanities and social sciences and putting it into STEM fields. "If I'm going to take money from a citizen to put into education," Scott said, "I want that money to go to degrees where people can get jobs in this state. Is it a vital interest of the state to have more anthropologists? I don't think so."[30] But naturally as trendy left-wing subjects have proliferated on campus, the university has only invited more criticism. Classes such as "The Problem of Whiteness" or "Food and Identity: Decolonizing our Food and Body" also double as invitations to cut university budgets. Public universities might very well believe that such classes are essential, but there is nothing that obligates the public to agree.

The political isolation of the academy also undermines the ability of scholarship to influence policy debates. It does so in two ways. First, when asked to weigh in on political and policy debates, it is tempting for academics to abuse their authority by speaking with certainty on questions that are, in fact, much in dispute. And second, when scholars primarily advocate for progressive positions, they risk being seen as ideologues masquerading as scholars. Policymakers will cast a jaundiced eye toward their claims of expertise and authority. Thus, if scholars believe they are producing research that should inform policy decisions, they should be concerned about how being in an overwhelmingly left-leaning institution marginalizes their scholarship.

CONCLUSION

If ideological homogeneity is a problem, there is unfortunately no straightforward or single solution. The most obvious one—instituting affirmative action for conservative scholars—would not work, since conservatives themselves find the idea offensive. In fact, the only supporters of the idea appear to be progressive scholars, like Jonathan Zimmerman, who think the logic of diversity applies as much to ideological diversity as it does to racial and gender diversity.

But there are a few simple things that can be done that at least would make a marginal difference. At a minimum, universities should stop censoring and disinviting conservative speakers. What could indicate epistemic closure more than excluding conservative opinions from your campus? Also, schools should consider creating more program like the School of Economic Thought and Leadership at Arizona State University. This program has already dramatically expanded the range of voices heard at ASU just through the speaker series which led to this volume.

Faculty members committed to intellectual diversity should also consider supporting organizations like the Heterodox Academy (HxA), to which I belong. HxA is a group of professors from across the political spectrum who came together in 2015 to enhance viewpoint diversity on campus. The hope is that signaling a desire to create a politically tolerant and pluralistic academic environment among faculty will help generate greater intellectual diversity and show that sharp but civil disagreement is possible—and necessary—on campus.

NOTES

1. Kevin Eagan et al., *Undergraduate Teaching Faculty: The 2013–14 HERI Faculty Survey* (Los Angeles: Higher Education Research Institute, 2014), 39. https://www.heri.ucla.edu/monographs/HERI-FAC2014-monograph.pdf

2. Alexander W. Astin et al., *The American College Teacher: National Norms for the 1989–90 HERI Faculty Survey* (Los Angeles: Higher Education Research Institute, 1990), 44. https://www.heri.ucla.edu/PDFs/pubs/FAC/Norms/Monographs/The AmericanCollegeTeacher1989To1990.pdf

3. Neil Gross and Solon Simmons, "The Social and Political Views of American Professors," Working Paper (2007): 41.

4. Mitchell Langbert et al., "Faculty Voter Registration in Economics, History, Journalism, Law, and Psychology," *Econ Journal Watch* 13 (3) (2016): 422–51.

5. Jonathan Haidt, "New Study Indicates Existence of Eight Conservative Social Psychologists," *Heterodox Academy*, January 7, 2016. https://heterodoxacademy.org/new-study-finds-conservative-social-psychologists/

6. Ethan Fosse and Neil Gross, "Why Are Professors Liberal?," *Theory and Society* 41, no. 2, (2012): 127–168.

7. George Yancey, *Compromising Scholarship: Religious and Political Bias in American Higher Education* (Waco, TX: Baylor University Press, 2011).

8. Yoel Inbar and Joris Lammers, "Political Diversity in Social and Personality Psychology," *Perspectives on Psychological Science* 7 (2012): 496–503.

9. Emily Esfahani Smith, "Survey Shocker," *Washington Times*, August 1, 2012.

10. Jon A. Shields and Joshua M. Dunn Sr., *Passing on the Right: Conservative Professors in the Progressive University* (New York: Oxford UP, 2016).

11. Russell Jacoby, "Academe is Overrun by Liberals. So What? *Chronicle of Higher Education*, April 6, 2016. https://www.chronicle.com/article/Academe-Is-Overrun-by/235898.

12. See for example, Jim Sedanius et al., *The Diversity Challenge: Social Identity and Intergroup Relations on the College Campus* (New York: Russell Sage Foundation, 2010), 323; and Lisa Legault, Jennifer N. Gutshell, and Michael Inzlicht, "Ironic Effects of Antiprejudice Messages: How Motivational Interventions Can Reduce (but Also Increase) Prejudice," *Psychological Science* 22 (2012): 1472–1477; and Stanley Rothman, April Kelly-Woessner, and Matthew Woessner, *The Still Divided Academy: How Competing Visions of Power, Politics, and Diversity Complicate the Mission of Higher Education* (Lanham, MD: Roman and Littlefied, 2011), 74–78. Also see Robert Whaples, "Changes in Attitudes Among College Economics Students About the Fairness of the Market," *Journal of Economic Education*, 26 (1995): 308–313.

13. Jonathan Haidt, *The Righteous Mind: Why Good People are Divided by Politics and*

Religion (New York: Pantheon Books, 2012), 288–294.

14. Mark Regnerus, "How Different Are the Adult Children of Parents Who Have Same-Sex Relationships: Findings from the New Family Structures Study," *Social Science Research* 41 (2012): 752–770.

15. Belinda Luscombe, "Do Children of Same-Sex Parents Really Fare Worse?," *Time*, July 11, 2012, available at http://healthland.time.com/2012/06/11/do-children-of-same-sex-parents-really-fare-worse/.

16. Michael Vitiello, "Liberal Bias in the Legal Academy: Overstated and Undervalued," *Mississippi Law Journal* 77 (2007): 541–542.

17. See for example, Geoffrey Weatherall et. al., "Discrimination Across the Ideological Divide: The Role of Value Violations and Abstract Values in Discrimination by Liberals and Conservatives," *Social Psychological and Personality Science* 4 (2013): 658–667; and Mark Brandt et al., "The Ideological-Conflict Hypothesis Intolerance Among Both Liberals and Conservatives," *Current Directions in Psychological Science* 23 (2014): 27–34.

18. Jon Shields, *The Democratic Virtues of the Christian Right* (Princeton: Princeton University Press, 2009), 2.

19. Peter Steinfels, "A Provocative Work About the Christian Right," *New York Times*, April 24, 2009. https://www.nytimes.com/2009/04/25/us/25beliefs.html.

20. Francis Bacon, *Novum Organum* (1620), Translated by James Spedding et al.: XLVI.

21. Phillip E. Tetlock and Gregory Mitchell, "Why So Few Conservatives and Should

We Care?," *Society* 52 (2015): 28–34.

22. James T. Patterson, *Freedom is Not Enough: The Moynihan Report and America's Struggle over Black Family Life from LBJ to Obama* (New York: Basic Books, 2010), 47–86, 129–165.

23. Shields and Dunn, *Passing on the Right*, 180.

24. Jose Duarte et. al., "Political Diversity Will Improve Social Psychological Science," *Behavioral and Brain Sciences*, *38*, E130. doi:10.1017/S0140525X14000430. https://www.cambridge.org/core/services/aop-cambridge-core/content/view/A54AD4878AED1AFC8BA6AF54A890149F/S0140525X14000430a.pdf/political_diversity_will_improve_social_psychological_science_1.pdf

25. See Olivia Goldhill, "(Un)Conscious Impact: The World is Relying on a Flawed Psychological Test to Fight Racism," *Quartz*, December 3, 2017, https://qz.com/1144504/the-world-is-relying-on-a-flawed-psychological-test-to-fight-racism/

26. Edouard Machery, "Should We Throw the IAT on the Scrap Heap of Indirect Measures?," *The Brains Blog*, January 17, 2017 http://philosophyofbrains.com/2017/01/17/how-can-we-measure-implicit-bias-a-brains-blog-roundtable.aspx. For a more comprehensive critique see Machery's "Anomalies in implicit attitudes research," *Wiley Interdisciplinary Reviews: Cognitive Science* 13, no. 1 (2022): e1569. https://doi.org/10.1002/wcs.1569.

27. http://newsroom.lmu.edu/2016/10/21/president-snyder-and-dean-waterstone-host-implicit-bias-retreats-for-faculty-and-staff/ and https://www.albany.edu/news/82883.php and https://news.wsu.edu/2018/04/06/national-expert-georgina-dodge-speak-implicit-bias-impact-leadership/

28. http://www.cavalierdaily.com/article/2017/10/implicit-bias-module-now-required-of-all-first-year-students.

29. Brian Leiter, "So it turns out implicit bias as measured by the Implicit Association Test (IAT) does not predict discriminatory behavior," *Leiter Reports: A Philosophy Blog*, January 9, 2017, http://leiterreports.typepad.com/blog/2017/01/so-it-turns-out-implicit-bias-as-measured-does-not-predict-behavior.html

30. Scott Jaschik, "Florida GOP vs. Social Science," *Inside Higher Ed*, October 12, 2011, available at www.insidehighered.com/news/2011/10/12/florida_governor_challenges_idea_of_non_stem_degrees#sthash.Kzp6BnIW.dpbs.

REFERENCES

Astin, Alexander W., et al. *The American College Teacher: National Norms for the 1989–90 HERI Faculty Survey* (Los Angeles: Higher Education Research Institute, 1990). https://www.heri.ucla.edu/PDFs/pubs/FAC/Norms/Monographs/TheAmericanCollegeTeacher1989To1990.pdf.

Bacon, Francis. *Novum Organum* (1620). Translated by James Spedding et. al.: XLVI.

Brandt, Mark, et al. "The Ideological-Conflict Hypothesis Intolerance Among Both Liberals and Conservatives." *Current Directions in Psychological Science* 23 (2014): 27–34.

Duarte, Jose, et al. "Political Diversity Will Improve Social Psychological Science." *Behavioral and Brain Sciences* 38, E130. doi:10.1017/S0140525X14000430. https://www.cambridge.org/core/services/aop-cambridge-core/content/view/A54AD4878AED1AFC8BA6AF54A890149F/S0140525X14000430a.pdf/political_diversity_will_improve_social_psychological_science_1.pdf.

Eagan, Kevin, et al. *Undergraduate Teaching Faculty: The 2013–14 HERI Faculty Survey* (Los Angeles: Higher Education Research Institute, 2014). https://www.heri.ucla.edu/monographs/HERI-FAC2014-monograph.pdf.

Fosse, Ethan, and Neil Gross. "Why Are Professors Liberal?" *Theory and Society* 41, no. 2 (2012): 127–168.

Goldhill, Olivia. "(Un)Conscious Impact: The World is Relying on a Flawed Psychological Test to Fight Racism." *Quartz*, December 3, 2017. https://qz.com/1144504/the-world-is-relying-on-a-flawed-psychological-test-to-fight-racism/.

Gross, Neil, and Solon Simmons, "The Social and Political Views of American Professors." Working Paper (2007).

Haidt, Jonathan. "New Study Indicates Existence of Eight Conservative Social Psychologists." *Heterodox Academy*, January 7, 2016. https://heterodoxacademy.org/new-study-finds-conservative-social-psychologists/.

Haidt, Jonathan. *The Righteous Mind: Why Good People are Divided by Politics and Religion* (New York: Pantheon Books, 2012).

Inbar, Yoel, and Joris Lammers. "Political Diversity in Social and Personality Psychology." *Perspectives on Psychological Science* 7 (2012): 496–503.

Jacoby, Russell. "Academe is Overrun by Liberals. So What? *Chronicle of Higher Education*, April 6, 2016. https://www.chronicle.com/article/Academe-Is-Overrun-by/235898.

Jaschik, Scott. "Florida GOP vs. Social Science." *Inside Higher Ed*, October 12, 2011. www.insidehighered.com/news/2011/10/12/florida_governor_challenges_idea_of_non_stem_degrees#sthash.Kzp6BnIW.dpbs.

Langbert, Mitchell, et. al. "Faculty Voter Registration in Economics, History, Journalism, Law, and Psychology." *Econ Journal Watch* 13, no. 3 (2016): 422–451.

Legault, Lisa, Jennifer N. Gutshell, and Michael Inzlicht. "Ironic Effects of Antiprejudice Messages: How Motivational Interventions Can Reduce (but Also Increase) Prejudice." *Psychological Science* 22 (2012): 1472–1477.

Leiter, Brian. *Leiter Reports: A Philosophy Blog*, January 9, 2017, http://leiterreports.typepad.com/blog/2017/01/so-it-turns-out-implicit-bias-as-measured-does-not-predict-behavior.html.

Luscombe, Belinda. "Do Children of Same-Sex Parents Really Fare Worse?" *Time*, July 11, 2012. http://healthland.time.com/2012/06/11/do-children-of-same-sex-parents-really-fare-worse/.

Machery, Edouard. "Anomalies in implicit attitudes research." *Wiley Interdisciplinary Reviews: Cognitive Science* 13, no. 1 (2022): e1569. https://doi.org/10.1002/wcs.1569.

Machery, Edouard. "Should We Throw the IAT on the Scrap Heap of Indirect Measures?" *The Brains Blog*, January 17, 2017. http://philosophyofbrains.com/2017/01/17/how-can-we-measure-implicit-bias-a-brains-blog-roundtable.aspx.

Patterson, James T. *Freedom is Not Enough: The Moynihan Report and America's Struggle over Black Family Life from LBJ to Obama* (New York: Basic Books, 2010).

Regnerus, Mark. "How Different Are the Adult Children of Parents Who Have Same-Sex Relationships: Findings from the New Family Structures Study." *Social Science Research* 41 (2012): 752–770.

Rothman, Stanley, April Kelly-Woessner, and Matthew Woessner. *The Still Divided Academy: How Competing Visions of Power, Politics, and Diversity Complicate the Mission of Higher Education* (Lanham, MD: Roman and Littlefield, 2011).

Sedanius, Jim, et al. *The Diversity Challenge: Social Identity and Intergroup Relations on the College Campus* (New York: Russell Sage Foundation, 2010).

Shields, Jon. *The Democratic Virtues of the Christian Right* (Princeton: Princeton University Press, 2009).

Shields, Jon A., and Joshua M. Dunn, Sr. *Passing on the Right: Conservative Professors in the Progressive University* (New York: Oxford UP, 2016).

Smith, Emily Esfahani. "Survey Shocker." *Washington Times*, August 1, 2012.

Steinfels, Peter. "A Provocative Work About the Christian Right." *New York Times*, April 24, 2009. https://www.nytimes.com/2009/04/25/us/25beliefs.html.

Tetlock, Phillip E., and Gregory Mitchell. "Why So Few Conservatives and Should We Care?" *Society* 52 (2015): 28–34.

Vitiello, Michael. "Liberal Bias in the Legal Academy: Overstated and Undervalued." *Mississippi Law Journal* 77 (2007): 541.

Weatherall, Geoffrey, et al., "Discrimination Across the Ideological Divide: The Role of Value Violations and Abstract Values in Discrimination by Liberals and Conservatives." *Social Psychological and Personality Science* 4 (2013): 658–667.

Whaples, Robert. "Changes in Attitudes Among College Economics Students About the Fairness of the Market." *Journal of Economic Education* 26 (1995): 308–313.
Yancey, George. *Compromising Scholarship: Religious and Political Bias in American Higher Education* (Waco, TX: Baylor University Press, 2011).

Chapter 12

Teaching Controversial Topics Such as Evolutionary Theory

Tips and Tools

Cristine H. Legare and David M. Buss

We are psychology professors at the flagship public research university in our state, The University of Texas at Austin. One of the core missions of this university is to educate the residents of the state of Texas. As faculty members and educators, we take that responsibility seriously.

The students at UT Austin come from every region of the state. Our state is highly diverse along many dimensions—ethnically, linguistically, religiously, socioeconomically, and politically. As a result, the intellectual diversity represented by students at UT Austin is substantial. We view this diversity as a strength and strive to make all students feel welcome and included in our classes.

Our students vary in the amount of exposure they have had to beliefs that differ from their own; they vary in their exposure to science. Many are still in the process of learning about different perspectives and developing their own views. Many have had little exposure to, or experience with, discussing controversial topics.

We both teach evolution in our psychology courses, which range from human cognition and culture to human sexuality. Teaching evolutionary science illustrates the challenge of teaching a conceptually difficult and controversial topic.[1] Evolution by natural selection is deceptively simple in theory, but it turns out to be one of the more difficult scientific concepts for students to understand; it requires the integration of subject expertise and skilled teaching methods for students to learn it effectively.[2] Students regularly misunderstand what evolution is and how it occurs. This is especially true for students living in a state like Texas, which has largely omitted evolutionary theory from K–12 education, largely due to ideological and religious objections. One of the implications of the omission of evolution from biological science curricula is that students often do not understand what evolution is, and thus cannot effectively assess why it is viewed by some as controversial. Students must have an accurate understanding of what evolution is to develop educated perspectives about how it is applied to explain human cognition and behavior.

In our courses on how evolutionary theory illuminates human nature, we've developed several teaching tools. One is to start with nonhuman animal examples. Animal examples help students think beyond their own species-centrism. Most species have predators that they have to defend against to survive. People can readily see that a porcupine's quills, a skunk's malodorous spray, and a turtle's hard shell are adaptations to defend against predators. These examples also illustrate the principle of natural selection. Turtles whose shells are a bit thicker and skunks whose spray is a bit more noxious to predators are more likely to survive long enough to reproduce, so their descendants inherit the qualities that led to the survival success of their parents. People then start to grasp the concepts of *variation* (individual differences in turtle shell thickness) and *differential reproduction* (turtles with thick shells leave more descendants than those with thinner shells)—the essence of Darwin's theory of natural selection.

By using animal examples, we illustrate that many adaptations are not invariantly expressed, but rather have evolved to be *context-contingent*, activated by specific features of the environment. Cats commonly grow longer fur in the winter, an adaptation to keep their bodies warm and insulated, but grow shorter hair in the summer when bitter cold does not pose a survival challenge. This example also hits home the core of natural selection—variation (individual cats differ in their ability to shift from short to long hair depending on the season) and differential reproduction (cats that survive the winter reproduce more), causing evolutionary change (cats in the next generation are descendants of the subset of cats that have better season-dependent hair growth abilities).

Once students start to understand the logic of adaptation and natural selection in animals, the next step is to shift to humans, beginning with the human body. Again, we begin by focusing on challenges of survival, such as adaptive problems of food selection or dangers that come from abrasions to the human skin. It's relatively easy to highlight evolved food preferences for substances rich in calories and food aversions to ingesting substances containing toxins—preferences for sweet things such as ripe fruit and aversions to ingesting bitter objects. Abrasions to the human skin caused by repeated friction activate the ingenious adaptation of a callus-producing mechanism, the ability to grow thicker skin in the precise locations of repetitive friction. This example also has the benefit of highlighting that many adaptations are context-specific, functioning to be activated only when confronted by specific environmental challenges.

While most people can comprehend evolution by selection in non-human animals and many can grasp that the same principles apply to the human body, by far the biggest hurdle comes from showing that precisely the same principles apply to the human mind. We point out that the mind is housed in the brain, and the brain is part of the body (a rather important part), so there is no reason to think that the brain has been exempt from evolutionary processes. A relatively easy example provides an entry point—*the behavioral immune system*. Just as humans have a physiological immune system (e.g., white blood cells called leukocytes that destroy disease-causing organisms) to fight off pathogenic dangers to the body, humans have a behavioral immune system that functions to avoid contact with those disease vectors to begin with. We have evolved the emotion of disgust, which causes us to be repelled by contaminated foul-smelling food; and we recoil from other humans who show symptoms of coughing and sneezing—two common disease vectors. This example highlights that those human emotions (e.g., disgust) and behaviors (e.g., avoiding contaminants)—adaptations housed in the brain—are also products of evolution by natural selection.[3] These fundamentals provide a much-needed scaffold for discussing a larger array of psychological adaptations—those for mating, parenting, cooperation, aggression, negotiating status hierarchies, and many other recurrent challenges of group living.

Teaching tools that follow this logical progression makes it easier to grasp the core evolutionary concepts of adaptation and natural selection. With these core building blocks in place, students are now primed to comprehend that variation and differential reproduction depend not just on survival success, but also on reproductive success. They are also prepared to reason about the brain as the product of evolution by natural selection, and thus to consider all of the implications of applying evolutionary theory to understanding human cognition and behavior.

Evolutionary theory is controversial, in part, due to misunderstandings about it. One is the misunderstanding that it's a theory of *genetic determinism*—the erroneous notion that genes determine human behavior with no input from the environment. Instead, evolutionary theory is an interactionist paradigm that invokes environmental causation at every step of the way—from the environments that are responsible for selecting adaptations, to the development of those adaptations over the lifespan, to their activation in the current environment. A second misunderstanding is the *naturalistic fallacy*, which assumes that what exists ought to exist in a moral sense. In fact, people decide that many products of evolution by selection should not exist, and we design interventions to ameliorate them. Examples include parasites dangerous to humans and adaptations for aggression; in both cases, interventions have been highly successful, as rates of violence have plummeted over the past few hundred years.[4] What ought to exist—a matter of values—should not be conflated with what does exist.

Another source of controversy is whether evolutionary theory is fundamentally incompatible with certain religious beliefs. In some cases, evolutionary theory is indeed fundamentally incompatible with beliefs such as the creation of all life forms in six days by a higher deity. Many people, however, easily reconcile their religious beliefs with evolutionary theory by positing that a higher deity created the laws of natural selection, and then let that natural causal process play out over millions of years.[5] Rather than telling students what they should believe, we present the range of positions regarding reconciling evolutionary principles with religious beliefs (or not) and let them decide for themselves.

It has been our experience that students in our courses enjoy the opportunity to engage in open dialogue about intellectual topics, including controversial topics such as evolution. We incorporate debate and discourse into our courses, as core activities central to our educational objectives. Facilitating respectful discourse based on evidence and critical thinking is an essential function of university education, and necessary for protecting and promoting an educated and democratic civil society.

We strive to develop critical thinking in our students in several ways. One way is to create a classroom environment that facilitates diverse opportunities for interaction and participation. We use critical thinking activities such as debates, problem-based group activities, thought-provoking films and videos, discussions about current events, and whole class discussion formats as tools to promote active participation. For example, we often assign students to groups on different sides of a controversial issue in evolutionary social science and have students work collaboratively to present the diverse perspectives to an audience of their peers. Following the in-class debate, we ask students to write a critical analysis of the issue by incorporating empirical data on the topic. To provide opportunities for students to develop analytical writing skills, we design creative writing assignments for students. To support empirically based appraisals and critical thinking, students contrast and compare scientific and popular media sources on an important educational issue such as evolution, review both, and come to an informed conclusion.

What are some key lessons that can be drawn from trying to teach students who have different political and religious beliefs, and come from diverse socioeconomic and ethnic backgrounds? One lesson is that active engagement is crucial. Learning occurs best when students actively grapple with the material rather than being passive recipients of lectures. A second is to recognize that students come to controversial topics with some beliefs already formed, such as misconceptions about the logic of evolutionary theory or the belief that it contravenes their religious teachings. This recognition requires a respectful, rather than dismissive approach. Some popular science educators, for example, denigrate religion as antithetical to science generally and to evolutionary science specifically. We have found that this stance alienates more than it educates. Genuine respect works better. A third lesson is that controversial topics need to be tackled head on. We believe that most students welcome and appreciate dispassionate discussion of scientific logic, cogent arguments, and high-quality evidence, even about hot-button topics. We have had success with these techniques in reaching and teaching students who come from a state as diverse as Texas.

NOTES

1. Cristine H. Legare, John Opfer, Justin T.A. Busch, and Andrew Shtulman, "A Field Guide for Teaching Evolution in the Social Sciences," *Evolution and Human Behavior* 39 (2018): 257–268.
2. Karl S. Rosengren, Sarah K. Brem, E. Margaret Evans, and Gale M. Sinatra, *Evolution Challenges: Integrating Research and Practice in Teaching and Learning about Evolution* (Oxford University Press, 2012).
3. Coren L. Apicella, Paul Rozin, Justin T.A. Busch, Rachel E. Watson-Jones, and Cristine H. Legare, "Evidence from Hunter-Gatherer and Subsistence Agricultural Populations for the Universality of Contagion Sensitivity," *Evolution and Human Behavior* 39 (2018): 355–363.
4. Steven Pinker, "Zoom Out, and You'll See People are Improving," *The New York Times*, May 31, 2016, https://www.nytimes.com/roomfordebate/2012/02/26/are-people-getting-dumber/zoom-out-and-youll-see-people-are-improving.
5. Cristine H. Legare, Evelyn M. Evans, Karl S. Rosengren, and Paul L. Harris, "The Coexistence of Natural and Supernatural Explanations across Cultures and Development," *Child Development* 83 (2012): 779–793.

REFERENCES

Apicella, Coren L., Paul Rozin, Justin T.A. Busch, Rachel E. Watson-Jones, and Cristine H. Legare. "Evidence from Hunter-Gatherer and Subsistence Agricultural Populations for the Universality of Contagion Sensitivity." *Evolution and Human Behavior* 39 (2018): 355–363.

Legare, Cristine H., Evelyn M. Evans, Karl S. Rosengren, and Paul L. Harris. "The Coexistence of Natural and Supernatural Explanations across Cultures and Development." *Child Development* 83 (2012): 779–793.

Legare, Cristine H., John Opfer, Justin T.A. Busch, and Andrew Shtulman. "A Field Guide for Teaching Evolution in the Social Sciences." *Evolution and Human Behavior* 39 (2018): 257–268.

Pinker, Steven. "Zoom Out, and You'll See People are Improving." *The New York Times*, May 31, 2016. https://www.nytimes.com/roomfordebate/2012/02/26/are-people-getting-dumber/zoom-out-and-youll-see-people-are-improving.

Rosengren, Karl S., Sarah K. Brem, E. Margaret Evans, and Gale M. Sinatra. *Evolution Challenges: Integrating Research and Practice in Teaching and Learning about Evolution* (Oxford University Press, 2012).

Chapter 13

Space, Speech, and Subordination on College Campus

Laura Beth Nielsen

INTRODUCTION

Questions about campus speech and policies around it have taken on new salience in recent years for several reasons, including the social and political environment in the United States, the use of social media to amplify speech events, and the dramatic increase in hate crimes. Considering how to balance the important democratic principle of free speech with other important constitutional values is difficult no matter the location and social context, but the unique case of college and university campuses provide additional challenges. Institutions of higher learning are unique in part because the free exchange of ideas is especially sacred there. Further, many of the controversies that ultimately are framed as controversies about speech begin as controversies about race, racism, and racial equality, or sex, sex discrimination, sexual assault, and rape.

These are not easy issues to discuss—especially when we disagree. And yet the current state of the free speech debate on college campuses often amounts to little more than a fruitless exchange about who is silencing whom, which distracts us from the issues that require our attention. Fundamentally, debates about free speech on college campuses often fail to recognize the inherently social nature of speech itself and neglect some of the most important reasons we value free speech, including listening and learning. By focusing on the multiple goals of the university, we can see a guiding set of principles for thinking through these issues which forefronts the social nature of speech and the hierarchical relationships that troubling speech makes salient.

This essay proceeds in three sections: a discussion of subordination, speech, and space; conversations about sex, sexual assault, and rape on campus; and an account of microaggressions related to race. My argument here is that in the United States we routinely balance equality with other important foundational principles. Although we often balance speech and harm, that balance is still very weighted in favor of people in power. If we took the substantive discussion of the difficult issues that underlie these debates seriously, we could make much more progress in constructing meaningful dialogue which is, after all, what we hope the First Amendment helps to foster.

SUBORDINATION, SPEECH, AND SPACE

Before thinking about the college context specifically, consider the importance of social context to our understandings of (and laws about) the regulation of speech. Space is not just a location. Rather, space is a social construct that affects how we understand race and gender relations, sex, consent, speech, and violence.

For example, consider the home. Our homes are a particular, special, and protected kind of space. There are jurisprudential and philosophical rationales that put the home in a special zone of law. Concepts of privacy, liberty, and property make state intrusion into the home (or into our affairs when we are in the home) subject to higher standards.

This conception of the home, the private space it evokes, and the relationships it assumes used to be premised on a male-oriented conception of property. A man's home was his castle (and his wife and family were inside its walls). Property rights still play a role in constructing the home as unique, but we now tend to think of this unique space as guaranteed by privacy and liberty. Inside the home (and the relations of marriage and family that exist there) is where we think of ourselves as the most secure from government intrusion.

And yet, feminists have made great strides in the past fifty years changing how we think about relationships in the home as well as the bright line of public versus private that previous conceptions supported. The criminalization of marital rape, for example, fundamentally rejected the idea that uninterrupted consent to sex is part of being married and in the home. Similarly, the laws against and prosecution of domestic violence also represented an interrogation of the idea that the privacy of the home should not be breached even when bodily integrity (most typically of women, although targets of domestic violence can be of any gender) is at stake. The results of these hard-fought feminist victories mean that—while enforced imperfectly—simply being in the private space of a home or the institutional relationship of marriage does not render a woman unable to revoke consent to sex or subject to being abused.

Some scholars argued at the time (and a few still might) that laws against marital rape and domestic violence represent an erosion of some conception of privacy and property, but most Americans understand these laws as protecting a vision of liberty and bodily integrity that we can appropriately balance (with some struggle to be sure) in society and in courts.

In the workplace, we have seen a similar change. The establishment of sexual harassment as a cognizable claim of sex discrimination under the Civil Rights Act of 1964 means that consent to sex or sexualized activity is no longer just "part of the working conditions" that people (mostly women, although again, targets of sexual harassment in the workplace often include men and among male targets are disproportionately LGBTQ) face if they want to work. We know sexual harassment and discrimination remain rampant in the workplace and the legal treatment of it leaves something to be desired, but ordinary people's expectations about freedom from workplace sexual harassment have changed dramatically in the last twenty years. My undergraduates at Northwestern University and public opinion polls demonstrate that most Americans understand that sexual harassment is a type of discrimination that the law has a legitimate role in prohibiting.

Like the "erosion" of property and privacy in the example of the home, some scholars thought (and a few still argue), that insofar as Title VII makes actionable "just" words, it is an infringement on private business interests or laissez-faire capitalism. But Americans increasingly understand Title VII as advancing other important shared social goals of democracy, equality, and opportunity at work.

The policy driver here is a conception of "harm." In other words, continually harassing an individual in the workplace is not "just" speech, it is doing something. It produces a harm, which is is gender subordination. It is the harm of perpetuating discrimination. Of creating inequality. The words can, in some circumstances, be doing discrimination by degrading white women, people of color, or gender non-conforming workers in ways that create inequality in pay and promotion for members of these traditionally disadvantaged groups.

A final example of debates about speech, government, and equality comes in the context of public spaces. Like the home, American legal and popular culture hold dear the concept of public space and free speech. We learn in our civics classes that the public sphere is shared by everyone and can be entered without reservation for purposes of civic participation. And since civic participation necessarily involves the robust exchange of (even unpopular or offensive) ideas, free speech is most unencumbered in public.

In the real world, being in public means something else entirely. Public space and interactions between strangers in public places are embedded in the locations in which they occur, the identities of the individuals involved, and the nature of the interactions.

Let's consider street harassment. Although there are not yet laws, there is a burgeoning movement for equality and freedom from harassment in public spaces. My own research on harassing street speech situates street harassment within a system of complex and connected physical and psychological acts designed to intimidate, exclude, subordinate, and reinforce relative group status and hierarchy in the United States.[1] In addition to the magnitude and pervasiveness of street harassment, we continue to live in a world where members of nontargeted groups do not appreciate the magnitude or frequency of street harassment. Americans do not know what it is like to do something as simple as walk down the street in the shoes of another. More specifically, 38 percent of people of color report being targeted for racist or race-related street speech "every day" but non-targets (whites) estimate this at about 8 percent. Similarly, male non-targets estimate that about 11 percent of women hear sexually suggestive comments from strangers in public places every day whereas about 20 percent reported that they do. These differences in reported and estimated frequency are statistically significant.[2]

There is a group of young, smart, creative, social movement actors who have begun to press for equality in the streets. Hollabacknyc[3] and Stop Street Harassment[4] both are premised on the need to bridge this experience gap by featuring the pervasiveness and harms of street harassment to nontargets. Hollabacknyc began by asking women to photograph street harassers and post photos on the blog. The public-shaming campaign received national attention when a target of street harassment turned to take a photo only to find her harasser exposing himself. When the police failed to arrest the individual despite the evidence, Hollaback was thrust into the spotlight.

And of course, understanding public speech is not complete without understanding the most famous expressions of racism/free speech in public including the now infamous Nazis marching through (predominantly Jewish) Skokie IL, KKK rallies, and the ultimate demonstration of racial threat/free speech, a burning cross. Cross-burning is important because it gives us the latest legal standard for restricting racist speech: racist speech can be limited when it is "done with the intent to intimidate," although generally it is protected speech.[5]

What about speech that targets traditionally advantaged groups like businessmen and soldiers? There we see a regime of free speech that protects the powerful or popular. For example, although there is not a definitive Supreme Court decision about panhandling,[6] there is a circuit court split meaning that restrictions on panhandling are considered constitutionally permissible in many parts of the country. Why? Because its targets have a legitimate purpose for being in public—to get to work.[7] Chambers of commerce and city governments interested in presenting customers with tidy shopping and tourism districts also have laws banning begging that have been upheld in the federal courts.

And finally, in one of the most recent First Amendment cases, the Supreme Court sided with protesters using soldiers' funerals to express their belief that homosexuality is a sin. One read of *Snyder* is that the court upheld abominable speech targeted at revered members of society—soldiers—as a demonstration that our Constitution protects the "speech we hate" the most. Or it could be read as another example of allowing hateful speech when targeted at members of traditionally disadvantaged groups (LGBTQ). Either way, the case inspired Congressional override in the form of the "Respecting America's Fallen Heroes Act," which prohibits any protests 300–500 feet around veterans' funerals 120 minutes before the start and 120 minutes after the ending of the funeral.[8]

Shifting the focus from the speaker to the target reveals a pretty clear pattern. We expect white women, people of color, and gender nonconforming individuals to tolerate public harassment, but we manage to look the other way when the targets are businesses, businesspeople, or soldiers.

Without even discussing conspiracy, obscenity, inciting lawless action, and the myriad other reasons courts have found compelling enough to justify the legal regulation of speech, I hope I have convinced you that, in the words of Stanley Fish, "there is no such thing as free speech and it's a good thing too."[9]

Or, as I would put it, our cherished values of speech often are and must be balanced with our values about equality, democratic participation, and liberty. When we take on this balancing task—in the courtroom or on a campus—speech, space, and subordination are connected. We have come to successfully balance these competing rights (not perfectly) at home and at work in ways that give white women, people of color, traditionally disadvantaged sexual minorities, and members of minority religions more voice. Although the "public sphere" remains a safer space for privileged members of society.

Returning to speech on campus, it is important to point out, that our schools are not *just* educational spaces but—for many of our undergraduates the campus is also their home—a place deserving special protections from intrusion, but one where movement toward gender equality has been made. Our campuses are the workplace for many students as well as all of our faculty and staff. And everyone must traverse public space to move about on campus. With the recognition that a college campus is a <u>work</u>place, a <u>living</u> space, and a <u>public</u> space, we should consider two controversies regarding campus free speech: sexual assault/trigger warnings and racial equality/ microaggressions. In both areas, students who are members of traditionally marginalized groups in education are voicing claims for equality as these groups enter higher education in greater numbers.

And this makes it feel like free speech is at risk on college campuses. It's been said that "when you are accustomed to privilege, equality can feel like oppression." Or, in the case of speech on campus, "When you are accustomed to privilege, movement toward equality can feel like oppression." Put differently, we are in a new era of being thoughtful about inclusion of people who have been historically excluded from institutions of higher learning. This inclusion—whether forced through protest and litigation or extended voluntarily—means taking claims about the harms of speech and the perpetuation of inequality seriously and balancing them with our desire for robust free speech.

Like in the so-called real world there is no such thing as an absolute right, including "free speech" for everyone. Like the contexts I started with, on college campus, we want to interrogate what is unique about this space. What do we do here? How do we want to ensure a free flow of ideas on campus? How can we best understand whose speech is being curtailed, and what can we do to ensure free speech for everyone on college campuses?

Of course, our first goal—our "core mission"—at a university is to teach and to learn. To hear, to take in, and to try out as many new ideas as we can. Lots of the time, we are trying to tackle serious social problems. That requires being in sustained dialogue about the kinds of difficult issues I discussed above. To learn, there must be speech. But when I think about free speech, I am not just thinking about my ability to speak, I am also thinking about my ability to hear—to take in the ideas of other people. And I want to hear as many as I can.

CONVERSATIONS ABOUT SEX, SEXUAL ASSAULT AND RAPE ON CAMPUS

Consider the example of campus rape and Title IX compliance. I hope we all agree—left and right—that campus sexual assault and the inadequate campus responses to it are serious social problems that we want to solve.

Whether you think the massive underreporting of campus rape is the problem (which peer-reviewed empirical research consistently demonstrates) *or* if you think the failure of university processes for protecting accused rapists is the problem (which some high profile media reports have highlighted in past few years and the reason that many on the Harvard Law faculty reject campus enforcement in such matters), we can all probably agree there is work to be done.

So here we are with a serious social problem in a place where we know *a lot* about the subject, and yet we find it difficult to have conversations about this in part because we get stuck on this issue of "trigger warnings." Do they violate free speech by "censoring" students who want to blame victims? Is asking professors to give them a waste of class time? Are we coddling students if we give trigger warnings?

I give brief trigger warnings before I speak about such matters in class. They take no time at all and yet, some would suggest that my exercise of this speech represents the "silencing" of someone else. That just doesn't make sense. Trigger warnings are given to make more people, especially targets of sexualized and racialized violence, more able to participate in our conversation.

In my courses, students learn about Title IX and sexual assault. I teach the peer-reviewed social science research on the topic to frame our policy and political theory debates. Before we decide what our policies should incentivize, we have to understand where we are. Somewhere between 20 and 25 percent of women report being sexually assaulted in college and about 1 in 20 men are sexually assaulted in their lives. How is that experienced by targets? I also want students—*men and women*—to know that rape is one of the most repeated crimes. The best research on the subject—using samples of college students—demonstrates that four percent of men are responsible for 28 percent of sexual violence on college campuses and the median number of sexually violent acts they report having perpetrated is six. These are some of the *lower* estimates.

A variety of factors prevent targets of sexual assault from being able to fully participate in these difficult conversations: shame; gendered and heteronormative power dynamics; and PTSD. Sex (a component of rape) is private and often stigmatized. The nature of a sexual assault defense is almost always consent. No rape shield law can prevent it.

Given all of this, it is not surprising that some targets of sexual assault feel systematically excluded from these conversations. The exclusion of their participation—their *speech*—means we are missing that important perspective about this serious social problem.

Conversations like these, like those about the Rolling Stone article about the University of Virginia, the mattress protest at Columbia, or the recent professor-undergraduate sex scandal at my own university, are *not* just chances to speak. They are opportunities to *listen*, to bridge the understanding gap highlighted by the research I have noted, and to make progress on these daunting social issues. When we focus only on our own speech, we miss these opportunities.

How can we maximize these opportunities? One answer is to give trigger warnings. The reason is not so that traumatized sex abuse survivors can run out of the room (although that is a legitimate response too), but so everyone is on notice that in my classroom troubling topics and ideas will be discussed and with civility.

To make it a conversation, we must understand the power dynamics and experiences of the people in the room in which the conversation is taking place. If that means designated safe spaces, women's centers, or trigger warnings, in the case of campus sexual assault, to compensate for the balance of power, I'll not just argue that they are a good idea but that they are *necessary*. But it is only necessary if we are actually interested in the listening part of speech.

One way in which campuses are trying to prevent sexual assault is by instituting "yes means yes" rules on campus (and laws in states). One of the first very public anti-rape movements on college campuses was the "no means no" movement, which sought to highlight the fact that rape need not include physical force. The concept of "date rape" or "acquaintance rape" was identified and named.

More recently, however, more colleges are moving to the "yes means yes" concept of consent. Most famously passed as SB 967 in California but becoming more prominent as the rule on college campuses, these affirmative consent rules say (and this is the exact language of the California law):

> "Affirmative consent" means affirmative, conscious, and voluntary agreement to engage in sexual activity. It is the responsibility of each person involved in the sexual activity to ensure that he or she has the affirmative consent of the other or others to engage in the sexual activity. Lack of protest or resistance does not mean consent, nor does silence mean consent. Affirmative consent must be ongoing throughout a sexual activity and can be revoked at any time. The existence of a dating relationship between the persons involved, or the fact of past sexual relations between them, should never by itself be assumed to be an indicator of consent.[10]

How does this relate to free speech on campus? This move to an egalitarian sex-positive way of expressing consent designed to protect all the parties in a sexual encounter is being met with a backlash by those who characterize these rules as "repressive" in their clarity. And, it has inspired backlash in the form of a now famous chant often directed at women during freshman orientation on college campuses. "No means yes and yes means anal."

Underreporting and failing to discuss these matters have the effect of making our colleges less able to detect and identify what scholars call the "undetected serial rapist." This should trouble everyone. When we consider the "inconvenience" of a trigger warning in the context of what we know about sexual assault on campus, the importance of full participation in the conversation should win.

RACIAL MICROAGGRESSIONS

A second challenge to free speech on campus often is made when (primarily but not exclusively) African American students organize to try to express the experience of being African-American in U.S. society and on university campuses. Described as fight, anxiety, fear, and failing to belong, student activists are attempting to bring the #blacklivesmatter movement to campus, to reinvigorate the race equality movement of the 1960s and '70s, and to advocate for equality at college.

In addition to systemic changes in curriculum, course offerings, student and faculty diversity, student activists often are asking for recognition of microaggressions and the harms they cause. Microaggressions, including racist street harassment, include the "brief and commonplace daily verbal, behavioral, and environmental indignities, whether intentional or unintentional, that communicate hostile, derogatory, or negative racial slights and insults to the target person or group."[11]

Discussion of microaggressions on college campuses are interesting because some free speech absolutists (the same ones that used to say the idea of "silencing" was absurd) claim that the discussion of microaggressions can be silencing of them! African American (primarily) students raise these issues and are told that discussion of microaggressions and asking faculty and administrators to avoid committing microaggressions is violating the free speech rights of those (mostly white) students and faculty members.

Like sexual assault, however, it is important to understand the social world in which microaggressions occur. Like sexual assault and street speech, racist microaggressions are part of a series of practices—often "just" speech—that are doing something. They are reinforcing racialized systems of inequality in the education context and with reference to the broader inequalities outlined here and have real physical and mental health effects.

Some free speech absolutists and other commentators who want to decry the current generation of college students say that complaining about microaggressions means students are "whiny" and want to be coddled.[12] I argue precisely the opposite. These students are bravely demanding to be heard about what it is like to be a member of a subordinated group on a college campus, which is an extension of what it is like to be an African American citizen of this country. A country where African American full-time, year-round workers make 60% of what white men[13] do and African American men make

70 cents for every dollar their similarly situated white male counterparts make.[14] A country where African Americans have a 30 percent greater chance of being stopped by the police while driving.[15] A country in which African American men are about 5 times more likely to have a felony conviction than their white counterparts[16] and are (controlling for myriad other factors) more likely to receive a longer sentence for the same crime.[17] A country in which state violence in the forms of police killing[18] and capital punishment[19] are disproportionally enacted on men of color. The discussion of microaggressions and their harms cannot and should not occur absent from this important social context.

In addition to that context, the impact of microaggressions should occur with the aid of empirical research about the harms of being the target of them. Experience with racial microaggressions is associated with a range of negative health outcomes.[20] Although microaggressions can be communicated subtly and often unknowingly, they can be stressors "that mediate the effects of racial minority status on physical and psychological health outcomes." We see associations between racial microaggressions and negative mental health outcomes,[21] including depression,[22] anxiety,[23] suicidal ideation,[24] alcohol and drug use, and high blood pressure.

Unfortunately, the free-speech debate often occurs without hearing what subordination through speech feels like. Instead, we devolve into a shouting match about who is "silencing" whom. That skips right over to the most important part of building better communities who are able to tackle these serious social issues—listening and understanding. One way of understanding how speech often is used to perpetuate inequality and subordination is listening—really listening—to the experiences of other people who are not like us.

CONCLUSION

A variety of factors shape how people understand social interactions. Law, space, and identity are implicated in ordinary citizens' assessment of social interactions and our understanding of speech rights. If students believe they must accept humiliating or threatening public speech, the law works—through "free speech"—to normalize or justify such interactions. And, insofar as the current state of the law is one of the many forces that normalizes such interactions, it is part of the construction of these acts of subordination as something that one does not have a "right" to be free from.

The First Amendment has always worked better for those with privilege. We "celebrate" difficult cases when it has been used to protect the speech we hate, like Nazi hate speech and KKK cross-burnings. Considered another way, what we see is our laws protecting the speech of those who violently demand the status quo of white domination over people of color.

As university administrators know, balancing speech and equality is a difficult task. To have any hope of achieving the proper balance, Americans must first try to listen to each other, so that we can understand the harms of hate speech. While "just speech," racist hate speech does the work of subordination and domination every day in public places by making salient the racist fissures undergirded by the violent past of slavery, lynching, and Jim Crow.

Instead of screaming about who is or is not being allowed to speak, which is ultimately ironic and circular, why don't we take the time to listen to those who are bravely advocating for equality on college campuses, instead of accusing those who have been silenced for generations of "silencing"? We are simply asking that America live up to a promise it made to white women and people of color long ago but has not yet fulfilled. That cannot be accomplished until we stop fighting about who is silencing whom.

NOTES

1. Laura Beth Nielsen, *License to Harass: Law, Hierarchy, and Offensive Public Speech* (Princeton, NJ: Princeton University Press, 2006).
2. Laura Beth Nielsen, "Subtle, Pervasive, Harmful: Racist and Sexist Remarks in Public as Hate Speech," *Journal of Social Issues* 58, no. 2 (Summer 2002): 265–280.
3. https://nyc.ihollaback.org/
4. http://www.stopstreetharassment.org/
5. *Virginia v. Black*, 538 U.S. 343 (2003).
6. The closest the Supreme Court has come to ruling on this issue is *Reed v. Town of Gilbert*, 576 U.S. ___ (2014), though it does not resolve the fundamental Circuit Court split.
7. *Loper v. New York City Police Dept.*, 785 F. Supp. 464 (SDNY 1992).
8. https://www.congress.gov/bill/109th-congress/house-bill/5037/text/eh
9. Stanley Fish, *There's No Such Thing as Free Speech . . . and It's a Good Thing, Too* (New York: Oxford University Press, 1994).
10. California Senate Bill 967, signed into law September 28, 2014, https://leginfo.legislature.ca.gov/faces/billNavClient.xhtml?bill_id=201320140SB967.
11. Derald Wing Sue et. al., "Racial Microaggressions in Everyday Life: Implications for Clinical Practice," *The American Psychologist* 62, no. 4 (2007): 271–286.
12. Greg Lukianoff and Jonathan Haidt, "The Coddling of the American Mind," *The Atlantic*, November 2015, https://www.theatlantic.com/magazine/archive/2015/09/the-coddling-of-the-american-mind/399356/.
13. "Highlights of Women's Earnings in 2014," *BLS Reports*, November 2015, https://www.bls.gov/opub/reports/womens-earnings/archive/highlights-of-womens-earnings-in-2014.pdf.
14. Ibid.

15. Jeff Rojek, Richard Rosenfeld, and Scott Decker, "Policing Race: The Racial Stratification of Searches in Police Traffic Stops," *Criminology* 50, no. 4 (2012): 993–1024.

16. Sara Wakefield and Christopher Uggen, "Incarceration and Stratification," *Annual Review of Sociology* 36 (2010): 387–406.

17. Besiki L. Kutateladze et al., "Cumulative Disadvantage: Examining Racial and Ethnic Disparity in Prosecution and Sentencing," *Criminology* 52, no. 3 (2014): 514–551.

18. Ryan Gabrielson, Ryann Grochowski Jones, and Eric Sagara, "Deadly Force, in Black and White," *Real Clear Policy*, October 13, 2014, https://www.realclearpolicy.com/blog/2014/10/14/deadly_force_in_black_and_white_1099.html

19. *McClesky v. Kemp*, 481 U.S. 279 (1987).

20. Ibid.

21. Kevin L. Nadal et al., "The Impact of Racial Microaggressions on Mental Health: Counseling Implications for Clients of Color," *Journal of Counseling and Development* 92 (1) (2014): 57–66.

22. Roxanne A. Donovan et al., "Impact of Racial Macro- and Microaggressions in Black Women's Lives: A Preliminary Analysis," *Journal of Black Psychology* 39, no. 2 (2013): 185–196.

23. Ibid.

24. Victoria M. O'Keefe et al., "Seemingly Harmless Racial Communications Are Not So Harmless: Racial Microaggressions Lead to Suicidal Ideation by Way of Depression Symptoms," *Suicide and Life-Threatening Behavior* 45, no. 5 (2015): 567–576.

REFERENCES

California Senate Bill 967, signed into law September 28, 2014. https://leginfo.legislature.ca.gov/faces/billNavClient.xhtml?bill_id=201320140SB967.

Donovan, Roxanne A., et al. "Impact of Racial Macro- and Microaggressions in Black Women's Lives: A Preliminary Analysis." *Journal of Black Psychology* 39, no. 2 (2013): 185–196.

Fish, Stanley. *There's No Such Thing as Free Speech . . . and It's a Good Thing, Too* (New York: Oxford University Press, 1994).

Gabrielson, Ryan, Ryann Grochowski Jones, and Eric Sagara. "Deadly Force, in Black and White." *Real Clear Policy*, October 13, 2014. https://www.realclearpolicy.com/blog/2014/10/14/deadly_force_in_black_and_white_1099.html.

"Highlights of Women's Earnings in 2014," *BLS Reports*, November 2015, https://www.bls.gov/opub/reports/womens-earnings/archive/highlights-of-womens-earnings-in-2014.pdf.

Kutateladze, Besiki L., et al. "Cumulative Disadvantage: Examining Racial and Ethnic Disparity in Prosecution and Sentencing." *Criminology* 52, no. 3 (2014): 514–551.

Loper v. New York City Police Dept., 785 F. Supp. 464 (SDNY 1992).

Lukianoff, Greg, and Jonathan Haidt, "The Coddling of the American Mind," *The Atlantic*, November 2015, https://www.theatlantic.com/magazine/archive/2015/09/the-coddling-of-the-american-mind/399356/

McClesky v. Kemp, 481 U.S. 279 (1987).

Nadal, Kevin L., et al. "The Impact of Racial Microaggressions on Mental Health: Counseling Implications for Clients of Color." *Journal of Counseling and Development* 92, no. 1 (2014): 57–66.

Nielsen, Laura Beth. *License to Harass: Law, Hierarchy, and Offensive Public Speech* (Princeton, NJ: Princeton University Press, 2006).

Nielsen, Laura Beth. "Subtle, Pervasive, Harmful: Racist and Sexist Remarks in Public as Hate Speech." *Journal of Social Issues* 58, no. 2 (Summer 2002): 265–280.

Reed v. Town of Gilbert, 576 U.S. ___ (2014).

O'Keefe, Victoria M., et al. "Seemingly Harmless Racial Communications Are Not So Harmless: Racial Microaggressions Lead to Suicidal Ideation by Way of Depression Symptoms" *Suicide and Life-Threatening Behavior* 45, no. 5 (2015): 567–576.

Rojek, Jeff, Richard Rosenfeld, and Scott Decker. "Policing Race: The Racial Stratification of Searches in Police Traffic Stops." *Criminology* 50, no. 4 (2012): 993–1024.

Sue, Derald Wing, et al., "Racial Microaggressions in Everyday Life: Implications for Clinical Practice," *The American Psychologist* 62, no. 4 (2007): 271–286.

Virginia v. Black, 538 U.S. 343 (2003).

Wakefield, Sara, and Christopher Uggen. "Incarceration and Stratification." *Annual Review of Sociology* 36 (2010): 387–406.

Chapter 14

Hiding behind Hate Speech

Heather MacDonald

In January 2018, over a hundred faculty and graduate students at the University of Chicago circulated a petition denouncing a planned campus debate.[1] Chicago business school Professor Luigi Zingales had invited Steve Bannon, former advisor to then president Donald Trump and former chairman of the Breitbart News website, to debate two key topics in the 2016 elections: globalization and immigration. According to the petition signatories, allowing Bannon on campus would threaten the safety of "people of color" at the university and in its surrounding community. The message was clear: President Robert Zimmer and Provost Daniel Diermeier should cancel the invitation if they cared about "diversity" and "inclusion." The debate never took place.

It is nevertheless worth examining the faculty petition in some detail. It is a locus classicus of contemporary arguments against free speech, echoing previous faculty petitions demanding the disinvitation of controversial speakers at Middlebury College and the University of California, Berkeley. Moreover, it emanates from an institution that has been lauded for its public stance against politically correct censorship. That so many faculty there nonetheless favor the suppression of ideas that challenge campus orthodoxies shows how deeply-ingrained the hostility to free expression has become.

The faculty petition begins with abysmal grammar and the usual Orwellian redefining of words to mean their opposites. "As faculty and others representing the breadth of the University's intellectual community and committed to critical and rigorous intellectual exchange," the letter opens awkwardly, "we are deeply concerned that Stephen Bannon . . . has been invited to speak at the University of Chicago." That commitment "to critical and rigorous intellectual exchange" is precisely what the letter writers abjure. They frame censorship as openness and the shutting off of speech as intellectual exchange.

"As academics," the letter-writers proclaim, "we understand that our work is only possible in a context where intellectual inquiry is afforded the space and freedom to push the boundaries of knowledge." So far, so good. It turns out, however, that that intellectual freedom only extends to a pre-approved set of ideas. "At the same time," the petitioners continue, "we believe that our mission of setting global standards for excellence in research and teaching is only possible in an environment where every member of our community is valued and hate speech that is meant to undermine their full participation is not tolerated." In other words, tolerance requires intolerance. Inclusion requires exclusion. "The university should model inclusion for a country that is reeling from the consequences of racism, xenophobia, and hate" by excluding Bannon, the petition argues. "We believe that Bannon should not be afforded the platform and opportunity to air his hate speech on this campus."

The key concept in this dizzying set of contradictions is "hate speech." The Chicago signatories claim to be all in favor of free speech, just not "hate speech." This carve-out amounts to the position: we will provide a forum for ideas that we agree with but not for ideas that we disagree with. But as free speech theorists from John Stuart Mill onward have stressed, freedom of expression only means something when confronting ideas with which one profoundly disagrees. There is no First Amendment exception allowing censorship of "hate speech." And the Chicago petition shows why there must never be such an exception. The signatories arrogate to themselves the boundless power to designate disfavored ideas as "hate speech," without any effort to define or limit the term. They simply declare over and over again that Bannon traffics in it.

Occasionally, they supplement their blanket "hate speech" designation with purported examples. These, too, show why the concept is so dangerous: it is merely a stand-in for political positions that the signatories oppose. Bannon, the petitioners write, "is cited[2] as the most consequential proponent of a recent ban on immigration, which is currently embroiled[3] in legal challenges for its discriminatory targeting of majority Muslim countries. He has unabashedly advocated[4] for more general restrictions of historically legal forms of immigration, in ways inconsistent with generally accepted ideals of openness embraced here on campus."

Even under the most expansive definition of "hate speech," it is a stretch to apply the term to the advocacy of temporary visa restrictions from terror-sponsoring countries or to the call for a skills-based immigration system. As hard as it might be for the Chicago faculty to grasp, "hate" was not involved in the development of those policy proposals. They grew out of a concept of the national interest different from the one current on the Chicago campus. To the stunningly parochial professoriate, however, hate speech equals any idea that is allegedly "inconsistent with generally accepted ideals . . . embraced here on campus."

The petition writers invoke the usual laundry list of America's discriminatory sins to further buttress the desired disinvitation of Bannon. "The defense of freedom of expression," they write, "cannot be taken to mean that white supremacy, anti-semitism, misogyny, homophobia, anti-Catholicism, and islamophobia must be afforded the rights and opportunity to be aired on a university campus." Assuming, for the sake of argument, that Bannon were credibly linked to these various isms and phobias, freedom of expression is directed squarely at such stigmatized ideas. In fact, however, the application of such terms as "white supremacy" and "misogyny" to policies disfavored by academia is precisely what needs debating, especially as the reach of those terms in the campus lexicon grows ever more totalitarian.

Two features of the Bannon disinvitation letter (besides its continuously appalling grammar) stand out most strikingly. The first is the faculty's lack of faith in the power of discourse. If Bannon's ideas are so dangerous, the faculty should welcome the opportunity to expose those ideas for the frauds that they are. The petitioners declare that Bannon's positions on immigration and terrorism "represent neither reasonable speech nor evidence-based and rigorous intellectual inquiry." Typically, they provide no supporting argumentation for that sweeping dismissal. But if Bannon's ideas are indeed so outside the realm of "evidence-based" speech, it should be easy to demolish them. This, the faculty demur from doing. Even more remarkably, the letter-writers adduce the alleged mainstream status of Bannon's ideas as further reason to cancel the debate: "The hate speech represented in Bannon's body of work are [sic] not the insignificant musings of a fringe political group, but rather the governing philosophy of the chief executive and a newly emboldened political movement based on white supremacy and religious intolerance." All the more reason to defeat that "hate speech" in a public forum. The response of the professoriate, however, is to carve out a protected sphere on campus where no one has to confront and rebut disfavored views but can simply rely on brute force to exclude them.

The faculty's low opinion of argumentation as a tool of social justice would have astounded Frederick Douglass. In 1860, a mob broke up a meeting in Boston held to commemorate the death of anti-slavery crusader John Brown. In response, Douglass penned "A Plea for Free Speech in Boston." Slavery "cannot tolerate free speech," he wrote. "Five years of its exercise would banish the auction block and break every chain in the South." Douglass understood that freedom of expression "is the dread of tyrants. It is the right which they first of all strike down," because it challenges authority. In Douglass's place, the Chicago faculty would have called for a ban on pro-slavery discourse. Douglass, by contrast, believed in the power of good ideas to overcome bad ideas, without the exercise of censorious force.

The other striking aspect of the disinvitation letter is the authors' child-like inability to abstract from their current position in the world. Right now, they have the power to control the definition of hate speech. Were they at a school other than the University of Chicago, they might also have to power to ban it. But what if the power balance shifts and the letter-writers' adversaries seize the authority to define and proscribe hate speech? By announcing the principle that hate speech can and must be silenced, the would-be disinviters are creating a precedent that can be used against their own cherished beliefs. It is not hard to imagine an anti-abortion political administration declaring that pro-abortion advocacy constitutes "hate speech" against the fetus. Or a declaration that advocacy of transgender rights constitutes "hate speech" against those who believe in the reality of biological sexual identity.

A concern for what political theorist John Rawls termed the "original position" argues for maximal free speech rights, not the opposite. (The original position refers to that arrangement of rights and economic structures that one would choose in the absence of knowledge about one's actual social and economic status in the world.) If you find yourself in the minority, you are going to want speech protections against the majority, as Brookings Institution fellow Jonathan Rauch has argued.

The disinviters' blindness to the reversibility of current power hierarchies and their disregard for the reach of abstract principles are either naïve or deeply cynical. It may be that they are fully aware that their hate-speech exception to freedom of expression could in theory be wielded against them, but they are confident that their control of elite culture will only solidify, buttressed by the very censoriousness they now exercise with near impunity. This is not an unjustified assumption.

Though the arguments for honoring the debating invitation to Bannon do not rest on the actual content of his thought, it bears noting that the disinviters' characterization of that thought is deeply tendentious. Bannon arguably showed more concern for the forgotten working class of all races than academic elites ever have. Bannon's sense of economic and patriotic nationalism is shared by millions of Americans, who also cannot fairly be characterized as "white supremacists." It might behoove the academic elites to try to understand how those alien beings think. A debate featuring Bannon would be a superb place to start. But the Chicago professoriate shows no curiosity about intellectual constructs radically different than its own, so confident is it in its own superiority and in everyone else's deplorable status.

The core idea driving the academy's assault on free speech is that to be a member of an ever-growing number of high-status victim groups on an American campus is to have your "rights and safety . . . routinely threatened," in the words of the disinvitation petition. That idea is patently delusional. Until it is overturned, however, no amount of arguments in favor of free speech will turn the tide. While such arguments are necessary, preserving as they do the intellectual patrimony that created our freedoms, they are not sufficient. The claim of life-threatening victimhood will, in the current environment, always prevail. To roll back the exercise of censorious power, it is essential to assert that there has never been a more resource-filled, bias-free environment in human history than the American campus and that American students, by virtue of their unfettered opportunities to learn, irrespective of race or other favored components of identity politics, are the most privileged human beings in history.

NOTES

1. Regrding Bannon at Chicago, January 18, 2018, https://docs.google.com/document/d/11HbJtIJkzMSF5aitP4Cy1YZmQUC1_70EX2or4oUOUdQ/edit

2. Zack Beauchamp, "Steve Bannon, the Trump adviser who helped craft the 'Muslim Ban,' explained," *Vox*, January 29, 2017, https://www.vox.com/world/2017/1/29/14431332/steve-bannon-muslim-refugee-ban-explained

3. Adam Liptak, "Supreme Court Allows Trump Travel Ban to Take Effect," *New York Times*, December 4, 2017, https://www.nytimes.com/2017/12/04/us/politics/trump-travel-ban-supreme-court.html

4. Tara Golshan, "Steve Bannon in 2016: legal immigration is the real 'problem,'" *Vox*, February 2, 2017, https://www.vox.com/policy-and-politics/2017/2/2/14472404/steve-bannon-legal-immigration-problem

REFERENCES

Beauchamp, Zack. "Steve Bannon, the Trump adviser who helped craft the 'Muslim Ban,' explained." *Vox*, January 29, 2017. https://www.vox.com/world/2017/1/29/14431332/steve-bannon-muslim-refugee-ban-explained.

Golshan, Tara. "Steve Bannon in 2016: legal immigration is the real 'problem.'" *Vox*, February 2, 2017. https://www.vox.com/policy-and-politics/2017/2/2/14472404/steve-bannon-legal-immigration-problem.

Liptak, Adam. "Supreme Court Allows Trump Travel Ban to Take Effect." *New York Times*, December 4, 2017. https://www.nytimes.com/2017/12/04/us/politics/trump-travel-ban-supreme-court.html.

PART IV

What Is to Be Done?

Chapter 15

A Free Speech Roadmap

How Universities Can Navigate the Current Campus Debates over Controversial Expression

Azhar Majeed

INTRODUCTION

Every day, seemingly, a new free speech controversy arises at one of our nation's colleges or universities. Whether it involves a student or faculty member being investigated and punished for speech labeled as offensive,[1] the invitation of a speaker to campus sparking outrage,[2] or students calling for censorship of their fellow students for espousing viewpoints with which they disagree,[3] campus free speech has become a hot-button issue and is now a greater part of the national consciousness.

In this climate, universities have grappled with the question of how to accommodate and balance all interests. College leaders who wish to uphold the freedom of expression at their school, while at the same time assuring students that the presence of allegedly divisive speakers and viewpoints should not make them feel unsafe or excluded, are placed in a difficult position at times. Added to this reality is the pressure faced from alumni and donors, who often react angrily to negative news coverage of their school and call upon its leadership to respond in a manner they personally deem best.

And, of course, the increased polarization of all things political in our country means that all too often, those on campus—whether they are conservative, liberal, or something else—fail to tolerate social and political viewpoints different from their own. Given these circumstances, how can university leaders respond to the free speech controversies that will inevitably arise at their institution?

This article proposes a few simple steps that seek to address this precise problem—steps that, while meaningful, are well within the means and resources of most colleges. These recommendations are informed by the actions of free speech advocacy groups such as First Amendment Watch (FAW) and the Foundation for Individual Rights in Education (FIRE).

This article is divided into four sections discussing substantive steps that colleges and universities can take, followed by a section with concluding thoughts.

I. ESTABLISH THE UNIVERSITY'S POSITION VIA A PRINCIPLED STATEMENT ON FREEDOM OF EXPRESSION

Among the most important steps a college or university can take to establish a culture of free speech on its campus is to set forth an institutional statement extolling the virtues of freedom of expression and inquiry. The adoption of such a policy statement can signal to students, faculty, staff, alumni, and the general public that the university is committed to protecting the free speech rights and academic freedom of its students and faculty, and that it will strive to do so in a manner that is both principled and neutral towards viewpoint and ideology.

This undertaking has tremendous value by itself, as it helps to inform stakeholders on and off campus that those offended by the presence of certain speakers or groups should not expect the university to step in to erase the controversy by engaging in censorial tactics.

Furthermore, university leadership will benefit from having a principled free-speech statement in place whenever a controversy arises, because it cannot—in good faith, at least—be accused of favoring certain viewpoints or ideologies if it allows the expression to stand.[4] That is, the administration would be able to simply point to its established statement and make clear that its approach is consistent with the values and principles espoused in that statement. In this manner, university leadership can signal that it treats all manner of free speech issues or controversies in the same fashion, regardless of ideology, so long as the expression in question is protected by the First Amendment.

As several campus free-speech advocates have pointed out, the model for such a policy statement exists in the form of the "Report of the Committee on Freedom of Expression" at the University of Chicago.[5] The "Chicago Statement," as it has come to be known, is an eloquent yet concise encapsulation of the importance of upholding freedom of expression in higher education, and why doing so benefits everyone in the campus setting. The Chicago Statement declares, in relevant part:

> Because the University is committed to free and open inquiry in all matters, it guarantees all members of the University community the broadest possible latitude to speak, write, listen, challenge, and learn. Except insofar as limitations on that freedom are necessary to the functioning of the University, the University of Chicago fully respects and supports the freedom of all members of the University community "to discuss any problem that presents itself."[6]

The statement goes on to provide:

> Of course, the ideas of different members of the University community will often and quite naturally conflict. But it is not the proper role of the University to attempt to shield individuals from ideas and opinions they find unwelcome, disagreeable, or even deeply offensive.[7]

Any university would benefit from making these declarations, as it would encourage students and faculty to speak freely. By reinforcing the idea that even "deeply offensive" speech will be protected as a matter of course, the institution fulfills its duty to provide a "marketplace of ideas," where ideas compete for prominence and speech with which one fundamentally disagrees is met with more speech, not calls for university intervention and censorship. Making these types of declarations part of official university policy can also help to prevent a harmful chilling effect on campus discourse, whereby students and faculty fear that holding a dissenting viewpoint or voicing the "wrong" opinion may lead to complaints, investigation, and disciplinary action. This lends itself to vital debate and dialogue, including on crucial matters of the day. The Supreme Court of the United States has made clear that speech related to social and political issues is at the core of the First Amendment's protections;[8] allowing such expression to flourish benefits not only the campus community, but also our democracy as a whole. The Chicago Statement adds, in pertinent part:

> In a word, the University's fundamental commitment is to the principle that debate or deliberation may not be suppressed because the ideas put forth are thought by some or even by most members of the University community to be offensive, unwise, immoral, or wrong-headed. It is for the individual members of the University community, not for the University as an institution, to make those judgments for themselves, and to act on those judgments not by seeking to suppress speech, but by openly and vigorously contesting the ideas that they oppose.

> As a corollary to the University's commitment to protect and promote free expression, members of the University community must also act in conformity with the principle of free expression. Although members of the University community are free to criticize and contest the views expressed on campus, and to criticize and contest speakers who are invited to express their views on campus, they may not obstruct or otherwise interfere with the freedom of others to express views they reject or even loathe.[9]

These provisions, too, have tremendous value. They help to inform the campus community that students, faculty, and others are expected to use the power of their own voice to respond to speech that upsets or offends others, rather than call on the institution to respond on their behalf. By managing expectations in this way, the adoption of such a policy statement can help to head off controversy before it gets underway. Moreover, under these provisions, students, faculty, and others are expected to exercise their expressive rights in a manner that respects the freedom of expression of others. Stated differently, their right to free speech ends where it interferes with the free speech rights of someone else.

It is worth noting that both the American Association of Universities (AAU) and the Association of Public and Land-Grant Universities (APLU) have come out with their own free speech statements. The AAU statement, released in April 2018 on behalf of the association's sixty-two member institutions, provides, in relevant part: "While we may deem some speech to be odious, disgraceful, and antithetical to our values, our campuses are and should remain places where ideas can be expressed free of disruption, intimidation, and violence."[10] Likewise, the APLU statement, released in April 2018 on behalf its 237 member institutions, declares, in pertinent part: "With a mission to advance the public interest, public universities have a responsibility to not just to be *[sic]* outspoken advocates for free speech, but leaders in providing a forum for civil discourse and disagreement."[11]

In the current climate, all colleges and universities should consider adopting their own policy statement on issues relating to free speech and campus discussion.

II. EDUCATE STUDENTS ABOUT THE VALUE AND EFFICACY OF FREE SPEECH

The second important strategy that universities can utilize is to make sure that their students—as well as other members of the university community—understand the many speech-related issues that may come up during their time on campus, as well as how those issues are part of a larger give and take that benefits all higher education.

Universities can accomplish this goal in several ways, including through programs that take place during freshman orientation and "welcome week" events at the beginning of a new academic year. They can also introduce a speaker series to bring in scholars and commentators on a wide variety of topics; create a debate series on campus; provide an alternate forum for students to discuss their views when a controversial speaker is invited to campus; and utilize other programs to ensure that free speech is at the forefront of students' minds throughout the academic year.

With respect to orientation activities, Purdue University provides a great example through its "Boiler Gold Rush" program, which incorporates a "Freedom of Expression" component for all incoming freshmen students.[12] Purdue's program provides valuable training to students by utilizing skits inspired by real-life events at the university, a faculty panel for discussion, and video clips showcasing speakers and commentators on the issue of campus free speech.[13] In this way, Purdue—which was one of the first universities to adopt its own version of the Chicago Statement—can bring its institutional commitment to open inquiry to real life before students. The program not only brings the words of Purdue's policy statement to action in common scenarios involving campus preachers, offensive expression in a student's dormitory, and more (thereby testing the resolve of the university's commitment to free speech), it creates discussion and reflection about how students themselves would respond to these controversial and sometimes-difficult issues.

Other colleges have found success via more regular programming on campus. Stanford University, for instance, introduced "Cardinal Conversations" in 2018, a "new series of conversations on burning issues of our time, featuring some of today's leading thinkers." In the university's own words, "At a time when attempts are being made on both the far left and the far right to limit what can be discussed on university campuses, Stanford's president, Marc Tessier-Lavigne, and provost, Persis Drell, have signaled their commitment to free speech."[14] The University of Illinois at Urbana-Champaign, similarly, instituted "Critical Conversations," "[a] series of discussions on potentially divisive issues involving campus and community stakeholders."[15] The university chancellor's remarks about the program reveal its core intent:

> "Public universities like ours have a responsibility to be the place where public and open conversations about even the most difficult ideas and issues take place," [Chancellor Robert] Jones said. "As a society, we will not find new solutions to our most pressing challenges if we cannot even talk about them. That's what we envision for this series. These conversations are a first step in

> understanding different perspectives and finding common ground to move us forward and beyond the issues that divide us."[16]

Other examples abound. Central Washington University hosted a six-day "First Amendment Festival," with a workshop on student activism, a panel discussion about investigative reporting, and a keynote address about how students can respond to "hate speech" without calling for censorship.[17] Winona State University hosted two "Free Speech Public Forums" on campus, inviting students and others to consider questions such as "What should be the role of the university in promoting/protecting free speech?" and "How should the campus deal with difficult, challenging and controversial ideas and speakers?"[18] Winona State even pledged that these forums were "the first step in a longer-term project to create a campus value statement covering academic freedom and free speech issues," tying in the recommendations covered in the first section of this article.[19]

The University of Michigan, for its part, offered a free online course about free speech on campus. The course called on participants to "think critically about the role free speech plays on university campuses and how this discourse shapes the broader narrative about free speech protection across the United States."[20] The course was part of the university's "Teach-Out Series," which it describes as "part of our deep commitment to engage the public in exploring and understanding the problems, events, and phenomena most important to society."[21]

As a final recommendation, universities may consider offering an alternate forum or event for discussion whenever either a controversial speaker is brought to campus or a student group is hosting a controversial event. This type of forum will provide students with a space to air their views and discuss why they may disagree with the speaker's beliefs (or with the choice of speaker in the first place) without resorting to tactics that may lead to disruption of the event or shouting down of the speaker. Of course, students would be well within their rights to protest or engage in other forms of counter-speech, provided they do not disrupt the event itself. However, providing an alternate forum may in some instances be more helpful to students, so that they can appreciate the fact that others on campus agree with them as well as speak frankly without feeling intimidated.

Colleges have a wide range of options available to them if they wish to create programs and events that address the topic of free speech. Doing so along the lines of any of the examples cited in this section will go a long way toward informing students about the principles behind the First Amendment and why they merit full protection in the higher education setting.

III. HAVE SOUND POLICIES IN PLACE TO PROTECT STUDENT AND FACULTY SPEECH RIGHTS

A third step that colleges can take is to ensure that their written policies and regulations fully uphold the First Amendment rights of students and faculty (or, in the case of private universities that are committed to freedom of expression, that their policies live up to that commitment).

Having sound policies in place will have numerous benefits, not the least of which is that university officials and administrators will only have permissible, constitutional regulations at their disposal. This will help to ensure that when they are responding to particular speech-related situations on campus—oftentimes without the luxury of much deliberation and reflection—they are informed and equipped with tools that will allow them to respect students' free speech rights.

Consider, for example, the case of Robert van Tuinen, a student at Modesto Junior College (MJC) in California who simply wished to distribute copies of the U.S. Constitution on campus to his fellow students. Despite the clearly protected nature of his expressive activity—as well as the fact that he was doing it on Constitution Day, of all days—van Tuinen was stopped by a campus police officer, who informed him that he could not distribute any written materials without registering his activity with the college's student development office.[22] Upon attempting to comply, Van Tuinen was further informed by a clerical staff member in the student center that he would need to stay within the college's "free speech area" and that he would need to wait until another day later in the month or potentially even the next month in order to distribute his copies of the Constitution.[23]

Cases like van Tuinen's should never make it to this point, and universities can better serve their administrators, staff members, and police officers by having well written policies and procedures on the books. Unfortunately for both van Tuinen and MJC, it took a federal lawsuit before he was able to vindicate his First Amendment rights. As part of his lawsuit, van Tuinen sued administrators at MJC as well as the Yosemite Community College District, alleging violations of his First Amendment right in both policy and practice.[24] Ultimately, MJC chose to settle the lawsuit, agreeing to pay Van Tuinen $50,000 in damages and to revise its policies to allow students to engage in expressive activity in open areas across campus.[25]

It goes without saying that this was an expensive lesson for MJC's administrators to learn—and for the taxpayers of California to foot the bill toward. Colleges can avoid a similar situation altogether by enacting, and periodically reviewing, speech policies that meet First Amendment standards. Moreover, such policies will properly inform students, faculty, and others about their speech rights, thereby encouraging them to speak freely and exercise their First Amendment rights. Conversely, having speech-restrictive policies on the books can create a harmful chilling effect on campus discourse.

Not only do restrictive policies poorly inform students and faculty about the extent of their speech rights, but they also contribute to a climate of censorship by providing university administrators with poor tools with which to regulate and take action in the face of campus expression deemed to be offensive or unwanted.

Again, the good news—as was the case in section I—is that colleges have a useful model to follow. Much as the Chicago Statement provides an excellent starting point for the enactment of a principled policy statement on campus free speech, a number of colleges and universities have in recent years demonstrated how easy and straightforward it is to bring their written policies and regulations in line with the requirements of the First Amendment.

Since 2015, institutions such as the University of North Carolina at Chapel Hill, the University of Florida, Emory University, Western State Colorado University, the University of Chicago, the University of North Dakota, the University of Maryland—College Park, State University of New York—Plattsburgh, Auburn University, and Claremont McKenna College have all revised their speech-related policies to earn FIRE's highest, "green light" rating,[26] indicating that their policies do not imperil the free speech rights of students and faculty.

These and all of the other green-light universities do more than pay lip service to the First Amendment. Their policies contribute to a campus climate that favors freedom of expression, allowing debate and dissent to flourish. Students and faculty members who are made aware of these policies and of their college's green light rating should feel encouraged to exercise their First Amendment rights free of the fear of administrative investigation, punishment, or censorship.

Additionally, such policies provide the requisite proper guidance to the administrators and staff members who will be charged with enforcing them. In contrast to the Modesto Junior College case discussed above, consider the policy on "Free Inquiry, Expression, and Assembly" maintained by the University of Mississippi, another one of the institutions earning a green-light rating from FIRE. The University of Mississippi's policy states, in relevant part:

> Speaker's Corners: To facilitate robust debate and the free exchange of ideas, the University has established high visibility areas on campus as "Speaker's Corners" that may be used for personal expression by any person including non-students and other campus guests. This use may be without permission from the University so long as the area has not been previously reserved or

> scheduled for a particular function, no sound amplification is used, and the participants do not violate other University policies. [. . .]

Designated Speaker's Corners include:

a. the Union Plaza adjacent to the Grove,
b. the area surrounding the flagpole in the Lyceum Circle, and
c. the plaza in front of Fulton Chapel.[27]

To make clear that these are not the only places on campus where students can engage in expressive activity—but rather are intended as "high visibility" areas where students can most effectively disseminate their message, without need to provide advance notice to the university—the policy further provides:

> Nothing in this section shall be interpreted as limiting the right of student expression elsewhere on the campus so long as the expressive activities or related student conduct do not violate any other applicable University policies.[28]

This approach opens up a great deal of the University of Mississippi's campus to student expression, particularly the open outdoor spaces that are well suited for this purpose. University officials enforcing this policy will have no legitimate reason, consistent with the policy's terms, to restrict student expressive activity to a particular "free speech zone" or to force students to wait a significant amount of time to engage in that expression, as took place in the Modesto Junior College case. As such, the policy will serve all members of the university community well, including those who wish to protest or speak out against a student's or student organization's initial expression.

All universities would be well advised to take the same approach with their speech codes, whether they be demonstration regulations, posting policies, harassment policies, bias incident protocols, residence hall policies, civility pledges, or other forms of speech codes.[29] The result would be an improved campus regulatory framework for administrators and students alike.

IV. BE PREPARED, AND HAVE PROTOCOLS FOR HANDLING THE INEVITABLE CONTROVERSY

The fourth major recommendation is that all colleges and universities should expect a campus controversy at some point—whether it involves an outside speaker or the expressive activity of a student or student organization—and should have their protocols prepared and in place in anticipation of such controversy.

For many colleges, this will entail having their campus security and other staff members on the ground trained to handle to a wide range of scenarios. While the specific training offered is best left to the discretion of each individual institution, any university will be well served by having well considered and clearly written protocols and procedures to guide on-the-ground decision-making.

Brown University, for example, has promulgated a useful set of "Protest and Demonstration Guidelines" that very specifically differentiate between constitutionally protected protest and unprotected disruption. The guidelines begin by declaring, in relevant part:

> Protest is a necessary and acceptable means of expression within the Brown community. However, protest becomes unacceptable when it obstructs the basic exchange of ideas. Such obstruction is a form of censorship, no matter who initiates it or for what reasons.
>
> Protests or demonstrations that infringe upon the rights of others to peaceful assembly, orderly protest, free exchange of ideas, or that interfere with the rights of others to make use of or enjoy the facilities or attend the functions of the University cannot be tolerated.[30]

The guidelines then move to a detailed discussion of what is and is not protected speech:

> Picket lines which permit free passage of those who wish to pass, and signs, banners and peaceful assemblies are all acceptable. [. . .] Actions such as the following, are unacceptable: blocking; obstructing or impeding passage of a person or vehicle; actions that result in bodily harm; erecting or placing of obstructions that result in depriving others of their rights.
>
> Halting a lecture, debate, or any public forum is an unacceptable form of protest. "Halting" means directly or indirectly preventing a speaker from speaking—even for a brief period of time—or seizing control of a public forum for one's own purposes.[31]

Through these guidelines, not only does the university provide sufficient explanation to its students, it instructs its administrators and campus police about the proper way in which to regulate student expression. Officials at Brown have little excuse, considering these guidelines, to misapply policy and restrict constitutionally protected protest activity.

The University of Missouri, meanwhile, has promulgated a comprehensive set of policies and procedures providing its staff members and campus security with specific guidance as to how they should handle various types of student expressive activity. To begin with, the university has set forth a "Guiding Principles" document, which helpfully includes discussion of the "right to dissent," the "[s]peaker's right to communicate" (both in terms of closed meetings and open meetings), true threats, the "legal distinction between outdoor space and indoor space," the extent of the right to use a "[v]ocal response" against a speaker, and more.[32] Critically, the "Guiding Principles" include a section relating to "[s]ecurity of attendees," providing, in relevant part:

- Upon making [the] determination that security measures are required, University officials, acting in consultation with the University of Missouri Police Department and other law enforcement agencies as appropriate, may determine the nature and extent of security measures required and should ensure their implementation in a way that does not unfairly discriminate against nor intimidate any participant. The University will fund these measures.
- Possible security measures may include, but are not limited to, (a) bags and other containers being subject to search by MUPD or other security officers; (b) bags and other containers being required to be put in a checkroom before entrance into an event; (c) coats or outerwear being required to be put in a checkroom before entrance into an event; (d) videotaping, audiotaping, and/or photographing of the event with prior notice to the audience.
- Only MUPD or another official law enforcement agency, or member of such agency, may use force as a security measure.[33]

In this way, the university provides a well planned-out and forward-thinking approach to its employees, thereby addressing potential problems before they ever present themselves. To complement the "Guiding Principles," the university has also put together policies governing a wide range of issues, from use of facilities to sound amplification to even camping on campus.[34] As is the case with Brown University, staff members and campus security at the University of Missouri should feel well equipped to handle the type of speech-related controversies or problems that may come their way.

Other institutions would be well advised to likewise provide detailed and informative guidance to their staff members in a proactive manner. In this way, schools can pre-empt free-speech controversies before they arise in the first place.

CONCLUSION

The foregoing discussion is intended as guidance that may help university leadership to navigate the often-treacherous waters of today's free-speech controversies. Of course, the steps outlined above are generalized guideposts, and the precise approach taken by an individual college or university will necessarily depend on the particulars of its institutional history and culture, student body composition, input from faculty members and staff, administrative preferences, campus location, and other pertinent factors.

The end goal, however, is roughly the same for all schools: to create a campus climate that respects freedom of expression and open inquiry, while at the same time providing students with an educational environment in which they feel welcome, safe, and able to carry about their scholarly pursuits.

Toward those ends, more discussion is always worthwhile, whether it is on the part of higher education leaders, civil liberties advocates, media commentators, or students and faculty themselves. This article seeks to join and contribute to that discussion so that, ultimately, those who depend on higher education for their learning and livelihood may be best served by its policies and practices.

NOTES

1. See, e.g., Press Release, Foundation for Individual Rights in Education, "'Too controversial': Polk State College rejects professor's anti-Trump artwork," February 20, 2018, www.thefire.org/too-controversial-polk-state-college-rejects-professors-anti-trump-artwork.

2. See, e.g., Samantha Harris, "'Stop Debating': CUNY Law Students Disrupt Speaker and his Critic," *FIRE Newsdesk*, April 12, 2018, www.thefire.org/stop-debating-cuny-law-students-disrupt-speaker-and-his-critic.

3. See, e.g., Brynne Madway, "Of Saltines and Speech Codes," *FIRE Newsdesk,* March 9, 2018, www.thefire.org/of-saltines-and-speech-codes.

4. Mary Zoeller, "Universities Should Endorse Free Expression Now, Avoid Criticism Later," *FIRE Newsdesk*, October 20, 2017, www.thefire.org/universities-should-endorse-free-expression-now-avoid-criticism-later.

5. Available at http://provost.uchicago.edu/sites/default/files/documents/reports/FOECommitteeReport.pdf.

6. University of Chicago, "Report of the Committee on Freedom of Expression," January 2015, https://provost.uchicago.edu/sites/default/files/documents/reports/FOECommitteeReport.pdf.

7. Ibid.

8. See, e.g., *Garrison v. Louisiana*, 379 U.S. 64, 74–75 (1964) (internal quotations omitted) (holding that "speech concerning public affairs is more than self-expression;

it is the essence of self-government," reflecting "our profound national commitment to the principle that debate on public issues should be uninhibited, robust, and wide-open.").

9. "Report of the Committee on Freedom of Expression," supra.

10. Association of American Universities, "AAU Presidents and Chancellors Reaffirm Commitment to Free Speech on Campus," April 18, 2018, www.aau.edu/newsroom/press-releases/aau-presidents-and-chancellors-reaffirm-commitment-free-speech-campus.

11. Association of Public and Land-Grant Universities, "APLU Statement on Public Universities' Commitment to Free Speech," April 2018, www.aplu.org/about-us/commitment-to-free-speech/index.html.

12. Purdue University, "Boiler Gold Rush: 2017 Activities and Schedule," www.purdue.edu/orientation/bgr/activities.html.

13. Alex Morey, "Free Speech Orientation Program Keeps Conversation Going at Purdue," *FIRE Newsdesk*, December 5, 2016, www.thefire.org/free-speech-orientation-program-keeps-conversation-going-at-purdue.

14. Stanford University, "A Free Speech Initiative at Stanford," www.hoover.org/cardinal-conversations.

15. University of Illinois News Bureau, "'Chancellor's Critical Conversations' series kicks off with Native imagery discussion," April 3, 2018, https://news.illinois.edu/view/6367/634563.

16. Ibid.

17. Yakima Herald, "CWU hosts First Amendment Festival," April 18, 2018, www.yakimaherald.com/news/local/cwu-hosts-first-amendment-festival/article_409fa4c8-4399-11e8-9164-63ee667f25a9.html.

18. Winona State University Events Calendar, https://w3.winona.edu/events/EventList.aspx?fromdate=4/12/2018&todate=4/18/2018&display=Week&view=DateTime.

19. Ibid.

20. Coursera, "Free Speech on Campus Teach-Out," https://online.umich.edu/teach-outs/free-speech-on-campus-teach-out/?

21. Ibid.

22. Press Release, Foundation for Individual Rights in Education, "Lawsuit! Student Ordered to Stop Handing Out Constitutions on Constitution Day Files Suit," October 10, 2013, www.thefire.org/lawsuit-student-ordered-to-stop-handing-out-constitutions-on-constitution-day-files-suit.

23. Ibid.

24. Press Release, Foundation for Individual Rights in Education, "Victory: Modesto Junior College Settles Student's First Amendment Lawsuit," Feb. 25, 2014, www.thefire.org/victory-modesto-junior-college-settles-students-first-amendment-lawsuit.

25. Ibid.

26. The full list of institutions earning a green light rating from FIRE is available at hwww.thefire.org/spotlight/?y=&speech_code=Green&institution_type=&type=advanced&submit=Search.

27. University of Mississippi, Policy on "Free Inquiry, Expression, and Assembly," https://policies.olemiss.edu.

28. Ibid.

29. For a rundown of these various speech code categories, see REPORT, Foundation for Individual Rights in Education, "Spotlight on Speech Codes 2018: The State of Free Speech on Our Nation's Campuses," www.thefire.org/spotlight-on-speech-codes-2018.

30. Brown University, "Protest and Demonstration Guidelines," www.brown.edu/about/administration/student-life/studentconduct/policies-regulations/protest-demonstration-guidelines.

31. Ibid.

32. University of Missouri, "Free Expression at Mizzou: Guiding Principles," https://freespeech.missouri.edu/principles.

33. Ibid.

34. University of Missouri, "Free Expression at Mizzou: Policies," https://freespeech.missouri.edu/policies.

REFERENCES

Association of American Universities. "AAU Presidents and Chancellors Reaffirm Commitment to Free Speech on Campus." April 18, 2018. www.aau.edu/newsroom/press-releases/aau-presidents-and-chancellors-reaffirm-commitment-free-speech-campus.

Association of Public and Land-Grant Universities. "APLU Statement on Public Universities' Commitment to Free Speech." April 2018. www.aplu.org/about-us/commitment-to-free-speech/index.html.

Brown University. "Protest and Demonstration Guidelines." www.brown.edu/about/administration/student-life/studentconduct/policies-regulations/protest-demonstration-guidelines.

Coursera. "Free Speech on Campus Teach-Out." https://online.umich.edu/teach-outs/free-speech-on-campus-teach-out/?

FIRE. "Lawsuit! Student Ordered to Stop Handing Out Constitutions on Constitution Day Files Suit." October 10, 2013. www.thefire.org/lawsuit-student-ordered-to-stop-handing-out-constitutions-on-constitution-day-files-suit.

FIRE. "Spotlight on Speech Codes 2018: The State of Free Speech on Our Nation's Campuses." www.thefire.org/spotlight-on-speech-codes-2018.

FIRE. "'Too controversial': Polk State College rejects professor's anti-Trump artwork." Feb. 20, 2018. www.thefire.org/too-controversial-polk-state-college-rejects-professors-anti-trump-artwork.

FIRE. "Victory: Modesto Junior College Settles Student's First Amendment Lawsuit." Feb. 25, 2014. www.thefire.org/victory-modesto-junior-college-settles-students-first-amendment-lawsuit.

Garrison v. Louisiana, 379 U.S. 64 (1964).

Harris, Samantha. "'Stop Debating': CUNY Law Students Disrupt Speaker and his Critic." *FIRE Newsdesk*, April 12, 2018. www.thefire.org/stop-debating-cuny-law-students-disrupt-speaker-and-his-critic.

Madway, Brynne. "Of Saltines and Speech Codes." *FIRE Newsdesk*, March 9, 2018. www.thefire.org/of-saltines-and-speech-codes.

Morey, Alex. "Free Speech Orientation Program Keeps Conversation Going at Purdue." *FIRE Newsdesk*, December 5, 2016. www.thefire.org/free-speech-orientation-program-keeps-conversation-going-at-purdue.

Purdue University. "Boiler Gold Rush: 2017 Activities and Schedule." www.purdue.edu/orientation/bgr/activities.html.

Stanford University. "A Free Speech Initiative at Stanford." www.hoover.org/cardinal-conversations.

University of Chicago. "Report of the Committee on Freedom of Expression," January 2015. https://provost.uchicago.edu/sites/default/files/documents/reports/FOECommitteeReport.pdf.

University of Illinois News Bureau. "'Chancellor's Critical Conversations' series kicks off with Native imagery discussion." April 3, 2018. https://news.illinois.edu/view/6367/634563.

University of Mississippi. Policy on "Free Inquiry, Expression, and Assembly." https://policies.olemiss.edu.

University of Missouri. "Free Expression at Mizzou: Guiding Principles." https://freespeech.missouri.edu/principles.

University of Missouri. "Free Expression at Mizzou: Policies." https://freespeech.missouri.edu/policies.

Winona State University Events Calendar. https://w3.winona.edu/events/EventList.aspx?fromdate=4/12/2018&todate=4/18/2018&display=Week&view=DateTime.

Yakima Herald. "CWU hosts First Amendment Festival." April 18, 2018. www.yakimaherald.com/news/local/cwu-hosts-first-amendment-festival/article_409fa4c8-4399-11e8-9164-63ee667f25a9.html.

Zoeller, Mary. "Universities Should Endorse Free Expression Now, Avoid Criticism Later." *FIRE Newsdesk*, October 20, 2017. www.thefire.org/universities-should-endorse-free-expression-now-avoid-criticism-later.

Chapter 16

Campus Free Speech, Hostage to Hecklers—Again

James M. Manley

Spring 2017 marked the end of a tumultuous year on American college campuses, with protests over invited speakers—both controversial and not-so-controversial—turning violent.[1] National Review writer Stanley Kurtz dubbed it the Year of the Shout-down.[2] Kurtz catalogued more than a dozen instances between September 2016 and May 2017—at least one a month—of hecklers shouting to silence invited speakers or barricading rooms to prevent an audience from assembling, which certainly qualifies the 2016–17 academic year for the dubious honor. But then came the fall of 2017. Halfway through the semester, the rate of shout-downs had nearly quadrupled that of the previous spring. Almost twenty events had been disrupted as winter break began—with a week of daily shout-downs in October.[3]

These anecdotes of intolerance are supported by empirical research. A March 2018 Gallup-Knight Foundation poll reported that about 30 percent of college students favor shout-downs, up from 22 percent two years ago.[4] More alarming, 1 in 10 approve of violent disruption, which amounts to approximately two million college students condoning violence against people based on their viewpoint.[5] More alarming still, 15 percent of college presidents agree that it is sometimes acceptable to shout-down a visiting speaker.[6] For more than half of college students, "promoting an inclusive society" is a higher priority than protecting free speech rights.[7]

Yet, inclusiveness should not be seen as incompatible with free speech; the history of higher education shows that these need not be seen as two competing values. Free speech requires inclusivity, because it requires tolerance to hear competing viewpoints and values. An institutional commitment to free speech is a commitment to welcoming genuine diversity of ideas, forms of expression, and values. The melting pot of ideas inevitably leads to conflict, but it is how we confront ideas we disagree with that defines us. Will students be encouraged to mount sonic and physical attacks against those with whom they disagree, or to engage in civil dialogue? The way universities answer that question will define the state of discourse as today's students become tomorrow's leaders.

Where this impulse to campus censorship arose is a complex question that needs answering. But in the short term, action is urgently needed to save the university's marketplace of ideas. This essay proposes one path for action to address the most immediate concerns created by the present censorship crisis. If two million students—and some portion of college presidents—cannot abandon support for violence in response to speech, understanding the root causes of the crisis will come too late. Whatever the cause, there are immediate actions that history tells us will stanch the impulse to censorship and give breathing room for free speech. Preventing the normalization of shout-downs will go a long way to restoring free expression as a living tradition on campus, regardless of whence the impulse to censor arises. Part one of this essay recounts historical lessons about linking free speech and intellectual tolerance. Part two illustrates ways those historical lessons have been learned, and not learned. Part three proposes an answer to the short-term problem of shout-downs and other manifestations of intolerance on campus.

I. THE CAMPUS SPEECH CRISIS IS NOT THE SNOWFLAKES' FAULT

It is fashionable to call sensitive students snowflakes when they respond to harsh ideas by retreating to "safe spaces" or calling for draconian speech codes or de-platforming a visiting speaker through shout-downs and other aggressive tactics.[8] Obviously, the image of frailty breaks down when we review the belligerent and violent tactics of the so-called snowflakes. Take the burning campus at the University of California, Berkley, in response to the prospect of hearing buffoon provocateur Milo Yiannopoulos. Snowflakes do not set fires. But there is a deeper reason to reject the pejorative term: the campus speech crisis is not their fault; it wasn't even their idea.

The shout-down, the speech code, the free speech zone are inventions at least 50 years old. The idea of imposing special restrictions on campus speech is older than even the parents of some of the so-called snowflakes. The way forward is not to denigrate students, but to attack the timeless impulse to censorship and the tools of censorship.

One recent example of so-called snowflake students calling for censorship occurred in 2015 at Yale. Erika Christakis, a faculty member and associate master of Silliman College, one of Yale's twelve undergraduate communities, wrote an email about Halloween costumes that would cost her and her husband their jobs.[9] Christakis's email criticized university guidelines on potentially offensive Halloween costumes; Christakis encouraged students to think for themselves and question assumptions about cultural appropriation and sensitivity: "Free speech and the ability to tolerate offence are the hallmarks of a free and open society."[10] Students protested Christakis's email and, faculty, deans, and nearly a thousand students called for her resignation. Her husband and master of Silliman College, Nicholas Christakis, defended his wife's views, which put him face-to-face with yelling students who also called for his resignation. Both resigned from their positions at Silliman within a year.[11] These students and staff were merely continuing a long tradition of stifling dissent at Yale.

Yale was opposed to diversity of expression from its very beginnings in 1701 as a Puritan cheerleader. Early faculty members swore allegiance to the strictly religious Connecticut "colony creed" and attendance at church services was required on penalty of a twenty-shilling fine. Using an Anglican phrase during a commencement service got the president of the university fired in 1722.[12]

In 1937, that reputation for not tolerating dissent led Provost Edgar S. Furniss to write a landmark memo to the new president, Charles Seymour. In words that might shock the modern ear, Furniss complained:

> [We] have acquired the reputation of being biased in favor of conservative opinion on current public issues, and of using administrative authority to prevent the expression of dissent whenever this takes an advanced liberal or radical form.[13]

It is worth pausing here to recognize that free speech is not a matter of promoting certain political views over others. The only value of the free exchange of ideas is in the free exchange of all ideas—regardless of which ideological orthodoxy predominates. Seymour agreed with Furniss's defense of intellectual diversity and communist, interventionist, isolationist, and anti-McCarthyist speakers engaged with the campus community.

But the "storms of controversy and crises of confrontation" of the 1960s would cause that administrative tolerance for controversial views to fade.[14] In 1963, the Yale Political Union—a debate society—invited Alabama Gov. George Wallace to speak. Provost Kingman Brewster successfully pressured the organizers to withdraw their invitation because of "the damage which Governor Wallace's appearance would do to the confidence of the New Haven community in Yale and the feelings of the New Haven Negro population."[15] The *Yale Daily News* reported that the reaction of the university community to the dis-invitation "appears almost overwhelmingly negative."

Unlike the Christakis fiasco, students and faculty were firmly on the side of free expression, because they realized that dis-inviting Wallace prevented either side from engaging on the issues. For that reason, the *Boston Herald* called the decision to silence a segregationist a "disservice to the cause of civil rights and liberties."[16]

The Era of "De-Platforming" Had Dawned

General William Westmoreland, Chief of Staff of the United States Army, was blockaded from giving a speech to the Yale Political Union in April 1972. The response was muted, from students, faculty, and administrators, and no groundswell of free speech sentiment occurred as had been the case nine years earlier with Governor Wallace. After General Westmoreland was silenced, Secretary of State William Rogers canceled a May appearance in the face of planned disruptions.[17]

Two years later, in April 1974, Stanford University physicist William Shockley was thrice disinvited before finally accepting an invitation to debate his eugenic views against William Rusher, the publisher of National Review. Shockley faced "open, determined, and menacing" protests, designed to prevent him from debating his views on genetic inferiority and voluntary sterilization.[18] Despite promises of "severe discipline" against students using "violent or coercive action," nary a word was heard from the dais; for over an hour, the speakers "were drowned out by derisive applause, insults chanted at Shockley, and shouted obscenities."[19]

The administration's response was languid and indecisive. Penalties were eventually meted out but immediately watered down and then eliminated after a probationary period. The campus press was equivocal about who was to blame for the shout-down. Few faculty members spoke out, but those who did spurred the administration into action.[20]

The Shockley shout-down prevented him from speaking, but it also saved him from the embarrassment of a debate; the real victim was the principle of free expression. Recognizing what was lost in the shouting and what the university administration and community had failed to defend, the faculty of Yale College passed a resolution to "reaffirm its adherence to the principles set forth in the Undergraduate Regulations" and "to appoint a faculty commission to examine the condition of free expression, peaceful dissent, mutual respect and tolerance at Yale, to draft recommendations for any measures it may deem necessary for the maintenance of those principles, and to report to the faculties of the University early next term."[21]

Partly in response to that resolution, President Brewster organized a Committee on Freedom of Expression, led by Yale historian C. Vann Woodward—who had criticized the Wallace disinvitation a decade before, after fighting for school desegregation on the *Brown v. Board of Education* legal team.[22] The Committee produced a report of its findings and recommendations, which would come to be known as the Woodward Report.

The Woodward Report eloquently upholds the principle of free speech, and it insists that students who shout-down visiting speakers must be disciplined. The Woodward Report establishes a sanctions policy, and a system for warning potentially disruptive students of disciplinary consequences. But only the first part of the report—a paean to free expression—was adopted as university policy. Although, the report's signers were clear that civility is necessary to protect free expression:

> In the room where the invited speaker is to talk, all members of the audience are under an obligation to comply with a general standard of civility. This means that any registration of dissent that materially interferes with the speaker's right to proceed is a punishable offense. Of course a member of the audience may protest in a silent, symbolic fashion, for example, by wearing a black arm band. More active forms of protest may be tolerated such as briefly booing, clapping hands, or heckling. But any disruptive activity must stop when the chair or an appropriate university official requests silence. Failure to quit in response to a reasonable request for order is a punishable offense.[23]

That lesson—that discipline is a necessary consequence for disrupting the free exchange of ideas—was and is a hard lesson for universities to learn. It is easier for administrators to stand on the sidelines and not defend the indefensible or even the controversial. It is easier still to call a shout-down "reasonable" or "limited" and forestall punishment. It happened in the Shockley shout-down, it happened in the Christakis incident, it happens nearly every time a shout-down occurs.[24] And so, we have seen shout-downs on and off ever sense, with a string of high-profile incidents in recent years.

II. CAMPUS ADMINISTRATORS NEED HELP TO ADDRESS THE CAMPUS SPEECH CRISIS

The Woodward Report makes a strong case that the credible threat of discipline—as a natural consequence of a robust institutional commitment to free expression—is the surest way to prevent shout-downs and preserve civil dialogue on campus. But, as with most commitments, it is easier made than kept.

University administrators face a push and pull from many competing factions: the faculty demanding freedom of expression; the legislature or the Regents calling for certain topics to be taught, or not taught; the students demanding luxury accommodations and safe spaces to avoid intellectual challenge. Administrators need guidelines, like those explained in the Woodward Report, so that they do not lose sight of the all-important role that free expression plays in the university setting. "Freedom of inquiry," according to University of Chicago President Edward H. Levi, "is our inheritance."[25] Administrators are squandering that inheritance for the sake of political and administrative expedience.

Two recent incidents illustrate the need for oversight from above the administrative level. One shout-down at City University of New York School of Law showed the need for holding administrators to disciplinary standards, while another shout-down that didn't happen at the University of Wisconsin-Madison illustrates the benefit of a firm commitment to discipline. Both the CUNY event and the Wisconsin non-event provide guidance about the way to protect free speech against intellectual intolerance.

At CUNY, Josh Blackman was shouted down trying to discuss the importance of free speech on campus.[26] Blackman, an Associate Professor of Law at the South Texas College of Law Houston, is a regular on the Federalist Society circuit and had been invited to CUNY by the local Federalist Society chapter to give a speech he had delivered without incident many times before, at Southern Illinois University, Texas Southern University, the University of Massachusetts, Barry University, the University of Oregon, and his home institution. As soon as the CUNY Federalist Society chapter began promoting the event, protestors started to organize.

On the day of the speech, Mary Lu Bilek, the dean of CUNY Law, sent an email to all students reminding them that CUNY was "committed to academic freedom, the free exchange of ideas, and expression of all points of view, including the freedom to disagree with the viewpoints of others" and providing a link to the "procedure for handling disruptive demonstrations," as detailed in CUNY's Policy on Freedom of Expression and Expressive Conduct.[27] Students gathered to draw-up signs and organize a demonstration. CUNY's chief of public safety met with Blackman to discuss his "exit plan" and then escorted Blackman to the classroom. Blackman began recording the events and what follows is based on his video, as well as video taken by the event organizers.[28]

As Blackman entered the classroom, several dozen students gathered outside with signs and chanted "shame on you," booed, and hissed. Inside, a handful of people were seated, but soon the sign-carrying protesters lined up on all four sides of the room—including about a dozen at the front of the room, directly behind Blackman. The Federalist Society chapter president asked the students to move away from the front of the room. They did not move. Instead, they began to shout rapid-fire: "Shame on you." "I don't understand how CUNY allows this." "There are students that are directly affected by this hate speech." "Legal objectivity is a myth." "You still have an opportunity to leave."

The heckling continued through an attempted introduction. After a stern warning from an administrator to allow Blackman to speak or face consequences, Blackman began to speak. He got through about a minute of extemporaneous remarks about the distinction between supporting a policy and supporting a law, when a law student responded, "fuck the law," and the censorship-by-sustained heckling resumed. After about eight minutes of this, an audience member spoke in Blackman's defense—by cogently attacking Blackman's views and asking the crowd to let Blackman respond. The hecklers left and a contentious but generally respectful conversation ensued for another hour as Blackman called on members of the audience.

The CUNY hecklers had commandeered the event for a little more than 10 percent of the total time. There should be little disagreement that their protest violated the student handbook, which states:

> a member of the academic community shall not intentionally obstruct and/or forcibly prevent others from the exercise of their rights. Nor shall she/he interfere with the institution's educational process or facilities, or the rights of those who wish to avail themselves of any of the institution's instructional, personal, administrative, recreational, and community services.[29]

But Dean Bilek disagreed. She characterized the disruption as "reasonable" because it was "limited": "This non-violent, limited protest was a reasonable exercise of protected free speech, and it did not violate any university policy."[30] This struck many in the academic community, including four CUNY professors, as a change in policy and an invitation to heckle and disrupt, so long as suppression of opposing views was kept to some arbitrary limit.[31;32] After Dean Bilek's surrender to the mob, hecklers know that eight minutes is an acceptable amount of time to silence a guest speaker. Will nine minutes be tolerated? Ten? Does it matter how long the event goes on after the shouting stops? Should CUNY professors now expect the same eight to ten minutes of heckling each class, à la protestors at Reed College who took over a western civilization class?[33] CUNY's handbook makes a commitment to free expression, but Dean Bilek's willingness to abandon that commitment has made those absurd questions relevant.

The Regents of the University of Wisconsin enacted a policy that gives clear answers to those questions. Faced with shout-downs on its campus—which were similarly "limited" and similarly disruptive[34]—the Regents acted decisively to protect free expression from the heckler's veto. In April 2017, State Representative Jesse Kremer introduced the Wisconsin Campus Free Speech Act.[35] The bill was based on Goldwater Institute model legislation that had been published that past January, which I coauthored with Jonathan Butcher and Stanley Kurtz.[36] As the bill moved through the legislature, the Regents moved more quickly and enacted a policy in October 2017 that echoed many of the policies contained in the bill.

The new Regents' policy, "Commitment to Academic Freedom and Freedom of Expression," reaffirmed the university's commitment to the "sifting and winnowing" of ideas through free and open scholarship. To protect open dialogue, the policy ensures punishment for students repeatedly found responsible for "violent or other disorderly misconduct that materially and substantially disrupted the free expression of others." It also ensures that "spontaneous" freedom of expression and assembly will be allowed and that "students and employees have the freedom to discuss any problem that presents itself." Each University of Wisconsin institution is also forbidden to "take action, as an institution, in such a way as to require students or employees to express a particular view on a public policy issue." And the Regents imposed new student orientation and annual reporting requirements to ensure those commitments are taken seriously.[37]

The Regents enacted the policy to reflect that "each institution in the University of Wisconsin System has a solemn responsibility not only to promote lively and fearless exploration, deliberation, and debate of ideas, but also to protect those freedoms when others attempt to restrict them."

The policy had its first measurable effect on free expression just three days after it was enacted. Gun-rights advocate and conservative pundit Katie Pavlich was invited to UW-Madison to talk about "campus carry" policies, which allow licensed adults to carry firearms for self-defense on campus, just as they do in most other parts of the state. Her talk was met with a protest, but unlike at CUNY—or even UW Madison before the new policy was in place—the protests were civil (if not particularly tasteful). Approximately twenty people waved dildos outside the event as part of a "Cocks not Glocks" protest. According to organizers of the demonstration, their decision to engage in peaceful protest rather than disrupt the event was a direct result of the Regents' new policy on "materially and substantially disrupt[ing] the free expression of others." The credible threat of discipline worked. [38]

The Pavlich event at UW Madison was a success for free speech not just because Pavlich was allowed to speak, but because protestors were able to deliver their message, too. Respecting each individual's right to peacefully present his or her views is what makes free expression essential to individual autonomy. It is the "sifting and winnowing" that results from multiple perspectives on a contentious issue that gives free expression its vitality and academic value.

III. A POLICY PROPOSAL TO RESTORE FREE SPEECH AS A LIVING TRADITION ON CAMPUS

As the contrast between the CUNY and Wisconsin examples demonstrates, a firm commitment to free expression can help check the impulse to censorship and incentivize students to consider peaceful forms of protest. Whether that commitment comes from the legislature (in the case of public schools) or the regents or trustees (in the case of public or private institutions), policy makers should follow the lead of the Wisconsin Regents and adopt the Goldwater Institute's model policy. Lawmakers in North Carolina, Arizona, Georgia, and Alabama have done just that in the past two years.[39]

To protect the increasingly imperiled principle and practice of campus free speech, the Goldwater model legislation is designed to ensure free expression at America's public university systems. Public debate over the policies contained in the model should strengthen freedom of speech at private colleges and universities as well. The key provisions in the model legislation were inspired by three classic defenses of campus free speech: Yale's 1974 Woodward Report, the University of Chicago's 1967 Kalven Report, and the University of Chicago's 2015 Stone Report. The Goldwater model legislation does several things:

- It creates an official university policy that strongly affirms the importance of free expression, nullifying any existing restrictive speech codes in the process.
- It prevents administrators from disinviting speakers, no matter how controversial, whom members of the campus community wish to hear from.
- It establishes a system of disciplinary sanctions for students and anyone else who interferes with the free-speech rights of others.
- It allows persons whose free-speech rights have been improperly infringed by the university to recover court costs and attorney's fees.
- It reaffirms the principle that universities, at the official institutional level, ought to remain neutral on issues of public controversy to encourage the widest possible range of opinion and dialogue within the university itself.
- It ensures that students will be informed of the official policy on free expression.
- It creates a special subcommittee of the university board of trustees to issue a yearly report to the public, the trustees, the governor, and the legislature on the administrative handling of free-speech issues.

- It requires security fees for invited speakers to be reasonable, and not based on the content of speech. The University may restrict the use of university facilities to invited individuals.
- It protects student organizations from discrimination based on the content of the organization's expression or membership requirements.

Taken together, those provisions create a system of interlocking incentives designed to encourage students and administrators to respect and protect the free expression of others. As Pavlich's experience in Wisconsin demonstrates, those incentives can work to foster freer and more civil debate and restore free expression as a living tradition on campus. That goal is not without risk:

> We take a chance, as the First Amendment takes a chance, when we commit ourselves to the idea that the results of free expression are to the general benefit in the long run, however unpleasant they may appear at the time. . . . If expression may be prevented, censored or punished, because of its content or because of the motives attributed to those who promote it, then it is no longer free.[40]

Freedom can be risky. But we must take that chance, because committing to freedom is essential to protecting individual liberty and fostering a civil society. It is, likewise, essential to maintaining the inheritance of free inquiry that defines the university.

NOTES

1. Mr. Manley is an attorney with Pacific Legal Foundation and a senior fellow at the Goldwater Institute. The views expressed are the author's own.

2. Stanley Kurtz, "Year of the Shout-Down: It Was Worse Than You Think," *National Review* (May 31, 2017), https://www.nationalreview.com/corner/year-shout-down-worse-you-think-campus-free-speech/.

3. Stanley Kurtz, "Campus Shout-Down Rate Nearly Quadruples," *National Review* (Nov. 2, 2017), https://www.nationalreview.com/corner/campus-shout-down-rate-quadruples-free-speech/.

4. Press Release, "College Students Show Strong Support for First Amendment, But Some Say Diversity And Inclusion Is More Important To A Democracy Than Free Speech, Gallup-Knight Survey Shows," Gallup-Knight Foundation (March 12, 2018), https://knightfoundation.org/press/releases/college-students-show-strong-support-for-first-amendment-but-some-say-diversity-and-inclusion-is-more-important-to-a-democracy-than-free-speech-gallup-knight-survey-shows.

5. Cathy Young, "Half of college students aren't sure protecting free speech is important. That's bad news," *Los Angeles Times* (April 8, 2018), http://www.latimes.com/opinion/op-ed/la-oe-young-free-speech-on-campus-20180408-story.html.

6. Scott Jaschik, "Presidents Back Free Speech," *Inside Higher Ed* (April 10, 2018), https://www.insidehighered.com/news/2018/04/10/survey-finds-strong-support-college-presidents-free-speech-campus.

7. Ibid.

8. Daily Wire, "Snowflake Alert: UC Berkeley Offers 'Support and Counseling' For Students Offended By Shapiro's Speech" (Sept. 8, 2017), https://www.dailywire.com/news/20818/do-snowflakes-exist-yes-they-do-uc-berkeley-offers-daily-wire.

9. Erika Christakis, "My Halloween email led to a campus firestorm—and a troubling lesson about self-censorship," *The Washington Post* (October 28, 2016), https://www.washingtonpost.com/opinions/my-halloween-email-led-to-a-campus-firestorm--and-a-troubling-lesson-about-self-censorship/2016/10/28/70e55732-9b97-11e6-a0ed-ab0774c1eaa5_story.html?utm_term=.3183ac52f501.

10. Erika Christakis, "Dressing Yourselves," email to Silliman College (Yale) Students on Halloween Costumes (Oct. 30, 2015), https://www.thefire.org/email-from-erika-christakis-dressing-yourselves-email-to-silliman-college-yale-students-on-halloween-costumes/.

11. Supra, n.9.

12. Gaddis Smith, "What can we say?," *Yale Alumni Magazine* (Jul/Aug 2011), https://yalealumnimagazine.com/articles/3236-what-can-we-i-say-i.

13. Ibid.

14. Yale College Dean's Office, "Report of the Committee on Freedom of Expression at Yale," (December 23, 1974), http:// yalecollege.yale.edu/deans-office/policies- reports/report-committee-freedom-expression-yale.

15. Ibid.

16. Ibid.

17. Ibid.

18. Ibid.

19. Ibid.

20. Ibid.

21. Ibid.

22. Bertram Wyatt-Brown, "In Memoriam: C. Vann Woodward (1908–99)," *Perspective on History* (March 2000), https://www.historians.org/publications-and-directories/perspectives-on-history/march-2000/in-memoriam-c-vann-woodward

23. Supra, n.14.

24. Supra, n.3.

25. University of Chicago, "Report of the Committee on Freedom of Expression," (2015), https://provost.uchicago.edu/sites/default/files/documents/reports/FOECommitteeReport.pdf.

26. Josh Blackman, "Students at CUNY Law Protested and Heckled My Lecture about Free Speech on Campus," *National Review* (April 12, 2018), https://www.nationalreview.com/2018/04/students-at-cuny-law-protested-and-heckled-my-lecture-about-free-speech-on-campus/

27. City University Of New York, "Policy on Freedom of Expression and Expressive Conduct," http://joshblackman.com/blog/wp-content/uploads/2018/04/CUNY-Policy-Freedom-of-Expression-Henderson-Rules-1.pdf.

28. Josh Blackman, "Importance of Free Speech on Campus," (April 12, 2018), https://youtu.be/kuWEFjnwLiA.

29. Supra, n.14

30. Scott Jaschik, "Shouting Down Talk on Campus Free Speech," *Inside Higher Ed* (Apr. 16, 2018), https://www.insidehighered.com/news/2018/04/16/guest-lecture-free-speech-cuny-law-school-heckled.

31. Josh Blackman, "CUNY Professors Write to CUNY Chancellor About Law School Protest and Heckling," Josh Blackman's Blog, (April 26, 2018), http://joshblackman.com/blog/2018/04/26/cuny-professors-write-to-cuny-chancellor-about-law-school-protest-and-heckling/.

32. David E. Bernstein, "CUNY Law Needs to Fire its Dean," *The Volokh Conspiracy* (Apr. 16, 2018), https://reason.com/volokh/2018/04/16/cuny-law-needs-to-fire-its-dean.

33. Lucía Martínez Valdivia, "Professors like me can't stay silent about this extremist moment on campuses," *The Washington Post* (October 27, 2017), https://www.washingtonpost.com/opinions/professors-like-me-cant-stay-silent-about-this-extremist-moment-on-campuses/2017/10/27/fd7aded2-b9b0-11e7-9e58-e6288544af98_story.html?utm_term=.c124a61622f9.

Lucía Martínez Valdivia is an assistant professor.

34. Dana Kampa, "Conservative pundit Ben Shapiro lectures to turbulent crowd on safe spaces, freedom of speech," *The Badger Herald* (Nov. 17, 2016), https://badgerherald.com/news/2016/11/17/conservative-pundit-ben-shapiro-lectures-to-turbulent-crowd-on-safe-spaces-freedom-of-speech/.

35. Stanley Kurtz, "Jesse Kremer's Wisconsin Campus Free Speech Act," *National Review* (May 2, 2017), https://www.nationalreview.com/corner/jesse-kremers-wisconsin-campus-free-speech-act-goldwater-proposal/.

36. Campus Free Speech: A Legislative Proposal, http://restorefreespeech.com.

37. Wisconsin Board of Regents, "Regent Policy Document 4–21, Commitment to Academic Freedom and Freedom of Expression," (Oct. 6, 2017), https://www.wisconsin.edu/regents/policies/commitment-to-academic-freedom-and-freedom-of-expression/.

38. Lawrence Andrea and Lilly Price, "Pro-gun speaker event goes on without a hitch despite Cocks Not Glocks protest," *The Daily Cardinal* (October 10, 2017), http://www.dailycardinal.com/article/2017/10/pro-gun-speaker-event-goes-on-without-a-hitch-despite-cocks-not-glocks-protest.

39. Stanley Kurtz, "Georgia Passes Goldwater-Based Campus Free-Speech Law," *National Review* (May 15, 2018), https://www.nationalreview.com/corner/georgia-campus-free-speech-bill-passes-fourth-state/.

40. Supra, n.14.

REFERENCES

Andrea, Lawrence, and Lilly Price. "Pro-gun speaker event goes on without a hitch despite Cocks Not Glocks protest," *The Daily Cardinal* (Oct. 10, 2017), http://www

.dailycardinal.com/article/2017/10/pro-gun-speaker-event-goes-on-without-a-hitch-despite-cocks-not-glocks-protest.

Bernstein, David E. "CUNY Law Needs to Fire its Dean." *The Volokh Conspiracy* (Apr. 16, 2018), https://reason.com/volokh/2018/04/16/cuny-law-needs-to-fire-its-dean.

Blackman, Josh. "CUNY Professors Write to CUNY Chancellor About Law School Protest and Heckling." Josh Blackman's Blog (Apr. 26, 2018). http://joshblackman.com/blog/2018/04/26/cuny-professors-write-to-cuny-chancellor-about-law-school-protest-and-heckling/.

Blackman, Josh. "Importance of Free Speech on Campus" (Apr. 12, 2018). https://youtu.be/kuWEFjnwLiA.

Blackman, Josh. "Students at CUNY Law Protested and Heckled My Lecture about Free Speech on Campus." *National Review* (Apr. 12, 2018). https://www.nationalreview.com/2018/04/students-at-cuny-law-protested-and-heckled-my-lecture-about-free-speech-on-campus/.

Campus Free Speech: A Legislative Proposal. http://restorefreespeech.com.

Christakis, Erika. "Dressing Yourselves," email to Silliman College (Yale) Students on Halloween Costumes (Oct. 30, 2015). https://www.thefire.org/email-from-erika-christakis-dressing-yourselves-email-to-silliman-college-yale-students-on-halloween-costumes/.

Christakis, Erika. "My Halloween email led to a campus firestorm—and a troubling lesson about self-censorship." *The Washington Post* (October 28, 2016). https://www.washingtonpost.com/opinions/my-halloween-email-led-to-a-campus-firestorm--and-a-troubling-lesson-about-self-censorship/2016/10/28/70e55732-9b97-11e6-a0ed-ab0774c1eaa5_story.html?utm_term=.3183ac52f501.

City University Of New York. "Policy on Freedom of Expression and Expressive Conduct." http://joshblackman.com/blog/wp-content/uploads/2018/04/CUNY-Policy-Freedom-of-Expression-Henderson-Rules-1.pdf.

Gallup-Knight Foundation. "College Students Show Strong Support For First Amendment, But Some Say Diversity And Inclusion Is More Important To A Democracy Than Free Speech, Gallup-Knight Survey Shows." (March 12, 2018). https://knightfoundation.org/press/releases/college-students-show-strong-support-for-first-amendment-but-some-say-diversity-and-inclusion-is-more-important-to-a-democracy-than-free-speech-gallup-knight-survey-shows.

Jaschik, Scott. "Presidents Back Free Speech." *Inside Higher Ed* (April 10, 2018). https://www.insidehighered.com/news/2018/04/10/survey-finds-strong-support-college-presidents-free-speech-campus.

Jaschik, Scott. "Shouting Down Talk on Campus Free Speech." *Inside Higher Ed* (Apr. 16, 2018). https://www.insidehighered.com/news/2018/04/16/guest-lecture-free-speech-cuny-law-school-heckled.

Kampa, Dana. "Conservative pundit Ben Shapiro lectures to turbulent crowd on safe spaces, freedom of speech." *The Badger Herald* (Nov. 17, 2016). https://badgerherald.com/news/2016/11/17/conservative-pundit-ben-shapiro-lectures-to-turbulent-crowd-on-safe-spaces-freedom-of-speech/.

Kurtz, Stanley. "Campus Shout-Down Rate Nearly Quadruples." *National Review* (Nov. 2, 2017). https://www.nationalreview.com/corner/campus-shout-down-rate-quadruples-free-speech/.

Kurtz, Stanley. "Georgia Passes Goldwater-Based Campus Free-Speech Law." *National Review* (May 15, 2018). https://www.nationalreview.com/corner/georgia-campus-free-speech-bill-passes-fourth-state/.

Kurtz, Stanley. "Jesse Kremer's Wisconsin Campus Free Speech Act." *National Review* (May 2, 2017). https://www.nationalreview.com/corner/jesse-kremers-wisconsin-campus-free-speech-act-goldwater-proposal/.

Kurtz, Stanley. "Year of the Shout-Down: It Was Worse Than You Think." *National Review* (May 31, 2017). https://www.nationalreview.com/corner/year-shout-down-worse-you-think-campus-free-speech/.

Smith, Gaddis. "What can we say?" *Yale Alumni Magazine* (Jul/Aug 2011). https://yalealumnimagazine.com/articles/3236-what-can-we-i-say-i.

"Snowflake Alert: UC Berkeley Offers 'Support And Counseling' For Students Offended By Shapiro's Speech." *Daily Wire* (Sept. 8, 2017). https://www.dailywire.com/news/20818/do-snowflakes-exist-yes-they-do-uc-berkeley-offers-daily-wire.

University of Chicago. "Report of the Committee on Freedom of Expression" (2015). https://provost.uchicago.edu/sites/default/files/documents/reports/FOECommitteeReport.pdf.

Valdivia, Lucía Martínez. "Professors like me can't stay silent about this extremist moment on campuses." *The Washington Post* (Oct. 27, 2017). https://www.washingtonpost.com/opinions/professors-like-me-cant-stay-silent-about-this-extremist-moment-on-campuses/2017/10/27/fd7aded2-b9b0-11e7-9e58-e6288544af98_story.html?utm_term=.c124a61622f9.

Wisconsin Board of Regents. "Regent Policy Document 4–21, Commitment to Academic Freedom and Freedom of Expression" (Oct. 6, 2017). https://www.wisconsin.edu/regents/policies/commitment-to-academic-freedom-and-freedom-of-expression/.

Wyatt-Brown, Bertram. "In Memoriam: C. Vann Woodward (1908–99)." *Perspective on History* (March 2000). https://www.historians.org/publications-and-directories/perspectives-on-history/march-2000/in-memoriam-c-vann-woodward.

Yale College Dean's Office. "Report of the Committee on Freedom of Expression at Yale," (December 23, 1974). http:// yalecollege.yale.edu/deans-office/policies-reports/report-committee-freedom-expression-yale.

Young, Cathy. "Half of college students aren't sure protecting free speech is important. That's bad news." *Los Angeles Times* (April 8, 2018). http://www.latimes.com/opinion/op-ed/la-oe-young-free-speech-on-campus-20180408-story.html.

Chapter 17

Statutory Protections for Public University Student Speech

Eugene Volokh

INTRODUCTION

What should we think about state laws that aim to protect speech at public universities?* The Goldwater Institute Campus Free Speech Act is one prominent recent proposal.[1] The Alabama, Arizona, Arkansas, Iowa, Louisiana, North Carolina, Ohio, Oklahoma, and South Dakota statutes are based on the Act but differ in some significant details;[2] a Tennessee statute also provides similar protection, sometimes using similar language.[3] California had long had a limited prohibition on public university campus speech codes.[4]

In principle, these laws can be helpful, in several different ways:

- They can valuably expand existing free speech protections.
- They can clarify those protections.
- Even if they just reaffirm the existing protections, they can offer support for administrators who want to follow the existing rules.
- They can offer focal points for decisionmakers who are trying to get things done, and who will comply with the rules if clearly told what they are.
- They can help public watchdogs argue against university misbehavior, by showing that the state university is violating the state's own clearly defined rules.
- They can help influence citizens, students, and faculty members, by harnessing people's tendency to view what the law is as some evidence of what the law should be.[5]

But as usual, the devil is in the details. In particular, the proposals can illustrate what common-law lawyers have long argued, and what codifiers have often stumbled on: The world is a complicated place, the rules that courts have created are thus necessarily complicated and incomplete, and trying to turn them into statutes can cause further problems.

This article will briefly discuss these matters, largely by walking through the proposed Free Speech Act but also by discussing some features of the Arizona and North Carolina implementations. I hope some of this analysis can help people evaluate the merits of the proposals and come up with still better versions.

I. STATEMENTS OF PRINCIPLE

The act begins,

> Section 1. The Board of Trustees of the state university system shall develop and adopt a policy on free expression that contains, at least, the following:
>
> A. A statement that the primary function of an institution of higher education is the discovery, improvement, transmission, and dissemination of knowledge by means of research, teaching, discussion, and debate. This statement shall provide that, to fulfill this function, the institution must strive to ensure the fullest degree of intellectual freedom and free expression.
> B. A statement that it is not the proper role of the institution to shield individuals from speech protected by the First Amendment, including, without limitation, ideas and opinions they find unwelcome, disagreeable, or even deeply offensive.

These statements that the Trustees are supposed to enact are hortatory; they don't create any binding rules. But I'm inclined to think that they are helpful, because they can remind administrators, faculty, students, and citizens—and the legislators themselves—about important principles. People often turn to official policies, even not strictly binding ones, for guidance and for support in debates. Having such policies on the books can be useful.

Likewise, establishing a Committee on Free Expression (as set forth in section 2) that has to report each year on the state of free expression at the university seems like a good idea. So does requiring that incoming students be informed about the policies (see section 3).

II. "FREEDOM TO DISCUSS ANY PROBLEM," SUBJECT ONLY TO CONTENT-NEUTRAL RULES

When we turn to Section 1(C), though, we see a requirement that the Trustees adopt a policy that is not just hortatory or educational. Rather, the required policy would be quite binding, and strikingly broad (I've separated and lettered the clauses for convenience):

> [a] Students and faculty have the freedom to discuss any problem that presents itself,
>
> [b] as the First Amendment permits [subject to the exceptions described in section 4] and
>
> [c] within the limits of reasonable viewpoint- and content-neutral restrictions on time, place, and manner of expression
>
> [d] that are consistent with this act and
>
> [e] that are necessary to achieve a compelling institutional interest;
>
> [f] provided that these restrictions are clear, published, and provide ample alternative means of expression.
>
> [g] Students and faculty shall be permitted to assemble and engage in spontaneous expressive activity as long as such activity is not unlawful and does not materially and substantially disrupt the functioning of the institution, subject to the requirements of this subsection.

Section 5(A) makes this enforceable through civil lawsuits, by providing,

> A state institution of higher education may restrict expressive conduct in the public areas of campus only if it demonstrates that the restriction:
>
> 1. Is necessary to achieve a compelling governmental interest;
> 2. Is the least restrictive means of furthering that compelling governmental interest;
> 3. Leaves open ample other opportunities to engage in the expressive conduct; and
> 4. Provides for spontaneous assembly and distribution of literature.

And Section 5(C), by providing for attorney fees for prevailing plaintiffs, makes it likely that these rules will be enforced.

Parts of this, of course, restate current First Amendment law. For instance, students do generally have the right to speak—so long as the speech doesn't fall within one of the First Amendment exceptions[6]—subject to content-neutral time, place, and manner restrictions that pass intermediate scrutiny and that leave open ample alternative channels (which is close to items [c] to [f]).[7]

But "generally" doesn't mean always, and existing First Amendment law recognizes that in many places content-neutrality and perhaps even viewpoint-neutrality are not sensible rules. For instance, in the classroom, the professor can sharply constrain student discussion by cutting off a student who is veering off-topic, or who is using personal insults instead of reasoned argument. Likewise, a law professor may ask for responses that convey a particular viewpoint, because he's trying to get students to think about how to craft a particular argument; if a student wants to discuss the question from the opposite viewpoint, the professor can cut that off, too.

And while professors should be open to a wide range of viewpoints, some viewpoints are so mistaken (e.g., if a student in a geology class wants to argue that the world is only 6,000 years old) that a professor might want to cut those off as well. Sometimes the class can benefit from hearing a discussion even about a clearly incorrect viewpoint—but sometimes the professor is just trying to convey information and doesn't want the class to get distracted by a discussion that some student is trying to start.

Indeed, professors teaching their classes also don't have "the freedom to discuss any problem that presents itself." Most obviously, they are supposed to stick to the topic; if they want to take time in their physics classes to talk about how horrible the election of President Trump or President Obama might be, the administration should be able to stop them.

All of these restrictions on class discussion are *not* content-neutral (even if some are viewpoint-neutral)—they distinguish among speech based at least on its subject matter (e.g., does it have to do with physics?).[8] Under First Amendment law, that is not a problem, because the classroom would be seen as a place for a government actor (the professor) to convey the speech he is paid to convey (a particular kind of class discussion), and the government actor is allowed to craft the discussion the way he thinks is best.[9] Content-neutrality is required only in "traditional public fora" and certain kinds of "designated public fora," and the classroom is neither.

But the Campus Free Speech Act lacks this nuance: It categorically requires content neutrality, with no flexibility for creating special rules for particular government-run places. Indeed, while it does provide latitude for instructors "maintaining order in the classroom," that is present only in Section 1(D), which deals with "protest[s] or demonstrat[ions]." Speech that falls short of protests or demonstrations is covered by Section 1(C), which lacks a "maintaining order in the classroom" exception.

Nor is this just limited to classes. Say that the university organizes a panel on some academic subject—for instance, free speech on college campuses. Students are invited to attend, and to ask questions.

Yet students would normally not be allowed to use the questions "to discuss any problem that presents itself." A student may genuinely think that the most important problem presented to the nation is gun crime or illegal immigration, and may want to discuss that problem everywhere, including the questions at the free speech conference. No, the moderator will say (or at least should say), please stick to the topic. Again, quite constitutional, because under First Amendment law the question period would likely be seen as a limited public forum, in which content-based but viewpoint-neutral rules (stay on topic) are allowed.[10] Yet the act has no such limitation, so presumably the off-topic questions couldn't be restricted.

And the list can of course go on. Under First Amendment law, faculty aren't allowed "to discuss any problem that presents itself" in, say, faculty or committee meetings; they can be required to stay on topic, and even to be polite to each other. The Act would eliminate that latitude.

I'm not sure that the drafters of the act intended to eliminate all these restrictions. Perhaps they just wanted to codify and clarify the existing First Amendment rules. But that would have taken a much longer statute.

To be sure, some might argue that one does need to have such broad restrictions on university power, even in the classroom, in conferences, in faculty meetings, and the like. Perhaps professors and administrators can't be trusted to fairly enforce content-based and especially viewpoint-based rules anywhere on campus. Perhaps it's better to strip them of this power, and leave any digressions, personal insults, and the like to be dealt with through social norms or argument, rather than restriction.

But I doubt that this is right. It seems to me that effective teaching, enlightening conferences, and successful faculty self-governance require some ability to at least keep people on-topic and polite. Turning every event at a university into a place for students and faculty to discuss whatever problems they please is neither necessary nor desirable.

Item [e] in this proposal also includes another departure from First Amendment law. Content-neutral speech restrictions that leave open ample alternative channels are usually permissible if they pass "intermediate scrutiny"—are "narrowly tailored to serve a significant government interest."[11] Item [e] requires that the restrictions be "necessary to achieve a compelling institutional interest." That is the language used for the much more demanding "strict scrutiny" test.[12]

This might substantially limit the university's power to impose content-neutral restrictions. We don't know quite how much, since the Court has never made clear just what interests are "important" but not "compelling." But the tone set by strict scrutiny is a much more restriction-invalidating tone than that set by intermediate scrutiny.

The proposal thus means that speech on university property is more protected against content-neutral restrictions than is speech on traditional public fora such as public streets and sidewalks. I doubt this is a good idea, though, because of the vagueness of the phrasing, it's hard to tell just what will happen until some cases come to court.

III. OUTSIDE SPEAKER RIGHTS

Now we move on to subsections 1(D) and 1(E), which require policies that say,

> (D) Any person lawfully present on campus may protest or demonstrate there . . . [P]rotests and demonstrations that materially and substantially infringe upon the rights of others to engage in or listen to expressive activity shall not be permitted and shall be subject to sanction. This does not prohibit professors or other instructors from maintaining order in the classroom.
>
> (E) The public areas of campuses of the institution are traditional public forums, open on the same terms to any speaker.

This deliberately goes beyond existing First Amendment rules, under which most public universities can exclude public speech by outsiders (people who aren't students, faculty, or staff), including in open space on those grounds.[13] Under the act, these outsiders would indeed be able to demonstrate on campus quads and walkways, and can presumably also orate, leaflet, and the like.

My sense is that this is, in large measure, a good development: If freedom of speech by members of the public on city sidewalks and in city parks is a net plus for society, why not allow similar free speech on university walkways and park spaces? True, those places are dedicated to a particular purpose—university education—but that purpose is generally compatible with speech by members of the public and is indeed likely furthered by such speech.

To be sure, some kinds of public speech may be inconsistent with some special features of the university. Loud demonstrations can threaten to interfere with students who are studying in the library or who are preparing for exams. Protests on a very busy sidewalk might block students from getting to class quickly. Protests may interfere with the quiet needed by patients at the university hospital.

Those concerns, though, can be dealt with using content-neutral time, place, and manner restrictions, much as they are on regular city streets. And indeed, the provision that "protests and demonstrations that materially and substantially infringe upon the rights of others to engage in or listen to expressive activity shall not be permitted" reflects this (though it may be good to more precisely define "materially and substantially infringe," as the Arizona statute does, see Part V below).[14]

But here too the codification might have some unexpected results, because not all places where a person is "lawfully present" are places where demonstrations are allowed. My law school, for instance, had long been open to the public, so visitors who just want to look around could lawfully be there (at least until access was restricted because of COVID); but I doubt that they should have been able to organize a demonstration in the foyer or in the hallways. Yet if "Any person lawfully present on campus may protest or demonstrate there" is read as meaning "Any person lawfully present on campus may protest or demonstrate *in any place where he is lawfully present*," then the protests inside the building would indeed be allowed, at least until they start actually interfering with classes or other expressive activities.

This could be avoided by reading "Any person lawfully present on campus may protest or demonstrate there" as meaning "Any person lawfully present on campus may protest or demonstrate *in the traditional public forums on the campus.*" But it would be better, I think, to have made this provision narrower and more explicit on this point. Perhaps to avoid this, the North Carolina proposal omits these subsections and simply says, "Access to campus for purposes of free speech and expression shall be consistent with First Amendment jurisprudence regarding traditional public forums, designated public forums, and nonpublic forums, subject to reasonable time, place, and manner restrictions."[15]

IV. INVITED SPEAKERS, AND PROTECTION FOR SPEAKERS

Under Sections 1(F) and 1(G), the policy must provide that:

> (F) The campuses of the institution are open to any speaker whom students, student groups, or members of the faculty have invited.
>
> (G) The [i]nstitution shall make all reasonable efforts and make available all reasonable resources to ensure the safety of invited speakers. An institution shall not charge security fees based on the content of the inviter's speech or the

content of the speech of invited speakers. The institution may restrict the use of its non-public facilities to invited individuals.

Now it's not clear what "campuses" means here. Presumably, it can't just mean that invited speakers must be allowed to speak in public places on campus—under Section 1(D), all people lawfully present on campus, whether specifically invited or not, are already allowed to do that.

Nor, I take it, would it mean that all interior spaces at the institution must be freely open to any invited speaker at any time. After all, the university may have its own plans for many of those rooms.

Rather, I assume this means that, when the university makes classrooms and auditoriums available to some invited speakers, it must make them equally available to other invited speakers. It cannot exclude speakers based on viewpoint (that's already existing First Amendment law[16]). It cannot exclude them based on content (that goes beyond existing law but is likely good for promoting campus speech[17]). And, probably most importantly, it presumably can't exclude them because of a concern that allowing them would require security that would be too expensive; First Amendment law probably already bans such exclusions, but that's not completely clear—the statute would clarify that.[18]

But does Section 1(F) also mean that the university can't even impose content-neutral rental fees for the spaces that it makes open? It looks to me like the provision could indeed be read as banning such fees, even if they apply equally without regard to whether the speaker is controversial and requires extra security. An auditorium, the argument would go, isn't "open to any speaker whom students, student groups, or [professors] have invited" if it costs thousands of dollars to rent it (and to provide cleanup services and normal security services), money that the inviters may well not have.

This too is a defensible position—perhaps universities should provide such space for free to promote public debate on campus, even when the market rent for the space would normally be substantial. Yet legislators may wonder whether they should indeed impose such a requirement or should instead bar universities only from excluding speakers (or charging extra money to allow them) based on their views or the expected security costs.

Moreover, Section 1(G) seems to suggest that security fees that are *not* based on the content of speech are permissible, for instance if the university generally requires student groups to pay security fees based on the size of the expected audience. Presumably the university's duty to provide "all reasonable resources to ensure the safety of invited speakers" thus doesn't extend to providing those resources for free. Might the university also not be required to provide the rooms themselves for free? The proposal seems unclear on this score.

V. PUNISHMENT FOR DISRUPTERS

Sections 1(H) and (J) provide that,

> (H) [Each university's disciplinary] policy shall include a range of disciplinary sanctions for anyone under the jurisdiction of the institution who materially and substantially interferes with the free expression of others.
>
> (J) Any student who has twice been found responsible for infringing the expressive rights of others will be suspended for a minimum of one year, or expelled.

Subsection (J) of course is a deliberate choice to go beyond the constitutional requirement; but it strikes me as an unwise choice.

People shouldn't interfere with others' expressive rights, whether by violence or true threat of violence, by vandalism, or by shouting down. Just as pro-choice speakers should be free to deliver their speech without pro-life activists shouting them down, for instance, so pro-Israel speakers should be free to do the same without anti-Israel speakers shouting them down.[19] Such interference with others' speech is constitutionally unprotected;[20] there are ample avenues for people to speak in venues that they have booked for the occasion (or during scheduled question periods for other events), without interfering with the speech of others.[21] And the interference should indeed be punished.[22]

But mandating a yearlong suspension, which is practically likely to cost tens of thousands of dollars for many students, as punishment for two violations strikes me as often likely to be overkill.[23] Some violations may be quite serious, for instance when students use violence or threats of violence to suppress speech. Others may be close to permissible speech: For instance, some amount of hissing or booing, like some amount of applause, is generally considered tolerable in many contexts, such as outdoor political rallies[24]—going slightly beyond that should lead to some punishment, but a year-long suspension for two incidents?

And this is especially so given how much can be classified as "infringing the expressive rights of others." Tearing down a properly posted leaflet in a moment of anger would presumably qualify. Scrawling an insult on it would, too. Again, these are not good behaviors, and should probably lead to some modest punishment—but likely not something this substantial.[25]

Likewise, a student who gets into fisticuffs with a classmate who insults the student's girlfriend twice would be guilty of "infringing the expressive rights of others." (Expression isn't limited to ideological expression.[26]) Here too, some punishment is justified, but a required one-year suspension seems to be going too far.

Of course, we might think that the university normally would exercise its discretion to make sure that only serious misconduct leads to a finding of "responsib[ility] for infringing the expressive rights of others." But the very premise of Section 1(J) is that we shouldn't trust the discretion of university administrators—or else why set up a mandatory punishment in a situation where the punishment would otherwise be left to administrators' discretion?

It's thus unsurprising, I think, that no state has chosen to implement this rigid requirement. North Carolina left the matter at requiring universities to:

> implement a range of disciplinary sanctions for anyone under the jurisdiction of a constituent institution who substantially disrupts the functioning of the constituent institution or substantially interferes with the protected free expression rights of others, including protests and demonstrations that infringe upon the rights of others to engage in and listen to expressive activity when the expressive activity has been scheduled pursuant to this policy or is located in a nonpublic forum.[27]

Arizona provided that "It is the sense of the legislature that if a student has repeatedly been determined to have materially and substantially infringed on the expressive rights of another person, a punishment of suspension or expulsion from the university or community college *may* be appropriate," and further limited "materially and substantially infringes" to cover only

> conduct by a person who, with the intent to or the knowledge of doing so,
>
> materially and substantially interferes with another person's or group's expressive activity, prevents the communication of a message or prevents the transaction of the business of a lawful meeting, gathering or procession by . . . :
>
> 1. . . . . fighting or violent or seriously disruptive behavior
> 2. . . . . any protracted commotion, utterance or similar action
> 3. [or] physically blocking, preventing or hindering any person from attending, listening to, viewing or otherwise participating in an expressive activity.[28]

Like the problems with Section 1(I) (see Part I), the problems with section 1(J) reflect the difficulty of codifying a complex decision-making process, though here the decision has to do with the magnitude of punishment rather than the scope of protection. If you think the university just can't be trusted to make decisions, you might want to create such rigid rules. But there are huge costs to this sort of rigidity, and it's unsurprising that states have sought to avoid them.

VI. DUE PROCESS

Section 1(I) provides,

> In all disciplinary cases involving expressive conduct, students are entitled to a disciplinary hearing under published procedures, including [the rights to] . . .
>
> 1. receive advanced written notice of the charges,
> 2. review the evidence in support of the charges,
> 3. confront witnesses against them,
> 4. present a defense,
> 5. call witnesses,
> 6. . . . an impartial arbiter or panel, . . .
> 7. appeal,
> 8. active assistance of counsel, [when suspension is for more than 30 days or expulsion are potential penalties].

This proposal would presumably apply both to cases involving punishment for expressive conduct that disrupts others' free expression, and to cases involving punishment for expressive conduct that fits within one of the other exceptions set forth in Section 4, such as defamation or true threats.

This is a good clarification of what the Due Process Clause may often require, and a good expansion beyond what the Due Process Clause requires. (For instance, the Due Process Clause doesn't secure the right to appeal even in criminal cases.[29]) As with many procedures, the additions have some costs—appeals can be time-consuming and expensive for an institution, for instance, and cross-examination of witnesses can be unpleasant for the witnesses and can deter some witnesses from coming forward. But, on balance, I think such procedural protections are necessary for fair decision-making.

One important question, of course, is whether "active assistance of counsel" simply requires students to be able to hire lawyers themselves or would require the university provide free legal assistance. If the university must provide free assistance, that can get quite expensive—especially since these rules, if adopted for "disciplinary cases involving expressive conduct," will likely be used in other disciplinary cases, too. (What plausible justification would there be for providing procedural protections for students charged with engaging in unprotected speech, or suppressing others' speech, and not for students charged with sex offenses or plagiarism or the like?)

On the other hand, if the university simply lets students hire lawyers if they can afford them, that will lead many to criticize the process as unduly favoring students with rich parents—a familiar feature of the civil justice system, but one that might be less politically sustainable in formal university disciplinary proceedings. Perhaps some compromise might be possible, for instance if a public university that has a law school could create a clinical class in which law students, under a trained lawyer's supervision, defend other students who are accused of serious misconduct. That's an imperfect solution, but perhaps the best one possible under the circumstances.

VII. INSTITUTIONAL NEUTRALITY

Section 1(K) provides that each public university (as opposed to individual student, faculty, and staff):

> should attempt to remain neutral, as an institution, on the public policy controversies of the day, except insofar as administrative decisions on such issues are essential to the day-to-day functioning of the university.

This, I think, is generally a sensible aspiration. The university, as an agency of the state, has no First Amendment rights of its own when it comes to restraints imposed by the state legislature;[30] and, by and large, university administrators shouldn't use the state institution's prestige to express views on controversial questions. Moreover, if a university takes stands on particular questions, that may in some measure discourage university employees—including especially untenured faculty, non-tenure-track faculty, and graduate students—from expressing contrary views.[31]

VIII. FREEDOM NOT TO EXPRESS A PARTICULAR VIEW

Section 1(K) also adds,

> The institution may not take action, as an institution, on the public policy controversies of the day in such a way as to require students, faculty, or staff to publicly express a given view of a public controversy.

This is likely a restatement of First Amendment compelled speech principles when it comes to students, and of well-accepted academic freedom norms when it comes to the faculty.

IX. STUDENT GROUP RIGHTS

Subsection 1(L) provides,

> No institution may deny a student organization any benefit or privilege available to any other student organization, or otherwise discriminate against a student organization, based on the content of the organization's expression, including any requirement that the leaders or members of such organization:
>
> 1. Affirm and adhere to the organization's sincerely held beliefs;
> 2. Comply with the organization's standards of conduct; or
> 3. Further the organization's mission or purpose, as defined by the student organization.

This departs from existing First Amendment law, in two ways.

First, while public universities can't discriminate against student organizations based on their *viewpoints* in distributing generally available benefits, they are allowed to discriminate in viewpoint-neutral ways based on the content of student speech.[32] Thus, for instance, universities likely can

- prefer student groups that are curriculum-related to ones that aren't,
- deny certain benefits to groups that are focused primarily on partisan politics,[33] or
- bar vulgarities in student organizations' promotional materials.[34]

But a legislature might, of course, choose to require universities to forgo any such power to engage in content discrimination, whether because the legislators think that universities should promote a maximum range of student groups, or because they worry that facially viewpoint-neutral content restrictions might hide attempts to discriminate based on viewpoint.

Second, public universities are allowed to impose "take-all-comers" rules on student organizations, requiring them to be open to all students.[35] They are likely also allowed to impose narrower nondiscrimination rules, which would bar groups from discriminating based on race, sex, religion, sexual orientation, and the like.[36] This proposal would change that.

I'm inclined to think that the change is sound. Atheist student groups should be free to exclude religious students, and vice versa; that will help those groups remain as distinctive voices on campus, voices that can better express a coherent view in support of a particular religious (or antireligious) perspective. Likewise, religious groups that oppose same-sex relationships (or remarriage following divorce, or interracial relationships) should be free to limit their members—especially their voting members—and their officers to those who agree with these ideas, who live their lives consistently with these ideas, and who can therefore more effectively advocate for those ideas.[37]

Though this means that some students may be excluded from some groups, the result will be a wider range of groups with a wider range of ideologies providing a wider range of perspectives for students. That a Christian group may want to exclude me, as a non-Christian, does not appreciably harm me, I think—but the possibility that many irreligious people like me might join a Christian group and thus change its ideological character may keep the group from being able to effectively promote its ideas both to the university at large and to Christian students. And to the extent that there needs to be a check on the use of such discriminatory criteria, I think that in the modern university social pressure will be an adequate check—except in situations where particular conditions really are important to the groups' ideals (e.g., when the groups are aimed at promoting particular religious traditions, however unpopular they may be in some institutions).

X. CONCLUSION

Most American free speech law comes from courts—but not all. Anti-SLAPP statutes, for instance, help protect speakers against abusive lawsuits.[38] Libel retraction statutes protect publishers under certain circumstances against potentially ruinous punitive and presumed damages.[39] Newsgatherer privilege provisions codify, clarify, and expand judge-made protections.[40] New Hampshire offers broad protection to speech by government employees.[41] Some state statutes protect speech by K–12 students beyond what the Supreme Court has provided;[42] the Leonard Law in California has long codified and clarified First Amendment protections for public university students, and even extends them to private university students.[43]

The Goldwater Institute proposal is a worthy part of that tradition. But it is unusually ambitious: It aims to protect students, faculty, staff, and invited speakers. It aims to prevent both discipline and exclusion from access to university property. It provides both protection against government suppression and protection against private suppression.

Unsurprisingly, this breadth has yielded some likely missteps, which I've tried to identify above, as well as a good deal that is valuable. I hope this analysis can help improve future legislative efforts (many of which are already in the works) that are based on the Goldwater proposal.

NOTES

* This paper was prepared in 2018 but has been updated in some measure to reflect more recent developments.

1. See, Goldwater Institute, "Campus Free Speech: Model Legislation," at https://www.restorefreespeech.com/the-answer.

2. Ala. Stats. §§ 16-68-1 to -8; Ariz. Rev. Stat. §§ 15–1861 to -1869; Ark. Code Ann. §§ 6-60-1001 to -1010; Iowa Code Ann. §§ 261h.1 to .8; La. Rev. Stats. §§ 3339.31 to .37; N.C. Gen. Stat. §§ 116–300 to -304; Ohio Rev. Code Ann. § 3345.0215; Okla. Stats. § 70–2120; S.D. Codified L. §§ 13-53-49 to -53.

3. Tenn. Code Ann. §§ 49-7-2401 to -2408; compare, e.g., § 49-7-2401(a)(5) ("It is not the proper role of an institution to attempt to shield individuals from free speech, including ideas and opinions they find offensive, unwise, immoral, indecent, disagreeable, conservative, liberal, traditional, radical, or wrong-headed") with Goldwater Institute proposal Section 1(B) ("It is not the proper role of the institution to shield individuals from speech protected by the First Amendment, including, without limitation, ideas and opinions they find unwelcome, disagreeable, or even deeply offensive.").

4. Cal. Educ. Code § 66301. Va. Code § 23.1–401.1 aims to protect speech at public universities, but only by reaffirming that they may not "abridge the constitutional freedom of any individual . . . to speak on campus," and by requiring them to create and publicize policies related to this principle.

5. See Eugene Volokh, "Mechanisms of the Slippery Slope," *Harvard Law Review* 116 (2003): 1026, 1080–81.

6. See, e.g., *DeJohn v. Tempe Univ.*, 537 F.3d 301, 314, 316 (3d Cir. 2008).

7. See, e.g., *Rock for Life-UMBC v. Hrabowski*, 411 F. App'x 541, 551 (4th Cir. 2010).

8. *Reed v. Town of Gilbert* reaffirms that subject-matter restrictions are content-based, 135 S. Ct. 2218 (2015).

9. See, e.g., *Forbes v. Arkansas Education Television Comm'n*, 523 U.S. 666, 674–75 (1998) (holding that programs in which the government is speaking, and selecting which speech from others to communicate, are generally not speech fora, and the government generally has a free hand in choosing what is to be included and how).

10. See, e.g., *Christian Legal Society v. Martinez*, 561 U.S. 661 (2010).

11. See, e.g., *Ward v. Rock Against Racism*, 491 U.S. 781 (1989).

12. See, e.g., *Arkansas Writers' Project, Inc. v. Ragland*, 481 U.S. 221, 231 (1987).

13. See, e.g., *Gilles v. Blanchard*, 477 F.3d 466, 470 (7th Cir. 2007). I say "most" because universities can't exclude people from the normal city sidewalks surrounding their buildings, though they can exclude people from the special-purpose spaces within the university campus. An urban university that has generally used city streets going through its campus thus can't exclude speakers from the sidewalks on those streets.

14. Eric T. Kasper, "Public Universities and the First Amendment: Controversial Speakers, Protests, and Free Speech Policies," *Capital University Law Review* 47 (2019): 529, at 564–71, suggests that this prohibition may be unconstitutionally vague and overbroad, but it seems to me that this prohibition is comparable to the criminal law upheld in *Grayned v. City of Rockford*, 408 U.S. 104, 108–12 (1972), which banned "willfully . . . making . . . any noise or diversion which disturbs or tends to disturb the peace or good order of [a] school session or class" "while on public or private grounds adjacent to any building in which a school or any class thereof is in session." Like that law, this provision should be read as focusing on harms unrelated

to content, such as excessive noise or the blocking of walkways (though including the language from the Arizona statute would make that even clearer); and if that criminal prohibition is valid, a university policy enforceable through internal disciplinary sanctions should be as well.

15. N.C. Gen. Stat. § 116–301(5).

16. See, e.g., *Giebel v. Sylvester*, 44 F.3d 1182, 1188–89 (9th Cir. 2001).

17. See Kasper, supra note 14, at 543.

18. *Forsyth County v. Nationalist Movement*, 505 U.S. 123 (1992), held that the government may not charge the organizers of controversial parades extra for police protection: "Speech cannot be financially burdened, any more than it can be punished or banned, simply because it might offend a hostile mob." Ibid. at 134–35. The parade was to take place on a public street, which is a traditional public forum, and auditoriums at universities are limited public fora. See, e.g., *Bowman v. White*, 444 F.3d 967, 976 (8th Cir. 2006); *Eichenlaub v. Township of Indiana*, 385 F.3d 274, 280 (3d Cir. 2004). But the logic of *Forsyth County* seems applicable to limited public fora, where viewpoint discrimination is generally forbidden, and courts have indeed so applied it. See, e.g., *Sonnier v. Crain*, 613 F.3d 436, 447–48 (5th Cir. 2010), *withdrawn as to another part of the opinion*, 634 F.3d 778, 779 (5th Cir. 2011); *College Republicans of Univ. of Wash. v. Cauce*, 2018 WL 804497, *2 (W.D. Wash. Feb. 9); Kasper, supra note 14, at 543.

19. See Press Release, Orange Cnty. Dist. Attorney, "10 Men Convicted and Sentenced for Conspiracy and Disrupting a Meeting During Speech by Israeli Ambassador at UCI" (Sept. 23, 2011), http:// www.orangecountyda.com/home/index.asp?page=8&recordid=2588.

20. See, e.g., *State v. Hardin*, 498 N.W.2d 677, 681 (Iowa 1993); *Morehead v. Texas*, 807 S.W.2d 577, 579 (Tex. Crim. App. 1991); *McIntosh v. Arkansas Republican Party–Frank White Election Committee*, 766 F.2d 337, 341 (8th Cir. 1985).

21. Even in traditional public fora, "the Court has recognized that government, in order to regulate competing uses of public forums, may impose a permit requirement on those wishing to hold a march, parade, or rally." *Forsyth County v. Nationalist Movement*, 505 U.S. 123, 130 (1992). It is at least as clear that, when it comes to university auditoriums, the government may allow groups to book a room for their invited speakers to speak and exclude others who might want to shout over the speaker.

22. Any prohibition should, of course, define the term properly, but because the Campus Free Speech Act doesn't establish any university policies but only commands universities to establish them, the policies can (and should) contain more precise definitions.

23. See also AAUP, "Campus Free-Speech Legislation: History, Progress, and Problems," 10 (2018), https://www.aaup.org/report/campus-free-speech-legislation-history-progress-and-problems; Charles Koch Foundation, "Keeping Universities Safe for Free Speech" (May 2, 2017), https://www.charleskochfoundation.org/story/keeping-universities-safe-for-free-speech/ ("Though measures like the Goldwater Institute's model policy may attempt to protect campus free speech, fear of punishment can have the opposite effect of chilling speech."); PEN America, "Legislative

and Political Action on Campus Free Speech: An Analysis," *Seton Hall Legislative Journal* 43 (2019): 405, 412; Timothy Zick, "The Costs of Dissent: Protest and Civil Liabilities," *George Washington Law Review* 89 (2021): 233, 294; Kasper, supra note 14, at 572–73; Katarina I. Chavez, "The Problems with the Solutions: Examining the Response from Universities, President Trump, and State Legislatures to Campus Free Speech Issues," *Ave Maria Law Review* 19 (2021): 146, 173–74; Sean M. Kammer, "The 'Intellectual Diversity' Crisis That Isn't: Liberal Faculties, Conservative Victims, and the Cynical Effort to Undermine Higher Education for Political Gain," *Quinnipiac Law Review* 39 (2021): 149.

24. *In re Kay*, 464 P.2d 142 (Cal. 1970).

25. Likewise, Kasper, supra note 14, at 574–75, notes that Section 5(B)–(C) mandates the award of damages (with a minimum of $1000) and "reasonable court costs and reasonable attorney fees" against anyone found to have violated the statute. This would usually be a damages award against a university, but it might also cover ordinary students and others who engage in "protests and demonstrations that materially and substantially infringe upon the rights of others to engage in or listen to expressive activity," Section 1(D). That magnitude of liability, based on conduct that may often be only a minor offense (such as excessive noise or minor blocking of passages), might similarly be overkill.

26. See, e.g., *United States v. Stevens*, 559 U.S. 460, 479–80 (2010).

27. N.C. Gen. Stat. § 116–301(7).

28. Ariz. Rev. Stat. §§ 15–1861(2), 15–1866(A)(4), (6) (emphasis added).

29. "[I]t is well settled that there is no constitutional right to an appeal. Indeed, for a century after this Court was established, no appeal as of right existed in criminal cases, and, as a result, appellate review of criminal convictions was rarely allowed." *Abney v. United States*, 431 U.S. 651, 656 (1977).

30. See *Ysursa v. Pocatello Ed. Ass'n*, 555 U.S. 353, 362–64 (2009).

31. This is the view famously, and I think correctly, expressed by the Kalven Report. See Univ. of Chicago, *Kalven Committee: Report on the University's Role in Political and Social Action* (Nov. 11, 1967), https://perma.cc/WL7J-HS3P; Keith E. Whittington, "Free Speech and the Diverse University," *Fordham Law Review* 87 (2019): 2453, 2459. I'm not claiming that this effect makes it unconstitutional for the university to take stands on controversial questions—but it does suggest that there are real costs to academic freedom from the university doing so. For the opposite view, see Kristine L. Bowman, "Universities' Speech and the First Amendment," *Nebraska Law Review* 99 (2021): 896; PEN America, supra note 23, at 412; Kasper, supra note 14, at 545–46.

32. See, e.g., *Forbes v. Arkansas Education Television Comm'n*, 523 U.S. 666, 674–75 (1998) (holding that programs in which the government is speaking, and selecting which speech from others to communicate, are generally not speech fora, and the government generally has a free hand in choosing what is to be included and how); see also Kasper, supra note 14, at 545.

33. *Cf. Minnesota Voters Alliance v. Mansky*, 138 S. Ct. 1876, 1888 (2018) (suggesting that clearly defined restrictions on election-related clothing and pins in polling places would be reasonable and viewpoint-neutral).

34. *Cf. Iancu v. Brunetti*, 139 S. Ct. 2294, 2303 (2019) (Alito, J., concurring) (taking the view that a restriction on vulgarities would generally be viewpoint-neutral); ibid. at 2303–4 (Roberts, C.J., concurring in part and dissent in part) (taking the same view); ibid. at 2308 (Sotomayor, J., joined by Breyer, J., concurring in part and dissenting in part); ibid. at 2302 n.* (majority opin.) (apparently reserving the question).

35. *Christian Legal Socièty v. Martinez*, 561 U.S. 661 (2010).

36. Ibid. at 698–703 (Stevens, J., concurring); Eugene Volokh, "Freedom of Expressive Association and Government Subsidies," *Stanford Law Review* 58 (2006): 1919.

37. See generally, John D. Inazu, "More Is More: Strengthening Free Exercise, Speech, and Association," *Minnesota Law Review* 99 (2014): 485.

38. See, e.g., Rodney A. Smolla, *Law of Defamation* (St. Paul, MN: Thomson Reuter, 2010-) §§ 9:107–110.

39. See generally *Lindey on Entertainment, Publishing & the Arts* (Clark, Boardman, Callahan) § 4:19 (3d ed.).

40. See, e.g., Rodney A. Smolla, *Law of Defamation* §§ 12:60–62.60.

41. N.H. Rev. Stat. § 98-E:2; *Appeal of Booker*, 653 A.2d 1084 (N.H. 1995).

42. See, e.g., Cal. Educ. Code § 48907; *Leeb v. Delong*, 198 Cal. App.3d 47 (1988).

43. Cal. Educ. Code §§ 66301, 94367.

REFERENCES

AAUP. "Campus Free-Speech Legislation: History, Progress, and Problems" (April 2018). https://www.aaup.org/report/campus-free-speech-legislation-history-progress-and-problems

Abney v. United States, 431 U.S. 651 (1977).

Appeal of Booker, 653 A.2d 1084 (N.H. 1995).

Arkansas Writers' Project, Inc. v. Ragland, 481 U.S. 221 (1987).

Bowman v. White, 444 F.3d 967 (8th Cir. 2006).

Bowman, Kristine L. "Universities' Speech and the First Amendment." *Nebraska Law Review* 99 (2021): 896.

Charles Koch Foundation. "Keeping Universities Safe for Free Speech" (May 2, 2017). https://www.charleskochfoundation.org/story/keeping-universities-safe-for-free-speech/.

Chavez, Katarina I. "The Problems with the Solutions: Examining the Response from Universities, President Trump, and State Legislatures to Campus Free Speech Issues." *Ave Maria Law Review* 19 (2021): 146.

Christian Legal Society v. Martinez, 561 U.S. 661 (2010).

College Republicans of Univ. of Wash. v. Cauce, 2018 WL 804497, *2 (W.D. Wash. Feb. 9).

DeJohn v. Tempe Univ., 537 F.3d 301, 314 (3d Cir. 2008).

Eichenlaub v. Township of Indiana, 385 F.3d 274 (3d Cir. 2004).

Forbes v. Arkansas Education Television Comm'n, 523 U.S. 666 (1998).

Forsyth County v. Nationalist Movement, 505 U.S. 123 (1992).

Giebel v. Sylvester, 44 F.3d 1182, 1188–89 (9th Cir. 2001).

Gilles v. Blanchard, 477 F.3d 466, 470 (7th Cir. 2007).

Goldwater Institute. "Campus Free Speech: Model Legislation." https://www.restorefreespeech.com/the-answer.

Grayned v. City of Rockford, 408 U.S. 104 (1972).

Iancu v. Brunetti, 139 S. Ct. 2294 (2019).

Inazu, John D. "More Is More: Strengthening Free Exercise, Speech, and Association." *Minnesota Law Review* 99 (2014): 485.

Kammer, Sean M. "The 'Intellectual Diversity' Crisis That Isn't: Liberal Faculties, Conservative Victims, and the Cynical Effort to Undermine Higher Education for Political Gain." *Quinnipiac Law Review* 39 (2021): 149.

Kasper, Eric T. "Public Universities and the First Amendment: Controversial Speakers, Protests, and Free Speech Policies." *Capital University Law Review* 47 (2019): 529.

Leeb v. Delong, 198 Cal. App.3d 47 (1988).

Lindey on Entertainment, Publishing & the Arts (Clark, Boardman, Callahan) (3d ed.).

McIntosh v. Arkansas Republican Party–Frank White Election Committee, 766 F.2d 337, 341 (8th Cir. 1985).

Morehead v. Texas, 807 S.W.2d 577, 579 (Tex. Crim. App. 1991).

Orange Cnty. Dist. Attorney. "10 Men Convicted and Sentenced for Conspiracy and Disrupting a Meeting During Speech by Israeli Ambassador at UCI" (Sept. 23, 2011). http:// www.orangecountyda.com/home/index.asp?page=8&recordid=2588.

PEN America, "Legislative and Political Action on Campus Free Speech: An Analysis," *Seton Hall Legislative Journal* 43 (2019): 405.

Reed v. Town of Gilbert, 135 S. Ct. 2218 (2015).

Rock for Life-UMBC v. Hrabowski, 411 F. App'x 541, 551 (4th Cir. 2010).

Smolla, Rodney A. *Law of Defamation* (St. Paul, MN: Thomson Reuter, 2010-).

Sonnier v. Crain, 613 F.3d 436 (5th Cir. 2010).

State v. Hardin, 498 N.W.2d 677, 681 (Iowa 1993).

United States v. Stevens, 559 U.S. 460 (2010).

Univ. of Chicago. *Kalven Committee: Report on the University's Role in Political and Social Action* (Nov. 11, 1967). https://perma.cc/WL7J-HS3P.

Volokh, Eugene. "Mechanisms of the Slippery Slope." *Harvard Law Review* 116 (2003): 1026

Ward v. Rock Against Racism, 491 U.S. 781 (1989).

Whittington Keith E., "Free Speech and the Diverse University." *Fordham Law Review* 87 (2019): 2453.

Ysursa v. Pocatello Ed. Ass'n, 555 U.S. 353 (2009).

Zick, Timothy. "The Costs of Dissent: Protest and Civil Liabilities." *George Washington Law Review* 89 (2021): 233.

Chapter 18

Legislative Remedies for Violations of Campus Free Speech

The View From 30,000 Feet

Larry Alexander

My intention is to discuss the general principles governing speech on campuses and what legislatures may do if freedom of speech is denied or if universities decide to further ideological as opposed to academic goals. The topic can be complex, but there are some basic points that provide the background for assessing university policies and legislative responses.

THE CLOSED CAMPUS

One thing a university may do is ban all outside speakers or itself invite only outside speakers who further the university's educational or research mission. Academic freedom is not the same thing as freedom of speech. A university may, and should, stifle classroom teaching that does not comport with the disciplinary standards that govern the subject matter. (No flat-earth espousal in geography classes. No holocaust denial in history classes.) What this means is that the university may restrict university funds to speakers who advance its academic agenda. (Flat-earthers and Holocaust deniers will not be invited to speak on campus on the university's dime.)

The position just adumbrated has been a recurrent theme in the writings of Robert Post.[1] Post argues that a university's academic mission entitles it to censor what gets said and by whom, at least when the university is footing the bill. Therefore, university-funded student groups may be restricted from inviting whomever they wish to hear to speak on campus—or, presumably, off-campus if financed by the group and thereby with university funds.[2]

Legislatures might choose to fund universities that adhere to disciplinary standards even if the universities strictly control which outside speakers whose appearances they will fund and for whom they will provide fora. A corollary to this point, however, is that legislatures may refuse to fund universities that choose to fund only a particular position—in the classroom, in research, and in hiring, promotion, and tenure decisions—even if those who do not endorse that position nonetheless are adhering to disciplinary standards. For even if every teacher and scholar who supports the university's position does so for reasons accepted by their disciplines, the exclusion of others, for ideological rather than academic reasons, is a violation of academic freedom. And that violation potentially chills and degrades the academic work of those who currently endorse the university's position. A violation of academic freedom undermines the integrity of the teaching and scholarship of everyone. And a legislature can rightly refuse to fund an institution that denies academic freedom.[3]

If that is true, then it follows *a fortiori* that legislatures can (and should) refuse to fund those departments that are ideological rather than academic. It is well known that some university departments make no pretense of adhering to disciplinary standards.[4] Their stock-in-trade is grievance polemics, often couched in postmodern jargon and reflecting the naïve assumption that there are political implications of the postmodern claim that standards are not objectively valid but merely reflect the views and interests of particular classes or identity groups.[5] And legislatures would be acting properly in withholding or withdrawing the funds that allow those departments to exist.

(It is an interesting question whether, if a legislature may permissibly refuse to fund ideological universities and ideological departments, it *must* refuse to fund them as a constitutional matter. This question is, in free speech parlance, a question of the free speech limitations of government speech. It is obvious that governments may take positions on controversial matters and may subsidize speakers who communicate the government's point of view.[6] But there must be limits. A government may endorse policy X, but it cannot say, "Vote for Joe because he supports policy X." How that line is to be drawn and defended is beyond my pay grade.[7] But the issue does bear on government support for universities and departments that are ideological. And note that if the legislature funds a university or department that takes a particular position P—perhaps because the legislature agrees with P—must it then fund ideological universities or departments that endorse not-P? And if it does not, has it engaged in the free speech's mortal sin, the sin of viewpoint discrimination?[8])

One final question regarding the closed campus: May a university ban not only all outside speakers but also all speech among students that does not serve the university's academic mission and that might offend or insult other students? Of course, a university might find it difficult to police inter-student speech to that extent. And it might find applications from prospective students declining if it attempts to ban too much extracurricular student speech. But one can imagine a university's banning student speech on political or sensitive cultural topics on the ground that such speech might offend (or harass?) students who hold different political, cultural, or, in the case of religiously affiliated universities, religious views.

I think such a ban would be terribly unwise. And I would not want my children to attend a university with such a policy. But neither do I see any constitutional violation, nor any reason why a legislature may not fund such a university, assuming the university is otherwise adhering to disciplinary standards in its teaching, scholarship, and personnel decisions.

THE OPEN CAMPUS

I want to turn now to the far more common case of a university that allows student groups to invite outside speakers to speak on topics in which the students are interested regardless of whether the speakers advance the university's academic objectives. The university may provide funds to student groups for such a purpose, or it may merely provide fora—lecture halls or classrooms. In either case it is allowing use of its resources for student-invited speakers.

If the university is a public institution—or if it receives public funds directly (rather than through programs that give students funds to use at whatever university they choose)—then the university must be viewpoint neutral in its decisions regarding outside speakers.[9] (The same is true for non-invited outside speakers who speak on the streets, sidewalks, and open areas that extend into the campus—that is, the traditional public fora.[10]) A violation of viewpoint neutrality is a quintessential free speech violation—unless, that is, it is interpreted as government speech, which, as stated above, is an interpretation that is always available and that therefore threatens to upend the viewpoint neutrality doctrine.[11]

A legislature surely may, even if it is not always true that as a constitutional matter it must, refuse to fund a university that violates viewpoint neutrality. And it surely should refuse to fund such a university. Not just the student Democrats and student Republicans, but also the student Marxists and student monarchists, should be able to invite their favorite speakers if outside speakers are allowed.

If viewpoint neutrality is respected, the final requirement universities must meet is protecting the invited speakers and their audiences. One aspect of that requirement is banning disruptive conduct, conduct that prevents a speaker from completing his remarks or the audience from hearing them. And of course, that means banning prolonged heckling, loud chanting, drum beating, screaming, threatening, and any other behavior that impedes the speaker's speaking or the audience's hearing. The students who invite a speaker have the right to hear that speaker and everything the speaker intends to say. Disrupting the speaker is equivalent to a legal nuisance, conduct that unduly interferes with others' ability to do what they otherwise have a right to do. The interference is undue because its only purpose *is* to interfere and not to engage in an activity that just happens to interfere with others' activities.

If the legislature is directly funding the university, then, as a condition on that funding, it may and should demand that the university sanction students who disrupt speakers. A first offense of serious disruptive behavior should merit suspension, at least if there has been adequate notice provided of that penalty. And a second offense should result in expulsion. The resources required to protect speakers and their audiences from disruptions by students should be minimal if students who disrupt are credibly threatened with meaningful sanctions.[12]

That brings me to what I believe is the hardest question. What should be done when the disrupters are not students at the university? Because threats of suspension or expulsion are meaningless to outsiders, the only way to prevent the disruption of the speech and, on occasion, protect the speaker and the audience from violence is to have an adequate number of law enforcement personnel present and prepared to arrest the disrupters.[13] If free speech requires this, then free speech is not only an immunity, a status which it and other constitutional rights share, but is also a claim right to resources—in this case, law enforcement resources. And resources always being finite and subject to competing claims, the question becomes how much in the way of resources does free speech demand to avoid the so-called heckler's veto?

In the case of *Feiner v. New York*,[14] a Supreme Court majority held that when the police presence on the scene was insufficient to control the crowd and prevent violence in reaction to the speaker's speech, the police could permissibly shut down the speaker and arrest him when he resisted being silenced. Essentially, too little police presence resulted in a heckler's veto and no violation of Feiner's free speech.

The Supreme Court has never repudiated its decision in *Feiner*, although neither has *Feiner* been followed in any of the Court's subsequent decisions.[15] And given that law enforcement resources are limited, have uses other than protecting speakers, and compete with the resource claims of education, health, parks, roads, and all other governmental functions, the *Feiner* claim right dilemma is inescapable. (It is testimony to the wisdom of our Constitution that the rights it proclaims are almost always immunities rather than claim rights, such as rights to education, employment, and housing, that are proclaimed in other countries' constitutions. The principal exception other than what we are discussing here is the right to appointed counsel in criminal and some civil cases.)

Almost every free speech theorist I'm aware of opposes allowing protesters to prevent speakers from speaking and audiences from hearing. In other words, they oppose the so-called heckler's veto.[16] They also recognize, however, that the resources required to prevent the heckler's veto are finite and compete with all other potential uses of those resources. This is what I deem "the *Feiner* dilemma."

The author who has most perspicaciously addressed the *Feiner* dilemma is Frederick Schauer.[17] Schauer notes:

> One thing that is now settled, if anything is settled, and that the post-*Feiner* cases make reasonably clear, is that law enforcement may not initially or prematurely arrest the speaker. It also appears settled that the state may not prosecute on grounds of incitement the speakers whose speech has prompted the reactions. . . . But although this much seems more or less clear, what is importantly not clear is just how much the authorities must do before taking some sort of action against the speaker or before bringing the entire event to a halt.[18]

Schauer goes on to point out the resource problem, endemic to any regime of affirmative rights, that preventing the heckler's veto entails.

> [A]t some point, although we do not know at what point, a city, county, or state will simply not have the available personnel and not have the available funds. When this point is reached, can a city then deny a permit, or otherwise prohibit the event? And assuming that such decisions will eventually come before the courts, can a city, county, or state argue that providing more than some amount will then take funds away from school lunches? From emergency medical services? From public housing? From low-income welfare assistance? From providing services that themselves have a constitutional aspect, such as providing a certain quality of unpaid legal assistance for defendants in criminal cases, or, in earlier times, providing police protection for African-American children seeking to attend previously segregated schools? Now that we know the actual costs involved in places such as Berkeley, Charlottesville, Gainesville, and the District of Columbia, we cannot avoid confronting the fact that protecting speakers exercising their First Amendment rights will come at some cost to other worthy municipal goals, including, at times protecting or enforcing other constitutional rights.[19]

Needless to say, what applies to the resources of cities, counties, and states applies to universities and their resources when the speakers in question are on university campuses.

I have no solution to the *Feiner* dilemma. As events at Berkeley made evident, protecting speakers and their audiences can be very expensive.[20] And those costs are paid at the expense of countless alternative ways that money could be spent.

NOTES

1. See, e.g., Robert C. Post, *Democracy, Expertise, Academic Freedom: A First Amendment Jurisprudence for the Modern State* (New Haven: Yale University Press, 2012); Robert C. Post, "Academic Freedom and the Constitution," in *Who's Afraid of Academic Freedom*, edited by Akeel Bilgrami and Jonathan R. Cole (New York: Columbia University Press, 2015), 123–152. See also, Larry Alexander, "Fish on Academic Freedom: A Merited Assault on Nonsense, But Perhaps a Bridge Too Far," *Florida International Law Review* 9 (2013): 1–8.

2. It will no doubt be difficult for courts to ascertain whether such censorship of outside speakers is in furtherance of disciplinary standards or an imposition of an ideological test. If it's the latter, then for reasons spelled out below, it may be unconstitutional.

3. It will be most difficult to determine if ideological discrimination is occurring when hiring, as opposed to promotion and tenure, is involved. I thank Jim Stoner for pointing this out.

4. I am here referring to all the departments that are defined by identity groups—e.g., women's studies, ethic studies, queer studies, and so on—and increasingly to departments like English and other modern language departments and to nonempirical ("interpretive") sociology and anthropology departments or parts thereof.

5. For why postmodernism, properly understood, is logically self-undermining and has no political implications, see Larry Alexander, "What We Do, and Why We Do It," *Stanford Law Review* 45 (1993): 1885, 1896–98. Postmodernism, as I described it in the cited article, is the modern heir to the Hegelian and later Wittgensteinian twist on Kant. Kant's universal categories of understanding . . . [are] relativized to culture and language, and the phenomenal world that they make a possible object of experience is cut loose from all moorings in the world of things in themselves, the world "as it really is" apart from our experiences of it. The postmodernist concludes that reality is nothing more than a matter of perspective, which varies from subject to subject, all of whose understandings are socially constructed. The postmodern view, like all thoroughgoing, skeptical views about knowledge, is ultimately self-undermining. Like all claims to knowledge it debunks, it also purports to know something about the world. Moreover, its view that our categories are socially constructed is an "is" from absolutely no "ought" follows. Ibid. at 1896–97.

6. See, e.g., *Rust v. Sullivan*, 500 U.S. 173 (1991).

7. See, Larry Alexander, *Is There a Right of Freedom of Expression?* (Cambridge: Cambridge University Press, 2005), Ch. 5. In that chapter I illustrate how difficult it is to come up with a principled limit on government speech.

8. See, e.g., *Reed v. Town of Gilbert, Arizona*, 576 U.S. ___ (2015). See generally, Alexander, *supra* note 7, at Ch. 4.

9. See, e.g., *Rosenberger v. University of Virginia*, 515 U.S. 819 (1995).

10. See, e.g., *Chicago Police Dept. v. Mosley*, 408 U.S. 92 (1992).

11. For a questionable extension of the notion of government speech in order to get around the requirement of content neutrality, see *Walker v. Texas Division, Sons of Confederate Veterans, Inc.*, 576 U.S. 200 (2015).

12. Faculty members who disrupt speakers should also face discipline and, in some cases, termination for cause.

13. It also may be helpful—and cheaper—to require that outsiders only attend if they have been invited, or if they purchase a ticket. I owe this insight to Jim Stoner.

14. 340 U.S. 315 (1951).

15. The Court refused to follow *Feiner* and allow a real or alleged threat of violence to justify gagging the speakers or demonstrators in three cases: *Edwards et al. v. South Carolina*, 372 U.S. 229 (1963), involving a demonstration on the South Carolina State House grounds by black students in the presence of 200 to 300 nonthreatening onlookers and thirty police; *Cox v. Louisiana*, 379 U.S. 536 (1965), involving a demonstration near a Baton Rouge courthouse by black students in the presence of a crowd of about 100 to 300, some of whom were "grumbling" and "jeering," and about seventy-five to eighty police; and *Gregory et al. v. City of Chicago*, 394 U.S. 111 (1969), involving a peaceful march to the mayor's residence in the presence of an unruly crowd of hecklers. These cases were similar in many respects to the pre-*Feiner* case of *Terminiello v. Chicago*, 337 U.S. 1 (1948), a case very similar to *Feiner* but decided in favor of the speaker. See also the California case of *In re Kay*, 1 Cal. 3d 930 (1970).

16. The "heckler's veto" literature is extensive. A recent sample includes, Keith E. Whittington, *Speak Freely: Why Universities Must Defend Free Speech* (Princeton: Princeton University Press, 2018), 94–116; Frederick Schauer, "Costs and Challenges of the Hostile Audience," *Notre Dame Law Review* 94 (2019): 1671; Timothy E. D. Horley, "Rethinking the Heckler's Veto After Charlottesville," *Virginia Law Review* 104 (2018); Suzanne B. Goldberg, "Free Expression on Campus: Mitigating the Costs of Contentious Speakers," *Harvard Journal of Law & Public Policy* 41 (2018): 163, 183–84; R. George Wright, "The Heckler's Veto Today," *Case Western Reserve Law Review* 68 (2017): 159, 169–71.

17. Schauer, *supra* note 16.

18. Ibid., at 1684–1685.

19. Ibid., at 1689.

20. See, e.g., Jocelyn Gecker, "The Cost of Free Speech Isn't Cheap at UC Berkeley," *U.S. News & World Report*, September 15, 2017, https://apnews.com/f2d6a139cd6b44d7a743932f2b913677. One possible solution, charging the speaker or the group inviting her for the costs of adequate policing, has been deemed unconstitutional by the Supreme Court. *Forsyth County v. Nationalist Movement*, 505 U.S. 123 (1992).

REFERENCES

Alexander, Larry. "Fish on Academic Freedom: A Merited Assault on Nonsense, But Perhaps a Bridge Too Far." *Florida International Law Review* 9 (2013): 1–8.

Alexander, Larry. *Is There a Right of Freedom of Expression?* (Cambridge: Cambridge University Press, 2005).

Alexander, Larry. "What We Do, and Why We Do It." *Stanford Law Review* 45 (1993): 1885.

Chicago Police Dept. v. Mosley, 408 U.S. 92 (1992).

Cox v. Louisiana, 379 U.S. 536 (1965).

Edwards et al. v. South Carolina, 372 U.S. 229 (1963).

Feiner v. New York, 340 U.S. 315 (1951).

Forsyth County v. Nationalist Movement, 505 U.S. 123 (1992).

Gecker, Jocelyn. "The Cost of Free Speech Isn't Cheap at UC Berkeley." *U.S. News & World Report*, September 15, 2017, https://apnews.com/f2d6a139cd6b44d7a743932f2b913677.

Goldberg, Suzanne B. "Free Expression on Campus: Mitigating the Costs of Contentious Speakers." *Harvard Journal of Law & Public Policy* 41 (2018): 163.

Gregory et al. v. City of Chicago, 394 U.S. 111 (1969).

Horley, Timothy E. D. "Rethinking the Heckler's Veto After Charlottesville." *Virginia Law Review* 104 (2018).

In re Kay, 1 Cal. 3d 930 (1970).

Post, Robert C. "Academic Freedom and the Constitution." In *Who's Afraid of Academic Freedom*. Edited by Akeel Bilgrami and Jonathan R. Cole (New York: Columbia University Press, 2015).

Post, Robert C. *Democracy, Expertise, Academic Freedom: A First Amendment Jurisprudence for the Modern State* (New Haven: Yale University Press, 2012).

Reed v. Town of Gilbert, Arizona, 576 U.S. ___ (2015).

Rosenberger v. University of Virginia, 515 U.S. 819 (1995).

Rust v. Sullivan, 500 U.S. 173 (1991).

Schauer, Frederick. "Costs and Challenges of the Hostile Audience." *Notre Dame Law Review* 94 (2019): 1671.

Terminiello v. Chicago, 337 U.S. 1 (1948).

Walker v. Texas Division, Sons of Confederate Veterans, Inc., 576 U.S. ___ (2015).

Whittington, Keith E. *Speak Freely: Why Universities Must Defend Free Speech* (Princeton: Princeton University Press, 2018).

Wright, R. George. "The Heckler's Veto Today." *Case Western Reserve Law Review* 68 (2017): 159.

Index

About the Contributors

Larry Alexander is Warren Distinguished Professor at the University of San Diego School of Law. He is the author or co-author of nine monographs and over 250 articles, essays and book chapters, and the editor or co-editor of seven anthologies, on topics relating to legal, moral, and constitutional theory. Among his many contributions dealing with freedom of speech is his 2005 Cambridge University Press monograph titled *Is There a Right of Freedom of Expression?*

Ulrich Baer, a graduate of Harvard College (BA) and Yale University (PhD), is University Professor at New York University. A recipient of Guggenheim, Getty, Daad, and Humboldt fellowships, he has written for the *New York Times*, the *New York Review of Books*, and the *Los Angeles Book Review*. His books include *What Snowflakes Get Right: Free Speech, Truth and Equality on Campus* (Oxford 2019); *Spectral Evidence: The Photography of Trauma* (MIT); *110 Stories: New York Writes After September 11* (editor); *The Dark Interval: Rilke's Letters on Loss, Grief and Transformation* (Random House); *Rainer Maria Rilke: Letters on Life* (Random House), and numerous new editions of classic works of world literature. He hosts two ideas podcasts, *Think About It,* and *The Proust Questionnaire* (with Caroline Weber).

David M. Buss is a Professor of Psychology at the University of Texas at Austin. Buss previously taught at Harvard University and the University of Michigan. He is considered the world's leading scientific expert on strategies of human mating and one of the founders of the field of evolutionary psychology. His books include *The Evolution of Desire: Strategies of Human Mating*; *Evolutionary Psychology: The New Science of the Mind*; *The Dangerous Passion: Why Jealousy is as Necessary as Love and Sex*; *The Murderer Next Door: Why the Mind is Designed to Kill*; and *Why Women Have Sex* (with Cindy Meston), and *When Men Behave Badly: The Hidden Roots of Sexual Deception, Harassment, and Assault* (2021). Buss has more than three hundred scientific publications. In 2019, he was cited as one of the fifty most influential living psychologists in the world.

Paul Carrese is the founding director of the School of Civic and Economic Thought and Leadership at Arizona State University. For nearly two decades he was a professor of political science at the United States Air Force Academy. He is author of *The Cloaking of Power: Montesquieu, Blackstone, and the Rise of Judicial Activism,* and co-editor of three other books—on George Washington, constitutionalism, and American grand strategy. His most recent book is *Democracy in Moderation: Montesquieu, Tocqueville, and Sustainable Liberalism*. He studied at Oxford University on a Rhodes Scholarship and has held fellowships at Harvard University, the University of Delhi (as a Fulbright fellow), and the James Madison Program, Politics Department, Princeton University.

Daniel Cullen is Professor of Philosophy at Rhodes College and directs the Project for the Study of Liberal Democracy. Cullen is Senior Fellow for Constitutional Studies at the Jack Miller Center for Teaching America's Constitutional Principles and History, and he serves on the Center's Academic Council. Cullen also serves on the board of the Association for Core Texts Studies and Courses, an international organization devoted to the advancement of liberal education. He is the author of *Freedom in Rousseau's Political Philosophy*, and has published various essays on Rousseau, Montaigne, democratic theory, liberal education and most recently, on the political philosophy of Roger Scruton. His most recent book is *Liberal Democracy and Liberal Education*, which he edited and co-authored. He is currently writing a book on the philosophy of Roger Scruton.

Donald Alexander Downs is the Alexander Meiklejohn Emeritus Professor of Political Science, and Emeritus Affiliate Professor of Law and Journalism at the University of Wisconsin-Madison. He has written about academic freedom, free speech; campus politics; American politics; political and legal thought and movements; citizenship; domestic violence, psychiatry, and the criminal law; and the relationship among the military, the university, and civic education. He has written several books, most recently *The Value and Limits of Academic Speech: Philosophical, Political, and Legal Aspects* (Routledge, 2018), Chris W. Surprenant, co-editor; and *Free Speech and Liberal Education: A Plea for Intellectual Diversity and Tolerance* (Cato, 2020). He served as secretary and then president of the independent Committee for Academic Freedom and Rights at Wisconsin from 1996 to 2016 and as faculty adviser to the Open Inquiry Project at the Institute for

Humane Studies, 2015–19. He currently serves on the Academic Affairs Committee of the national Academic Freedom Alliance.

Joshua M. Dunn is a professor of political science and director of the Center for the Study of Government and the Individual at the University of Colorado Colorado Springs. He is the coauthor of *Passing on the Right: Conservative Professors in the Progressive University.*

Jonathan Haidt is a social psychologist at New York University's Stern School of Business. His research examines the intuitive foundations of morality, and how morality varies across cultural and political divisions. Haidt is the author of *The Happiness Hypothesis* (2006), *The Righteous Mind* (2012), and *The Coddling of the American Mind* (2018, with Greg Lukianoff). He is a cofounder of HeterodoxAcademy.org.

Steven F. Hayward is senior resident scholar at the Institute of Governmental Studies at UC Berkeley, and a visiting lecturer at UC Berkeley Law School. He was the inaugural visiting scholar in conservative thought and policy at the University of Colorado at Boulder in 2013–14. From 2002 to 2012 he was the F.K. Weyerhaeuser Fellow in Law and Economics at the American Enterprise Institute in Washington, DC, and has been senior fellow at the Pacific Research Institute in San Francisco since 1991. He writes daily on Powerlineblog.com, one of the nation's most read political websites, and is the author of *Churchill on Leadership: Executive Success in the Face of Adversity*, *Greatness: Reagan, Churchill, and the Making of Extraordinary Leaders*, and *The Age of Reagan: The Conservative Counterrevolution: 1980–1989*.

Cristine H. Legare is a professor of psychology, a faculty affiliate of the Population Research Center (PRC), and the founder and director of the Center for Applied Cognitive Science (CACS) at The University of Texas at Austin. Her research examines how the human mind enables us to learn, create, and transmit culture; her core areas of expertise include global public health, international education, child development, and cognitive science. Her work has been widely published in a number of high-impact journals, and has been covered by a range of media outlets, including *NPR, Nature, The Wall Street Journal,* and *Scientific American.*

Heather MacDonald is the Thomas W. Smith fellow at the Manhattan Institute and the author of *The Danger of Disparate Impact* (forthcoming); *The Diversity Delusion*; and *The War on Cops*.

Azhar Majeed is the Director of Government Affairs at the Center for Inquiry (CFI), where he handles various legislative matters at both state and federal levels. Prior to that, he spent fourteen years at the Foundation for Individual Rights in Education (FIRE), defending campus free-speech rights at colleges across the country. Azhar is a graduate of the University of Michigan–Ann Arbor as well as the University of Michigan Law School.

James M. Manley is an attorney at Pacific Legal Foundation, where he serves as an Attorney Manager and litigates in defense of free speech and economic opportunity. He is also a senior fellow at the Goldwater Institute, where he co-authored the Institute's Campus Free Speech Act, winner of the 2017 Bob Williams Award for Outstanding Policy Achievement from the State Policy Network. A native of Michigan, he graduated from Arizona State University, with a double major in Political Science and Journalism. He earned his JD from the University of Colorado Law School.

Harvey C. Mansfield is the William R. Kenan Jr. Professor of Government at Harvard University, where he has taught for sixty years. Mansfield is a recipient of the 2011 Bradley Prize. He has held Guggenheim and National Endowment for the Humanities Fellowships, has been a fellow at the National Humanities Center, and in 2004 received the National Humanities Medal. He is the author of studies of Aristotle, Burke, Machiavelli, Tocqueville, Hobbes, constitutional government, and, most recently, manliness.

Carol McNamara is the associate director for public programs for the School of Civic and Economic Thought and Leadership at Arizona State University. Her research focuses on politics and literature, ancient Greek political thought, and the American presidency. She is the coeditor, with Trevor Shelley, of the first volume in this set of books based upon the School's Civic Discourse Project, *Citizenship and Civic Leadership in America.*

Laura Beth Nielsen is a Research Professor at the American Bar Foundation as well as a Professor of Sociology and Director of the Center for Legal Studies at Northwestern University. Her research focuses on the sociology of law, with particular interests in legal consciousness (how ordinary people understand the law) and the relationship between law and inequalities of race, gender, and class. Her first monograph, *License to Harass: Law, Hierarchy, and Offensive Public Speech* (Princeton University Press, 2004) studies racist and sexist street speech, targets' reactions and responses to it, and attitudes about using law to deal with such speech. Professor Nielsen is an expert in the areas of sexual harassment in the workplace and beyond, employment civil rights of all sorts including pregnancy, pay, race, sex, national origin, and is a scholar of the legal profession.

Robert C. Post is Sterling Professor of Law at Yale Law School, and served as the School's sisxteenth dean, from 2009 to 2017. He has written and edited numerous books, including *Citizens Divided: A Constitutional Theory of Campaign Finance Reform* (2014), which was originally delivered as the Tanner Lectures at Harvard in 2013, and *Democracy Expertise, Academic Freedom: A First Amendment Jurisprudence for the Modern State* (2012), and he publishes regularly in legal journals and other publications. He is a member of the American Philosophical Society and the American Law Institute and a fellow of the American Academy of Arts and Sciences. He is a former member of the Board of Directors of the American Constitution Society.

Geoffrey R. Stone is the Edward H. Levi Distinguished Professor of Law. He has written and edited many books and articles about the First Amendment. The two most recent are *Social Media, Freedom of Speech and the Future of Our Democracy* (2022) and *Free Speech and National Security: The Pentagon Papers Fifty Years On* (2021).

James R. Stoner, Jr. is the Hermann Moyse, Jr., Professor and Director of the Eric Voegelin Institute in the Department of Political Science at Louisiana State University. He is the author of *Common-Law Liberty* and *Common Law and Liberal Theory*, and co-editor of four books, most recently *The Political Thought of the Civil War*. He earned his AB from Middlebury College and his MA and PhD from Harvard University and has been a visiting professor and fellow in the James Madison Program at Princeton University.

Norma Thompson is Senior Lecturer in the Humanities at Yale University. Her scholarship and teaching are in the humanities, with special interests in political philosophy and politics and literature. Her books include *Unreasonable Doubt: Circumstantial Evidence and the Art of Judgment*, *The Ship of State: Politics and Statecraft from Ancient Greece to Democratic America*, and *Herodotus and the Origins of the Political Community: Arion's Leap*. Among her articles, she has published chapters in *Western Civilization and the Academy* and *Symposium on Arthur Melzer's Philosophy Between the Lines*.

Eugene Volokh is the Gary T. Schwartz Distinguished Professor of Law at UCLA School of Law. He is the author of over fifty law review articles about the First Amendment and related topics, and a casebook on the subject (now in its seventh edition); he is also the founding editor-in-chief of the *Journal of Free Speech Law*.

www.ingramcontent.com/pod-product-compliance
Ingram Content Group UK Ltd.
Pitfield, Milton Keynes, MK11 3LW, UK
UKHW041833031026
15587UKWH00002B/733

9 781666 900705